Read This First:
ASIA &
INDIA

CHRIS ROWTHORN
PETER CRUTTENDEN

LONELY PLANET PUBLICATIONS
◆melbourne ◆oakland ◆london ◆paris

D1098369

SOUTH-EAST ASIA

SUGGESTED REGIONAL ITINERARIES
The Hippie Trail: Europe to Australia   Trans-Siberian Railway   Routes in North-East Asia
Karakoram Highway   Routes in South-East Asia   Routes on the Indian Subcontin

Read This First – Asia & India
1st edition

Published by
Lonely Planet Publications Pty Ltd ACN 005 607 983
192 Burwood Rd, Hawthorn, Victoria 3122, Australia

Lonely Planet Offices
Australia PO Box 617, Hawthorn, Victoria 3122
USA 150 Linden Street, Oakland, CA 94607
UK 10a Spring Place, London NW5 3BH
France 1 rue du Dahomey, 75011, Paris

Printed by
The Bookmaker Pty Ltd
Printed in China

Designed by
Penelope Richardson

Photographs by
Eddie Gerald; Mick Elmore; Andrew Brownbill; Stan Armington; Richard I'Anson; Penelope
Richardson; Juliet Coombe; John Hay; Mark Kirby; Greg Elms

Published
November 1999

ISBN 1 86450 049 2

text, maps © Lonely Planet 1999

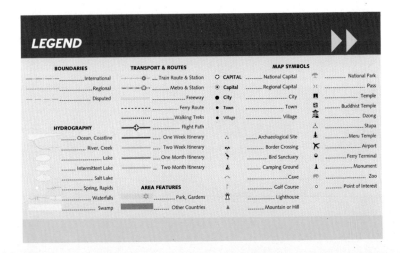

LEGEND

BOUNDARIES
International
Regional
Disputed

HYDROGRAPHY
Ocean, Coastline
River, Creek
Lake
Intermittent Lake
Salt Lake
Spring, Rapids
Waterfalls
Swamp

TRANSPORT & ROUTES
Train Route & Station
Metro & Station
Freeway
Ferry Route
Walking Treks
Flight Path
One Week Itinerary
Two Week Itinerary
One Month Itinerary
Two Month Itinerary

AREA FEATURES
Park, Gardens
Other Countries

MAP SYMBOLS
CAPITAL — National Capital
Capital — Regional Capital
City — City
Town — Town
Village — Village
Archaeological Site
Border Crossing
Bird Sanctuary
Camping Ground
Cave
Golf Course
Lighthouse
Mountain or Hill

National Park
Pass
Temple
Buddhist Temple
Dzong
Stupa
Meru Temple
Airport
Ferry Terminal
Monument
Zoo
Point of Interest

CONTENTS

THIS BOOK

This book is designed to help you to research and prepare for a trip to Asia and the Indian subcontinent. It contains much of the advice that we'd like to include in our regular travel guides, but cannot due to space limitations. It's a compilation of lessons learned by Lonely Planet travel writers and readers on innumerable trips across Asia, and includes detailed advice on planning your route, buying your ticket, choosing and packing your gear, and surviving your first night on the road. Even more importantly, it contains plenty of advice on day-to-day living while you're on the road – things that hold true across the continent – from finding a decent room, eating a good meal, keeping your valuables safe and getting around on some very different forms of transport. In short, this book is the one we wish we'd had before we set out on our first trip to Asia.

This book includes country profiles that provide the basic details and highlights of each country in Asia. These can be used to plan your route, calculate your travel budget and figure out what visas you must get before setting out. These sections will not replace the greater detail you'll need from guidebooks once you're in Asia, but they should serve as a solid start to planning your trip and learning about the cultures you are heading to.

We've also included itineraries for each of the countries. The routes we've selected take in the major sights and attractions, plus a few places further off the beaten track, but if you do some further research and come up with your own specific route, you'll encounter the aspects of the region that appeal most to your particular tastes and you'll generally have a more rewarding time.

A couple of other things – for reasons of simplicity, throughout the text we refer to the whole region of Asia and the Indian subcontinent as 'Asia'. We have also included loads of web site references and addresses in recognition of the increasing role these resources play in travel planning and information. Inevitably, by the time you read this book, some of these links will have changed or disappeared. A simple keyword search should furnish you with the site's new address.

If you combine the information in this book with some imagination and a healthy sense of adventure, you can't help but fall in love with Asian travel. Remember, the sooner you get started the sooner you'll be stepping off a plane into your first Asian adventure.

THE AUTHORS

Chris Rowthorn

Chris was born in England and grew up on the east coast of the USA. He moved to Japan in 1992 and immediately fell in love with the country. After doing the obligatory few years as an English teacher, he landed a job at the *Japan Times*, which eventually led to a job at Lonely Planet. He has worked on Lonely Planet's *Japan, Tokyo, Hiking in Japan, Malaysia, Singapore & Brunei* and *South-East Asia on a shoestring* guides. He has travelled widely in Asia and escapes whenever possible to Thailand or Nepal. When not travelling, he lives a quiet domestic life in Kyoto with his wife Chiori, commuting to the public bath and eating at yakitori restaurants.

Peter Cruttenden

Born in Perth, Western Australia, and raised for a time in England, Peter worked in daily journalism, magazines and desktop publishing in Canberra and Melbourne before heading off to see the world at the less-than-tender age of 28. On his return to Melbourne, he joined the Asia unit at Lonely Planet where he has worked on titles including *China, Indonesia, Korea, Japan, Bali & Lombok, Indonesia's Eastern Islands, Vietnam, Hong Kong* and *South-West China*, as well as contributing reviews to the *Out To Eat: Melbourne* restaurant guide. He lives with his partner in inner-city Melbourne.

FROM THE AUTHORS

From Chris

I would like to thank the travelling companions with whom I shared good times in Asia: Paul Carty, Steve Levine, Sarah Downs, Anthony Weersing, Denise Wallace, Chip Weintraub and, of course, my wife Chiori.

From Peter

Thanks to everyone at LP who helped get this new project off the ground, as well as to the many LP authors and staffers whose work we've used and adapted for this guide. To my co-author Chris, a million thanks for your professionalism, diligence and willingness to supply extra material on very short notice. Finally, thanks to my partner Rebecca for her company on the road and tolerance during the long hours of writing and production, and to my many other friends for keeping me sane.

FROM THE PUBLISHER

This book, the first title in Lonely Planet's new series of introductory travel guides, has been a long time in the planning, writing and production. The structure and content of the series was developed by Pete Cruttenden and the internal and cover design by Penelope Richardson, but loads of other LP people have contributed to the project along the way. Anne Mulvaney edited this first title, made many useful suggestions on content and consistency, and contributed enormously to the quality of the series. She was assisted by proofers Alan Murphy and Graham Fricke. Cartographer Jim Miller produced the excellent colour maps throughout the book, with the assistance of Jackie Rae, Paul Piaia, Paul Clifton and David Golding. Paul Piaia and Tim Fitzgerald supplied the climate charts, Tim Uden helped out with Quark and Quentin Frayne advised on language matters. Thanks again to design manager Tass Wilson for her timely assistance.

Thanks also to Isabelle Young and Leonie Mugavin for their work on the health content, and to staff writers Alex Landrigan, John Ryan, Lisa Kerrigan, Nick Tapp and Andrew McKenna for their contributions, along with LP authors Paul Greenway, Joe Cummings, Marie Cambon, Michelle Coxall and James Lyon, and freelancers Robyn Coventry and Gareth McCormack. Thanks also to the following LP readers who contributed stories (and apologies to those whose pieces didn't make it into print): Margaret Wilson, Francois Lasalle, Jo Higgs, Johan Guillaume, Linda Burlinson, Louise Hamer-Keijser, Thomas Anderson, Peder Bisbjerg, Andre Desnoyers, Ryan Aldred, Jeff Rothman, Anna Trahair, Mark Princi, Carol Huxley, Dik Klop, Nadia Meyercord, Orna Mayzel Oreg, Nathan Lee and Michael Cridland.

Finally, thanks to Sue Galley, Jeff Trounce, Graham Imeson, Alastair Stott, Jennifer Cox, Carolyn Miller, John Dennithorne, Laurence Billiet, Anna Bolger, Fiona Kinniburgh, Richard Everist, Charlotte Hindle and Eric Kuttenen variously for good ideas, assistance and feedback.

Much of the information in this guide (particularly the country profiles) has been drawn and adapted from existing Lonely Planet titles. Thanks to the following authors for their fine work: David Andrew *(Malaysia, Singapore & Brunei)*, Stan Armington *(Bhutan)*, Marie Cambon *(China)*, Michael Clark *(Myanmar)*, David Collins *(India)*, Joe Cummings *(Laos, Myanmar and Thailand)*, Brendan Delahunty *(Indonesia)*, Alex English *(China)*, Richard Everist *(Nepal)*, Hugh Finlay *(Nepal)*, Mason Florence *(Japan and Vietnam)*, Rob Flynn *(India)*, Nicko Goncharoff *(China and Japan)*, Paul Greenway *(Indonesia and Mongolia)*, Damian Harper *(China)*, Paul Hellander *(Malaysia, Singapore & Brunei and Singapore city guide)*, Thomas Huhti (China), John King (Pakistan), Gabriel Lafitte (Mongolia), Clem Lindenmayer (Malaysia, Singapore & Brunei), Caroline Liou (China), James Lyon *(Indonesia)*, Bradley Mayhew *(Pakistan)*,

Jon Murray *(Bangladesh)*, Alex Newton *(Bangladesh)*, Christine Niven *(India)*, Nick Ray *(Cambodia)*, Daniel Robinson *(Cambodia)*, Chris Rowthorn *(Malaysia, Singapore & Brunei* and *Japan)*, Sarina Singh *(India)*, Robert Storey *(China, Mongolia, Taiwan* and *Vietnam)*, David St Vincent *(Pakistan)*, Chris Taylor *(Cambodia, China, Indonesia* and *Japan)*, Bryn Thomas *(India)*, Peter Turner *(Indonesia* and *Singapore city guide)*, Dani Valent *(India)*, Betsy Wagenhauser *(Bangladesh)*, Tony Wheeler *(Cambodia* and *Nepal)* and David Willett *(Indonesia)*.

Warning & Request

Things change – prices go up, schedules change, good places go bad and bad places go bankrupt – nothing stays the same. So, if you find things better or worse, recently opened or long since closed, please tell us and help make the next edition even more accurate and useful. We genuinely value all the feedback we receive. Julie Young coordinates a well travelled team that reads and acknowledges every letter, postcard and email and ensures that every morsel of information finds its way to the appropriate authors, editors and cartographers for verification.

Everyone who writes to us will find their name in the next edition of the appropriate guidebook. They will also receive the latest issue of *Planet Talk*, our quarterly printed newsletter, or *Comet*, our monthly email newsletter. Subscriptions to both newsletters are free. The very best contributions will be rewarded with a free guidebook.

Excerpts from your correspondence may appear in new editions of Lonely Planet guidebooks, the Lonely Planet web site, *Planet Talk* or *Comet*, so please let us know if you *don't* want your letter published or your name acknowledged.

Send all correspondence to the Lonely Planet office closest to you:

Australia: PO Box 617, Hawthorn, Victoria 3122
USA: 150 Linden St, Oakland, CA 94607
UK: 10A Spring Place, London NW5 3BH
France: 1 rue du Dahomey, 75011 Paris

Or email us at: talk2us@lonelyplanet.com.au

For news, views and updates see our Web site: www.lonelyplanet.com

THE LP STORY

The story begins with a classic travel adventure – Tony and Maureen Wheeler's 1972 journey across Europe and Asia to Australia. Useful information about the overland trail did not exist at that time, so Tony and Maureen published the first Lonely Planet guidebook to meet a growing need among the backpacker community.

Tony and Maureen fresh off the boat at Exmouth on Western Australia's North-Western Cape at the end of their overland journey from Europe to Australia in 1972.

Written at a kitchen table and hand collated, trimmed and stapled, *Asia on the Cheap* became an instant local bestseller, inspiring thoughts of another book. A further 18 months in South-East Asia resulted in their second guide, *South-East Asia on a shoestring*, which they put together in a backstreet Chinese hotel in Singapore in 1975. The 'yellow bible' as it quickly became known to backpackers around the world, soon became *the* guide to the region. As we go to print, it has sold almost 750,000 copies, still retaining its familiar yellow cover. A 10th anniversary edition has recently been released and includes a story and photographs by Tony recalling the 1975 trip.

Today Lonely Planet publishes more than 450 titles, including travel guides, city guides, diving guides, city maps, phrasebooks, trekking guides, wildlife guides, travel atlases and travel literature. The company is the largest independent travel publisher in the world; an international company with offices in Melbourne, Oakland, London and Paris.

However, some things haven't changed. Our main aim is still to help make it possible for adventurous travellers to get out there – to explore and better understand the world. At Lonely Planet we believe that travellers can make a positive contribution to the countries they visit – if they respect their host communities and spend their money wisely. Since 1986 a percentage of the income from each book has been donated to aid projects and human rights campaigns across the world.

INTRODUCTION

Everyone has their own image of Asia. Perhaps it's terraced rice paddies lining steep Himalayan valleys. Or mist-shrouded peaks straight out of a Chinese ink painting. Or chaotic streets crammed with rickshaws and wailing street vendors. Whatever it is, there's a good chance that the Asia of your imagination actually exists. More importantly, there's an Asia out there that you can't possibly imagine. The hot, sweaty, pungent, vibrant, swirling Asia that surpasses the expectations of veteran travellers and first-timers alike.

If you're planning your first trip to Asia you are indeed lucky, for all of this is waiting to be discovered and experienced. This is not to say all your experiences will be good. Far from it; you will encounter things that challenge you, distress you and perhaps even sicken you. You will be exasperated, fed up, worn down and perhaps even ripped off. But you will not be bored. And more than likely, when it's all over, you'll find yourself counting the days till you can get back there and do it all over again.

How is it that a place can hold such allure? The answer is quite simple: Asia is so different from the places you know that it can't help but fascinate. From the high peaks of the Himalaya to the coral-rimmed islands of Indonesia, from the *Blade Runner* metropolis of Tokyo to the stone-age villages of Irian Jaya, Asia contains enough wonders to stagger even the most sophisticated of souls. Indeed, it's hard to imagine a place that fulfils all the requirements for good travel the way Asia does.

Best of all, Asia is affordable. There are few places in the world where you can travel as long and as widely on as little money. Provided you avoid some of the pricier countries, you can work your way around the continent for as little as US$10 a day. This means that it may be cheaper to holiday in Asia than in popular tourist spots closer to home – and that's with the price of your air ticket figured in.

With so much to offer at such a reasonable price, it's only natural that Asia is now fairly well trodden by travellers of all sorts, from low-budget backpackers to well heeled package tourists. This makes it surprisingly easy to travel in many parts of the continent, and if you stick to the backpackers trail, you'll find it almost as easy as travelling in Europe. And if you want to get off the beaten path, you can just about walk off the map in Asia.

Now, just to whet your appetite, here are a few of the attractions waiting for you out there ...

ISLANDS AND BEACHES – Hedonists of the world unite on the islands and beaches of Thailand, Indonesia, Malaysia and the Philippines. When you see the turquoise waters, white sands and swaying palms, you'll know why.

MOUNTAINS – You'll never be able to look at mountains the same way again after seeing the Himalaya. These mountains begin where all others leave off and a trek among the soaring peaks is the literal and figurative high point of many an Asian trip.

PEOPLE – Asia is a kaleidoscope of faces. From the easy-going folk of the Philippines to the exasperating cab drivers of India, you'll find the people of Asia to be as diverse as the landscapes and equally memorable.

TEMPLES – From the austere temples of Japan to the riotous colours and shapes of Hindu temples in Nepal and India, Asia is home to some of the world's most stunning examples of religious architecture.

FOOD – Eating is half the fun of travelling in Asia and you'll no doubt have some memorable meals; some memorably good and some memorably bad. Whatever the case, you'll have a lot of fun if you approach eating with a sense of adventure.

CITIES – You'll probably be spending a lot of time in cities, and you'll find that each has its own distinctive character. Some are nightmare snarls of congestion and crowds, while others are charming cultural centres where you can comfortably settle down and soak up the atmosphere for a few days.

MARKETS – The markets of Asia are a world unto themselves, filled with all manner of goods, from the familiar to the downright incomprehensible. Among the highlights are Tokyo's Tsukiji market (the world's largest fish market), Kuala Lumpur's bustling Chinatown market and Bangkok's sprawling weekend market.

And this is just the beginning. Whatever your tastes, you will certainly find that Asia satisfies and then some. For this reason, people who love travelling do a lot of their travelling in Asia. It's simply addictive. Don't say you weren't warned …

PLANNING

WHAT KIND OF TRIP?

Organised Tours

Many travellers tend to dismiss organised tours as only for older people and the terminally unadventurous; certainly, organised tours can be restrictive and overly planned, but they do have some advantages. The main one is obvious: you don't have to work out the details yourself – you simply pay your money and let the tour company take care of the rest.

Tours are also fantastic ways to meet people and provide ready-made travelling companions; they can be highly informative, especially if run by a well trained guide; and they can take you to places that would be difficult to reach as an independent traveller, such as long treks in the Himalaya requiring porters and guides, or rafting trips in places like northern India and Nepal that require specialised equipment.

Unfortunately, organised tours are often prohibitively expensive, usually costing several times the amount an independent traveller would spend visiting the same places. It's possible that accommodation costs might be cheaper overall, but tours often bed down in some unattractive places that, if you were on your own, you could just walk away from.

Another drawback is that organised tours rob you of your freedom of movement, and bind you to people you may not like. On your own, or with a companion, you can go where your whim takes you. You can stay put in places you especially like for as long as you please, track down unexplored destinations you hear about through fellow travellers, and leave those that don't measure up to your expectations.

If you decide on an organised tour, try to find a company that will suit your style of travel and appeals to your interests. If you're into mountain climbing or river rafting, for example, such a tour will increase your chances of meeting like-minded people. A few of the more interesting tour operators include:

AUSTRALIA
Intrepid Travel (☎ 1300-360 667; fax 03-9419 4426; www.intrepidtravel.com.au) 11 Spring St, Fitzroy, Vic 3065

UK
Encounter (☎ 020-7370 6951; fax 7244 9737; www.encounter.co.uk) 267 Old Brompton Rd, London SW5 9LA
Exodus (☎ 020-8675 5550; fax 8673 0779; www.exodustravels.co.uk) 9 Weir Rd, London SW12 OLT

USA

Global Exchange (☎ 415-255-7296; www.globalexchange.org) 2017 Mission St #303, San Francisco, CA 94110

Journeys International (☎ 1-800-255-8735; www.journeys-intl.com) 107 April Drive, Suite 3, Ann Arbor, MI 48103

INTERNATIONAL

Ecotour (www.ecotour.org/ecotour.htm)

Serious Sports (www.serioussports.com/core.html)

Specialty Travel (www.specialtytravel.com)

Going it Alone

The prospect of travelling on your own in Asia can be daunting. You will have to be self-reliant, make decisions single-handedly, and you may spend a lot of time alone. Equally important is the financial aspect of solo travel. Single rooms cost almost as much as double rooms, and clearly you'll get a cheaper deal if you can split restaurant bills and transport fares with a travelling companion.

Still, the luxury of being free to go where you want, and when you want, can more than outweigh these considerations. On your own, you'll probably find yourself being more receptive to new experiences and you'll also have the time to absorb them. You may end up meeting more people than if you were travelling with a friend, since you'll be forced to be more outgoing to find company. In fact, you probably won't stay solo for long anyway. A real delight of Asian travel is meeting and travelling with new people for a while, then going solo again.

If you're tempted by the idea of totally independent travel, but are unsure as to whether you have the temperament for it, why not give it a trial run before traipsing all the way to Asia? Try a brief solo trip at home; if you find yourself going psycho after a few days alone, then it's time to start looking for a travel companion.

Travelling with Friends

Travelling with a friend or two eliminates the potential isolation of solo travel. It has practical advantages too: you can split into teams when looking for rooms, or one person can guard the bags while the other searches; you'll save money on accommodation, food and taxis; and, most importantly, you will have moral support when facing unfamiliar or tricky situations. The key is finding the right person to travel with.

Surprisingly, a good friend doesn't necessarily make a good travel companion. Your travel partner is someone you'll be spending most of every day with. Add to this the stresses of Asian travel, and even the greatest friendships will be tested. Think carefully about the personality of your prospective travel partner, and whether you're compatible. In particular, discuss how each of you envisages travelling. Some people like to move slowly and plonk down in a nice spot for a while; others want to take in a new sight every day. Likewise, some people plan every aspect of their itinerary to the last detail, while others prefer to leave events to chance. Sometimes these different approaches can complement each other, but more often than not they will lead to friction and arguments.

If you're travelling as part of a larger group, things can get out of hand fast. A group of three people is probably the desirable limit. Beyond that, you'll start to resemble a lost boy scout troop, and all those conflicting personalities and travel aims are going to be impossible to satisfy. Think carefully about bringing your whole gang of friends with you. If you are travelling in a large group, try to operate as two or more separate groups most of the time.

Travelling with your partner or spouse can be the most sensitive travel arrangement of all. At its worse it could be a very good way of turning your significant other into your significant ex-other. Spending every moment of the

TESTING THE RELATIONSHIP

Lots of young couples set off together to foreign climes, but many come back separately – travel can be a tough testing ground for personal relationships. People who have lived together for years suddenly discover glaring incompatibilities as they set out on their trip of a lifetime.

When you're travelling together, you probably spend more time in each other's company than any couple ever would at home. Some of this time will be spent in difficult circumstances – on long, uncomfortable bus trips, or in cramped and sweaty hotel rooms – sometimes tired, hungry or exasperated. And how will you cope with all the shared decisions? Is it worth US$12 to stay in the concrete boxes called Paradise Bungalows? Do we trust a guy selling Rolex watches on the street? Will we get cholera eating this stuff? The couples who have it together agree on most things, whether it's trying street-stall noodles or a seven day jungle trek. The feuding couples bicker over a 10 rupee trinket, and spend the evening sniping at each other as the sun sets superbly behind the snowcapped Himalaya.

As at home, a partner offers security, emotional support and financial advantages. The security of a relationship really means something when you're in a crowded, chaotic bus station, and one person can sit on the luggage while the other buys the tickets. As for the economics, two people can't travel as cheaply as one, but they can often travel as cheaply as one-and-a-half.

The greatest advantage of travelling with your partner comes when you see something intriguing or really amazing. It's pretty much an instinct to turn to the person next to you and say, 'Isn't that whatever?!', and it's sure nice if that person gives a damn.

And if your relationship survives the road test, you might just look back on that marathon bus trip with the crazy driver, the inquisitive kids and the sleazy passengers as a high point of your life together. And that none-too-clean little guesthouse, with the flickering light and the swaying mosquito net, may yet be one of the most romantic places on earth.

JAMES LYON
LP AUTHOR, AUSTRALIA

day together in strange and stressful circumstances can pull hard at the seams of a relationship. If, however, you have travelled together before and are prepared to be a little flexible, then by all means give it a try – if your relationship can survive six months in Asia, there's no stopping you.

Staying Friends on the Road

It's only realistic to expect that you will have some arguments while you're on the road. Even the saintliest of folks might lose their cool when the thermometer is peaking at 45°C and the train is five hours late. These reactions to stressful circumstances are normal, just try not to hold a grudge against each other for too long.

You will probably find it helpful to build some space into your routine so that you can regularly have time alone, or at least away from each other. Some experienced travellers make a habit of separating for a few days and then meeting at a predetermined point a little further down the road. This breathing space can help keep the relationship alive, and allows you to pursue your own interests. If you have had an argument or are simply getting on each others' nerves, an afternoon spent apart is often enough to clear the air. If this doesn't work, bite the bullet, sit down together and discuss your problems. If there is no apparent solution, you can always continue on alone.

Finding Suitable Travel Partners

Ideally, your best friend has the next year off and is dying to join you on your Asian sojourn. If so, you've got a ready-made travel partner. If your friend can't join you and you're tentative about going it alone, try searching travel magazines and newspapers, which are loaded with advertisements for prospective travel partners. Similar notices are posted on university and community centre message boards and on Internet travel posts (or post your own ad through any of these mediums). Make a point of meeting your prospective travel partner before you set off, and perhaps do a short tour together to ensure you're compatible.

A convenient way of meeting a travel partner is to join an organised tour (see Organised Tours earlier in this chapter). If you choose your tour carefully, you may find someone to team up with for further travel when the tour finishes.

Another option is to set off solo and head to a spot with the specific intention of finding someone to travel with. Bangkok's Khao San Rd, Kathmandu's Thamel district and Ho Chi Minh City's Pham Ngu Lao Rd area are all crawling with backpackers looking to team up with other travellers. Introduce yourself to people in the backpackers cafes and hostels in these districts. If you feel shy about this, you could join a short organised tour, such as a rafting trip or mountain trek, and meet partners for ongoing travel this way.

PERFECT STRANGERS?

You're at Yogyakarta station, it's midnight, you're tired, you're dirty and you're by yourself. This is one of those times when you get misty-eyed at the thought of a travelling companion.

Apart from having a shoulder to cry on, there are many other advantages to hooking up with a another traveller. For one, your wallet will get a boost. Going dutch on taxis, food, car rental, rickshaw fares and, of course, accommodation, will significantly decrease your daily costs. Another is that ordinary activities that are a breeze back home can turn into minor Greek epics when you're travelling. For the solo traveller saddled with a backpack, a money belt and a daypack, simply going to the toilet can be an exercise in lateral thinking. This is when a companion-come-baggage minder is invaluable. The system can be adapted for any activity that involves queuing (buying tickets, asking for information).

Even a relative stranger is comforting when you're heaving your guts up into a squat toilet in Thailand; there's always a back-up decision-maker when your own brain's shut down for the day; you can pool your collective knowledge about a particular place; two people are less vulnerable than one when it comes to standing up to unscrupulous hostel owners; and finally, there's someone to talk to during the tedious hours of waiting for transport, the in-between hours on a long trip, or the delightful hours over a drink and a meal at the end of the day.

But there can be pitfalls to throwing your lot in with a stranger: being on the road can cause your bullshit meter to go on the blink, your judgement gets fogged by too much road food and too little sleep and you end up travelling with a cross between Arthur Daley and Ferris Beuller. Before you know it they've shot off with your money, your camera and your one clean shirt.

Other travellers aren't concerned with your valuables at all – they just want to steal your sanity. Too late you realise that your newest friend is a panpipe enthusiast, and from Orbost to Orbetello you are treated to excerpts from the 72 hour Peruvian Panpipe Festival. Sometimes your companion suffers from the opposite extreme – they're way too 'interesting' – which is why you end up in the boondocks of outer Mongolia, attending a ritual that involves nudity (usually yours) and a yak breathing down your neck, when what you really wanted to do was soak up some sun or wander around a Hindu temple.

Then there's the bludger (short on ready cash, but long on stories of a cheque waiting for them at the next city); the whinger (who cannot bear anything foreign, especially the food), the old hippy (tripped out from too many years in Goa) and the freshly minted ingenue (who chatters for days without drawing breath). The trick is to find a travel companion with a similar budget, compatible interests, a modicum of dependability and a compass pointing in the same vague direction as yours.

From the very beginning, be clear on where you stand in relation to money, sex and destinations. These rules don't have to be written in blood, but you both need space to work into a common groove. And once you do hook up with someone, there's a certain etiquette that should be observed. You do not leave a fellow traveller stranded in the backwaters of China because you've got a sudden urge for a Thai green curry. Any parting of the ways should be done in a civilised manner and with reasonable notice. Any outstanding debts should be payed off, borrowed items returned and an attempt made at forgiving past transgressions.

Sometimes meeting and travelling with a complete stranger can leave you with a load of good memories, a lot of laughs and a lifelong friend. Sometimes it even leaves you with a lifetime partner. It's all about making an informed choice, taking a few precautionary measures, and then road-testing the relationship. If it doesn't work out, give notice and move on.

LISA KERRIGAN
LP MELBOURNE

YOUR ROUTE

Only the trip itself can beat the excitement of spreading out all the maps, opening the guidebooks and just imagining the possibilities. Needless to say, in a continent the size of Asia, the possibilities are just about endless. Unfortunately, for most of us time is limited. To get the most out of your Asian adventure it pays to do some careful planning to ensure you take in at least some of the places that fascinate you, while having the leeway to linger in those spots that unexpectedly take your fancy.

The first decision to make is whether to do a point-to-point trip or fly into one city and use that as a base. Point-to-point trips include overland routes like the famous 'hippie trail' from Europe to Australia via India, and less rigorous and probably shorter trips that make use of round-the-world or open-jaw tickets (see the Air section of the Tickets & Insurance chapter for details).

If you're going to use one city as a base, the city you choose will depend on where you fly from. Most Europeans fly into Bangkok, Delhi or perhaps Kathmandu. Of these, Bangkok is probably the most convenient base from which to tour Asia as it is centrally located and has plenty of budget accommodation and travel agents selling cheap flights to other places within Asia. From North America you can approach either via Europe (from most east coast cities) or across the Pacific (from the west coast). If you go via Europe you'll probably land in one of above-mentioned cities, while from the west coast you'll find it cheapest to fly into Seoul, Bangkok or Hong Kong. As for Australians and New Zealanders, the most common gateway is Bali, but you'll also find inexpensive tickets to Bangkok, Kuala Lumpur and even Singapore.

You will also need to decide on your mode of transport. If you're travelling an overland route, you may want to consider your own motorcycle or car,

ACROSS ASIA ON YOUR OWN WHEELS

If you're planning on taking your own car or motorbike across Asia, you're going to have to deal with some serious paperwork in order to transport your vehicle across international borders. Most importantly, you will need a *carnet de passages en douane* (also known as a CDP). These can be obtained from automobile associations in your home country. The bad news is that in addition to taking a month or more to process, a CDP costs about US$175. Furthermore, you have to leave a deposit with the agency that provides your CDP and this deposit must be enough to cover any duties imposed on your vehicle by the countries into which you take your car – possibly up to 600% of the vehicle's value.

For more details of what's involved, contact your own country's automobile association or check out the Canadian Automobile Association's web site at www.caa.ca/CAAInternet/travelservices/frames14.htm. For more details on vehicles and documentation see *Russia and Central Asia by Road* by Hazel Barker & David Thurlow (1997). For details on International Driving Permits, see the Other Paperwork section in the Passports & Visas chapter. See also the Car & Motorcycle section in the While You're There chapter for some suggestions on day-to-day road travel in Asia.

although this can involve huge hassles with paperwork and documentation. For more details on doing the overland route in your own vehicle, see the boxed text 'Across Asia on Your Own Wheels' in this section.

The alternative is public transportation, although this brings its own brand of frustrations and will inevitably require more time. A good compromise would be to use surface transport most of the way and fly over some sections. Remember, you don't have to buy all legs of your plane ticket before leaving home. Flights within Asia are often surprisingly cheap, and flying is a feasible option if you just can't handle another long bus or train ride (see Getting Around in the While You're There chapter for transport details).

The following sections outline various route options for travelling to and across Asia. South-East Asia and the Indian subcontinent are quite separate areas geographically, but there's nothing to prevent you from joining them to create longer, more involved routes (the hippie trail is the ultimate example of this). When planning your route, make sure it is based on the way you want to travel and includes the sights and activities that interest you. Conditions in Asia can change rapidly, so it's important to check on the latest travel conditions before you leave home (see the Online Resources section later in this chapter).

For specific highlights and suggested itineraries within individual countries, see the country profiles later in this book.

Overland Routes

For an indelible impression of the landscape and cultures of Asia, overland travel is unbeatable. Instead of the jarring juxtapositions of air travel, you are able to watch the seamless flow of one landscape slowly transforming into another. After taking a back seat to air travel during the past decade, overland travel is regaining popularity as more borders open to allow fairly free surface travel over most parts of Asia. Overland travel requires careful research into current visa situations, travel advisories and border crossing regulations to ensure your proposed route is feasible (see Online Resources in this chapter, plus the Passports & Visas chapter and the country profiles for advice). The routes mentioned in the section appear on the colour map at the front of the book.

The Hippie Trail: Europe to Australia

This legendary overland route is the path carved out by all those hippies searching for enlightenment and good times in India, Kathmandu and Bali back in the 60s. It can be travelled from Europe all the way down to Australia, or just as easily in the opposite direction. Only two parts of the route cannot be covered by surface transport: the crossing from Bangladesh to Myanmar (Burma) and the ocean leg from Indonesia to Australia.

Many travellers still prefer to travel this route the old-fashioned way by driving their own vehicle for the leg of the route between Europe and India. This involves some serious research into the paperwork needed (see the boxed

text 'Across Asia on Your Own Wheels' earlier in this section for details on taking your own vehicle). You can do this trip in as little as three months with your
own transport, but six months to a year is a much more reasonable time frame.
No matter how you travel, you must start the visa application process long
before departing (particularly for your Iranian visa).

From Europe, the route starts in Istanbul, Turkey, and then crosses into Iran
at Gurbulak. From Iran, you enter Pakistan at Mirjave. You can then head north
and east into China via the Karakoram Highway (see the following Karakoram
Highway section) or press on into India, crossing from Wagah to Attari.

You could spend months exploring India and taking side trips north into
Nepal (probably crossing at the border village of Sunauli), before going back
into India and crossing into Bangladesh, either at Benapol-Haridaspur or
Chilahati-Haldibari. In Bangladesh, you must fly from Dhaka to Yangon
(Rangoon) in Myanmar, from where you can cross into Thailand at Tachilek
or Kawthoung (by boat at the latter). Many travellers spend a few months
exploring Thailand and nearby Laos, Cambodia and Vietnam before picking up
the route again, which now heads southward to Malaysia via the Thai Isthmus
of Kra. After traversing the length of Peninsular Malaysia, the Causeway leads
into Singapore, from where a ferry or speedboat will take you to Batam or
Bintan islands in Indonesia's Riau Archipelago, and on to Sumatra. From
Sumatra, it's a matter of island-hopping through Indonesia to East Timor. A
flight from Kupang to Darwin in Australia is the final leg of this well beaten
travellers trail.

Karakoram Highway

The Karakoram Highway connects northern Pakistan with far north-western
China via the Khunjerab Pass (4730m) and is the ideal way to link a northern
Asia-Indian subcontinent route. Theoretically you could cover the 1300km trip
in 48 hours, but it would be more realistic to allow two to three weeks. The
pass is open only from 1 May to 30 November and is usually traversed by bus,
although some adventurous souls have made the trip by bicycle or motorcycle.
The highway begins in Rawalpindi in Pakistan and ends at Kashgar in China,
from where a 36 hour bus ride will take you to Ürümqi, the capital of China's
Xinjiang Province. On the Pakistan side, the closest city to the pass is Gilgit,
which is a good base for expeditions to the Karakoram Range (home to K2, the
world's second highest peak).

Travelling the Karokoram Highway requires some preparation, as you
must arrange your China visa in advance. You should do the same for your
Pakistan visa, as the 36 hour transit visa you will otherwise get upon entry will
barely allow you enough time to reach Islamabad to extend it.

Trans-Siberian Railway

Few rail journeys can conjure up mystery and romance like the Trans-Siberian
Railway. It actually comprises three separate rail routes. The 'true' Trans-Siberian

trip takes seven days to travel from Moscow to the eastern Siberian city of Vladivostok, and ferries leave from the nearby port of Nakhodka for Niigata in Japan. The Trans-Manchurian line crosses the Russia-China border at Zabaikalsk-Manzhouli before arriving in Beijing, and the Trans-Mongolian line connects Moscow and Beijing, via the Mongolian capital of Ulaan Baatar. Both these routes take six days.

Conditions aboard the trains are rough, and theft is rampant. If you can afford to, travel deluxe class, which has two-bed cabins, showers and better security. Economy-class cabins will do in a pinch. In Europe, you can purchase tickets through The Russia Experience in the UK (☎ 020-8566 8846; www.travel.world.co.uk) and STA Travel (www.sta-travel-group. com), among others. In China, try China International Travel Service in Beijing (☎ 010-6515-8570) or Monkey Business in Hong Kong (☎ 852-2723-1376; www.monkeyshrine.com). The *Trans-Siberian Handbook* (Trailblazer Publications) by Bryn Thomas is a useful and detailed guide.

Routes in South-East Asia

Bangkok is by far the most convenient starting point for trips around South-East Asia. It's cheap to fly to from most parts of the world, is packed with budget accommodation and is a gentler introduction to Asia than a city such as Delhi. It's also easy to get cheap flights to all parts of the region from here.

Bali is another good starting point. From here you can island-hop northward through Indonesia and Malaysia to Thailand and from there explore the countries of Indochina.

The Philippines, which lies off the main tourist route in South-East Asia, is less convenient to visit. Unless you fly there directly from your home country, you'll have to fly from another Asian

ROUTES IN ASIA

Two Weeks to One Month

- Any single country in Asia
- Thailand & Malaysia
- Japan & South Korea
- Northern India & Nepal
- Malaysia & Singapore

Two to Three Months

- Japan, South Korea & China
- Vietnam, Laos & Cambodia
- India, Nepal & Bangladesh
- Thailand, Malaysia & Singapore

Three to Six Months

- Vietnam, Laos, Cambodia & China
- India, Pakistan & China (via the Karakoram Highway)
- Vietnam, Laos, Cambodia, Thailand & Indonesia

Six Months to One Year

- Europe to Australia (overland)
- Subcontinent & North-East Asia (via the Karakoram Highway)

19

country (common departure points are Bangkok, Kuala Lumpur and Hong Kong). It may also be possible to take a boat from northern Sabah (in East Malaysia) to Zamboanga, Mindanao in the Philippines (though this route is sometimes shut down due to pirates in the Celebes Sea).

Thailand. Malaysia & Singapore   These three countries are easily visited in a trip of one to three months, facilitated by the excellent rail line that runs south from Bangkok all the way to Singapore. Starting in Bangkok, you can travel to Chang Mai in Northern Thailand for some hill trekking, before heading to any of the Thai islands for some serious relaxation. From Thailand you can catch a bus or train to Padang Besar in Malaysia.

In Malaysia, you have the choice of an east cost route, with the better beaches and islands, or a west coast route, with Malaysia's more cosmopolitan cities. Either way you should be able to take in the capital city, Kuala Lumpur, and the stunning jungle in the Taman Negara National Park. From Kuala Lumpur, it's an easy bus or train ride to Singapore, from where ferries continue down into Indonesia via Batam or Bintan.

Vietnam. Laos & Cambodia   This area, often referred to as Indochina, has opened its doors to foreign travellers in recent years. New border crossings are opening each year, so check on the latest conditions when planning your route. Many of the overland crossings are still difficult, so consider flying between countries on parts of this route (for details see the relevant country profiles later in this book).

The main option is to fly from Bangkok to either Ho·Chi Minh City or Hanoi in Vietnam. You can travel from Vietnam north into China via the crossings at Dong Dang or Lao Cai. An interesting trip is to travel as far as Beijing on the international express that runs from Hanoi via Dong Dang twice a week. You can also enter China from Laos, at Boten.

The main overland option from Thailand is to enter Laos via the Nong Khai crossing near Vientiane. From Laos you can travel overland to Vietnam via the Lao Bao border crossing. No border crossings are permitted between Laos and Cambodia, but buses run regularly between Phnom Penh in Cambodia and Ho Chi Minh City in Vietnam.

Routes in North-East Asia

Due to the greater expense of travelling in North-East Asia, extensive overland travel is not as common as in South-East Asia. If you want to travel through this region, an obvious route would cover China, Japan and South Korea, adding Mongolia if you have the time and energy. You could begin by flying into Japan, which is a good option as there are lots of cheap flights to Osaka and Tokyo from the west coast cities of North America. Tour Japan for as long as you can afford it, then take a ferry from Shimonoseki in western Honshu to Pusan in South Korea.

It's virtually impossible to travel overland into China via North Korea, but plenty of ferries depart from the port of Inch'on, near Seoul, to Tianjin in China. You could cut out the Korea leg entirely by taking a ferry from Kobe to Shanghai (flying is also an option).

An interesting North-East Asia route starts in South Korea (flying into Seoul), then crosses from Pusan to Shimonoseki in Japan. You can head down through Kyushu to Naha on Okinawa and catch a ferry to Keelung in Taiwan. From nearby Taipei you can catch flights to any South-East Asian country or back home.

Routes on the Indian Subcontinent

The Indian subcontinent forms almost a separate block in Asia as it is cut off from the rest of the continent by the Himalaya to the north and travel restrictions in Myanmar to the east. To travel here from other parts of Asia, you must either traverse the Karakoram Highway (see that section earlier in this chapter), make the difficult land crossing from Kathmandu to Lhasa in Tibet (this route is closed to independent travellers) or fly (there are lots of cheap flights between Delhi and Bangkok or Hong Kong, and between Bangkok and Kathmandu). Thus, a trip combining the subcontinent with other parts of Asia will entail significant extra amounts of both time and money. Alternatively, a trip around the subcontinent alone can be extremely satisfying and can easily fill months of travel. For details on each country in the subcontinent, see the country profiles later in this book.

A popular route is to fly into Delhi and then journey overland by train and bus to Kathmandu, the base for trekking and rafting trips in Nepal. From Kathmandu, it's fairly easy to take a combination of buses back across the border to the Indian hill station of Darjeeling. From Darjeeling, you can travel into Bangladesh, or head further into India, taking in major attractions such as Varanasi and the Taj Mahal before returning to Delhi. A second option is to travel from India into Pakistan via the crossing at Attari (Wagah on the Pakistan side) to explore the Hindukush and Karakoram ranges, or continue over the Khunjerab Pass into north-western China.

For details on travelling overland from Europe via Turkey, Iran and Pakistan, see The Hippie Trail: Europe to Australia earlier in this chapter.

Thematic Trips

You could almost guarantee a memorable Asian holiday by building it around a favourite activity or interest. If you're a diving, trekking or surfing enthusiast, you'll find world-class destinations in various parts of the continent. Likewise, myriad opportunities exist for pursuing wildlife spotting, birdwatching, white-water rafting, kayaking, meditation or even cooking. Consult the activities section of a good guidebook for detailed options. As well, there are specialised guides available covering Asia's more popular trekking and diving destinations. The Researching Your Trip section later in this chapter lists resources useful in planning an activity-based trip. Have a look also at our Ecotourism Guidelines in the Issues & Attitudes chapter, to ensure you are sensitive to the preservation of the ecosystems of the places you are visiting, especially while trekking or wildlife spotting.

Trekking

The Himalaya, the 'abode of the snows', is the highest chain of mountains on earth, and is largely the birthplace of trekking. The Nepal Himalaya provides ample opportunity for trekking, as do Pakistan, Japan and the other countries listed below. An alternative to higher-altitude trekking is jungle trekking, which is especially popular in Thailand and other tropical regions of Asia. Don't under-estimate the endurance needed for jungle trekking. It's infinitely more strenuous than many people expect and temperatures can fall surprisingly low in tropical mountains, even those near the equator.

If you're planning on trekking in Asia, get into shape beforehand. For camping or technical climbing, you should bring most of your equipment from home as rental equipment is often inferior. You may also need to hire a guide and porters, depending upon your route. Regional highlights include:

NEPAL – The world's highest mountains, stunning scenery and friendly people combine to create the world's best trekking terrain. The fascinating city of Kathmandu, the main base for trekking in the Himalaya, is an added bonus.

PAKISTAN – Though less famous than the Himalaya, the Hindukush and Karakoram ranges provide spectacular trekking, including the long trek up to the K2 base camp. Less affected by the seasonal monsoon that drenches Nepal, these mountains are good for mid to late-summer trekking.

INDIA – The north Indian areas of Ladakh, Kashmir, Himachal Pradesh, Uttarakhand and Sikkim all boast excellent Himalayan trekking, whether to the source of the Ganges or as a rugged trek around the high moonscapes of Ladakh. We recommend extreme caution in this area due to political unrest in Kashmir.

MALAYSIA – Gunung Kinabalu (4101m) in East Malaysia is a fascinating mountain climb, allowing you to ascend from tropical rainforest to a barren alpine zone over a couple of days. In addition, you'll find great jungle trekking in the Taman Negara and Gunung Mulu national parks.

JAPAN – This mountainous archipelago is covered with fine trails. In particular, the 3000m-plus peaks of the Japan Alps are both challenging and beautiful.

PHILIPPINES – There is plenty of good trekking for those who don't mind pursuing these activities in often extremely hot weather. There are some great treks in Quezon Province on Luzon Island, and you can also scale some of the Philippines' 37 volcanoes (check with local authorities as to whether any eruptions are predicted).

INDONESIA – Some great walks and climbs can be found in the national parks of Gunung Leuser on Sumatra and Dumoga Bone on Sulawesi. You can scale dormant volcanoes, such as Gunung Batur on Bali and Gunung Ijen on Java, or for a wilder experience, head to the more remote Baliem Valley on Irian Jaya.

SOUTH KOREA – Every province of South Korea offers good trekking and you'll even find challenging walking and climbing areas in suburban Seoul. If you prefer less travelled regions, head to the Soraksan or Ch'iaksan national parks. You can use South Korea's excellent system of mountain huts, but be prepared for crowds in summer.

THAILAND – Wilderness trekking is one of Northern Thailand's biggest drawcards. Most treks last from four to 10 days. During the day you climb through forested hills and each evening you stay in hill-tribe villages. You can also trek in many of Thailand's national parks including Khao Yai, Kaeng Krachan, Khao Sam Roi Yot and Khao Sok.

Diving & Snorkelling

Asia abounds with exotic and excellent dive sites. Generally, you'll find the best diving in South-East Asia – particualrly the Similan Islands in Thailand, Manado in Indonesia and Pulau Sipadan in Malaysia – although there is some diving off Sri Lanka and the Maldives in the Indian Ocean, and Okinawa in Japan. The Association of Professional Diving Instructors (PADI) certification is the most widely recognised, but some operators will allow you to dive with certification from other organisations, such as NAUI, BSAC, FAUI and SSI. Remember to get a medical diving check before you leave home, as you'll need a certificate of fitness before any dive centre in Asia will let you dive.

You might also want to do a diving course before you leave, although any people obtain their diving certification in Asia; Thailand in particular has plenty of low-cost courses. Prices for PADI open-water dive certification courses generally cost around US$200 and two-dive packages for certified divers around US$50 including equipment. Try bargaining during the off season.

Rental equipment is widely available at dive centres, though quality varies. If you're a serious diver, consider bringing your own mask, regulator, BCD and fins. Likewise, if you're a serious snorkeller you might want to bring your own mask, snorkel and fins.

THAILAND – With the Andaman Sea to the west and the South China Sea to the east, Thailand has superb diving and a well developed diving industry. Popular spots include Ko Tao, Ko Samui, Phuket, Ko Phi Phi and Pattaya. Live-aboard boats allow you to journey out to top spots such as the Similan and Surin islands and the Burma Banks (famous for whale shark sightings in late spring). For cheap certification, head to Ko Tao, where courses cost as little as US$100.

INDONESIA – Indonesia is a diver's paradise, with sites up and down the archipelago. Better known spots are off Bali, Lombok, Maluku and, most famously, off Manado in northern Sulawesi. Irian Jaya has excellent wreck dives in Cenderawasih Bay. The cheapest certification rates are on Bali.

MALAYSIA – World-famous Pulau Sipadan, boasting steep wall dives, impressive coral and myriad colourful tropical fish, is off the south-east coast of Sabah. Other top sites are Pulau Perhentian and Pulau Tioman (both with inexpensive dive centres for certification), Pulau Redang and the smaller islands of the Seribuat Archipelago.

PHILIPPINES – Better dive sites among the 7000-plus islands of the Philippines are in the Mindoro Strait, the Calamian Group, the Bacuit Archipelago, Honda Bay (off Palawan) and off Sumilon Island (in the Visayas). More adventurous souls can sample the spectacular diving on the Tubbataha Reef in the Sulu Sea, and there are heaps of WWII wrecks in Subic Bay north-west of Manila and in the sound between Busuanga and Culion islands.

Surfing

If you're a surfer, you'll probably already know about the legendary breaks to be found in Indonesia, such as Pulau Nias off Sumatra. There are also some decent breaks in the Philippines, Japan and even Vietnam. In recent years, surfing has really taken off, particularly in Indonesia, and visitors will often find themselves sharing the line-up with hot locals – remember, if you treat locals with respect, and avoid confrontations with a smile, you should get lots of waves.

It's possible to rent boards in some of the more popular spots, but serious surfers should bring boards from home. In South-East Asia, waves tend to break sharply over shallow coral reefs, so you'll probably need a slightly longer board (seven feet or more), plus accessories as surf shops are rare. A rash shirt or short-sleeve spring wetsuit, and high-protection sunscreen, are a good idea.

INDONESIA – Among these reef-rimmed islands, world-class surfing can be found at Ulu Watu on the south coast of Bali, Grajagan (G-Land) and Pulau Panaitan on Java, and Pulau Nias off the west coast of Sumatra. Many surfers camp on the beaches at the more remote spots, and cheap *losmens* (guesthouses) are available at popular spots. (If you decide to camp, ask about local conditions as surfers have, at times, been attacked by machete-wielding thieves.) You can visit some outlying breaks by chartered yacht, advertised in surfing magazines.

PHILIPPINES – The surf scene is just developing here and the waves generally can't compete with those in Indonesia. However, there are some decent breaks on the Pacific coast of Luzon, at Puraran on Catanduanes, and on Siargao Island north-east of Mindanao. Try also the south-east coast of Samar.

JAPAN – It's certainly not the place to visit just for the surf, but there are some breaks around Shikoku, Wakayama and south of Yokohama. Unless a typhoon is blowing in, don't expect much in the way of big waves.

White-Water Rafting & Kayaking

White-water rafting and kayaking are still in their infancy in much of Asia, but the industry is developing quickly. Adrenaline junkies will find plenty to satisfy them on the mighty rivers of Nepal, northern India and Pakistan, while Thailand, Indonesia and Malaysia also boast some excellent rafting and kayaking through jungle environs. However, be wary of tour operators throughout the region, as many have substandard equipment and use poorly trained guides; ask fellow travellers to recommend a trustworthy operator. It's difficult to rent equipment outside Nepal, so serious kayakers will have to lug their own boats from home.

NEPAL – The Karnali, Sun Kosi, Kali Gandaki, Bhote Kosi and Seti rivers draining the high Himalaya provide superb white-water rafting and kayaking. Numerous tour companies are based in the Thamel district of Kathmandu, so shop around. Expect to pay from US$40 to US$70 per day for a good trip with a reputable operator.

INDIA – Rafting expeditions are conducted on the Beas River in Manali, the Ganges and its tributaries in Himachal Pradesh, the Indus and Zanskar in Ladakh and Zanskar, and the Teesta in West Bengal. These sports are very new to India, so you may have to look around for a decent operator. Prices are significantly lower than in Nepal, with one operator in Manali offering two-week trips for US$140.

PAKISTAN – It's possible to raft or kayak the Indus, Kunhar, Swat, Gilgit, lower Ishkoman, Shyok and Hunza rivers in northern Pakistan. However, there are few operators running these rivers commercially, so you may have to organise a trip yourself. Ask around Gilgit to see what's available.

INDONESIA – The Sungai Hamputung in Kalimantan, the Sungai Sa'dan in Sulawesi and the Ayung in Bali are open for rafting, but have few commercial operators. Ask around when you get there, and you may find new options.

THAILAND – Rafting is rapidly gaining popularity in Thailand. While most rafting here can't really be called 'white-water' it is nonetheless very enjoyable. Most trips are fairly gentle floats down jungle rivers with stops to enjoy nearby waterfalls, caves and hot springs. Most raftable rivers are in the north and these include the Kok, Mae Hong Son, Mae Klong, Mae Taeng and Pai.

Wildlife Spotting & Birdwatching

Wildlife and birdwatching enthusiasts will be dazzled by the options in Asia. While some of the larger endangered mammals, such as the Bengal tiger, the snow leopard and the Asian rhinoceros, are rarely (if ever) seen, smaller creatures abound in natural parks and reserves across the continent, including varieties of deer, monkey, fox and rodent. In particular, the parks of India, Malaysia, Indonesia and Nepal are fertile ground for both wildlife spotting and birdwatching. To maximise your chances of seeing wildlife, you may want to join a safari or similar tour that sets out with the express purpose of finding game. These are widely available in both Nepal and India.

Of the many specialist guides available about the wildlife and birdlife of Asia, the Insight and Periplus series are particularly useful. In addition, the better guidebooks to the individual countries in Asia have sections on where to spot wild animals and birds.

INDIA – There are numerous national parks, wildlife sanctuaries and nature reserves in India. The top ones include: Corbett Tiger Reserve in Uttar Pradesh; Sunderbans Wildlife Sanctuary in West Bengal, which has one of the largest tiger populations of any of the Indian parks; Kaziranga National Park in Assam, famous as the last major home of the rhinoceros; and Similipal National Park in Orissa with tigers, elephants and several types of deer. A popular way to see wildlife in India is to take an elephant safari; operators are based in towns near the major parks. At Keoladeo Ghana National Park, painted storks are a spectacular feature of the bird sanctuary, while Vedan-tangal Bird Sanctuary harbours a variety of Indian waterbirds, including cormorants, egrets, storks, ibises and spoonbills.

NEPAL – Nepal has an astonishing variety of wildlife, especially on the southern plains of the Terai which is home to the two best places to spot large mammals: the Royal Chitwan and Royal Bardia national parks. Here, if you're especially lucky, you may glimpse a Bengal tiger or a rhinoceros. Bardia also has leopards, jungle cats, mongoose, sloth bears and langur and rhesus monkeys, among other types of wildlife. Keep your eyes open when trekking in the Himalaya, and you'll spot a surprising variety of birds, such as the golden eagle, the Himalayan griffon and the lammergeier.

MALAYSIA – For some of the best wildlife spotting in South-East Asia, head straight to Malaysia's excellent national parks. Taman Negara in Peninsular Malaysia is a haven for endangered species such as elephants, tigers and leopards, and the birdlife is prolific. Gunung Mulu and Gunung Kinabalu mountains in East Malaysia are other highlights.

INDONESIA – Because the islands of western Indonesia were once linked by land to the Asian mainland, they still contain some large mammals such as elephants, tigers, rhinoceros and leopards, though all are exceedingly rare. The orang-utan is most accessible at the Bukit Lawang Orang-utan Rehabilitation Centre in north Sumatra. Another good place to spot wildlife is in Ujung Kulon National Park, best known as the last refuge on Java for the one horned rhinoceros, and home to wild pigs, otters and gibbons. As for birdwatching, adventurous types will find plenty of interesting species in Irian Jaya, including the bird of paradise and cassowary.

BANGLADESH – Home to almost half of all bird species found on the subcontinent, it's hard to imagine a better place for birdwatching. In the Dhaka area, the Madhupur Forest is home to several species of owls, thrushes and raptors. In the north, the Sylhet area has extensive wetlands which are home to several species of wildfowl, including Baer's pochard and Pallas' fishing eagle. Other important areas include the Indian border near Srimangal, the coastal regions near Hoakhali and the marshy Sundarbans near the Indian border, which is home to eight varieties of kingfisher, among many other species.

CHINA – Birdwatchers will find the long trip to Qinghai Lake, west of Xining in northwestern China, well worth the effort. In particular, visit Bird Island on the western side of the lake, where thousands of wild geese, gulls, cormorants and extremely rare blacknecked cranes come to breed between March and early June.

Spiritual Trips

Many of the travellers who pioneered the overland route to Asia in the 1960s came looking for spiritual wisdom. While the search for enlightenment is no longer such a popular travel aim, you can still study meditation and other aspects of spirituality in several Asian countries. India remains the dominant focus for spiritual trips, and you can also study at temples in Nepal, Thailand and Japan. While study is generally free of charge, you should make a donation to the temple or ashram where you are staying. Wherever you study, don't expect it to be a cakewalk. Most places will require that you wake before dawn, work around the grounds, meditate for several hours during the day, and then study aspects of the practice for several more hours. This rigorous discipline will come as a shock if you've previously been partying your way around Asia.

It pays to ask around about the course you're thinking of enrolling in – there are many sham gurus out there and some groups are dangerously close to cults. Others are just money-making fronts selling pseudo-spirituality to gullible westerners. If the place you're looking at seems more interested in the contents of your wallet than in the welfare of your soul, look elsewhere.

INDIA – If you come to India looking for spiritual wisdom you'll be following in the footsteps of such luminaries as the Beatles, who studied in Rishikesh, and the American poet Allen Ginsberg, who spent time in Varanasi. Ashrams can be found throughout the country. Most do not require prior notice of your arrival, but it might be worth checking in advance. See the Lonely Planet *India* guidebook for a detailed section on gurus and ashrams in India. These include the Sai Baba ashram in Puttaparthi and the Poonjaji ashram in Lucknow.

NEPAL – Unlike India, where study focuses on an individual teacher, spiritual practice in Nepal is largely centred on different schools of thought. There are several ashrams and temples in the Kathmandu Valley where you can study yoga and meditation. Some places are advertised in the Thamel district in Kathmandu, while others are advertised by word of mouth.

THAILAND – The most common form of meditation practised in Thailand is Vipassana, which is a Pali word usually translated as 'insight'. Thai language is often the medium of instruction, but you will find temples and meditation centres that offer courses in English scattered throughout the country. New age spas on touristed islands like Ko Samui gently school foreigners in meditation, fasting and exercise (all for a princely price, of course).

JAPAN – Many foreigners come to Japan to study the austere form of Buddhism known as Zen. These courses are exceedingly strict (lax students who nod off during meditation can expect to be rapped over the shoulder with canes). While most courses are given in Japanese, some specifically aimed at foreigners are given in English. Kyoto is the most popular place to study and courses are offered to foreigners at Myoshin-ji Temple, Zenjo-ji Temple, Gesshukai Sesshin and the Kyoto Soto Zen Center. For information on all these places, contact the Kyoto Tourist Information Office (☎ 075-371 5649). You can also study Zen at Sogen-ji Temple in Okayama and Eihei-ji Temple in Fukui (check out its web page at www.zendo.com/eiheiji.html).

Learning a Skill

You'll find courses of every type, duration and cost in Asia. There are casual places where you just show up and enrol, and more serious courses for which you must apply in advance. Study options include cooking, language, batik, pottery, martial arts, music and traditional dance, as well as diving, meditation and yoga. Some places where courses are easily found are Cherating in Malaysia (for batik), Chang Mai in Thailand (for Thai cooking), Bali (for various Indonesian arts), Kyoto (for various Japanese arts) and Kathmandu in Nepal (for *thangka* painting). For more course details, consult a good guidebook, or look for advertisements in popular backpacker hang-outs and tourist information centres.

Other Activities

The activities discussed in this chapter only scratch the surface of what's possible in Asia. You can rock climb in Thailand, ski in the Indian Himalaya, windsurf in the Philippines, bungee jump in Bali, play golf in Japan or mountain bike just about anywhere. For some pointers on finding the right place to indulge your favourite activity, see Researching Your Trip later in this chapter. Also see Work & Travel later in this chapter for advice on finding paid and volunteer work.

WHEN TO GO

Asia is so vast that at any time of year you'll find good weather, entertaining festivals and budget accommodation somewhere on the continent. While no one should forego a trip to Asia because it doesn't appear to be the 'ideal' time to visit, if possible you want travel when the weather is moderate, the prices are low and the crowds aren't too thick. If you can enjoy some good festivals on the way, that's icing on the cake.

Weather

Asia extends from the subarctic conditions of northern China all the way down into the tropics. Name a climate or a season, and odds are you will find it somewhere on this massive continent. Weather patterns change dramatically throughout the year. For the traveller, planning your trip so you arrive in each country on your route during fine weather is a major challenge, although it's possible to just about follow an endless spring across the continent if you really work at it.

Many of the countries in Asia embrace several climates within the one country at the one time. India, China and Japan in particular suffer harsh variations in temperature. The June heat in Delhi may be so intense that you can barely move; way up in Ladakh in India's north, however, the snow might just be melting on some of the higher roads. Likewise, in Japan, Hokkaido in January could be in the grip of subzero temperatures, while down in Okinawa the mercury is rising to the mid-30°s Celsius. So if time constraints mean you can only travel during a certain period, look closely at the weather details of your favoured destination to find areas of good weather, even if the rest of the country is freezing, boiling or drenched with rain.

Asia can be divided into three broad climatic groups – four-season, three-season and two-season countries. For information on the climates of specific countries, see the When to Go sections of the country profiles.

Four-Season Countries

North & North-East Asia   China, Japan, Korea, Mongolia and Taiwan have the yearly climatic changes that are familiar to many western travellers: cold winters and hot summers with moderate spring and autumn seasons in between. The difference is that temperature fluctuations can be far more severe. Also, extreme humidity affects most of these countries during summer, and Japan and South Korea are hit by heavy rainy seasons around June or July.

The best time to visit northern Asia is in spring (late February to May) and autumn (late September to early December). At these times, you're pretty much guaranteed clear skies, moderate temperatures and reasonable humidity. The exceptions are outlying regions such as Mongolia, Tibet, western China and Hokkaido, which all have longer winters and will be unpleasantly cold and snowy from early November to late March.

If you are travelling in northern Asia during summer or winter, try to focus on the coastal areas, which are much more temperate than those inland. Japan, Taiwan, South Korea and coastal China will be far more comfortable to travel in than western China and Mongolia during summer and winter. Indeed, some travellers find winter is the perfect time to visit southern areas such as Kyushu in Japan or Hong Kong because temperatures are cool, but not prohibitively cold, and the crowds of tourists are absent. Conversely, in summer, temperatures in places like Mongolia and Hokkaido will be warm, but not unbearably hot.

Three-Season Countries

Indian Subcontinent Most of the Indian subcontinent is far enough south to avoid a real winter, except for the Himalaya, where altitude creates an alpine microclimate. In the lowland areas of Bangladesh, India, Nepal and Pakistan there are three main seasons: the hot season (around late February to June); the wet season (heralded by the south-west monsoon and lasting until September); and the cool season (October to late February).

Without question, the cool season is the best time to travel in these lowland regions. India in particular is stiflingly hot during the premonsoon period and then miserably hot, wet and humid during the monsoon itself. During these periods you'll find it just about impossible to enjoy yourself on the plains of India. This is when the Himalaya is at its most appealing; do like the British colonials used to, and escape to the northern hills.

TOP 10 TIPS FOR
FIRST-TIME TRAVEL IN ASIA

1 Travel light – You can always buy things you need on the road (usually for a lot less than you'd spend at home).

2 Don't try to do too much – You'll have other opportunities to see the places you miss this time round.

3 Get off the beaten track – Even if you spend most of your time on the tourist trail, try at least once to get somewhere that few foreigners visit.

4 Get out of the cities – It's all too easy to tramp from one city to the next, and yet some of the most beautiful sights are in rural areas.

5 Splurge once in a while – Don't get too hung up on penny-pinching. When you're feeling run-down, treat yourself to a fantastic meal or a nice hotel.

6 Know yourself – Plan a trip that takes into account your comfort level.

7 Try some unusual foods – Eating exotic cuisines is part of the fun of being in Asia.

8 Learn a few words of the language of the countries you visit – With language, a little can go a long way.

9 Seek advice from other travellers – There's nothing like a first-hand account from someone who's just been there and done that.

10 Give yourself a break from time to time – If you've just spent two months haggling your way around India, why not spend a week lying on a Thai beach to recover?

The best conditions in the Himalaya are during the postmonsoon period from late September to December, when the rains have washed most of the summer dust from the air and the mountain views are spectacularly clear. This is less true of the western Himalaya in Ladakh and Pakistan, which are beyond the reach of the monsoon and offer their best trekking from mid-June to mid-September (when the eastern Himalaya experiences heavy rainfall). See the Nepal and Pakistan profiles for more climate details.

Continental South-East Asia   Cambodia, Laos, Myanmar, Thailand and Vietnam have a climatic cycle similar to that of the Indian subcontinent, although the rainy season is less pronounced and the heat not quite as extreme. These five countries generally have a cool season (November to late February), a hot season (March to June) and a rainy season (starting in June and petering out by September or October). Fortunately the rainy season is not as severe as the drenching India monsoon, and travel is still possible in most of the region at this time. The cool season is the ideal time to travel in continental South-East Asia (it will still be very warm by most people's standards), but you can travel relatively comfortably here at any time of year. Thus, when planning your trip, festivals and crowded periods can be as much a consideration as the weather.

Two-Season Countries

Oceanic South-East Asia   Malaysia, Singapore, Indonesia and the Philippines are in the tropics and surrounded by sea, which keeps temperatures fairly consistently hot. These countries are affected by two monsoons (one from the north-east generally falling between October and April and one from the south-west the rest of the year), although neither is severe enough to preclude travel. Often you can simply cross from one side of the island or country to the other to find better weather. Festivals and peak travel periods are worth taking into account as much as the weather when planning your trip.

Special Events

Many travellers regard festivals and special social events as serendipitous events to be enjoyed if your paths cross, while others build as many as possible into their itinerary. Festivals can be major highlights of your trip, so try to incorporate at least a couple into your plans.

Major festivals and special events attract huge numbers of both foreign and domestic travellers, so you may not be able to find accommodation unless you book well in advance. Furthermore, transport will probably be congested and prices may double, so make sure your budget can handle the extra stress. Making a day trip to the event from somewhere less affected by the crowds is often a good solution. See the boxed text 'Festivals in Asia' over the page, plus the country profiles, for details of some of the continent's more spectacular events. *World Events Calendar* (www.travel.epicurious.com) has a huge list of events which can be searched by theme, country or date.

Travel Periods

When planning your arrival in and departure from Asia, you will need to take into account peak, off-peak and shoulder travel periods. Peak periods are when the majority of travellers want to fly. In your home country, these periods usually coincide with the school holidays, and with certain holidays such as Christmas, New Year and Easter. The country you are flying to will also have its own peak periods, such as Chinese New Year or Ramadan. Flights to these countries will be heavily booked at these times and air fares expensive.

For Asia, the peak period generally covers December to January and July to August; the shoulder period is November and February; and the low season takes in the remaining months. The cheapest time to travel is during off-peak periods, when air fares are significantly lower (sometimes less than half the price of peak periods) and you will have less difficulty getting the departure date of your choice. Shoulder periods, when prices are about midway between peak and off-peak prices, are the obvious second choice of travel period. Find out from a travel agent when the peak, shoulder and off-peak periods are for the countries you plan to visit. Even one day can make a huge difference in the price of tickets. For details, see the Air section in the Tickets & Insurance chapter.

Bad Travel Times

The tourist season in any part of Asia can result in high prices and scarcity of rooms. More importantly, the presence of so many foreign tourists can keep you from enjoying the real flavour of the countries you've come so far to visit. In October, for example, Nepal's most popular treks will be inundated with foreign trekkers. Try the same treks in late December, and you're likely to be the only foreigner in sight. This is just one instance of where, if you are able to travel out of season, your enjoyment of Asia will be greatly enhanced. If you are travelling during the high season, make a special effort to travel off the beaten path. Even when the better known destinations are awash with foreign tourists, you can almost always uncover much less crowded spots and cheaper rooms elsewhere. Alternatively, if you want to see the major sights, make advance reservations or show up early in the day to guarantee yourself a room.

It is not just foreign tourists that can jam up an otherwise pleasant destination – local travellers, especially during school holidays, will descend on tourist sites in hordes. Unless you're partial to sharing your digs with dozens of screeching children, try travelling outside these times, or head for the more inaccessible mountains or islands of a country, where families are less likely to holiday.

National holidays, public events and religious observances can all make travel difficult. Many places (such as Hong Kong, Malaysia and Singapore) just about shut down for Chinese New Year; if you haven't stocked up, you may find yourself dining on dear convenience store goodies for a few days. Muslim countries, such as Pakistan, Malaysia and Indonesia, can be difficult to travel in during Ramadan, because locals are following a strict regime of fasting and prayer.

FESTIVALS

There are myriad Asian festivals celebrating religious and political events. Exact dates for festivals may vary from year to year, either because they are based on the lunar calendar or because local authorities decide to alter dates. The following is our pick of some of the major festivals across the continent:

ATI-ATIHAN FESTIVAL (PHILIPPINES) — Held at Kalibo on the island of Panay for three days in January, this is the Mardi Gras of the Philippines. Vibrant tom-toms signal the beginning of a colourful open-air extravaganza with people bedecked in bizarre costumes and celebrating around the clock.

BIRTHDAY OF CONFUCIUS (CHINA) — The birthday of the great sage occurs on 28 September and is an interesting time to visit Qufu (the birth and death place of Confucius) in Shandong Province. The giant open-air festival held here attracts travellers, entertainers and merchants. A ceremony is held at the Confucius Temple, starting at around 4 am.

BON OM TUK (CAMBODIA) — The Water Festival begins in late October or early November, when the Tonlé Sap River reverses its flow and begins to empty into the Mekong River. Pirogue races are held in Phnom Penh at this time.

BUN BANG FAI (LAOS) — The Rocket Festival takes place every May and features processions, music, dancing and folk theatre, before culminating with bamboo rockets being fired into the sky to encourage the heavens to send rain for the upcoming rice harvest.

DURGA PUJA (BANGLADESH) — This is the country's most important Hindu festival. Statues of the goddess Durga (the Inaccessible, a form of Siva's wife) astride a lion are placed in every Hindu temple. Celebrations last for four days, culminating on the day of the full moon when each statue is moved to the banks of a river or pond; sometime after sunset the goddess is carried into the water to dissolve. A huge festival takes place along the Buriganga River in Dhaka.

DUSSEHRA (INDIA) — The most popular of India's almost countless festivals takes place over 10 days, beginning on the first day of Asvina (September/October). It celebrates the victory of Durga over the buffalo-headed demon Mahishasura. In many places huge images of the demon king Ravana and his accomplices are burned, to symbolise the triumph of good over evil. In Delhi the festival is known as Ram Lila (Life story of Rama), with fireworks and re-enactments of the *Ramayana*.

EID-UL-FITR (PAKISTAN, BANGLADESH, INDONESIA, MALAYSIA, BRUNEI AND PARTS OF THE PHILIPPINES, VIETNAM AND SINGAPORE) — This major two to three day holiday is held to celebrate the end of Ramadan (the Muslim month of austerity and ritual fasting), with alms-giving, prayer, feasting, merriment, new clothes and gift-giving.

FESTIVAL OF LIGHTS (MYANMAR) — Held over three days during September/October, this festival celebrates Buddha's return from a period of preaching. The entire country is lit by oil lamps, fire balloons, candles and even mundane electric lamps, while every house has a paper lantern hanging outside.

GAWAI DAYAK (SARAWAK IN EAST MALAYSIA) — The festival of the Dayaks marks the end of the rice season in early June. Events include war dances, cockfights and blowpipe competitions.

HANAMI (JAPAN) — The Japanese delight in celebrating the appearance of plum, peach and cherry blossoms between February and April. The parties begin on the southernmost island, Okinawa and continue northward to match the progress of the opening of the blossoms. This is a time for frequent picnics and riotous behaviour.

HOLI (INDIA) — During this exuberant Hindu festival people mark the end of winter by throwing coloured water and *gulal* (powder) at one another. In tourist places this might be seen as an opportunity to take liberties with foreigners, so don't wear your good clothes on this day, and be ready to duck. On the night before Holi, bonfires are built to symbolise the destruction of the evil demon Holika.

ICE LANTERN FESTIVAL (CHINA) – Held in Harbin, capital of the northern Heilongjiang Province, in the depths of its winter (January/February). The abundant ice and snow in Zhaolin Park is carved and sculpted into extraordinary shapes – animals, plants, and even a miniature Great Wall of China and Forbidden City. The sculptures are illuminated at night to create an absolute fantasy land.

KANDY ESALA PERAHERA (SRI LANKA) – On the Esala full moon (usually July but occasionally early August) this spectacular festival in Kandy is the climax of 10 days and nights of increasingly frenetic activity, held to honour the sacred tooth enshrined in the Dalada Maligawa temple. A great procession includes thousands of dancers, drummers and temple chieftains, plus 50 or more magnificently decorated elephants. Smaller festivals are held around the island.

LUNAR NEW YEAR (CAMBODIA, CHINA, LAOS, MALAYSIA, SINGAPORE AND VIETNAM) – This three day event, which goes under various names from country to country, is held in either February or April (again depending on the country). It variously involves offerings to gods and ancestors, gifts to family and the needy, the settlement of debts, celebratory dinners, street parades and a ritual cleaning of one's house to usher in the new year on the right note.

NAADAM (MONGOLIA) – This festival showcases Mongolia's finest in the three 'manly sports' of horse racing, archery and wrestling. It is the biggest event of the year for foreigners and locals alike and is held around the country, usually between 11 and 13 July.

NYEPI (INDONESIA) – This celebration on Bali marks the Hindu New Year and virtually the entire island closes down. The celebrants dress in traditional garb, play instruments and offer gifts of food and flowers to a huge doll known as an *ogoh-ogoh*. They then march around the village, pray and make speeches, chase away evil spirits, burn the ogoh-ogoh and get down to some serious revelry.

O-BON (JAPAN) – Held on 13 to 16 July and in August, according to Buddhist tradition the Festival of the Dead is a time when ancestors return to earth. Lanterns are lit and floated on rivers, lakes or the sea to signify the return of the departed to the underworld.

THAIPUSAM (MALAYSIA) – During this dramatic Hindu festival devotees honour Lord Subramaniam with acts of amazing masochism, including driving metal hooks and spikes into the flesh, skewering cheeks and tongues, and lining sandals with nails.

THIRD MOON FAIR (CHINA) – Held in Dali in Yunnan Province for five days in April/May, this festival originated to celebrate the fabled visit of Guanyin, the Buddhist Goddess of Mercy, to the Nanzhao kingdom. Today, thousands of people from the province converge on Dali to buy and sell horses and take part in wrestling matches and other performances.

TSAGAAN SAR (MONGOLIA) – After months of enduring the bitter winter, Mongolians love to celebrate White Month in January or February. Food is central – if you can't eat 10 *buuz* (steamed mutton dumplings) you are deemed to be inadequate – and a cast-iron liver is also required to cope with the amount of alcohol which is consumed.

TSECHU (BHUTAN) – Most *dzongs* (fort-monasteries) and many monasteries have an annual festival, the largest of which is the tsechu, honouring Guru Rimpoche, the 8th century founder of Mahayana Buddhism and the second Buddha. The festival involves a long and complicated series of traditional dances which depict 12 episodes of the life of the Guru. It's held on or around the 10th day of the month throughout the year in the Bhutanese calendar.

WATER-SPLASHING FESTIVAL (CHINA) – Held in the Xishuangbanna region of Yunnan Province, this event falls around mid-April. The purpose is to wash away the dirt, sorrow and demons of the old year and bring in the happiness of the new. Events include a giant market, dragon-boat races, games, dancing and fireworks, before the drenching begins on the third day.

RESEARCHING YOUR TRIP

Research can be a bit of drag, especially when you have a thousand other details to attend to, but focused reading, web exploration, film watching and discussion with travel experts and friends can greatly enhance your trip. This is particularly true if you're basing your trip on a particular theme (such as religious architecture, birdwatching or diving). Proper research can help you maximise your time away, prepare you for the quirks and rigours of different countries and ensure you get to experience most things on your wish list. Even if you're planning a rambling, extended stay in the region, some minimal research is still important. You'll need to know the various border crossings between countries, visa requirements, the easiest and cheapest ways to get around, plus the health and safety risks.

Many of Asia's highlights – such as a trek in Bhutan, a boat trip to Indonesia's Bandas islands or entry to Tibet – are virtually impossible without organising the time-consuming paperwork beforehand.

Guidebooks

Travel guides are invaluable tools, particularly when you're travelling in a country for the first time. They'll help you find places to stay and eat, describe popular attractions, provide vocabulary lists, give you an insight into the local culture, and include all the transport options between and within countries.

Try to decide on a rough route before you buy your guidebooks and allow yourself plenty of time to read them. Some visas can take up to a couple of weeks to organise, which is bad news if you have four or five to arrange two weeks before you're due to leave (see the Passports & Visas chapter and the country profiles for details). Similarly, some immunisations must be administered over a period of weeks (see the Health chapter and country profiles).

If you decide you want a detailed guide to each country you plan to visit, don't necessarily buy them all before you go. Guidebooks can be expensive, and quite a weight to lug around. You can pick up new or second-hand guides in many countries, or swap them with fellow travellers on the road.

Selecting a Guidebook

The travel guide market has mushroomed over the past 20 years and there are thousands of titles available. Before you buy, ask your friends which books they used – a personal recommendation is often the best. Then spend time in a local bookshop browsing the guides to a particular destination. Read the author biographies, assess the quality of the maps, look at the edition date, flick through the photographs, and compare some hard information – how each guide describes a particular town, the number of places to stay and eat that are covered, and the tone of the writing. If you're basing your trip on a particular activity, read the section that covers it and see how much prominence is given to it in the index.

Consider also how long you plan to spend in each country, as this will influence the level of detail you'll need from a guide. For example, in Lonely Planet's *South-East Asia on a shoestring*, Singapore merits 31 pages; in the *Malaysia, Singapore & Brunei* guide the coverage is expanded to 93 pages; and the *Singapore city guide* runs to 196 pages. As the focus is sharpened, a greater level of information is provided; recommendations are more expansive; a larger number of maps is included; and cultural, historical and artistic issues are given more prominence. At Lonely Planet we seek to strike the right balance between background and hard information, adding detailed maps, full-colour photos to evoke the essence of each destination and a style of no-nonsense advice that still inspires a sense of adventure. Have a look across the market and make your own decision.

Complementary Guides

As well as a day-to-day practical guide, consider bringing a more general cultural guide. Odyssey, Periplus and Insight provide quality books in this genre, with loads of full-colour plates and very detailed information on religion, architecture, arts, history and other social and cultural aspects of the countries of Asia.

Specialist Guides

If you plan to indulge a particular activity, such as trekking, surfing or diving, check out the specialist guides devoted to them. Also see the Magazines section later in this chapter.

Cycle Touring   There are very few cycling guides to Asian destinations on the market. Ask at your nearest cycling shop or run a search at your local library for individual titles. Even those that are in print generally cover little more than the route, so accommodation, food and transport will require extra research. A useful magazine is *Bicycling* (☎ 800-666-2806; www.bicyclingmagazine.com; 135 N Sixth St, Emmaus, PA 18098, USA), a leading monthly covering destinations, training, nutrition, touring, racing, equipment and clothing, maintenance and new technology. For some tips on bicycle touring, see the Getting Around section of the While You're There chapter.

Diving & Snorkelling   Lonely Planet's *Pisces* diving and snorkelling series covers many of the world's premier dive spots, including Bali and the Komodo region. The series includes detailed information on dive sites, marine life, dive operators, safety, conservation, history, weather, accommodation, transport, dining and money matters. Similar publications include those by Passport/New Holland (international destinations), Periplus Action Guides and Asian Diver Scuba Guides.

Surfing   There's no comprehensive worldwide series of guides, although there are many one-off guides to particular destinations such as Indonesia. Check out your local surf shop or contact *Surfer Magazine* (☎ 1-714-496-5922;

www.surfermag.com), which has information on breaks around the world, equipment, clothing, courses and tours. It publishes *The Surf Report – Journal of World-wide Surfing Destinations*, and will send you a copy for about US$5 per destination. Order at PO Box 1028, Dana Point, CA 92629.

Trekking Lonely Planet publishes specialist walking guides to the Nepal and Indian Himalaya, and the Karakoram and Hindukush ranges. There is also a *Hiking in Japan* guide that will be published mid-2000. These guides include all the information contained in LP country guides, plus detailed maps of routes, day-by-day descriptions of treks and information on preparation, equipment, food, transport, accommodation, guides and health. Cicerone and Interlink Books produce notable walking guides, although few of their titles cover Asia.

Using Your Guidebook

A guidebook is not intended as a 'bible' to be unquestioningly followed every step of the way. Guides are written by people who bring their own experiences and interests to the text, and these may not necessarily coincide with your own. Also, the 'hard' information such as prices and schedules tends to date quite quickly, so don't go into a blue funk if a bus timetable has changed or a hotel has raised its prices, or the standard of its rooms has changed since your guide was published. A good guide will give you all the information and advice you need, but there's no substitute for your own research.

It's easy to stay safely within the boundaries laid down by a guidebook, but you'll be tied firmly to a 'tourist trail' which is increasingly tailoring its services to western visitors, and which will inhibit your experiences of the real, day-to-day life of the country you are visiting. For a few pointers to your own explorations, see Off the Beaten Track in the While You're There chapter.

Also, treat your guide as expendable. Don't be afraid to rip out the sections covering regions you won't visit, or to ditch (or better still, swap) a book once you've finished with it. If you want to retain your guide as a keepsake, mail it home once you've finished with it.

Maps

If your main method of getting around is public transport, then the regional and city maps in your guidebook should meet your needs. If you plan to hire a car or motorbike, do some independent trekking or an extensive cycle tour, then you'll need to purchase more detailed maps either at home or once you arrive.

By western standards, Asia is not well mapped. Most major cities and towns will have maps in English available either free from local tourist agencies or for sale in bookshops and newsagencies, but once you get away from the popular tourist areas, maps can be thin on the ground or nonexistent.

If you're after a large-scale map, don't bother too much with a continental map of Asia as the scale won't show enough detail, but use a regional map such as one for the Indian subcontinent or South-East Asia. Nelles produces an excellent series of country maps, which often include a map of the capital city centre. Lonely Planet also produces detailed country maps, including Thailand, India & Bangladesh, Laos and Vietnam. Otherwise look at the maps published by Periplus, Kümmerly & Frey, Geocenter or Bartholomew. Contoured maps for cycling or trekking should definitely be obtained before you leave home as these are very difficult to find in Asia. A good place online is *Mapquest Mapstore* (www.mapquest.com). Regular shops with good stocks of maps include:

AUSTRALIA

Mapland (☎ 03-9670 4383) 372 Little Bourke St, Melbourne, Vic 3000
The Travel Bookshop (☎ 02-9241 3554) 20 Bridge St, Sydney, NSW 2001
Nev Anderson Maps (☎ 02-9878 2809) 30 Fawcett St, Ryde, NSW 2112

CANADA

World of Maps & Travel Books (☎ 613-724-6776; maps@magi.com; www.worldofmaps. com) 118 Holland Ave, Ottawa, Ontario K1Y 0X6

NEW ZEALAND

Map World (☎ 03-374 5399; maps@mapworld.co.nz) PO Box 13-833, Christchurch
Whitcoulls (☎ 09-356 5400) 210 Queen St, Auckland

UK

Stanfords Map Centre (☎ 020-7836 1321) 12-14 Long Acre, London WC2E 9LP
The Map Shop (☎ 06-846 3146) AT Atkinson & Partner, 15 High St, Upton-on-Severn, Worcestershire WR8 OHJ

USA

Traveller's Bookstore (☎ 212-664-0995) Time Warner Building, 22 E 52nd St, New York, NY 10019
Rand McNally – The Map & Travel Store (☎ 212-758-7488; www.randmcnallystore.com) 150 East 52nd St, New York, NY 10022; (☎ 415-777-3131) 595 Market St, San Francisco, CA 94105-2803

Travel Agencies

Brochures distributed by travel agents can be good, free sources of information. Even if you have no intention of going on an organised tour, you can get a good feel for a country's major sights from the full-colour images in these publications. Travel consultants are often widely travelled and most will be happy to share their experiences with you. Just remember that many consultants work on commission, so don't take up too much of their time if you're not planning to book through them (see also Buying from Travel Agents in the Tickets & Insurance chapter).

International Tourist Offices

A good percentage of countries in Asia maintain tourist offices in western countries and these can provide destination information, maps and lists of domestic tour operators. See the Tourist Offices Overseas sections in the country profiles for details or go to *Tourism Offices Worldwide Directory* (wsww.towd.com), which has regularly updated links to almost every tourist office web site.

Newspapers

Many major western newspapers include good-quality weekly or monthly travel sections carrying advertisements for special travel deals and packages. Check out the following papers in your country or access the content on their web site:

AUSTRALIA
The Age (www.theage.com.au)
The Australian (www.news.com.au)
Sydney Morning Herald (www.smh.com.au)

CANADA
The Globe & Mail (Toronto; www.theglobeandmail.com)
Vancouver Sun (www.vancouversun.com)

UK
The Independent (www.independent.co.uk)
Southern Cross (www.southerncross.co.uk)
Time Out (www.timeout.com/london)
TNT (www.tntmag.co.uk)

USA
Chicago Tribune (www.chicagotribune.com)
LA Times (www.latimes.com)
New York Times (www.nytimes.com)
San Francisco Examiner (www.examiner.com)

Books

Books are an excellent way to research a potential travel destination. As a result of the extensive colonisation of Asian countries by western powers over the past few centuries, there's a wide body of western literature set in these countries. Apart from being excellent yarns, they can offer a fascinating insight into the way western writers interpreted Asian societies. Translations of Asian authors afford an equally tantalising glimpse into the structure and mores of various societies, although the quality of translation can vary – it's always preferable to read a book in the language it was written, if possible.

Travelogues are another way to learn about the history and society of a country, and to gain an understanding of life as a traveller in a particular country or region, at a particular time in history. For the hardcore enthusiast, there are reams of speciality books available, covering subjects as diverse as religion, food, trekking, arts, architecture, diving and wildlife.

Finally, academic treatise on subjects such as sociology, politics, culture or diplomacy can be heavy going, but will give you a good intellectual assessment of the issues. See Books in the country profiles for recommended reading lists.

Magazines

Many travel magazines are directly targeted at a particular market and include a combination of holiday and country profiles; comparative pieces on flights, accommodation and cuisine; articles on specialist activities such as diving, surfing or birdwatching; tips on equipment and clothing; readers' letters; competitions; and reams of travel-industry advertisements. Many publications have an e-zine component that you can access on the web (addresses appear below). Also look at the magazines produced by travel organisations, like STA's *Escape*, Intrepid Travel's *The Intrepid Traveller* or Trailfinders' *Trailfinder Magazine*.

- *Action Asia Magazine* (☎ 852-2521 6377; www.actionasia.com; 8th floor, Al Aqmar House, 30 Hollywood Rd, Central, Hong Kong, China) – A bimonthly magazine with a focus on action travel, plus good general information on Asian travel.

- *Adventure Magazine* (☎ 800-846-8575; PO Box 461270, Escondido, CA 92046-1270, USA) – A full-colour glossy offering in-depth articles on adventure travel options and practical advice on doing it yourself.

- *Big World Magazine* (☎ 717-569-0217; orders@bigworld.com; www.bigworld.com; PO Box 8743, Lancaster, PA 17604-8743, USA) – A no-frills approach offering the independent budget traveller a fresh look at the adventures and joys of travel.

- *Escape: The Global Guide for the Adventurous Traveler* (☎ 800-738-5571; EscapeMag@aol.com; PO Box 5159, Santa Monica, CA 90409-5159, USA) – An excellent quarterly featuring out-of-the-way destinations, reviews of equipment, books and music, and advertising for US-based tour companies.

- *Geographical Magazine* (☎ 020-7938 4011; geogmag@gn.apc.org; 47c Kensington Court, London W8 5DA, England) – The magazine of the Royal Geographical Society (UK) focuses on cultural, anthropological and environmental issues, with beautiful photographs, book and television reviews and some advertising for tour companies.

- *National Geographic* (☎ 1-800-647-5463; www.nationalgeographic.com; PO Box 98198, Washington, DC 20090-8198, USA) – The magazine of the US National Geographic Society with great photos and excellent background information.

- *Outside* (☎ 800-678-1131; outside.starwave.com; PO Box 54729, Boulder, CO 80322-4729, USA) – For travel by bike, skateboard, kayak or any other means that requires some physical effort. It has a US bias, but includes international destinations.

- *Travel Unlimited* (subscription by mail from PO Box 1058, Allston, Mass 02134, USA) – Publishes details of cheap air fares, special deals and courier options.

- *Traveller Magazine* (☎ 020-7589 3315; mship@wexas.com; www.travelmag.co.uk; 45-49 Brompton Road, Knightsbridge, London SW3 1DE, England) – A quarterly with an emphasis on anthropology, exploration and adventure travel, plus travellers health, book reviews, travel hot spots and advertising for UK-based tour operators.

- *Wanderlust* (☎ 01753-620426; PO Box 1832, Windsor, Berkshire SL4 6YP, England) – Concise general travel information on both out-of-the-way and routine destinations. Has heaps of ads for tours and tour companies.

Films

There are two types of film that can be useful to your research – western films set in Asian countries and home-grown films made by Asian film industries.

Western efforts can be lamentably inaccurate, coloured by a western interpretation of culture and history, and often shot outside the country in which they are fictitiously set. Sarawak in Malaysia, for example, has been the site for films set in Vietnam, Cambodia, Myanmar and even South America and Africa. Still, if you can find out the shooting location of a film, you can get a good appreciation of the landscapes and cities of a country. Check out the *Internet Movie Database* (www.imdb.com), which allows you to search by title, director, actor, genre, year of release, location, country, language, awards, quote, keyword and much more.

Asian films, by contrast, provide a more accurate picture of the society, culture, scenery and social issues of a country, and many countries in Asia have a rich cinematic tradition. There may still be an element of fantasy (witness the idealised extravagance of many of India's 'Bollywood' productions or the straight-laced revisionism of Japan's historical epics), but even these unlikely efforts will give you some information about a society, and there are many fine films dealing with contemporary issues.

For recommended films from each country in Asia, see the Films sections in the country profiles.

Useful Web Sites

The following is a small selection of web sites covering common travel-related issues and information to help you decide which countries you'd like to visit in Asia. There are scores more sites mentioned throughout this book, and all appear in the appendix 'Internet Addresses' at the back of the book.

- *Lonely Planet* (www.lonelyplanet.com) – Destination information, health advice, photographs, bulletin boards and links to all topics travel related.

- *British Foreign & Commonwealth Office* (www.fco.gov.uk) – Official travel advisories written for Brits, but relevant for most travellers.

- *Hiking & Walking Homepage* (www.teleport.com/-walking/hiking.html) – Excellent information on international trekking spots, tours and clubs.

- *Internet Guide to Hostelling* (www.hostels.com) – Details of hostels across the world, with a good travellers news section.

- *Internet Traveller Information Service* (www.itisnet.com) – Destination information and advice.

- *Rain or Shine* (www.rainorshine.com) – Five-day weather forecasts for 800 cities around the world.

- *Travelocity* (www.travelocity.com) – General travel information, bookings, equipment and links.

- *US State Department Travel Warnings & Consular Information Sheets* (travel.state. gov/travel_warnings.html) – Mildly paranoid warnings about world trouble spots written principally for American citizens.

- *World Events Calendar* (travel.epicurious.com) – Huge list of festivals, events and other festivities, which can be searched by theme, country or date.

- *World Tourism Organization* (www.world-tourism.org/ows-doc/wtich.htm) – The United Nations international organisation dealing with travel and tourism policy and development, with members in 138 countries representing local government, tourism associations, airlines, hotel groups and tour operators.

LANGUAGE

There's no doubt that being able to speak the language of the country in which you're travelling makes life easier – from asking directions on the street to ordering in a restaurant. More importantly, it allows to you get 'inside' a culture and not just view it from the outside. Most of us don't have the time or energy to acquire more than the basics of a foreign language, let alone the several you might need in Asia, but don't throw your hands up in despair or consign yourself to six months of intensive study – it's more than possible to get by in Asia on English alone.

English is by far the most common second language in Asia; it is spoken by most locals involved in tourism and almost all western travellers. In Malaysia and India you will find English-speakers in even the smallest towns, although there are places, such as Laos and Tibet, where you will be reduced to using sign language and phrasebooks (see Learning a Language below).

Whatever country you visit, you'll find English more widely spoken in cities than in rural areas. In addition, you'll find rural dialects of any language to be maddeningly different from the standard form of that language. However, the locals will almost certainly understand the standard phrases of their national language, and this will usually be enough to break the ice.

Learning a Language

Asian languages range from among the world's easiest (Bahasa Indonesia) to among its most difficult (Mandarin Chinese and Japanese). Balance the difficulty of learning a language against the benefits you will gain from being able to speak it. Many travellers make a point of learning a few words of the local language of the country they are visiting. The basic pleasantries (hello, please, thank you, excuse me and goodbye) can go a long way. Add a few simple phrases such as 'Where is the … ?', 'How much does this cost?' and so on, plus learn to count to at least 10, and you will find day-to-day survival infinitely easier. Even if you can speak only a few words, locals will often appreciate that you have bothered to make the effort.

To make headway in learning a language, you will need a textbook, with tapes to assist with pronunciation (for study before departure) and a phrasebook (for use on the road; see Phrasebooks later in this section). Good textbook titles include Teach Yourself, Berlitz, Barrons and Routledge.

Set yourself some goals and sit down with the book on a regular basis. Just running your eyes over the words is not only boring, but a waste of time. Take the phrases you want to learn and make flashcards. Drill yourself.

You could supplement your study with private tutoring or language classes. Many local universities offer extension courses and night classes in foreign languages, and community centres also often offer foreign-language classes. These places are also useful resources for finding a private tutor; also try the embassy or consulate of the country you plan to visit, look for newspaper advertisements or search the Internet under the name of the language you want to learn. Private language schools are another option, though these can be frightfully expensive.

Finally, if you intend spending a decent amount of time in a particular country, consider taking a language course there after you arrive. This is the fastest way to learn any language since you can put into practice what you learn as soon as you step outside the classroom. Check the local English-language newspaper for listings.

Phrasebooks

Phrasebooks should be compact and have comprehensive reverse vocabulary lists. Most importantly, they should offer easy reference, so look for books that are arranged in clear and logical sections. Lonely Planet publishes phrasebooks for most of Asia's major languages with an emphasis on useful, current expressions, and words and phrases written in local script for countries like China, Japan and Thailand. Also, don't forget the language sections of your guidebooks. These can be used for learning the basics of a language and come in very handy while you're on the road.

WORK & TRAVEL

People work in Asia for different reasons. Some want to gain a deeper experience of a culture that particularly fascinates them and others want to save money so they can continue their travels. Still others do some kind of volunteer work in hopes of making a positive contribution to the country in which they're staying.

Whatever the case, it's a good idea to do some research and make some contacts before you leave home. It is possible to simply turn up and get work in some countries, but the plum positions generally go to those who have put in a bit of effort before their arrival.

English Teaching

The most common job for westerners in Asia is teaching English. Sure, it's none too glamorous, but there's a steady demand for it and you don't need an advanced degree to qualify. However, to get a decent job you will need to get the ball rolling before you leave home. This means researching the opportunities available, writing letters to prospective employers, getting letters of recommendation written by former teachers and bosses, obtaining copies of your university transcripts, writing resumes and perhaps even doing some study of the English language.

A university degree of some sort is almost essential, without which you have no hope of obtaining a work visa. Useful credentials are the RSA Cambridge certificate, a master's degree in a subject at least somewhat related to teaching or, even better, a master's or doctorate in TEFL (Teaching English as a Foreign Language) or TESOL (Teaching English to Speakers of Other Languages). A little experience will be a big asset when interviewing for positions. Many community centres and schools in the west have programs where you can teach English as a volunteer to recent immigrants.

In almost all the countries in Asia, it's possible to work legally (with a work visa) or illegally (on a tourist visa). With a work visa, you'll be able to relax and you'll almost certainly make more money. Working illegally is quite common and involves teaching off the books, mostly through private lessons. However, when your tourist visa runs out you'll have to leave the country and re-enter on a new tourist visa – not only is this expensive, but you may get caught upon re-entry as most countries are wise to this game.

HONG KONG – Though the situation is unclear, it appears there are still jobs available for English teachers. At the time of writing, most teachers in Hong Kong were earning a little over HK$200 (US$26) per hour. Both school lessons and private lessons are available. School lessons often come with housing or a housing allowance. Check the South China Morning Post's classified section for ads, or the Hong Kong school board's offerings at www.info.gov.hk/ed/teacher/elt. net.htm.

JAPAN – With Japan in the grip of a recession, jobs are difficult to come by, and you'll be looking at around ¥2500 (US$21) per hour. Private lessons are an option, but they do not qualify you for a work visa, about which the Japanese are very strict. Start your search in the *Japan Times* classifieds.

SOUTH KOREA – With good luck and a few connections, you might find yourself making close to what you'd earn in Japan, though South Korea is also in a recession and jobs for teachers are pretty thin on the ground. Also unfortunate is that language schools in South Korea have a nasty habit of cheating their foreign staff of salary. Having a proper job that qualifies you for a work visa is a tremendous asset. Check the *Korea Herald* or *Korea Times*.

TAIWAN – Typical pay in Taiwan is about NT$400 per hour (US$12). You can teach privately in schools, universities or companies. Only the school jobs qualify you for a work visa, and some may help with housing. Check the *China Post* or *China News*.

OTHER COUNTRIES – If it's culture, not cash, you're after, you can also teach English in Cambodia, China, Laos, Nepal, Pakistan, Thailand and Vietnam. You'll find you usually

A ROSE BY ANY OTHER NAME...

As a first-time visitor to Thailand I didn't realise I had to reconfirm my flight out. I got to the airport in what I thought was good time only to be informed I wasn't on the flight list and couldn't get a seat for at least a month. Fortunately I got on a flight a few days later, but I had a few days to kill in Bangkok with my travelling companion. A very friendly and helpful tuk-tuk driver (who called me 'Lobyn') made himself our tour guide and convinced us to go to the mysterious and ancient-sounding 'Lost Garden' with him. The Lost Garden wasn't in the guidebook and we hadn't heard other travellers mention it, so we decided, after much cajoling, to investigate. We bounced along a freeway in his rattly old three-wheeled tuk-tuk for 45 minutes only to arrive dishevelled and hot at the very commercial and very touristy Rose Garden. If I had reconfirmed my departure in time I would have missed this altogether forgettable place, but I did learn a lesson in phonetics – listen carefully to the pronunciations of the locals and you'll hopefully avoid misunderstandings.

ROBYN COVENTRY
AUSTRALIA

have a choice between legal and illegal work, and between school and private lessons. Either way you can expect to earn between US$2 to US$8 per hour, which may just cover your expenses. To find work, search the Internet or check the English-language papers and magazines once you arrive.

Teaching Resources

The Internet is awash with English-teaching sites. Some of the best are:

- *TEFL Job Centre* (www.jobs.edunet.com) – English-teaching positions all over the world, including lots in Asia.

- *EFL in Asia* (www.geocities.com/Tokyo/flats/7947/elfasia.htm) – Some really annoying advertising, but good info on English-teaching books and web pages.

- *English Expert Page* (www.englishexpert.com) – Good general information on teaching in Asia and some job listings.

- *International House* (www.international-house.org) – A good source of information on RSA Cambridge certification.

There are lots of good books available about teaching English. A few of the best Asia-specific ones are:

- *Teaching English in Asia* by Galen Harris Valle (Pacific View Press)

- *Teaching English in South-East Asia* by Nuala O'Sullivan (Passport Books)

- *Now Hiring! Jobs in Asia* by Jennifer Dubois et al (Perpetual Press)

Bar & Restaurant Work

Foreigners can often find work in western-style restaurants and bars in Japan, South Korea, Taiwan, Hong Kong and Singapore, generally earning subsistence pay of between US$5 and US$10 per hour. Check the English-language newspapers or ask around the local expat community for jobs. Bar and restaurant work may also be available in resort areas, such as Ko Tao, Ko Samui and Ko Phi Phi in Thailand or Bali in Indonesia. Though you may earn only room and board, this can be a cheap way to spend a few months in the islands.

HOSTESSING

In Japan, and to a lesser extent Hong Kong, there are openings for western women to work as bar hostesses. A hostess is paid to chat up male bar customers, light their cigarettes and pour their drinks. While this does not entail prostitution, it is a dubious business and you'll definitely be subjected to almost nonstop sexual innuendoes and probably minor physical harassment. Pay starts at around ¥10,000 (US$83) per night and can go a lot higher. In Japan, this work is almost exclusively found in the bigger cities like Osaka and Tokyo – check the classifieds of the *Japan Times*. In Hong Kong, you'll find most jobs by word of mouth.

Dive Masters

A very popular way to spend a year or two in the islands is to obtain your dive master certification and work at a dive shop in Thailand, Malaysia, Indonesia or the Philippines. The competition for this is pretty stiff and you'll need good connections or decent experience to land a good job. For information on obtaining dive master certification and employment opportunities, check the *PADI* web site (www.padi.com).

Travel Writing & Photography

You may be able to defray some of your travel costs by getting articles and/or photos published of the places you visit. If you have ambitions of being a photographer, invest in the appropriate equipment (see the Camera section in the What to Bring chapter) and consider taking a course in photography. The field of travel photography is very competitive. Typically, if you submit 100 shots to a photo library, it might accept fewer than 10. Be sure to use slide film, as transparencies are the industry standard.

The same professional approach should be brought to travel writing. Research the potential markets for your stories and even send away for writers' guidelines before hitting the road. Newspaper travel pages should be your first stop, as many large daily papers need to fill several pages each week and are always on the lookout for new material. However, your work will be much more saleable if you have high-quality colour slides to accompany it. When you're on the road, research your material thoroughly and keep good notes. It might not be feasible to return to Asia to fill in the gaps!

Other Professional Work

Japan, South Korea, Hong Kong, Singapore and Taiwan have openings in journalism, copy-editing, proofreading, translating, computer science, and business and trade-related fields if you have a university or more advanced degree and some professional experience. Many employers do their recruiting overseas, so start searching in your home country. Within Asia, look in the classified sections of the major English-language newspapers.

Volunteer Work

Volunteer work allows you to help address one of Asia's social or economic ills and simultaneously become involved in a foreign culture. Most international aid organisations concentrate their efforts in Bangladesh, Bhutan, Cambodia, India, Laos, Mongolia, Thailand and Vietnam, though volunteer work can be found in most parts of Asia. Most organisations will cover food and lodging expenses, but not your transport from home.

Research thoroughly the sort of work you're interested in before setting out. Volunteer work can be tough, dispiriting and very uncomfortable. There is a great variety of work available, from teaching English in rural villages to attending the dying in India's slums, so choose what you're most comfortable with.

Below are some international aid organisations and placement organisations to get you started. Also consult country-specific guidebooks and search the Internet.

AUSTRALIA

Earthwatch Institute (☎ 03-9682 6828; www.earthwatch.org/australia/html) 126 Bank St, South Melbourne, Victoria 3205

Australian Volunteers International (☎ 03-9279 1788; www.ozvol.org.au) PO Box 350, Fitzroy, Victoria 3065

NEW ZEALAND

Volunteer Service Abroad (☎ 04-472 5759; www.tcol.co.uk/comorg/vsa.htm) PO Box 12-246, Wellington 1

UK

Earthwatch Institute (☎ 01865-311 600; www.earthwatch.org) 57 Woodstock Rd, Oxford OX2 6JH

International Voluntary Service (☎ 0131-226 6722; www.ivsgbn.demon.co.uk) St John's Church Centre, Edinburgh EH2 4BJ

Voluntary Service Overseas (VSO; ☎ 020-8780 7200; www.oneworld.org/vso) 317 Putney Bridge Rd, London SW15 2PN

USA

Earthwatch Institute (☎ 800-776-0188; www.earthwatch.org) 680 Mt Auburn St, PO Box 9104, Watertown, MA 02272

Global Volunteers (☎ 612-482-0915; www.globalvolunteers.org) 375 E Little Canada Rd, St Paul, MN 55117-1628

Peace Corps of the USA (☎ 202-606-3970; www.peacecorps.gov) 1990 K St NW, Washington, DC 20526

MONEY MATTERS

Asian countries range from among the world's most expensive (Japan) to among the cheapest (Bangladesh). Overall, however, travel in the Asia is good value. Depending upon where you go, it may even be cheaper to travel in Asia than to visit tourist destinations closer to home, and that's including the cost of your plane ticket. This is especially the case for North Americans and Europeans. Indeed, once you have covered your ticket and other predeparture expenses, the rest of the trip may seem incredibly cheap. Favourable exchange rates in place in Asia since the currency crash of 1998 add to this rosy situation.

Travel, however, is fraught with unforeseen expenses and you should leave some money aside to deal with these. Furthermore, currencies in Asia are highly volatile. For up-to-the-minute exchange rates, check the Oanda online currency converter (www.oanda.com/site/cc_index.html).

Keep in mind also that travel costs vary from season to season. If you're travelling during the tourist high season you can expect to pay up to 50% more than during the low season, especially for accommodation, so when calculating your budget be sure to take this into account.

The following sections will give you an idea of how much a trip to Asia will cost. These are rough estimates only – depending on your budget, it's possible to spend a little less or whole a lot more.

PRETRIP EXPENSES

A good portion of your travel budget will be spent before you leave home. Your main expense will be your plane ticket, but purchasing equipment and travel insurance will also make a dent in your savings. Don't let the compulsion to save money get the better of you – look for a cheap plane ticket, but make sure it's from a trustworthy agent and on a safe airline. The same goes for gear; there's no point buying junk if it's only going to fall apart in your first week on the road.

Plane Tickets

Assuming you fly into Bangkok – a common gateway city to Asia – and you shop around for a decent deal, you could plan on spending the following for a return ticket:

From Australia

East Coast – Bangkok	A$1000 to A$1250
Perth – Bangkok	A$950 to A$1100

From Canada

Vancouver – Bangkok	C$900
East Coast – Bangkok	cheapest to go via New York (see From the USA below)

From New Zealand

Auckland – Bangkok	NZ$1450

From the UK

London – Bangkok	£350 to £500

From the USA

East Coast – Bangkok	US$950 to US$1000
West Coast – Bangkok	US$800 to US$900

Online information on air fares can be found at *Flight Info.Com* (www.flifo.com), *Expedia* (www.expedia.msn.com/daily/home/default.hts) and *Travelocity* (www.travelocity.com).

For more information on buying plane tickets, see the Tickets & Insurance chapter; for details on air fare prices within Asia, see the Getting Around section in the While You're There chapter.

Insurance

Good travel/health insurance is an absolute necessity. If you really want to skimp, buy a fake personal stereo, but don't neglect your insurance. If your country has socialised health care, you may be covered while travelling overseas, thus saving on some elements of an insurance package. Typical rates for a basic travel insurance package (including health, accidental death, baggage and cancellation insurance) are: one week (US$35), one month (US$115), two months (US$180) and six months (US$400). See the Tickets & Insurance chapter for details on buying insurance.

Visas

Visas for many countries in Asia are free, and the cost of those you must pay for averages around US$25. Notably expensive visas are India (US$50 for six months) and Laos (US$50 for 15 days). In other cases, such as China and Vietnam, the visa may be free but you'll probably want to pay a travel agent to get it for you to avoid bureaucratic hassles. Not all the visas you need will be a pretrip expense: you will be able to get some at your point of entry, or in neighbouring countries.

See the Passports & Visas chapter and the country profiles for details on visas to individual countries.

Immunisations

You'll probably have to pay for the pleasure of getting an armful of immunisations. You can expect to pay between US$50 to US$100 for a full course. See the Health chapter for details.

Equipment

What you spend on equipment will depend to a large extent on how you like to travel (or how much you can borrow from friends and relatives). Some folks make it around Asia with little more than a knapsack, while others bring most of their worldly goods. Be careful not to load yourself down too much. If you're travelling with a friend, you could share some items to save weight and money, but don't rely too heavily on your companions for everything. Following are typical prices for items you may need (also see the What to Bring chapter for more details on equipment):

Backpack	US$150 to US$300
Tent	US$150 to US$250
Sleeping bag	US$150 to US$250
Camera (automatic)	US$50 to US$300
Camera (SLR)	US$250 to US$800
Torch (flashlight)	US$10 to US$20
Pocketknife	US$20 to US$50
Hiking boots	US$80 to US$200

Average Pretrip Expenses

The following figures are rough estimates for a two month trip to assist planning for your trip. In reality, your actual expenses may vary quite a bit.

Plane ticket (return)	US$900
Insurance	US$180
Visas	US$75
Immunisations	US$50
Gear	US$490
Total	US$1695

DAILY ON-ROAD COSTS

Your daily travel expenses will depend on the level of comfort you require, how much you move around, and the cost of living in the countries you visit.

Comfort Levels

Some people regard travel in Asia as an exercise in masochism – the more suffering they endure the better they imagine their trip is. These travellers stay only in dormitories, travel only 2nd or 3rd class, eat the most basic food and don't purchase a single souvenir. If you travel like this in inexpensive countries, you can get by in Asia on US$10 a day, perhaps even less.

Remember, though, that travel in Asia can be very trying. You need to preserve your sanity as much as your money, and you will probably have a far more enjoyable time if you're not too hard on yourself. The whole point of travel is the pleasure of experiencing new places and meeting new people – it shouldn't be a contest to see who can survive the longest time on the least money. The occasional treat can make the difference between losing your mind

TREATING YOURSELF

Perhaps you've just been on a bus for the last 24 hours and you're so tired you can barely move. Maybe you've got a high fever and a raging case of diarrhoea. Or maybe you're just sick and tired of grotty guesthouse rooms and bad food. Whatever the case, there are times when you should forget about the money and give yourself a treat. Splurging on the occasional feast, comfy hotel room or cross-town taxi ride can make the difference between losing it or having a great trip. If you need a break, heed the call, even if it means digging deep into your budget and perhaps even cutting your trip short by a few days.

The perfect example of this is if you've been travelling in India and are feeling run-down after weeks of noisy dorm rooms, cheap food and 2nd class train journeys. Rather than continue and risk falling sick, pamper yourself – find a comfortable room in a nice hotel and chill out for a few days. Or, if you're really at the end of your tether, splurge on a ticket to Bangkok and spend a week or two recuperating on a sunny Thai island. In the long run, it's better to spend the money and stay well, than to pinch pennies until you've run yourself into the ground.

The great thing about Asia is that in most countries you can indulge yourself without blowing the bank. An excellent meal can be had in the restaurants of most South-East Asian and Indian top-flight hotels for less than US$15. An air-con room in a fine hotel in the same countries can be had for around US$75, perhaps less, depending upon the season. And best of all, you can live in relative splendour on a beach in South-East Asia for around US$10 a day.

All of which means you don't have to limit the occasional splurge to those times when you're feeling tired or sick. If you're not prepared to spend the money, how will you enjoy the experience? If you're aching to go on that rafting trip, desperate for that souvenir, or feel life just wouldn't be worth living if you never taste some first-class sushi, then go ahead and lash out – in most cases, you'll find it was worth it. Remember, with the low prices in Asia, this may be one of the only chances you'll have in life to live like the jet set.

and having a blast, so plan your budget with this in mind (see also the Cost of Living section below).

Moving vs Staying Put

Transportation expenses can eat up a lot of your budget, especially if you're travelling 1st or 2nd class on trains, or flying from one place to another. If you're on a tight budget, try to avoid too many expensive train journeys or plane flights. Alternatively, you may be able to buy a plane ticket that includes several flights within Asia for little more than the cost of the flight there. Likewise, a rail pass like Japan's JR Railpass may be worthwhile if you plan to move around a lot. For more details, see Getting Around in the While You're There chapter.

Don't despair if you can't afford to visit lots of countries. It's often more enjoyable to stay for a while in one place and soak up the atmosphere, than to hurtle from place to place barely seeing anything. Besides, Asia isn't going anywhere – the countries you miss this time around will be there for your next trip, and your next …

Cost of Living

The amount you spend will depend very much on where you go. A cup of coffee in Tokyo could buy you dinner and a hotel room in parts of India. Likewise, a night in a fancy Hong Kong hotel could fund a month of travel in Indonesia. If you are on a tight budget and want a lengthy trip, you'll need to stick to Asia's cheaper countries.

Generally, those countries with a lower cost of living are in South-East Asia (such as Thailand, Laos and Vietnam) and on the Indian subcontinent. The more expensive destinations are clustered in North-East Asia (Japan, Korea and Taiwan). China manages to cover both categories – the north-eastern coastal areas are as expensive as Japan, while the interior and western regions are almost as cheap as Thailand.

The major cities in any country are likely to be much more expensive than the rural areas. In Kathmandu you might pay US$10 a night in a decent hotel, but spend only US$1 a night for a room in a teahouse while you're trekking in the Himalaya. Furthermore, you might be able to save money by camping in rural areas.

The countries of Asia fall roughly into three price categories (see the accompanying table). These figures are a rough estimate of the minimum you can expect to spend each day if you stay in hostels and cheap hotels, travel on public transport and eat local food. You can easily spend twice or three times these amounts if you require a higher level of comfort. Inflation and fluctuating exchange rates can dramatically alter these figures, so check newspapers or the Internet for the latest exchange rates before departure. See also the Money sections of the country profiles.

Inexpensive	Moderate	Expensive
← US$20/day	US$20-$40	US$50 →
Bangladesh	Brunei	Bhutan
Cambodia	West China	Coastal China
India	Korea	Hong Kong
Indonesia	Malaysia	Japan
Laos	Mongolia	Singapore
Myanmar	Philippines	
Nepal	Taiwan	
Pakistan	Thailand	
Sri Lanka		
Vietnam		

Saving Money on the Road

While you're travelling, it can be very alarming to see your hard-earned cash trickling away faster than you expected. To prevent serious cash shortfalls, follow some of these thrifty spending policies:

- Eat local food – You can get three or four local meals for the price of one western-style meal.

- Take public transport – Even though the prospect can be daunting, you'll save heaps of money by taking buses instead of taxis.

- Shop in markets – You can buy almost anything in Asian markets and you'll always pay less than in the shops, especially if you bargain.

- Ask for a discount – You'll be surprised how many hotels will reduce room rates if you ask.

- Learn to bargain effectively – This is a real skill and a little practice can save you a lot of money.

- Get out of the cities – Prices are almost always cheaper in rural areas.

- Camp – If you have a tent, you'll save heaps on accommodation.

CARRYING YOUR MONEY

The US dollar is the major currency in Asia and is likely to remain so for some time, despite the introduction of the Euro. This means you should carry your money in US dollars, either as cash or travellers cheques. If you cannot get US dollars, you'll be able to get by with any other major world currency most of the time. As a rule, the less developed a country is the more difficult it is to exchange currencies other then US dollars. It is generally also more difficult to exchange other currencies in rural areas.

The main options for carrying money are travellers cheques, credit and/or debit cards and cash. Each has advantages, and most experienced travellers carry a combination of all three (see the following sections).

Always keep your money and other valuables where no one can get them, preferably in a money belt worn under your clothing as unobtrusively as possible. Be absolutely sure that the belts and clasps are secure, and that you can feel it against your skin (see the Money Belt section in the What to Bring chapter for some advice). You will also need a purse or change pouch to carry your daily spending money, for convenience and to make sure you have some money on hand if your money belt is lost or stolen. See the Hazards & Safeguards section in the Issues & Attitudes chapter for more advice on protecting your valuables against theft.

Travellers Cheques

Tried and true, travellers cheques are still the most popular way to carry money while travelling. The main advantage is that if they are stolen they will be replaced by the issuing bank within a few days. Also, in many places, you'll get better exchange rates for travellers cheques than for cash.

To facilitate replacement if your cheques are lost or stolen, always keep the purchase agreement of the cheques with you and keep accurate records of the serial numbers of the cheques as you spend them, so you can tell the bank which ones are missing. Keep the purchase record, spending records and the credit card company's emergency contact number in a separate place, so that they are not lost or stolen along with the cheques.

In Asia, US dollar travellers cheques issued by American Express or Thomas Cook are the most commonly accepted. Other major banks and credit card companies issue travellers cheques, but you may have trouble changing these cheques in out-of-the-way places. It's a good idea to carry large-denomination cheques (say US$100 or US$50) since some places charge a per-cheque cashing fee and this can really add up if you're constantly cashing smaller cheques. However, anything greater than $100 is likely to leave you with too much cash to carry comfortably.

Credit Cards

Credit cards are becoming more and more popular in Asia. While they are fairly useless for small purchases, many budget travellers use them to get cash advances from local banks, thereby eliminating the need for travellers cheques. This is indeed convenient, but you will find places where you cannot get cash advances or where it is very time-consuming to do so. Thus, we recommend using credit cards in conjunction with travellers cheques. You can also use credit cards to pay for more expensive items, such as plane tickets, and the occasional splurge. They are also invaluable in an emergency.

In Asia, MasterCard and Visa are both widely accepted and handy for cash advances. As many local banks are affiliated with either MasterCard or Visa, but not both, get both cards if possible. American Express credit cards are less useful in Asia.

With your PIN number, you can withdraw cash from automatic teller machines (ATMs) in some countries (see the country profiles for details). Only the ATMs in bigger, more touristy areas are linked to international networks. Check the back of your card to see if it matches any of the network stickers displayed on the ATM in question. You can search for ATMs that accept Visa or MasterCard on www.mastercard.com/atm or www.visa.com/pd/atm/main.html.

The downside of credit cards is the risk they pose of putting you into heavy debt. On most cards – including Visa and MasterCard – if you don't pay the account in full each month, you'll be charged interest and the rates can be exorbitant. Finally, always check the invoice and the receipt when you buy something with a credit card, and check your account statement when you get home. Credit card fraud is rare, but it does happen (see Scams in the Issues & Attitudes chapter for further details).

Cashed Up But Cashless

I was prepared for a few hassles during my first days in India, but I was alarmed at how my plans unravelled before I had even left Delhi airport. The cashier at Thomas Cook pushed my brand-new, unswiped, unclunked Visa card back at me: 'MasterCard only please,' he explained.

So there we were, myself and two friends with three Visa cards and three healthy but utterly unreachable accounts, and not a single travellers cheque or American dollar between us. Rummaged pockets turned up a couple of sterling pound coins which came back to us as rupees – enough for the grimy bus ride to the centre of Delhi.

We were hesitant to arrive penniless at our hostel at two in the morning and gave in meekly to a rickshaw driver's insistence that our hostel was full and that he could take us to a Visa-accepting hotel. Off we went through the dark backstreets of the Old Bazaar, plagued by fears of robbery, to arrive at another robbery (of sorts) at an overpriced and underappointed hotel. This place gladly clunked our cards and swallowed a week's accommodation budget.

The next morning we began a confused search for an ATM or bank, our dilemma compounded by back-to-back public holidays and a curious lack of Visa ATMs. Eventually a visit to a 'Government Approved' travel agent put hard cash in our pockets. We paid airline prices for a few train tickets and received the balance in cash. Two days later we were back in the office shouting ourselves hoarse to have the dud tickets refunded.

Leaving Delhi at the end of the week for the tranquillity of the Himalaya, we all had renewed faith in travellers cheques and cash – sometimes the most flexible of friends.

Gareth McCormack
Ireland

Debit Cards

With a debit card, the money you spend or withdraw is taken straight from your savings or cheque account. If you don't have enough money in your account, you can't make the transaction. Debit cards can be used to withdraw cash from ATMs and to make purchases at some stores, though you'll find this is possible only in the bigger cities of the more developed countries in Asia. The largest networks in Asia are Cirrus, Plus, Star, Interlink, Accel, Exchange and Explore, roughly in that order. If you have a MasterCard or Visa debit card, you can search for ATMs using the web sites included in the Credit Cards section earlier in this chapter.

A drawback with debit cards is that once money is taken out of your account, it cannot be replaced. If your card is stolen and transactions or withdrawals are made, you won't see that money again. By contrast, if a credit card is stolen, and you inform the provider immediately, you can request a 'charge back' and have the money returned to you.

Cash

Obviously, you don't want to carry a lot of US dollar cash around – if it's stolen or lost you'll never see it again. However, it's a good idea to have some of your money in cash, for the following reasons: you will inevitably find places that only exchange cash; you can change a small denomination of cash when you don't want to cash a big travellers cheque; some countries require that you pay for visas in cash (eg Nepal demands payment in US dollars at Kathmandu airport); and some countries use foreign cash as their principal source of exchange (eg Vietnam and Laos, where US dollars are the unofficial currency).

Many experienced travellers carry a few hundred dollars in cash, as it is usually both difficult and expensive to buy US dollars cash in Asia. Keep your cash in a very safe place, perhaps carrying some in your money belt and stowing some away as an emergency stash (eg inside a backpack frame). If you are planning to spend a long time in countries that use US cash as their main currency, you probably won't need to bring as much cash from home, but can change travellers cheques for cash after you arrive.

International Money Transfers

If you're going to be on the road for a long time and don't want to carry too much money at the start of your trip, or if you run out of money while on the road, you can have money sent by wire from your home country to a local bank. It is advisable to do this only in Asia's more developed countries like Japan, Singapore and perhaps Thailand, and in Hong Kong. In other countries, such as India, not only will the paperwork be hellish, but you may never see the money anyway.

If you arrange a transfer, you will have to wait a few days for it to clear.

You'll be usually be given your money in local currency, either as cash or travellers cheques. Bring the details of your home bank account (account number, branch number, address and telephone number) to speed up the process.

Running Out of Money

This is something none of us likes to think about, but it is a real possibility so it helps to be prepared. If you realise you are running out of money, do something before you go flat broke, or you'll have no money to make arrangements for more. If the worst comes to the worst, you may be able to borrow money from a fellow traveller.

There are two ways to have money sent from home. The first is an international money transfer (see that section above). The second is through a service like Western Union, which specialises in sending cash to all parts of the world. To receive cash this way, you'll have to arrange for someone in your home country to take cash to one of their offices. This is a convenient service, though the rates are significantly higher than those charged by banks for international money transfers. For more information, call Western Union (☎ 0800-833833 in the UK or ☎ 1-800-325-6000 in the USA).

Another option if you're running out of money is to find a job. For more details, see Work & Travel in the Planning chapter.

CHANGING MONEY

Changing money is one of those little chores that you'll have to attend to every few days or weeks while you're on the road. You can change money at banks, moneychangers, hotels and on the black market (in a few countries).

Before you change money, check in your guidebook or ask other travellers where the best place is to change money in a particular country. In some countries, banks are the best or only places to change money, while in others you'd be crazy not to use a moneychanger. Also check a local newspaper for the official exchange rate, and compare the exchange rates and commission fees of several places before deciding where to change. You may have to do some calculations here, as the rate offered and the commission charged will vary from place to place. Be sure to ask when cashing travellers cheques if the commission is per check or per transaction.

Save the foreign exchange certificates every time you change money to prove you've exchanged your money legally. Although you will rarely be asked to produce receipts for this purpose, in countries such as Nepal and China you'll need the foreign exchange certificates to reconvert leftover local currency. Following are some basic pointers for changing money in Asia:

- In general, you'll find moneychangers and banks offer the best exchange rates. Moneychangers are often more convenient because they require less paperwork. Hotels usually offer poor exchange rates and high commissions.

YOUR SPENDING POWER

Money is power and this is never so evident as when travelling in Asia. As a western traveller you will be regarded as having a bottomless well of resources at your disposal (whether or not this is actually the case) and your dealings with locals may well be coloured by this attitude. Hotel owners, tour operators, cyclo drivers and others in the travel industry are legendary for the range and cleverness of their strategies to separate you from your hard-earned cash, but it's worth putting yourself in their place every now and again.

Most countries in South-East Asia and the Indian subcontinent lack the government-funded social security systems, charity-run support services and private philanthropy that we take for granted in western countries. If people don't earn any money, they're likely to starve, especially in the cities where they might be separated from the family or village-based networks that would normally look after them during difficult times. It's a sad fact of life that many of Asia's less educated and poorer people work very long hours, yet have very little in terms of personal possessions.

Compared with this, even the meanest western traveller looks wealthy. Your clothes, backpack, watch, personal stereo and constant spending on food, accommodation and souvenirs mark you as a person of wealth. The fact that you may have spent years saving for your trip – and are trying to minimise your expenses to stay on the road for as long as possible – is unlikely to register with locals. The mere fact that you can afford to travel at all places you in a different league from them.

The envy this can produce is often aggravated by the never-ending flow of tourists (who are often demanding, rude and heedless of local customs) and the changes that the travel industry works on local cultures, from inappropriate redevelopment to the breakdown of family and societal values.

So it pays to keep some sort of perspective on your financial dealings with locals while on the road. Being 'ripped off' can leave you feeling foolish and unworldly, especially if the amount is significant, but beware of adopting a siege mentality. Many travellers fall into a mind-set of never wanting to pay more than the local price for anything, but end up spending ridiculous amounts of time and effort trying to achieve this, to the detriment of their enjoyment of the country and its people.

Similarly, bargaining is part of the fun of travelling in Asia, but try not to be too niggardly, particularly with people running small businesses or selling their wares at a market. Take a moment to work out just how much that extra 2000 dong or five rupees is really going to cost you. A quick calculation will probably reveal that you are arguing over 10 or 15 cents – a paltry sum that you would never miss at home, but which could make a real difference to the life of the person you're dealing with.

In short, show a little panache and a trace of empathy for the other person's circumstances. They'll be happy with the transaction and you can travel on with a clear conscience.

- In some countries, such as Nepal, Vietnam and India, it's possible to change money on the black market, though this is illegal and leaves you vulnerable to arrest or bribery attempts from local police. If you're ripped off, you'll have no legal recourse and all sorts of scams exist to short-change you. Ask other travellers for advice about a trustworthy person to change money with, and keep your wits about you.

- You'll usually get the best exchange rates in main cities, so change your money before heading to rural areas, where you may find it impossible to change money at all.

- Try not to change at border crossings, where exchange rates are often very low, or change just enough to get you into a major city. In some countries, airports offer poor exchange rates, though moneychangers at some airports will offer the same rates as those in the city centre.

- Each time you change money at a moneychanger or bank, you will be given a slip with the details of the transaction for you to sign. Inspect it carefully. If anything is amiss, you can terminate the transaction immediately.

- Before you sign a travellers cheque, make completely sure that the changer will accept it, as you will probably find the signed cheque difficult to change elsewhere.

- If you're using a credit card for a cash advance, shop around for the best rates and lowest commission fees. Also, check that the figures are correct on the credit card slip before you sign it.

- Always count the bills carefully after you change your money, cash a travellers cheque or get a cash advance to ensure you haven't been sort-changed.

- Exercise extreme caution when changing money. This is one of the few times when you'll have your money belt out in public; you'll be particularly vulnerable at street-side moneychangers. Keep everything together and where you can see it, and check you have it all before walking away from the counter.

- Don't change a large-denomination bill or travellers cheque just before leaving a country as you'll lose on commissions and exchange rates when you reconvert unspent money. Also some currencies, such as those of Nepal and China, are not convertible outside the country, so you'll have to reconvert it just before you leave.

BARGAINING

Many travellers approach Asia with a sense of dread knowing they're going to have to bargain for many goods and services. If you've grown up in the west, it's likely the only chance you've had to bargain is at neighbourhood rummage sales – not the best preparation for going up against people who have been bargaining their whole lives. You'll save yourself a lot of anguish by accepting the fact that you'll never pay what the locals do. The best you can hope for is a price reasonably close to that. There's nothing more pathetic than those travellers who are obsessed by paying only the 'local price' and whose trip has been reduced to a series of bitter negotiating sessions.

It's important to know where in Asia it's appropriate to bargain. Bargaining is widely practised in South-East Asia, the Indian subcontinent and China. In these countries, you can and should bargain in markets and small stores and for private transportation such as unmetered taxis, tuk-tuks and rickshaws. You can also bargain in guesthouses and hotels, especially in the low season (bargain out-right at cheap hotels, but in expensive places simply ask for a discount). In these countries, you cannot bargain for public transportation, or in most restaurants or department stores (although you can try asking for a discount in department stores).

In Japan, South Korea and Taiwan, bargaining is much less widely practised. You could try bargaining in markets, especially flea markets, but you'll often find that vendors are unwilling to negotiate. You could also ask for a discount in hotels and department stores, and perhaps will receive a 10% reduction.

There are lots of implicit rules pertaining to bargaining. Most importantly, try to conduct the procedure in a friendly, polite way – getting angry won't result in a better price and will usually just bring the negotiations to a halt. Also, never offer a price unless you're willing to go through with the transaction if that price is accepted – bargaining for sport is cruel (the vendors are trying to

TIPS FOR EFFECTIVE BARGAINING

1. Be polite, friendly and even playful when you bargain. Try not to think of the other person as an adversary (a lot easier said sometimes, but do your best).

2. Do some research on what a reasonable price would be for the item in question. This is your best guarantee against being fleeced.

3. Take your time. If you'll be in the area for a while, you could even stretch out a bargaining session over several days.

4. Never quote the first price. Let the other person start and work from there. If the seller starts with an outrageous price, as taxi and rickshaw drivers are fond of doing, just walk away.

5. If you're planning to make several purchases, buy everything at once to get a quantity discount. The more you buy, the more bargaining power you have. You can also pool your purchases with another traveller.

6. Give reasons for asking for a lower price, such as everyone on the block is selling similar goods, or the item is flawed.

7. Decide in advance the price you'd like to pay and the top price you'll accept.

8. Do your shopping in the morning. Many vendors in Asia believe the first sale of the day is lucky and ensures a good day's business, so if you're the first customer you might get a special 'morning price'.

9. The walking-away tactic is one of the best in the book, especially if you're close to the price you're willing to pay. You'll usually be called back to close the deal.

earn a living, after all) and can even lead to violence. And never lose a sense of how much money you're haggling over. It makes no sense to spend half an hour fighting over the equivalent of 20 cents

TIPPING

Tipping is not nearly as common in Asia as it is in the west. Indeed, there are very few situations when you will be expected to tip, with the major exceptions porters who handle your luggage in an airport or a hotel, and porters or guides you have hired for a trek in Nepal (a tip of 10% of their total pay is standard).

Otherwise, tipping is a discretionary matter. If you feel that someone has rendered you a particularly good service, especially for a low price (or free), then by all means leave a tip – it will always be appreciated. Consider tipping people who clean your room, efficient waiters and waitresses, honest taxi and rickshaw drivers who have gone out of their way for you, and station masters and conductors who perform miracles with tickets and so forth. Try not to tip if a service has been poor, or you will only create a false expectation for tips that other travellers will have to meet.

BARGAINING POWER

Kathmandu is the Tiger balm capital of the world. Apparently, some residents believe that westerners coat themselves from head to foot with the stuff at least three times a day. Or so you would think, judging from the sheer number of Tiger balm vendors in the city and their endless calls of `Tiger balm, sir?'

I met an Australian man in Kathmandu who'd had an interesting encounter with a young Tiger balm salesman. He had just arrived in Thamel, fresh off the plane. It was his first time in Asia, and he was prepared to bargain for everything. He had spoken to friends. Consulted guidebooks. Even practised a few bargaining routines in his head. No one was going to play him for a fool.

The young boy sprang out of an alley, as he made his way through the streets searching for a hotel. `Tiger balm, sir?' The Australian stopped. `Hmm. Tiger balm. That could come in handy on the trek,' he thought. `OK, how much?' The salesman's eyes lit up – once the bargaining starts a sale is almost assured. `Only 500 rupees, sir.'

The Australian knew the way these things worked – you name a figure half the original starting price and go from there. `No. Too much. I'll give you 250.' The salesman thought for a moment then came out with 450. The Australian countered with 300. The salesman sighed and begrudgingly lowered his price to 350. The Australian did some simple arithmetic and came back with a figure of 325 rupees. The salesman acquiesced. `OK, I give to you for 325 rupees.' Perhaps it was his first sale of the day. Or perhaps the Australian was just too shrewd. Anyway, it was a deal. The Australian paid his money and received a thumbnail-sized jar of the stuff – 25g at best. Anyway, he had done it. He had bargained successfully. He pocketed the jar and continued on his way. Around the next corner, a pharmacy came into view. In the window was a large vat of Tiger balm, a few hundred grams of the stuff, with a large price tag for all to see – 40 rupees.

CHRIS ROWTHORN
LP AUTHOR, JAPAN

PASSPORTS & VISAS

PASSPORTS

Your passport is your one indispensable travel document. While you are overseas, it's your principal means of identification, as well as your main evidence (via visa stamps or papers) that you have the legal right to be in a country.

Losing your passport is not the end of the world, but it is a serious inconvenience and will take time and money to replace. Always keep your passport on your person (preferably out of sight in a money belt) and try to avoid situations which require you to hand it over for any length of time – whether to a foreign bureaucrat or a hotel proprietor. See Hazards & Safeguards in the Issues & Attitudes chapter for some tips on keeping your valuables safe.

Photocopy the front page and all pages with prearranged visa stamps on them, and carry these separately from your passport (see the Photocopies section at the end of this chapter).

If You Have a Passport...

If you already hold a passport, check its expiry date. If it expires within six months of the date when you plan to enter the final country on your itinerary, then get it replaced – most Asian countries will refuse you entry if you have less than six months left on your passport. Even if you have a couple of months' leeway, it would still be sensible to get a new one. Passports of most western countries are valid for 10 years and are generally much easier to replace in your home country. In addition, if your passport has a few years to run, you'll be in a better position to take up any personal or business opportunities that come your way during your trip. Also check how many blank pages you have left for visas and entry and exit stamps. It would be very inconvenient to run out of spare pages when you are too far from an embassy to have a new passport issued or extra pages added to it.

Applying for a Passport

Make sure you arrange for a passport well in advance. In fact, this should be your first piece of business for a few reasons: you will have to submit your passport for each visa application (these can take anywhere between three and 14 days each); possibly quote its number to pick up your plane ticket; and present it to buy duty-free goods.

Conditions and requirements for passport issue vary between countries, but most agencies require you to submit the following with the application form:

• Proof of citizenship – Such as a birth, naturalisation or registration certificate.

- Photographs – Two recent head-and-shoulder shots of you taken against a white background; signed and identified.

- Proof of identity – Someone must vouch for your identity on the application form and on your photographs. This can be either the holder of a current passport from your country who has known you for two years (but is unrelated to you) or a citizen of good standing such as a Justice of the Peace (although this category can somewhat arbitrarily include employers, teachers, doctors and lawyers!).

- Proof of any name change – Such as a marriage or deed poll certificate.

- A fee – This starts at around A$125, C$60, NZ$80, UK£21 or US$65 for a standard adult passport of the minimum number of pages, issued within the usual processing time.

Issuing Periods & Rush Jobs

Most agencies will issue your passport within 10 days, assuming you have provided everything they need. If you've left your application until the last moment, or your passport inexplicably isn't where you left it after your last trip, then you might need to get a new or replacement passport in a hurry. This process is called expediting, and you'll generally pay plenty for it. Expediting fees can be paid directly to the national issuing agency, or a commercial agency can do it for you, but even then an expedited passport may take a couple of days to get to you.

A simple search on the web or in the phonebook will give you plenty of options for commercial expeditors.

Issuing Agencies

The government agencies responsible for issuing passports in Australia, Canada, New Zealand, the UK and the United States are listed below. However, you can often submit your application to other authorised agencies such as post offices or banks instead.

AUSTRALIA
Passports Australia, Department of Foreign Affairs & Trade (☎ 131232; www.dfat.gov.au/ passports/passports_faq_contents.html)

CANADA
The Passport Office, Department of Foreign Affairs & International Trade (☎ 1-800-567-6868; www.dfait-maeci.gc.ca/passport/paspr-2.htm)

NEW ZEALAND
The Passport Office, Department of Internal Affairs (☎ 0800-22 5050; inform.dia.govt.nz/ internal_affairs/businesses/doni_pro/fees.html)

UK
UK Passport Agency, The Home Office (☎ 0870-521 0410; www.open.gov.uk/ukpass/ ukpass.htm)

USA
Passport Services, The State Department (☎ 1-900-225-5674; http://travel.state.gov/ passport_services.html)

Dual Citizenship

Being able to carry two passports is a very valuable asset, as it allows you to select the passport which will get you the better (and cheaper) visa and which will be better received by each country you enter. For example, you may hold British and Australian passports. Brunei will require a visa from an Australian, but not from a Brit. Similarly, South Korea does not require a visa from either nationality, but will issue a 90 day visa to a Brit while an Australian will have to make do with 15 days.

Check out your own situation, and if you decide to travel under two passports, keep your wits about you: it's wise not to let on to immigration officials that you have dual citizenship. Try also to stick to the same passport when travelling between neighbouring countries – if you've entered Thailand on your British passport and then try to enter Malaysia on your Australian passport, the officials are going to wonder how you managed to get into the region.

Hostile Home Countries

For most western travellers, your home country shouldn't affect your reception by officials when you try to enter a country in Asia. Most countries are crying out for western tourist dollars and are easing restrictions, particularly following the currency crisis. Israeli passport holders are, however, a major exception. Malaysia and Indonesia will refuse an Israeli entry point-blank and nothing can be done about it. Historical factors might also result in a less-than-welcoming reception – you might have the misfortune to encounter a South Vietnamese official who believes the USA abandoned them, a Laotian who has issues with the former French colonial government, or a Chinese who resents the imposts of the British in the 19th century. Just smile and make the best of it.

Lost or Stolen Passports

Losing your passport while you're on the road is a major headache and can lead to interminable bureaucratic hassles, both with the government of the country you're in at the time and with your own embassy or consulate.

If you do lose your passport, contact your embassy immediately. If your home country does not have diplomatic representation where you are, then contact the embassy in the nearest neighbouring country. Seek advice from the embassy staff on whether you need to notify the local government of the loss, and how to handle it if you do. It may be that a new passport can be arranged within the time limits of your visa. If, however, your visa is due to expire (and you were due to fly out) the day after your passport is lost, you'll need a visa extension until your new passport is ready and you can leave the country.

If your passport is stolen, also inform the local police and get a police report before heading to your embassy. You'll need some form of identification to satisfy the embassy staff before they'll issue a replacement. You should carry a photocopy of your passport with you, as well as a driver's licence, student card, an old passport, your birth certificate or some other form of ID, including something with your photo on it. Your embassy should be able to issue a new passport within a couple of days, but you may pay handsomely for the privilege.

VISAS

Visas are stamps or documents in your passport that permit you to enter a country and stay for a specified period of time. It's best to research your visa requirements when you're planning your itinerary. Wait, however, until you have booked your ticket before you start approaching embassies or consulates, as some countries will not issue a visa until you can produce your plane ticket.

Very few countries will refuse entry to independent travellers (Bhutan is a notable exception, and will only issue a visa if you are part of a package tour), but all enforce a range of restrictions, such as time limits or the border points where you can enter and leave the country. Countries such as Mongolia and Myanmar place almost overwhelming bureaucratic obstacles in your path, but these countries are among the most bewitching destinations in the region. Persevere if you're set on getting there; you won't be disappointed.

Home or Away?

You often have the option of obtaining visas in your home country or when you arrive at your destination. If you're planning to travel in North-East Asia, Myanmar or Bhutan, it's better to get your visas before you leave home. If you're intending to travel mostly in South-East Asia or the Indian subcontinent, it's generally easier to apply for visas while you're over there. Vietnam, for example, demands the exact days that you plan to enter and leave the country, so unless you have planned your itinerary to the nth degree, it's best to arrange your visa in a neighbouring country.

Another factor is that not all countries will have an embassy in your home country. Mongolia, for example, does not maintain embassies in Australia, New Zealnd or Canada, so you may have to go to a travel or visa agent, or wait until you arrive in the region to apply for your visa. See the Embassies sections in the country profiles later in this book for contact details.

Planning Your Visas

Every country differs in the price, length of stay and extension requirements it offers. Bear the following in mind when you're planning your visas:

- Find out whether your visa is activated on entry or on issue. In some countries (eg India and Pakistan) visas are activated as soon as the stamp appears in your passport so if you wait too long before you enter the country, you'll be left with little time to explore the place.

- The time period can differ depending on whether you arrange the visa at home or on entry. Laos, for example, will give you a 30 day visa if you apply in your home country, but only 15 days at the border.

- Check whether you can extend your visa once you're in the country. If this is pretty straightforward, you might opt for a cheaper, shorter-stay visa at the border. If it's going to be difficult, consider a longer-term visa arranged outside the country.

- Try to have some idea whether you're going to want to enter the country more than once. If you've decided on a loop-style itinerary where you arrive and depart from the same airport, you may need a multiple-entry visa. These are best applied for in your home country.

- Make sure you know the approved entry and exit points for each of your visas. Some countries (eg Vietnam) will ask you to stipulate which town or airport you plan to arrive and depart from, and will make it difficult for you to change your plans. In other countries, the visa type will differ depending on whether you're arriving by air or overland.

The Visa Requirements table in this section will give you an idea of which countries you will need a visa for. For further details, see the country profiles. Visa requirements change without notice, so always check with the country's embassy or consulate in your home country. There's a reasonably reliable web site (www2.travel.com.au/cgi-bin/clcgi?E=bevisreq) that provides visa requirements by country of origin and destination.

Visa Requirements

	Australia	Canada	NZ	UK	USA
Bangladesh	yes (3 months)	yes (3 months)	yes (3 months)	yes (3 months)	yes (3 months)
Bhutan	yes (15 days)	yes (15 days)	yes (15 days)	yes (15 days)	yes (15 days)
Brunei	yes (14 days)	no (14 days)	no (14 days)	no (30 days)	no (90 days)
Cambodia	yes (30 days)	yes (30 days)	yes (30 days)	yes (30 days)	yes (30 days)
China	yes (30 days)	yes (30 days)	yes (30 days)	yes (30 days)	yes (30 days)
India	yes (6 months)	yes (6 months)	yes (6 months)	yes (6 months)	yes (6 months)
Indonesia	no (60 days)	no (60 days)	no (60 days)	no (60 days)	no (60 days)
Japan	no (90 days)	no (90 days)	no (90 days)	no (90 days)	no (90 days)
Laos	yes (30 days)	yes (30 days)	yes (30 days)	yes (30 days)	yes (30 days)
Malaysia	no (60 days)	no (60 days)	no (60 days)	no (60 days)	no (30 days)
Mongolia	yes (90 days)	yes (90 days)	yes (90 days)	yes (90 days)	yes (90 days)
Myanmar	yes (28 days)	yes (28 days)	yes (28 days)	yes (28 days)	yes (28 days)
Nepal	yes (60 days)	yes (60 days)	yes (60 days)	yes (60 days)	yes (60 days)
Pakistan	yes (90 days)	yes (90 days)	yes (90 days)	yes (90 days)	yes (90 days)
Philippines	yes (59days)	yes (59 days)	yes (59days)	yes (59 days)	yes (59 days)
Singapore	no (30 days)	no (30 days)	no (30 days)	no (30 days)	no (30 days)
South Korea	no (30 days)	no (90 days)	no (90 days)	no (90 days)	no (15 days)
Sri Lanka	no (90 days)	no (30 days)	no (90 days)	no (30 days)	no (90 days)
Taiwan	no (14 days)	no (14 days)	no (14 days)	no (14 days)	no (14 days)
Thailand	no (30 days)	no (30 days)	no (90 days)	no (30 days)	no (30 days)
Vietnam	yes (30 days)	yes (30 days)	yes (30 days)	yes (30 days)	yes (30 days)

The Application Process

No matter where you apply for your visa, you're likely to face short opening hours, long queues (especially in London) and stone-faced or unhelpful staff. To make this tedious process as hassle-free as possible, consider the following strategies:

- Phone in advance to find out the embassy's opening hours and requirements for costs, photographs, identification and documents. Check out the country's public holidays too, when the embassy is likely to be closed.

- Leave yourself plenty of time as your visa may not be processed on your first attempt.

- Arrive early and be prepared to queue. Bring a book or stereo to help pass the time.

- Have all your documentation in order and ready to present to the clerk, including your planned entry and departure dates. There's no need to dress up, but don't look too scuzzy either. Embassies are not obliged to grant you a visa, so it helps to make a good first impression.

- When you pick up your visa, be on time and don't leave until you've checked that the dates, length of stay and other details are correct.

Photographs

Whether you decide to arrange your visas in advance or on the road, bring plenty of passport-size photographs with you. Many countries will require two or three photos to process a visa, and not all Asian cities will have cheap and accessible instant-photo booths.

OTHER PAPERWORK

Hostelling International Card

Membership of Hostelling International (HI) is relatively cheap, but it's not particularly useful in Asia. Accredited hostels are scarce and tend to be a lot more expensive than local budget accommodation. If you plan to continue to Europe or the USA, a HI card can be useful, but you'd be better off saving your cash if you're staying within Asia. Membership costs around US$25 per year. See the HI web site (www.iyhf.org) for full details.

International Student Card

The International Student Identity Card (ISIC) is the most widely recognised student card in the world. It qualifies the holder for discounts on airline tickets, rail passes, accommodation, shopping and entrance to museums and cultural events, although the availability and level of discounts varies from country to country. This card is available only to full-time students (there is no age limit) and is issued by accredited travel agencies (such as STA) through the International Student Travel Confederation (ISTC; www.isic.org/index.htm) in Copenhagen,

Denmark. You'll need documentary proof of your full-time student status from your university.

If you're over 25 years old, your card will be of only limited use in most Asian countries, where many student concessions have been either eliminated or replaced by 'youth rates' or similar age-based concessions (although some services in Japan, South Korea, Malaysia and Pakistan will still honour the card). However, it's a useful form of secondary identification if you don't have a driver's licence or another form of ID that contains your photograph.

If you're not a full-time student but are under 25 years of age, you'll qualify for the International Youth Travel Card (IYTC), which is also issued by ISTC. It has similar benefits, but is recognised by fewer countries around the world. A similar card is the GO 25 International Youth Travel Card (known as the GO 25 Card), which is issued by representative offices of the Federation of International Youth Travel Organisations (FIYTO; www.fiyto.org/index-old.html). These cards offer essentially the same benefits as the ISIC card.

International Teacher Card

If you're a full-time teacher at a recognised educational institution, you'll qualify for the International Teacher Identity Card (ITIC). Also issued by ISTC, it offers similar discounts as the student cards, and is distributed in more than 40 countries and recognised by educational institutions worldwide. For full details visit the ISTC web site (www.isic.org/index.htm).

International Driving Permit

If you want to drive a car or ride a motorbike in Asia, you'll probably need an International Driving Permit (IDP). These are issued only by automobile associations in your home country – occasionally a web site appears that claims to provide IDPs, but these are likely to be counterfeit and far more expensive than going through the authorised organisations.

To qualify, you normally have to be 18 years of age or over and the holder of a valid driver's licence from your home country. You'll have to supply a couple of passport-type photographs and pay a nominal administrative fee.

In many western countries, IDPs are only valid for one year, so there's no sense getting one too far in advance of your departure (check with your local authority). Make sure your permit states that it is valid for motorbikes if you plan to ride one.

Not all Asian countries recognise IDPs – for example, in China it's very difficult to get permission to drive at all, while Malaysia and the Philippines will only accept your home licence – but you will need one for the majority of countries. Even if you get an IDP, bring your home licence with you as well. Contact details for major issuing agencies are:

- **American Automobile Association**
  (☎ 1-888-859-5161; ww.aaa.com/vacation/idp.html)

- **Australian Automobile Association**
  (☎ 02-6247 7311; www.aaa.asn.au – for links to the state-based automobile associations that issue IDPs)
- **British Automobile Association** (☎ 0990 500 600; www.theaa.co.uk/membership/offers/ idp.html)
- **Canadian Automobile Association** (☎ 613-247-0117 ext 2025; www.caa.ca/CAAInternet/ travelservices/frames14.htm)
- **New Zealand Automobile Association** (☎ 0800-500 444; www.aa.org.nz)

Name Cards

You might feel a bit like a travelling salesman, but it can be worthwhile having cards printed with your name, address and email address to give to people you meet along the way. This is preferable to writing your details out by hand for each person you want to keep in touch with. Cards can also be useful when dealing with officialdom, as many Asian cultures set great store by business cards.

You can get cards printed very cheaply in most Asian countries, and local printers will be able to make bilingual cards. Needless to say, if you're going to job-hunt in Asia, cards are essential.

Yellow Fever Vaccination Certificate

This certificate is needed if you are entering Asia after a recent trip to a country where yellow fever is prevalent (sub-Saharan Africa and tropical South America). Border officials will want to see the Yellow Fever Vaccination Certificate that was issued to you after you received your jab. This used to be covered by International Health Cards, but these are no longer issued in all countries, mainly because they were so easy to forge. See the Health chapter later in this book for details on predeparture vaccinations.

Photocopies

Make sure you make two sets of copies of all your important documents, such as your passport (including any visa stamps), tickets, travel insurance, travellers cheques receipt and serial numbers, International Driving Permit, birth and marriage certificates (if you bring them) and credit cards. Keep one copy in your main luggage (assuming the originals are in your money belt) and give the other to a friend or family member at home. If you lose any of the original items, having copies will make them much easier to replace, particularly if you have to deal with local officialdom. The copy at home is further insurance, just in case something goes horribly wrong and you manage to lose both sets on the road.

TICKETS & INSURANCE

YOUR TICKET

Air

Most travellers to South-East Asia or the Indian subcontinent will arrive by air. It's worth thinking about buying your ticket as soon as you've decided to go, as the best deals tend to be available well in advance of your departure date. You can get spectacularly cheap tickets at the very last moment, but this strategy is fraught with danger. If you do manage to find such a ticket, you probably won't get the routes you're seeking and you may struggle to arrange insurance and visas in time. If you can't find a good deal, you'll either have to pay full price or delay your departure.

Airlines

Like most industries, the airline industry has operators catering to the full range of standards and budgets – from top-end outfits such as Singapore Airlines, which boasts a modern fleet with high-quality service and personal movie and games screens (even in economy class), to cut-rate domestic Asian airlines with old fleets and shoestring services.

The adage that 'you get what you pay for' certainly applies to airlines. Cheaper operators have older fleets which tend to have greater safety risks, lower levels of comfort and a lower level of reliability, making cancellations and delays more frequent. However, there are many good options in the middle ground, particularly within the European and American carrier markets.

Before you get caught up in the finer details of your route, pick up information on several airlines from a travel agency. Check out the age of the fleet, frequent flyer programs, options for booking, payment and alteration of prebooked tickets, and the cancellation policies of each airline.

Most airlines have a web site providing information on the routes they fly, their schedules and their frequent flyer programs. A few to try include:

- **Air New Zealand** (www.airnz.com)
- **Alitalia** (www.alitalia.com/english/index.html)
- **American Airlines** (www.americanair.com)
- **Ansett Australia** (www.ansett.com.au)
- **British Airways** (www.british-airways.com)
- **Canadian Airline** (www.cdnair.ca)
- **Cathay Pacific** (www.cathaypacific.com/index.html)
- **Continental Airlines** (www.flycontinental.com)
- **Qantas** (www.qantas.com)

- **Singapore Airlines** (www.newasia-singapore.com; www.singaporeair.com)
- **United Airlines** (www.ual.com)
- **Virgin** (www.fly.virgin.com)

Partnerships   The airline you choose to fly with will affect your route options, since no airline can fly between all destinations. Access to sectors is jealously guarded and almost always favours the home country airline. To deal with this, most airlines negotiate reciprocal arrangements, or partnerships, with a series of other airlines to allow them access into designated sectors of each other's markets. This allows both airlines to offer a much broader range of flight options, particularly for special fares such as Round-the-World (RTW) tickets. If you opt for a single, multisector fare with a particular airline, you will almost certainly fly part of the route with partner airlines, so check them out as well beforehand.

Frequent Flier Programs   Most airlines offer frequent flier programs that can earn you free plane tickets or other benefits. Rewards are based on the number of miles or kilometres you fly with that airline (or its partners), although you can also gather frequent flier points by using associated travel services such as designated car rental companies or hotel chains.

Points generally must be used within five years from the time of your flight, and most airlines will allow you to redeem them for members of your family. The downside is that you'll be locked into one airline, or a group of airlines, which may not always have the cheapest fares or most convenient flight schedule. There is also a joining fee, and some airlines are introducing annual maintenance fees too. Obviously you'll want to sign up with the airline that will carry you the greatest distance during your trip, but keep in mind that if you choose one of your home country's carriers, you may be able to use your frequent flier points for domestic travel on your return.

There are various rules governing frequent flier flights. Most flights will have only a small number of seats allocated for 'freebies', so book well in advance. Many airlines also have blackout periods where no free seats are available (such as Christmas and Chinese New Year).

When you receive your frequent flier member number, keep a record of it with your other documents as you must quote it every time you book a ticket or use an associated service, in order to get your points credited to your account.

Tickets & Restrictions

There is a bewildering variety of tickets and deals on the market and all are governed by complicated rules and restrictions. Common restrictions include:

- Cancellation or change penalties – Cancelling your ticket or altering your route once it's booked may incur financial penalties (most travel insurance policies will protect against unavoidable cancellations).

- Directional limits – Round-the-World tickets usually allow you to travel only in one direction.

- Minimum or maximum limits – You may have to be away a minimum of 14 days or a maximum of 12 months, for example.

- Refund policy – Some refunds can only be made through the travel agency where the ticket was purchased, which is not much good to you while you're in Asia.

- Seasonal limits – A ticket may only be available in off-peak or shoulder periods (see When to Go in the Planning chapter for details).

- Stopover limits – There may be a maximum number of stopovers attached to your ticket.

The basic ticket is a full-price one-way or return ticket between two cities. Airlines typically offer 1st class (coded F), business class (coded J) and economy class (coded Y) tickets. Once the discounting starts, the conditions become ever more complicated and restrictive as the price drops. Some of the common deals are:

Discount Return Tickets If Asia is the only continent you plan to visit, then a plain old return ticket might be your best option. If you can get a cheap return ticket to an Asian transport hub such as Bangkok, Hong Kong or Delhi, you could use a combination of local flights, boats, trains and buses to visit the countries on your itinerary. This assumes you have time on your side and that you're not planning to travel massive distances, as you'll have to return to your entry point to fly home. For more flexibility, you may be able to include one or more stop-offs at cities en route to your destination. Stop-offs can last several weeks, allowing you to explore one region before you resume your journey. A good example would be a London-Bangkok ticket with a stop-off in Delhi, so you can travel through the subcontinent and South-East Asia for a single fare.

Open-Jaw Tickets These are return tickets which allow you to fly to one destination, but return home from another, thus saving you a lot of backtracking and time. Open-jaw tickets are generally more expensive than standard return fares, but can allow you to see a lot more of a region, especially if the distance between the two cities on your ticket is great. For example, if you can arrange a ticket that arrives in Hong Kong and departs from Bangkok, you'll be able to explore a huge section of South-East Asia without having to put aside the time to return to Hong Kong.

One-Way Tickets These tickets tend to more expensive than return tickets, but are useful if you are unsure of your itinerary or return date. Knowing you have no deadlines or definite places to be – and complete freedom to follow your whims – is very liberating. The drawback is that many countries require an onward ticket before they'll issue you a visa (see the Passports & Visas chapter and the country profiles for more details on visas). However, if you know which route you'll use to leave the country (be it by rail, bus or air) and you can prove you have the cash reserves to keep you solvent during your stay, you should be able to convince most officials to grant you a visa.

Round-the-World Tickets If you plan to travel to more than one continent, a Round-the-World (RTW) ticket is a very good deal. This fare gives you a limited period (usually 12 months) to circumnavigate the globe, and you can only go in one direction (which means no backtracking).

There'll be a predetermined number of stop-offs, but these can often be increased for an extra charge per stop. The biggest constraint is that you're limited to the flight paths of the airline and its partners, but these fares tend to be such good value that paying for a sector fare to another destination during one of your stop-offs doesn't seem too hard to swallow. The other great advantage is the air mileage you accumulate for your frequent flyer program, even though RTW fares collect points at the lowest rate.

Circle Asia Fares If you are intending to make a number of stops across Asia, it would be well worth considering a Circle Asia ticket. These are deals put together for you by a travel agent linking key cities. The cheapest deals will usually involve 'surface sectors', meaning that you must make your own way by land – or sometimes by sea – between two cities. For example, you might be flown to Kuala Lumpur, but must then travel overland under your own steam to Singapore, before taking the next leg of your Circle Asia ticket on to another major city, such as Bangkok. Once you've constructed a route and paid for your ticket, the route is fixed. It may be possible to change the day on which you fly out of a particular city, although this can incur a penalty. Another downside to the Circle Asia deal is that fares have a 60 day limit. Consult your travel agent before you leave for the best and most suitable deal.

Group Tickets You may be able to get a discount if you ostensibly travel with a 'group'. These groups can be brought together by a travel agent for the sole purpose of selling a block of cheap fares, and there's certainly no need to stay with your group once you've touched down. These fares do tend to be restrictive and inflexible. Check carefully with your travel agent.

APEX Tickets Advance Purchase Excursion (APEX) tickets also lock you into a fairly rigid schedule. APEX tickets must be purchased at least two or three weeks before departure, they do not permit stopovers and may enforce minimum and maximum stays, as well as fixed departure and return dates. There are also usually stiff cancellation fees. Unless you have a definite return date, it's often best to purchase an APEX ticket on a one-way basis only.

Student. Teacher & Youth Fares Some airlines offer discounts of up to 25% for holders of student, youth or teacher cards (see Other Paperwork in the Passports & Visas chapter). In addition to the card, some airlines may ask for a letter from your school. These discounts are generally only available on ordinary economy class fares. You wouldn't get one, for instance, on an APEX or RTW ticket since these are already discounted.

Courier Flights Courier flights are a great bargain if you travel ultralight and are lucky enough to find one. The deal is that an air freight company takes over your entire checked baggage allowance. You are permitted to bring along a carry-on bag, but that's all. In return, you get a steeply discounted fare. There are other restrictions – courier tickets are sold for a fixed date and schedule, so changes can be difficult or impossible. If you buy a return ticket, your schedule will be even more rigid; and don't expect any refunds. Booking a courier ticket takes some effort. They are limited in availability, and arrangements have to be made a month or more in advance. You won't find courier flights on all routes – major routes such as London-Hong Kong or New York-Shanghai offer the best possibilities.

Courier flights are occasionally advertised in the newspapers, or you could contact air freight companies listed in the phonebook. One possibility for US residents is to join the International Association of Air Travel Couriers (☎ 561-582 8320; www.courier.org/index.html).

Tickets to Avoid

Back-to-Front Tickets   These tickets are return fares purchased in your desti-nation city, rather than your home city. For example, if you are living in Sydney (where tickets are relatively expensive) and you want to fly to Bangkok for a holiday (where tickets are much cheaper), theoretically you could buy a ticket by phone using your credit card and get a friend to mail it to you in Sydney. The problem is that the airlines have computers, will know that the ticket was issued in Bangkok and will probably refuse to honour it. Be careful that you don't fall foul of these back-to-front rules when purchasing plane tickets by post or on the web.

Second-Hand Tickets   You'll occasionally see advertisements on youth hostel message boards and sometimes in newspapers for 'second-hand tickets', mean-ing that somebody purchased a return ticket or one with multiple stop-offs, and now wants to sell the unused portion of the ticket.

The prices offered can look very attractive indeed. Unfortunately, these tickets are usually worthless, as the name on the ticket must match the name on the passport of the person checking in. Some people reason that the seller of the ticket can check you in with their passport, and then give you the boarding pass. Usually, however, immigration officials will check that the pass matches the name in your passport, and will stop you from boarding the flight.

If you purchase a ticket and then change your name, make sure you have documentary proof (marriage, divorce or deed poll certificate, or your old pass-port) to prove that the old you and the new you are the same person.

Buying Your Ticket

Try to have a clear idea about the kind of trip you're looking for before you buy your ticket (see What Kind of Trip? in the Planning chapter for some pointers). If you're after an organised tour or package holiday, then your ticket will be included in the price and your decision will be much more influenced by factors such as the age of your fellow travellers, standards of food and accommodation, and the destinations you want to visit. If you're planning to travel independently, ensure you have a reasonably clear idea of your route and the time you wish to be away, as these will greatly affect the type of ticket you purchase and its cost.

Buying from Airlines   You can buy your ticket directly from an airline, but you probably won't get a discount, as airlines use travel agencies to dispose of tickets they are not confident of selling directly to the public at full price. These tickets are generally sold in discounted blocks to the travel agent and part of these savings are passed on to the traveller. So, unless you're trying to organise your ticket at the very last minute, it's almost inconceivable that you won't get a better deal by going through a travel agent.

Buying from Travel Agents   The air travel market is highly lucrative and has attracted a swag of commercial service providers, from respectable travel agency chains to 'bucket shops' specialising in discounted tickets. The former group is 'bonded' to a national association that imposes ethical constraints on their members, including the all-important guaranteed refund if the agent goes into liquidation before you've picked up your ticket. Bucket shops, by contrast, are generally unbonded so you run the risk of losing your money, though they are likely to offer better deals.

If you buy your ticket from an unbonded agency, it's safer to pay by credit card, as the card company will cover the loss if the agency goes bust. If you do pay by cash, make sure the ticket is handed over straightaway; don't agree to pick it up tomorrow or next week. Once you have the ticket, call the airline and confirm that the booking was made. This might sound a trifle paranoid, but it's your money that's at stake. Good, reputable bonded travel agencies include:

AUSTRALIA
STA Travel (☎ 1300 360 960; www.sta-travel.com)
Flight Centre (☎ 131600; www.flightcentre.com)

CANADA
Travel CUTS (☎ 1-800-667-2887; www.travelcuts.com)

NEW ZEALAND
STA Travel (☎ 0800 100 677; www.sta-travel.com)

UK
Trailfinders (☎ 020-7938 3366; www.trailfinder.com)
STA Travel (☎ 020-7581 4132; www.sta-travel.com)

USA
Council Travel (☎ 1-800-226-8624; www.counciltravel.com)
STA Travel (☎ 1-800-781-4040; www.sta-travel.com)

Buying Online   The Internet boom has created a new market for plane tickets. You can find astonishing bargains on the web if you spend a lot of time online (the really amazing deals do not last long), but equally you can spend an awful lot of time tracking down the ticket you want, when you could have found a cheaper option in half the time through a travel agent.

Nevertheless, a few hours of web surfing can help you find out what you can expect in the way of budget fares. This can be a good start for negotiating with your travel agent. Try *Expedia* (expedia.msn.com/daily/home/default.hts), *Flifo* (www.flifo.com) or *Travelocity* (www.travelocity.com).

Getting a Good Deal Start your research by browsing the advertisements in travel magazines and major newspapers (see Researching Your Trip in the Planning chapter) and contacting a few of the major airlines to see which routes they fly. Together with the web sites listed in the previous Buying Online entry, you will get a good idea of the bargains available (always check the conditions and restrictions).

Buy your ticket as early as possible, preferably more than three months before you plan to depart. Most of the really good deals will be quickly snapped up, while others may require full payment well in advance of your departure date. You will also have plenty of time to arrange visas and immunisations (see the Passports & Visas and Health chapters for more details).

Check out a few travel agencies and try to find a well travelled agent of about the same age or inclination as yourself. Finding the good deals among the complex network of databases and promotions requires an agent with computer skills and imagination, so be prepared to go elsewhere if you're not satisfied. Here are a few tips on getting the cheapest fare available:

- Decide whether you're prepared to accept a roundabout journey to reach your destination. Talented travel agents may get you a dirt-cheap fare which is made up of several flights (rather than one direct flight), transiting in different countries over a few days. This is a pretty exhausting way to travel, and you'll spend many empty hours in transit lounges, but if you're looking for every option to keep your costs down, this could be for you.

- Be flexible about your departure date. If you were planning to leave in the peak season, see if you can delay or bring forward your departure date to take advantage of deals in the shoulder season. Alternatively, if you're planning to be away for several months, consider leaving in the low season, when fares are be cheaper and special deals available.

- Be prepared to alter your itinerary to take advantage of a particularly good deal. If you're set on visiting a place that cannot be accommodated by the deal, check out the options for taking a separate sector air fare, or an even cheaper train, boat or bus ride.

Once you've decided on a fare type, get a quote from your travel agent and take it to several other agencies to see if they can beat it. The travel industry is not a level playing field – some airlines have preferred agents and send their best deals through them, so different agencies don't necessarily have access to the same flights and deals. Also check out the payment options – most fares only require full payment around six weeks before departure, so many travel agents will request a small, nonrefundable deposit to ensure that you're a serious buyer.

Your Arrival Time If you can, get a flight that will arrive during daylight hours. If you arrive at lunchtime or early in the afternoon, you'll have time to clear customs and immigration, change some currency, get into the city centre and arrange your first night's accommodation (see Your First Night below) before night falls. You can do all this even if you arrive after dusk, but more services will be open during daylight hours, and arriving in a strange city in the middle of the night can be quite daunting.

It's generally easier to adapt to a new time zone if you arrive during the day – most people find they can manage to stay awake several hours longer than usual, but it can be difficult to fall sleep when your body is convinced it's another six or seven hours till bedtime. For more advice on your arrival, see the Touchdown chapter.

Your First Night

Even if you're the type of person who never plans ahead, you should consider making an exception and research where you plan to spend your first night. Depending upon where you're landing and what time you're arriving, you may want to make a hotel reservation before leaving home, so you don't have to worry about finding a place when you arrive. The disadvantage is that you'll probably have to book mid-range accommodation, as budget places in Asia rarely accept reservations, and this will generally set you back at least US$40.

In most cases, reservations are not necessary. The bigger cities in Asia all have travellers ghettos where you'll find lots of budget hotels and guesthouses clustered together. A good guidebook is handy here. Choose the area in which you want to stay and find out how to get there from the airport. Pick a few decent-looking hotels or guesthouses. You can simply show up and choose the one that looks the best. This simple preparation will probably make the difference between a smooth introduction to Asia and a nightmare of hassles, rip-offs and dodgy accommodation.

Bikes & Surfboards

If you plan to take a bike, surfboard or any other bulky specialised equipment with you, you'll need to notify the airline when you book your ticket. Most airlines are surprisingly easy-going about accommodating extra gear, as long as they've been given enough notice. They'll probably charge you a nominal fee (often as little as US$10), normally to cover the packing materials. Remind the airline of your extra requirements when you reconfirm your ticket, and get to the airport a little earlier so you can pack your equipment well before the rush – it will be better stored in the luggage compartment if it's not last on the plane.

Bikes   Most airlines won't make you take a bike to pieces, as their packages are generally big enough to take the whole bike. You will have to loosen the nut on the stem (to turn your handlebars 90°), remove the pedals and any attach-ments such as lights, bottles and speedos. It's also a good idea to wrap your bike in bubblewrap to protect it from denting or scratches while it's being moved by handlers or if it's poorly stowed during the flight. Alternatively, you can put your bike into your own package and turn up with it ready to go.

Surfboards   Airlines are unlikely to have special packaging for surfboards, so look into getting a travel board cover. These cost around US$200 to US$300 and have extra padding, and the more expensive models can take up to three boards. It's a good idea to wrap your boards in foam or bubblewrap to prevent damage. Some destinations (such as Indonesia) may charge a special import fee, but this seems to depend on the mood of the customs official you deal with.

Other Considerations

Apart from booking tickets, travel agencies may be able to reserve a particular seat on your flight if you are exceptionally tall, afflicted with chronic travel sickness or travelling with a young child. They may also be able to inform the airline if you have a particular dietary requirement and help book your first night's accommodation. See the Take-Off chapter for coverage of these issues, and advice for travellers with a disability.

Land

Trans-Siberian Railway

The Trans-Siberian Railway connects Europe to Asia on a journey of several days crossing several thousand kilometres. Its popularity has declined in recent years, due to the general state of chaos in Russia and continually rising prices, but it remains an intriguing option. For details, see Your Route in the Planning chapter.

Bus & Train

There are plenty of options for getting to Asia overland from Europe, using a mix of buses and trains, and perhaps with an occasional sector flight to avoid parts of the Middle East or to speed up your journey. Map out your preferred route and then check with your travel agent to see what is possible. With this sort of travel the adventure of your trip to Asia will be greatly enhanced: you'll see many varied landscapes, pass through (albeit briefly) many towns and cities, and have opportunities to mix with the locals along the way. If you plan your route and tickets well, you may be able to stop for a while if a place particularly appeals to you. Bear in mind that travelling overland can be expensive, and will certainly be time-consuming. You'll have to do plenty of research and be prepared to cope with numerous visas, border crossings and changes in currency (see Your Route in the Planning chapter for details on overland travel from Europe).

TRAVEL INSURANCE

A travel insurance policy is essential. Depending on your policy, it can protect you against medical costs through illness or injury, ticket loss, cancellation penalties on advance-purchase flights, theft or loss of possessions, and the cost of additional plane tickets if you are so sick that you have to fly home.

There are some very good medical facilities in Asia – particularly in Singapore, Japan, Hong Kong and Malaysia – but elsewhere they vary from mediocre to abysmal (see Medical Services in the Health chapter). If you contract any serious disease or sustain a major injury you may have to be flown to one of these countries or to Darwin in northern Australia. If you do have to undergo medical treatment in Asia, be sure to collect all receipts and copies of your medical report for your insurance company. Similarly, if you are robbed, you'll almost certainly need a police report to be able to claim on your insurance.

You may already have personal medical insurance in your own country, either private or government funded, so check whether it applies internationally. You also might be automatically covered if you hold an International Student Identity Card (ISIC), GO 25 Card or International Teacher Identity Card (ITIC ;for details on these cards see Other Paperwork in the Passports & Visas chapter).

Travel insurance policies are offered by travel agencies and student travel organisations, as well as general insurance companies. Have a good look at what's available – some policies are very cheap, but only offer minimal coverage. Read the small print carefully to avoid being caught out by exclusions.

TIPS ON BUYING TRAVEL INSURANCE

1 Buy your travel insurance as soon as you've settled on your departure date and itinerary. If you buy just before you depart, you may find, for example, that you're not covered for flight delays caused by industrial action that started before you took out the insurance.

2 Credit card companies may provide limited insurance if you pay for your airline ticket with their card. You may be able to reclaim the payment if the operator doesn't deliver. Ask your credit card company what it's prepared to cover.

3 See whether you can extend your policy if you decide to stay away for a longer period than you anticipated, and whether you can get a cheaper family policy if you're travelling with your partner or a friend.

4 An 'excess' (an agreed amount of money you must cough up for each claim) will be imposed by almost all policies. Find out the amount, because in some situations it may be cheaper and quicker for you to bite the bullet and pay all expenses out of your own pocket.

5 Find out whether your policy obliges you to pay on the spot and redeem the money later, or whether the company will pay the providers direct. If you have to claim later, make sure you keep all documentation. If you have a medical problem, some policies will ask you to call back (reverse charges) to a centre in your home country where an immediate assessment of your problem will be made.

6 Be upfront with the insurance company about any pre-existing medical condition you may have. If you gloss over a problem in the quest for a cheaper deal, the company will have grounds not to honour your claims.

7 Some policies specifically exclude 'dangerous activities', which can include scuba diving, motorcycling, and even trekking. A locally acquired motorcycle licence may not be valid under some policies. Also check that the policy covers ambulances or an emergency flight home, especially if you plan to trek or cycle tour in remote areas.

HEALTH

Health issues can loom large when you're thinking about going to Asia. Alarming stories abound in travellers circles, and sensational news reports of disease epidemics can make travel in the region seem at best masochistic and at worst positively life-threatening. The reality is much more mundane. The risks obviously vary according to your destination (Japan and Singapore, for example, are unlikely to present much more risk than holidaying at home), but with a little preparation, some basic precautions and a whole heap of common sense, the worst your trip is likely to entail is a couple of days of the runs. Inconvenient perhaps, but hardly fatal. And what else are you going to talk about on those long bus rides? This chapter discusses general health issues related to travel in Asia; for details on specific destinations, see the country profiles.

BEFORE YOU GO

Information Sources

You can get up-to-date information on the health risks of your destination, as well as advice on immunisations and other preventive health measures, from your family doctor, travel health clinics, government health departments and the web. Specialist travel health clinics are probably the best places to visit. Some have phone, fax or email information lines, so you could get a health brief from them which you could then take to your usual doctor. Most travel clinics sell travel health products such as insect repellent and needle and syringe kits. In the UK, some good places to try include the following:

- **British Airways Travel Clinics** (☎ 01276-685040; www.britishairways.com/travelqa/fyi/health/health.html); countrywide network of clinics (plus three in South Africa); you don't need to be travelling on British Airways to use them.
- **Hospital for Tropical Diseases Travel Clinic** (☎ 020-7388 9600) Mortimer Market Centre, Capper St, London WC1E; it also has a healthline (☎ 0839-337733).
- **Malaria Healthline** (☎ 0891-600 350); recorded information on risks and avoidance from the Malaria Reference Laboratory at the London School of Hygiene & Tropical Medicine.
- **Medical Advisory Services for Travellers (MASTA;** ☎ 020-7631 4408) London School of Hygiene & Tropical Medicine, Keppel St, London WC1E 7BR; provides information and travel health products; its healthline on ☎ 0906-8 224100 has detailed health information on Asian destinations.
- **Nomad Travellers Store & Medical Centre** (☎ 020-8889 7014) 3-4 Wellington Terrace, Turnpike Lane, London N8 0PX; travel healthline on ☎ 0891-633414, email nomad.travstore@virgin.net.

In Australia and New Zealand, the Travellers Medical and Vaccination Centre has a network of clinics in most major cities – use the phonebook to find your nearest clinic or check out its web site (see the following section). TMVC also has clinics in Bangkok and Singapore. They can provide an online personalised travel health report (for a fee) via the web site.

In North America, the central source of travel health information is the Centers for Disease Control (CDC). It has travel health information lines by phone (☎ 888-232 3228) and fax (888-232 3299), and publishes an excellent booklet, *Health Information for International Travel* (☎ 202-512 1800; order from the Superintendent of Documents, US Government Printing Office, Washington, DC). CDC can also advise you on travel medicine providers in your area.

Alternatively, for a comprehensive list of travel health providers in your area you could contact the International Society of Travel Medicine (☎ 770-736 7060; www.istm.org) PO Box 871089; Stone Mountain, GA 30087 or the American Society of Tropical Medicine & Hygiene (☎ 847-480 9592; fax 847-480 9282; www.astmh.org) 60 Revere Drive, Suite 500, Northbrook, IL 60062

The web is also a great source of information on travel health issues, both before you go and when you are on the road. Two authoritative web sites are the first point of call:

• **WHO** (www.who.ch) – The official site of the World Health Organization, this has all the information you'll ever need on the state of the world's health, including disease distribution maps and all the latest health recommendations for international travel. The section that's probably going to be most useful to you is at www.who.int/emc – it has disease outbreak news and health advice for travellers.

• **CDC** (www.cdc.gov) – The official site of the US Centers for Disease Control & Prevention, this has loads of useful information, including disease outbreak news and disease risks according to destination.

Other sites you could try include:

• **MASTA** (www.masta.org) – This highly recommended site of the Medical Advisory Services for Travellers (see earlier) is easy to use and provides concise readable information on all the important issues. It also has useful links, including to the Foreign and Commonwealth Office for advice on safe travel.

• **Medical College of Wisconsin Travelers Clinic** (www.intmed.mcw/travel.html) – This site has useful information on all the usual travel health issues, and an impressively comprehensive list of links to a variety of other travel health information sites. Browse till you drop.

• **Shorelands** (www.tripprep.com) – This well organised site is easy to navigate and has lots of good travel health information, as well as a comprehensive directory of travel medicine providers around the world and handy country profiles that include US State Department travel advisory information.

• **Travel Health Information Service** (www.travelhealth.com). This chatty site, run by US-based Dr Stephen Blythe, is easy to navigate and has loads of good information and links.

• **Travellers Medical and Vaccination Centre** (www.tmvc.com.au/info.html) – This Australian-based site has lots of useful information, including disease outbreak news and good sections on travelling while pregnant and with children.

There are also plenty of good books for further information, including:

- *CDC's Complete Guide to Healthy Travel* – US Centers for Disease Control & Prevention recommendations for international travel.

- *Staying Healthy in Asia, Africa & Latin America*, Dirk Schroeder – Concise, practical and easy to use.

- *Travellers' Health*, Dr Richard Dawood – Comprehensive and authoritative, this is an excellent reference source.

- *Where There Is No Doctor*, David Werner – A very detailed guide intended for some-one, such as a Peace Corps worker, going to work in a developing country.

- *The World Travellers Manual of Homoeopathy*, Dr Colin B Lessell – This impressively comprehensive guide is a good reference even if you're not into homoeopathy.

You might want to consider taking a small health guide with you. Some options are:

- *Healthy Travel Asia & India*, Isabelle Young, Lonely Planet – Provides practical guidance on dealing with various travellers ailments.

- *The Pocket Doctor*, Stephen Bezruchka – A great little book, but let down by its nonuser-friendly design.

- *The Travellers Healthbook*, ed Miranda Haines & Sarah Thorowgood – Small, but surprisingly comprehensive, it contains lots of practical travel health information.

Immunisations

Immunisations help protect you from some diseases you could be at risk of while on the road. Once you have a rough idea of where you're heading, go to your doctor or a travel health clinic for the lowdown on which immunisations you'll need.

Be wary of advice on immunisations given to you by a travel agent or an embassy. For example, you may be told that no immunisations are needed for a certain country, but what they actually mean is that you won't be asked for proof of immunisation when you roll up at the border. You will still need immunisations to protect yourself.

Make sure all your immunisations are recorded on an official certificate – your doctor or travel health centre should issue you with one – so you know what you're protected against and when you're due for a repeat.

Ideally, you need to have your immunisations sorted out at least six weeks before you travel, to give yourself the best chance of developing full protection before you go, and so you don't end up feeling like a human pincushion. This also gives you time to have a full course if necessary, and to get over any possible reactions. Some immunisations are best not given together, so the more time you've got to arrange all this, the better.

Don't panic if you have left it to the last minute. Schedules can be rushed if necessary, it just means you may not be quite as well protected.

If you are interested in homoeopathic immunisations, discuss this with your practitioner or your doctor, or consult the *The World Travellers Manual of Homoeopathy* (see Information Sources earlier).

Which Immunisations?

Working out which immunisations you need depends not only on where you're going but on how long you're planning to travel, if you're travelling in rural areas or sticking to the resorts, or if you're planning to work or just holiday.

IMMUNISATION DETAILS

If you're an adult, you will probably have had the full course of an immunisation before, usually as a child. With most immunisations, it takes two to three weeks to build up

VACCINE	FULL COURSE
• Tetanus	three doses given at four-week intervals (usually in childhood); usually given with diphtheria
• Polio	three doses given at four-week intervals (usually in childhood)
• Hepatitis A vaccine	single dose
• Hepatitis A immunoglobulin	single injection; needs to be given close to departure
• Typhoid	single injection, or three or four oral doses
• Meningococcal meningitis	one dose
• Hepatitis B	two doses one month apart plus a third dose six months later
• Rabies (pre-exposure)	three doses over one month
• Japanese B encephalitis	two doses over a month
• BCG (for tuberculosis)	single dose

Other factors that need to be considered are what immunisations you've had in the past, any medications you're taking and any allergies you have.

All vaccines can cause side effects, usually minor (sore arm, feverish for half a day) but very occasionally serious allergic reactions can occur. There is no evidence that immunisations damage your immune system in any way. Note that some immunisations are best avoided in pregnancy, and there are special considerations in babies and children.

Recommendations change, so you'll need to discuss these with your doctor

maximum protection. There are currently no immunisations available for travellers diarrhoea, dengue fever or malaria.

BOOSTER	COMMENTS
every 10 years	full course usually given in childhood
every 10 years	full course usually given in childhood
booster at six to 12 months	gives good protection for at least 12 months; with booster, protects for more than 10 years
gives protection only for two to six months, depending on dose	because it's a blood product there's a theoretical risk of HIV and hepatitis B or C
injection: every three years; oral: every one to five years	the old injectable vaccine was notorious for producing unpleasant side effects, but the new one causes few side effects
protection lasts three years	protects against the major epidemic forms of the disease
three to five years	more rapid courses are available if necessary
two to three years booster at six to 12 months	the old vaccine was extremely unpleasant as it had to be injected into the stomach, but the new vaccine is injected under the skin, and has few side effects
three years	should be avoided if you have multiple allergies (eg to bee stings or drugs)
immune for life; no booster required	often given in childhood, so you may already be immune

or travel health clinic. However, whatever your travel plans, you'll need to be up to date with the following:

- **Tetanus** – Usually given with diphtheria.

- **Hepatitis A** – If you're going to Japan only, this may not be necessary.

- **Polio** – Usually given orally

Other travel-related immunisations you may need include:

- **Typhoid** – If you're going for more than a couple of weeks to most parts of Asia, except Japan.

- **Meningococcal meningitis** – For Nepal, northern Pakistan, parts of India, Mongolia and, in certain circumstances, Vietnam.

- **Hepatitis B** – If you'll be working as a medic or nurse, or if needle-sharing or unprotected sexual contact is a possibility where you're going.

- **Japanese B encephalitis** – You may need this if you're planning to spend time in rural, rice-growing areas of Asia.

- **Rabies** – This expensive vaccine doesn't prevent rabies totally but it does give you more time to get medical help. It's recommended for travel off the beaten track or for handling wild animals in high-risk areas. Rabies hotspots in Asia currently include the Indian subcontinent, Thailand and the Philippines. Countries reportedly free of rabies are Japan, Malaysia and Taiwan. Whether you have been immunised or not, you need to have booster injections as soon as possible after a suspect bite – you will need more if you haven't been immunised.

- **Tuberculosis** – You probably won't need this unless you're going to be living with local people for three months or more.

Note that immunisation against cholera is no longer recommended, except in special circumstances, because it provides only short-lived, poor protection.

Malaria Pills

If you're going to a malarial area (see the map on the opposite page), you need to get expert advice on preventing this potentially fatal mosquito-borne disease – a travel health clinic is the best place to go. You're not generally at high risk of malaria in Asia, and in many popular tourist areas the risk is very low. However, malaria is very difficult to treat in some parts of South-East Asia because of the development of resistance to the principal drugs used to prevent and treat malaria.

Remember, if you need to take malaria pills, they generally need to be started at least one week before you leave (ideally two to three weeks for mefloquine) and it's very important to keep taking them for four weeks after returning home. For the best protection, you need to take antimalarials regularly. Minor side effects are common with all the drugs but if you get major side effects that make you unsure about continuing the drug, seek advice about

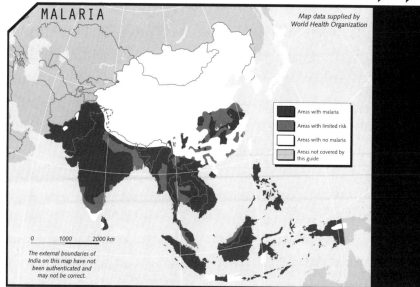

MALARIA

Map data supplied by
World Health Organization

Areas with malaria

Areas with limited risk

Areas with no malaria

Areas not covered by
this guide

0   1000   2000 km

*The external boundaries of
India on this map have not
been authenticated and
may not be correct.*

changing to a medication that suits you better. Some malaria pills are not suitable for everyone, so check this with your doctor.

Some points to bear in mind are:

• No antimalarial provides 100% protection, especially now that resistance to many antimalarials is increasing, so it's important to reduce your risk further by protecting yourself
against mosquito bites (see Insect Bites in the Everyday Health section).

• If you get malaria, taking your normal prevention medicine won't treat it.

If you do need to take malaria pills, you will probably be offered one of three
main options: mefloquine (trade name Lariam), chloroquine with proguanil or
doxycycline. Mefloquine and chloroquine are taken weekly, whereas proguanil
and doxycycline are taken daily. Resistance to chloroquine is well established,
and resistance to mefloquine is on the increase, so it's best to get the latest
information on this from your travel health clinic, or the CDC or WHO web
sites (see Information Sources earlier). Doxycycline is a relatively new option for
malaria and drug resistance hasn't been reported, although it's probably only a
matter of time. Doxycycline is a useful option if mefloquine-resistant malaria is
present or you would prefer not to take mefloquine.

All antimalarials have side effects (see the boxed text 'Afraid To Take Your
Medicine?' on the next page), and minor reactions are common with all of them.

Emergency Treatment

If you're going to a high-risk malarial area without access to medical assistance
or you are going to a low-risk area and prefer not to take antimalarials, you

should consider taking emergency treatment for malaria plus a malaria diagnosis kit with you. This is something you should discuss when you are getting your antimalarial medication. You will need a different medication from that used for prevention.

Travel Insurance

However lucky (or poor) you're feeling, you don't want to be without this for all sorts of reasons. For details, see the Tickets & Insurance chapter earlier in the book.

Check-Ups

General Health

It may be worth making an appointment with your doctor to discuss some of the following issues:

- If you suffer from any ongoing conditions such as asthma, hay fever or dermatitis, try to clarify any specific problems travelling may cause and what to do about them.

- To get supplies of prescription medicines you might need and to discuss taking emergency treatment for diarrhoea or chest infections.

- To discuss problems that travel may pose to any contraceptives you are using, or to discuss options if you want to start contraception.

- Stopping your periods temporarily, for example if you're going to be trekking in a remote area at an inconvenient time (also see the Women's Health section later in this chapter).

If you're going on a long trip and planning to spend time in remote areas, especially if you're going trekking, you might want to consider doing a first-aid course before you leave. Asia has some fantastic diving sites – you'll need a diving medical check before you go.

AFRAID TO TAKE YOUR MEDICINE?

Which malaria pills to take and whether to take them at all can be a hot topic of conversation among travellers, especially as the risk of malaria in Asia is quite variable. Mefloquine is one of the most effective antimalarials available, but it's also one of the most controversial, and there has been much discussion in the media and among travellers about its side effects. These range from common side effects such as sleep disturbance (especially vivid dreams) to uncommon but more serious effects such as panic attacks, hallucinations and fits. Most people who take mefloquine do not, however, have any problems. Perhaps it's simply a case of bad news travelling faster than good.

You can get information on mefloquine and alternative antimalarials from travel health clinics, your doctor or any of the web sites listed under Information Sources at the beginning of this chapter. For a discussion of the issues surrounding mefloquine, check out the web sites at www.travel health.com/mefloqui.htm or www.geocities. com/TheTropics/6913/lariam.htm. Or you could visit Lariam Action USA's web site on www.suggskelly.com/lariam.

If you cannot (or would prefer not to) take mefloquine, there are other options, eg chloroquine plus proguanil, or doxycycline, and these may be better than taking nothing at all.

Dental

It's definitely worth making time for this before you go, especially if you have not been for a while. You don't want to find you need a filling when you're in a remote area far from the nearest pain-killing injection. Your teeth can take quite a battering when you're travelling because you often end up drinking gallons of sweet drinks, and inadequate water supplies may mean you can't keep up your usual dental health routine.

Optical

If you wear contact lenses, your optometrist can advise you about hygiene on the road; you'll want to take a plentiful supply of any cleaning solutions you use. If you wear glasses, consider taking a replacement pair or take your prescription with you, as in many Asian countries you can have prescription lenses made up quite cheaply.

Medical Kit

For details on what to include in your medical kit (a vital piece of equipment), see the Equipment section in the What to Bring chapter.

EVERYDAY HEALTH

As only a small percentage of travel-related illness is preventable with immunisations, maintaining good health also means taking basic precautions to prevent illness and accidents. Everything that makes travelling exciting can also make it both physically and mentally stressful, particularly at the beginning of the big trip. There's a new physical environment to get used to as well as a new lifestyle, and you are likely to experience some culture shock too. It's worth taking some time out in the first week for a breather, to catch up on sleep or missed meals and to recover from jet lag.

Sun & Heat

If you're heading somewhere hot and sunny, allow at least a week to acclimatise, and bear in mind some of the following:

- **Footwear** – Too big is better than too small because your feet can swell up in the heat, and blisters or chafing can easily become infected.

- **Safe sun exposure** – The sun can be surprisingly strong in the tropics and subtropics, especially at high altitudes or near water; avoid long-term skin damage, including skin cancer, by covering up, staying out of the midday sun and using lots of sunscreen.

- **Take it easy** – Help your body out by not doing too much during the heat of the day, and avoid large heavy meals and excess alcohol during the hottest part of the day.

- **Hot climates** – These can make you sweat profusely, so dehydration is a risk. You'll need to drink lots of fluids, although your sweating mechanism becomes more efficient as you acclimatise.

- **Muscle cramps** – If your salt and water balance are out of kilter, you may need to add extra salt to your food or drinks to avoid cramping (salt is added to fresh lime sodas in some countries).
- **Prickly heat and fungal infections** – Avoid these by washing regularly (but avoid over-using soap, which makes it worse) and drying yourself carefully.
- **Heat exhaustion and heat stroke** – These are serious conditions that can occur if you don't recognise the dangers of heat exposure.

MEDICINES

In many Asian countries, medicines are much more freely available than they are in the west, where medicines deemed to be potentially risky are available only on prescription. Not so in places like the Philippines, India and Thailand where medicines of all kinds are often sold at roadside stalls or in the village store. Although this is great if you need to replace a medicine, it does have a downside:

- medicines may not have been kept in optimum conditions or may be past their expiry dates

- they may not be what you think they are; fake medicines are a major problem in the region

- you may not be able to get any guidance on when and how you should be taking a medicine

- your brand may not be available

- drugs no longer recommended in western countries may still be sold in Asia

For all these reasons, it's best to take plentiful supplies of any medication you think you'll be needing, with you. To avoid potential problems at customs, ask your doctor to prepare an official letter explaining why you need them with you.

Food

The classic travellers conundrum is whether to enhance the travelling experience by tasting every roadside snack, or to be obsessively selective and possibly avoid getting sick? The answer is probably neither. The risk of becoming ill from food varies with your destination – for example, there's generally a low risk in Japan and Singapore, and a higher risk in Bangladesh and India. Overall, contaminated food is the most common source of illness in travellers.

When you're eating out three meals a day for weeks, maybe months, and you don't have any control over how your food is prepared, it makes sense to take some basic precautions. Hot, freshly prepared food is usually fine, whether it's served at a roadside stall or in a restaurant. Hotel star rating is no guarantee of food safety. Food that has sat around with the possibility of flies and dust landing on it is dubious. If a restaurant looks dirty or is staffed by an unwashed chef, then avoid it.

Fruit is fine as long as you can peel it yourself, as are vegetables if they've been peeled and/or cooked. Eating salads is just asking for trouble because they may have been washed in polluted water or not at all. Shellfish can transmit hepatitis A and cholera, and raw fish, a delicacy in countries like Thailand, can transmit intestinal parasites. Raw meat can transmit various tapeworms. It's best to avoid unboiled milk as it may not have been pasteurised, though powdered or UHT milk should be OK.

If you're on a long trip, or you're budgeting hard, you'll need to take care that your diet is balanced and that you don't lose a huge amount of weight. Consider taking multivitamins with you in case you get run-down.

Water

With a few exceptions (for example Japan, South Korea and Singapore), you should assume that you cannot drink the tap water in Asia, as you can't be sure it hasn't been contaminated by human or animal waste somewhere down the line.

MALADY A DAY

When asked for travel advice, there is one mantra which I always try to drum into a new traveller's head. Be cool, no matter what insanity you find yourself embroiled in, and you'll be amazed at how smoothly things can go.

Health is often the most pressing concern for first-time travellers to Asia. Months of immunisations, stop-gap prescriptions and World Health Organization reports can engender hyperventilation in even the hardiest traveller. But if you let this hypochondriac bug into your brain, you risk what I call 'terminal malady'. You'll either make yourself sick or, if you truly are sick, you'll make yourself even sicker. Every bout of diarrhoea becomes dysentery, and every mosquito bite augurs malaria.

An acquaintance once came down with an acute case in South-East Asia. Before she left, I had detected a slight obsessiveness with all things health-related. A dutiful researcher, she tracked down all the things that could kill her (down to plague in south-west China!). By the time she left, she toted every pharmaceutical panacea known to western medicine and had a pincushion arm numb from inoculations. I believe she had also half-convinced herself she was going to fall sick.

First country, first malady. She spent days holed up in a guesthouse in Bangkok, suffering from gastrointestinal onslaught. No problem; the first few days are always tough when acclimatising. But over the next two months, each successive country brought on more ailments and mysterious symptoms. She seemed to be incessantly bedridden in low-rent guesthouses. Postcards became more graphic in relating symptoms and the bureaucracy of Asian clinics. I actually jumped up from my desk when I read in one letter that she had collapsed at the Hong Kong airport and had to be rushed to hospital. After a barrage of tests, which took up her entire stay in Hong Kong, puzzled doctors could find absolutely nothing wrong with her.

She had proved that you can get every shot, swallow every horse pill, and carry every fix-all, and they won't necessarily help you. Her travel partner had prepared little but came away absolutely unscathed. So, in reverse order of importance: do what you can preventively, use your common sense, but above all relax.

THOMAS HUHTI
LP AUTHOR, USA

This means not having ice in your drinks and not brushing your teeth with tap water. Bottled water is widely available throughout Asia, although it's probably best to stick to major brands as there have been scares over the quality of some bottled water. Choose a bottle with an unbroken seal so you can be confident it's not just an empty bottle refilled with tap water or worse.

You may want to consider an alternative to bottled water, as the cost can be quite substantial over a long trip and you may not want to contribute to Asia's growing mountain of unrecyclable plastic. Simplest is to boil all your water – in some countries boiled water is often provided routinely, or you could use a small heating coil (widely available from hardware shops in India). Alternatively, you could treat your drinking water with chlorine tablets or iodine, which is more effective and available as drops or tablets. Another option is to invest in a water filter, a big outlay but possibly worth it for a long trip or for trekking in remote areas.

BREAKBONE FEVER

Breakbone fever, as dengue used to be known, is the current scourge of Asia, and the indications are that it will stay that way for the foreseeable future. Dengue is a viral disease transmitted by mosquitoes which tend to be most active during the day, and are found mainly in urban areas. It starts like flu (or malaria) with a high fever, headache, joint and muscle pains (hence its old name), nausea and vomiting, and sometimes a rash. It can progress to a much more severe illness, dengue haemorrhagic fever (DHF), but this is rare and very unlikely in travellers. Recovery even from simple dengue fever may be prolonged, with tiredness lasting for several weeks.

There is no immunisation or specific treatment for dengue. The best prevention is to avoid mosquito bites .

If you have dengue fever don't take aspirin, as it increases the risk of haemorrhaging. You should seek medical attention as soon as possible if you think you may be infected.

Personal Hygiene

Maintaining good personal hygiene is important because standards of public hygiene can be low in many parts of Asia, and this is one reason why diseases like diarrhoea are so common. It goes without saying that you should wash your hands before you eat (there's usually a basin or jug for this in most restaurants) as well as after using the toilet, and keep your hands away from your mouth and eyes, especially on public transport.

Taking your own plate, cup and cutlery can be handy, especially for street food or meals on trains. You may notice that when drinking from a shared jug or cup people pour the water into their mouths rather than letting the vessel touch their lips. You could adopt the widespread local custom of using one hand (usually the left) for toilet duty and the other for eating.

Insect Bites

An impressive range of diseases are transmitted through insect bites – dengue fever, malaria, Japanese B encephalitis (which are all transmitted by mosquitoes), leishmaniasis (sandflies), typhus and other fevers (ticks and mites). The itch from some bites can drive you to distraction, and scratched bites can easily become infected.

To cut down on bites stay in well screened rooms, use mosquito nets and cover up (malaria mosquitoes are night-biters, but dengue mosquitoes bite during the day). Wearing light-coloured clothing may also help. Insect repellents containing the compound DEET are thought to be the most effective against mosquitoes, flies, midges, ticks, bedbugs and leeches, so take a good supply with you. Although there is no evidence that DEET is harmful, it's best to be cautious, especially with children – follow the instructions carefully and don't exceed the recommended dose.

Natural remedies include citronella, eucalyptus, and pyrethrum flowers. However, you will need to reapply them regularly as they generally have a very short time of action (up to an hour).

You'll find that the quality of mosquito nets and insect screening provided varies depending on the amount you're paying for a room. Consider taking a mosquito net with you. Nets soaked or sprayed with permethrin give even greater protection, and you could consider treating your clothes too, especially if you're trekking in tick-infested areas. You can buy treated mosquito nets at most travel equipment stores.

You could also consider using insect sprays, mosquito coils or electrical devices for heating small insect repellent pads, all of which are widely available throughout Asia.

Cuts & Scratches

Dust, dirt, lack of washing facilities and hot, humid conditions all make infection of any break in the skin more likely when you're travelling. Infections make wounds less likely to heal. Also, infections can spread and cause blood poisoning, which is a serious illness.

It's worth taking care to prevent infection by avoiding cuts, scratches and insect bites, and to keep skin breaks as clean as possible. Coral cuts can be very troublesome as the coral injects a weak

THE INJECTION QUESTION

Lack of resources and less rigorous sterilisation (if any) procedures in many less developed Asian countries mean that injections carry a risk of transmission of HIV/AIDS or hepatitis B or C. Ways to minimise this risk are to avoid injections where possible – ask if there's a tablet you can take instead – and to carry sterile needles and syringes with you just in case. You can get AIDS packs from most travel health clinics.

If you're basically healthy, not pregnant and you take sensible precautions to avoid accidents, it's very unlikely that you would need a blood transfusion while you are away. However, it's worth being aware that in most Asian countries (except Japan) blood is not screened adequately.

It's worth taking all reasonable precautions to avoid situations in which you might need a blood transfusion, but if you do need one, remember that safe blood supplies can generally be found in most major cities.

poison, and cuts are difficult to clean thoroughly. Wear shoes if necessary or, better still, don't walk on coral at all.

Accidents & Injury

Accidents are the most common cause of death in travellers and are more likely to affect younger travellers. It's a curious fact that when you're on holiday you tend to take risks that you probably wouldn't take at home, even though safety standards are often less rigorous in many countries in Asia. Here are a few pointers to help you to avoid accidents:

- Avoid alcohol when swimming or driving, and don't dive into shallow water
- Beware of strong currents at the seaside; check the local situation and don't swim alone
- If you're riding a motorcycle or moped, wear a helmet and protective clothing
- Hire cars from reputable firms, wear a seatbelt, try not to speed and avoid travelling at night
- Check your hotel room for safety features; in particular, avoid rooms with fires for heating as this may carry the risk of carbon monoxide poisoning if the ventilation is poor

Safer Sex

While it's true that sexually transmitted infections (STIs), including HIV/AIDS and hepatitis B, are a risk anywhere if you're having casual sex, it seems that you're more likely to throw caution to the wind when you are away from home, and are therefore more at risk. Added to this, levels of STIs in the countries you are visiting may be higher than at home.

Avoiding casual sex altogether is the safest option; otherwise, remember to practise safer sex by using a condom. Condoms are widely available in most Asian countries but you may prefer to take a familiar, reliable brand with you. Rubber condoms disintegrate in the heat, so take care to store them deep in your pack and to check them carefully before use.

Alcohol & Drugs

Be a wary of local brews, especially distilled spirits, as they may contain undesirable additives or methanol, a highly toxic form of alcohol which can cause permanent blindness.

Other mind-altering substances are readily available throughout much of Asia, and in tourist haunts especially you'll be offered drugs at every opportunity. If you decide to use drugs, be aware that there's no guarantee of quality, and locally available drugs can be unexpectedly strong or mixed with other harmful substances. Acute anxiety and panic attacks are common with many drugs, especially if you're taking them for the first time under stressful conditions. Acute paranoia can occur with cocaine, amphetamines and ecstasy, and can be very frightening. If you opt to take drugs intravenously, remember that needle-sharing carries the risk of HIV or hepatitis B or C infection. Because unexpected reactions can occur, never take drugs when you are alone. For a discussion of the possible legal ramifications of drug use in Asia, see Drugs in the Issues & Attitudes chapter.

Medical Services

Even if you take all reasonable precautions against illness and accident, you may still become sick and need to find a doctor. Other travellers may be able to recommend a doctor or clinic, and your guidebook will probably list some options. You could consider joining an organisation like the International Association for Medical Assistance to Travellers (☎ 519-836 0102; www.sentex.net) 40 Regal Rd, Guelph, Ontario N1K 1B5, Canada. This nonprofit organisation can provide you with a list of reliable doctors in the countries you're planning to visit. Otherwise, your embassy or travel insurance hotline should be able to provide you with the name of a local doctor. Upmarket hotels can often recommend a doctor, and may even have a doctor attached to the staff.

Depending on where you are, medical services may be very different to what you are used to, and language difficulties can exacerbate problems. However, most doctors in touristed areas will be used to treating common travellers ailments, and doctors in tropical areas will have considerable experience diagnosing and treating tropical diseases. If you are uncertain of the treatment or diagnosis offered, don't be afraid to ask for a second opinion.

In general, public hospitals in Asia are underfunded and understaffed, and are probably best avoided unless they are affiliated to a university. Most large towns will have private clinics or hospitals providing adequate to good medical services, although they can be quite expensive. Mission hospitals often have extremely high standards, and may be the only option in more remote areas. Medical care in Japan, Singapore and Hong Kong is excellent but expensive. Check your guidebook for specifics about medical services in individual countries.

Be prepared to pay upfront; this may also be more expensive than you're used to. Make sure you have travel insurance (see the Tickets & Insurance chapter), and keep an emergency stash of money in case you have to pay on the spot and claim later.

WOMEN'S HEALTH

Period Problems

You may find that your periods stop altogether when you're away – a result of the physical and mental stresses of travelling (but have a pregnancy test done if you think you may be pregnant). You're just as likely to find, however, that travelling brings on the worst period of your life, at the most inconvenient time. If you suffer from PMT, be prepared for it to be worse while you are away and take plentiful supplies of any painkiller or other remedy you find helpful. If you think you may need contraception, you could consider starting the pill before you leave – it greatly reduces PMT and gives lighter and regular periods. Alternatively, you might want to consider stopping your periods altogether for a short time. It's best to discuss this with your doctor well in advance of travelling.

Vaginal Infections

Hot weather and limited washing facilities make thrush (yeast infection) more likely when you're travelling. If you know you are prone to thrush, it's worth taking a supply of medication with you. Unprotected sex with a new partner makes a sexually transmitted infection a possibility. Get any symptoms like an abnormal vaginal discharge or genital sores checked out as soon as possible. Some STIs don't cause any symptoms, even though they can cause long-term fertility and other problems, so if you have unprotected intercourse while you're away, be sure to have a check-up when you return home.

Oral Contraception

If you think you'll need this while you are away, see your doctor, family planning clinic or local women's health organisation before you leave. The Marie Stopes web site (www.mariestopes.org/uk) has useful information on your options.

The timing of pill-taking can be tricky if you're crossing time zones, and diarrhoea, vomiting and antibiotics used to treat common infections can all reduce its effectiveness. Take a plentiful supply of your medication with you, as it may be difficult to get your brand. In some countries, oral contraceptives may not be readily available. The International Planned Parenthood Federation (☎ 020-7487 7913; www.ippf.org) at Regent's College, Inner Circle, Regent's Park, London NW1 4NS can provide information on the availability of contraception and local attitudes towards birth control and termination of pregnancy in various countries in Asia.

MEDICAL PROBLEMS & TREATMENT

Altitude Sickness

The lack of oxygen at altitude (usually over 2500m) affects most people to varying degrees, especially if you fly straight there. If you're travelling to the Himalaya, the Karakoram range, Tibet or Mongolia, or in the higher-altitude areas of Borneo, Irian Jaya or Japan, you'll need to be able to recognise the symptoms of acute mountain sickness (AMS) and know what to do about them.

You can get advice on preventing AMS from a travel health clinic or expedition organiser, or read up about it in your guidebook or one of the travel health guides listed earlier. Two authoritative web sites with information

TRADITIONAL ASIAN MEDICINE

In most Asian countries, traditional healing systems that have evolved over hundreds or thousands of years are practised alongside western-style medicine, the relative newcomer. While in Asia, you should not find it difficult to set up an appointment with a traditional practitioner, though stick to those with recognised accreditation, or someone who has been recommended to you through word of mouth. Your travel guidebook should have more details.

Most traditional Asian medical systems consider your whole body and spirit, and use a combination of techniques including herbal remedies, dietary manipulation, massage, acupuncture and meditation. All systems are based on quite complex underlying philosophies that may be hard for westerners to fully understand.

For most types of Asian medicine, the first session is the longest, lasting about an hour, during which you'll be asked lots of questions (language difficulties may shorten this!) about your physical and mental health, your family's health, your lifestyle, your diet etc, before the practitioner examines you. Finally, a diagnosis is made and treatment is recommended.

Ayurveda

This is practised widely in India and Sri Lanka. It's thought to have originated in India in 5000 BC, making it one of the oldest of all medical systems. A state of health is achieved through a combination of meditation, massage (Ayurvedic massage or marma is a particular speciality of practitioners in Kerala), yoga, astrology, herbal medicine and diet; it's a preventive rather than curative philosophy. Underlying it is the belief that the body is governed by energies and that a balance of these energies is needed for good health. We are all made up of five basic elements, fire, water, earth, air and aether, which are converted into three humours: *vata* (wind), *pitta* (digestive juices) and *kapha* (phlegm). A person's character is determined by their dominant humour, and an imbalance of the humours results in ill health or disease.

Traditional Chinese Medicine

This ancient system comprises herbal medicine, diet, massage, acupuncture, acupressure, relaxation and exercises. The body is thought to have a network of invisible pathways called meridians, along which *qi*, the life energy, flows. Qi has two components, *yin* and *yang*, which are opposites: dark and light, female and male etc. Illness is a result of blocked qi or perhaps an imbalance in yin and yang, and balance is restored through herb treatments and acupuncture. In acupuncture, the meridians are unblocked by placing needles at points along them; in herbal medicine, herbs with particular attributes are used. Other techniques include a variant of acupressure in which bamboo suction cups are used, and moxibustion, where herbs are rolled up into a ball, held near the skin and ignited.

Thai Medicine

This system is closely related to both Ayurvedic and Chinese medicine, and aims to restore the balance of four body elements — earth, water, fire and air. Treatments are herbal, spiritual (meditation) and, perhaps best known, massage. Thai massage consists of a variety of techniques and combines elements of massage, chiropractic and acupressure.

Tibetan Medicine

This is an interesting combination of Ayurvedic, Chinese and perhaps ancient Greek influences. As with most Asian systems, it is based on maintaining a balance of humours in the body. Pulse and urine analysis are the cornerstones of diagnosis in Tibetan medicine. Therapy is through a combination of herbal remedies, moxibustion and a type of acupuncture.

about AMS and other altitude-related problems are www.princeton.edu/~oa/altitude.html and www.gorgr.net/hamg/AMS.html.

Before you leave, it's a good idea to check that your insurance covers altitude sickness. If you have any ongoing illnesses like asthma or diabetes, or you're taking the oral contraceptive pill, discuss with your doctor the possible effects altitude may have.

Symptoms of mild altitude sickness are common when you first arrive at altitude and include headache, nausea and loss of appetite, difficulty sleeping and lack of energy. They usually respond to rest and simple painkillers. More serious forms of altitude sickness occur less commonly but can be fatal. Each year, a few travellers to Nepal die from the effects of altitude.

The best way to prevent AMS is to ascend slowly. Try to sleep at a lower altitude than the greatest height you reached during the day, and make sure you allow extra time in your schedule for rest days. Drugs such as acetazolamide (trade name Diamox) are sometimes used to prevent AMS, although this is controversial. The most important point to remember is that taking drugs is no substitute for proper acclimatisation.

The best treatment for AMS is descent, and the golden rule is never to continue to ascend if you have any symptoms of AMS. If mild symptoms persist or get worse, you must descend.

Cholera

This serious diarrhoeal illness receives much publicity but, as a rule, is unlikely to affect travellers. Cholera is caused by poor sanitation, spread through contaminated food and water, and usually affects the poorest of the poor in developing countries. The best prevention is to take care with food and water. Dehydration is the main risk, and the mainstay of treatment is fluid replacement.

Diarrhoea

This is a great conversation-starter in travellers circles – and sometimes a stopper too. Although the risks vary with your destination, the fact is that diarrhoea affects between 20% and 50% of all travellers. Even if it's relatively mild, you're probably going to feel a tad sorry for yourself for a day or so as it passes through your system, so it's worth building a few rest days into your travel schedule to allow for this.

Taking basic precautions with food and drink and paying attention to your personal hygiene are the most important preventive strategies. There are a couple of drug possibilities, but neither are viable options for most travellers. Bismuth (Pepto-Bismol), which is not an antibiotic, can be helpful, but at the quantities required should not be taken for more than three weeks and has potential side effects. Certain antibiotics can be used to prevent travellers diarrhoea, but this is a controversial issue and they are generally not recommended.

Diarrhoea tends to strike about the third day after you arrive and lasts about three to five days. It can be caused by a whole heap of factors, including jet lag, new food, a new lifestyle and new bugs. It sometimes returns in the second week, although you may develop immunity to some of the causes (but not the serious types). Symptoms are usually diarrhoea without blood, mild fever, some nausea and stomach cramps.

The most important aspect of treatment is to prevent dehydration by replacing lost fluid – and to rest. You can drink most liquids, except alcohol, very sugary drinks or dairy products. Oral rehydration sachets can be useful but aren't essential if you're young and otherwise healthy. Starchy foods like potatoes, plain rice or bread are good, and you'll need to stick to a bland diet until things are back to normal.

Antidiarrhoea tablets are of limited use as they prevent your system from clearing out the toxin and can make certain types of diarrhoea worse, though they can be useful as a temporary stopping measure, for example if you have to go on a long bus journey. They should be avoided in children. Antibiotic treatment for simple travellers diarrhoea may shorten the illness but side effects are possible, so you might want to discuss this with your doctor before you leave.

Sometimes diarrhoea can be more serious, with blood, a high fever and cramps (bacterial dysentery), or it can be persistent and bloody (amoebic dysentery) or persistent, explosive and gassy (Giardia). These types need treatment with specific antibiotics.

If you're going to a remote area far from medical help, you may want to consider taking antibiotics with you for self-treating diarrhoea. However, it's generally better to seek medical advice to diagnose which type of diarrhoea you have and decide which antibiotics you should be taking. .

Heat Exhaustion & Heat Stroke

Heat can cause a range of conditions from heat cramps and fainting to heat exhaustion and potentially fatal heat stroke. Even if you don't feel too bad, heat and dehydration can affect your physical performance and mental judgement. In a hot climate you can lose an astonishing 2L of sweat in an hour, more if you're doing strenuous physical activity. Sweat contains water and salts, which you need to replace, so drink a lot more than you would in a cool climate, even when you have acclimatised. An adult needs to drink about 3L of fluid a day in a hot climate, or 5L or more if doing a strenuous physical activity such as trekking or cycling. Take a water bottle with you wherever you go, and remember to drink frequently from it.

Both heat stroke and heat exhaustion are caused by prolonged exposure to high temperatures and inadequate fluid intake. With heat stroke, sweating stops and the body temperature rises dangerously, which can be fatal. Severe, throbbing headaches and lack of coordination occur, and the sufferer may be confused or aggressive. Eventually the sufferer becomes delirious or convulses. You must seek medical care urgently in this situation, but in the meantime get the sufferer out of the sun, remove their clothing, cover them with a wet sheet or towel and fan them continually. Give them fluids to drink if they are conscious.

Symptoms of heat exhaustion are headache, dizziness, nausea and feeling weak and exhausted. You may get muscle aches or cramps. If you notice these symptoms in yourself or your travel companions, rest in a cool environment and drink lots of cool fluids.

Hepatitis A

This common, vaccine-preventable viral infection of the liver is spread through contaminated food and water – make sure you're immunised against it and take care with food, especially shellfish, and water. Symptoms are fever, jaundice and diarrhoea (sometimes). It can leave you feeling weak for some time after, but has no other long-term effects.

Hepatitis B

This viral infection of the liver is transmitted via blood (transfusions, injections etc) and body fluids (for example, by sexual intercourse). The number of carriers of hepatitis B is generally high in most Asian countries. The best prevention is to avoid risk situations eg unprotected sexual contact, razor blades, tattooing or body piercing. Symptoms are similar to hepatitis A but are often more severe and, unlike hepatitis A, the disease can lead to chronic liver damage, liver cancer or a long-term carrier state.

HIV/AIDS

There's no vaccine currently available against this life-threatening disease caused by the human immunodeficiency virus. In Asia, HIV is mainly spread by hetero-sexual sex, and preventive measures include avoiding casual sex or practising safer sex by using latex condoms. It can also be transmitted through exposure to contaminated blood, blood products or body fluids. It is not spread by mosquitoes, swimming pools, by sharing cups or by toilet seats.

Hypothermia

Too much cold can be just as dangerous as too much heat, so be prepared if you are trekking at high altitudes or simply taking a long bus trip over moun-tains, particularly at night. Hypothermia occurs when the body loses heat faster than it can produce it, causing your core body temperature to drop. You can easily go from being very cold to dangerously cold with a combination of wind, wet clothing, fatigue and hunger, even if the air temperature is above freezing.

It's a good idea to dress in layers – silk, wool and fleeces are all good insulating materials. A hat is important, and a strong, wind and waterproof outer layer (and perhaps a space blanket for emergencies) is essential. You should always carry some basic supplies with you, including sugary foods and fluid to drink. Make sure you have a sleeping bag appropriate for the conditions.

The symptoms of mild hypothermia are exhaustion, numb skin (particularly toes and fingers), shivering, slurred speech and stumbling. If you notice any of these signs in yourself or your travelling companions, get the person out of the wind and/or rain, and replace any wet clothing with dry, warm clothing. Give them hot liquids – not alcohol – and some high-kilojoule, easily digestible food. Severe hypothermia is a potentially fatal condition.

Japanese B Encephalitis

This mosquito-transmitted viral infection of the brain is a risk only in rural, rice-growing areas, and is thought to be a very low risk for travellers. It can be fatal, and may cause permanent brain damage in those who recover. There is an effective vaccine, and you should take measures to avoid mosquito bites.

Malaria

The malaria map earlier in this chapter shows the areas where this serious, mosquito-transmitted disease is a risk. Prevention is important, and consists of avoiding mosquito bites and taking antimalarial tablets. Symptoms can be non-specific and include fever, chills and sweating, headache, diarrhoea and abdominal pains – or just a vague feeling of ill-health. Without treatment it can rapidly become more serious and can be fatal, but if treatment is started promptly, most people recover.

Meningococcal Meningitis

This vaccine-preventable infection attacks the lining of the brain, and can be fatal if not treated rapidly. There are recurring epidemics in parts of Asia, notably Nepal, Mongolia and northern India. Symptoms include fever, headache, neck stiffness and sensitivity to light; a skin rash may appear later. Meningococcal meningitis is spread by close contact with healthy carriers.

Rabies

This is a fatal viral infection that causes horrific symptoms, including hydrophobia (fear of water). It's found in virtually every part of Asia, with Japan and Taiwan the only exceptions. Many animals can be infected, including dogs, cats, bats and monkeys and it is their saliva which is infectious. Once symptoms have appeared, death is inevitable, but the onset of symptoms can be prevented by a course of injections, which you need whether or not you have been immunised previously.

Schistosomiasis (Bilharzia)

The parasite that causes this disease multiplies in freshwater snails, and occurs in limited pockets of Asia, notably the Yangzi River basin in China, the Mekong Delta in Vietnam, the southern Philippines and central Sulawesi. It may cause few symptoms at first, but can lead to long-term damage of internal organs. Avoid swimming, bathing or even paddling in fresh water in risk areas.

Tetanus

This vaccine-preventable disease occurs worldwide and is caused by a germ that lives in soil and in the faeces of horses and other animals. It enters the body via breaks in the skin. Its common name is lockjaw because it causes stiffening of the jaw and neck followed by painful convulsions.

Tuberculosis

Although there is currently a worldwide resurgence of this bacterial infection, mainly due to drug resistance, travellers are not thought to be at a high risk. It's usually transmitted from person to person by coughing but also through unpasteurised milk. The lungs are the primary site of infection but any organ in the body can be affected, including bones and the brain. The best prevention is the vaccine; also avoid unpasteurised milk.

Typhoid

This vaccine-preventable disease is transmitted through contaminated food and water, and is a risk worldwide where hygiene standards are low. Symptoms are initially similar to flu, with headache, aches and pains and a fever. Abdominal pain, vomiting and either diarrhoea or constipation can occur. Serious complications such as pneumonia, perforated bowel or meningitis may develop. It can be effectively treated but medical help must be sought.

Typhus

This disease is spread by ticks, mites and lice, and may be a risk for trekkers in tick-infested areas, usually dense tropical forests. It causes fever, headache and muscle pains, and often a rash. It can be treated effectively. The best prevention is to avoid tick bites.

WHEN YOU RETURN

If you were away for a short time only and had no serious health problems, there's probably no need to get a medical check-up when you return, unless you develop symptoms. If you become sick in the weeks following your trip, be sure to tell your doctor that you have been away, which countries you have visited and any antimalarials you may have been taking. Remember that you need to keep taking antimalarials for four weeks after you leave a malarial area.

If you've been on a long trip or are concerned that you may have been exposed to a disease such as bilharzia or an STI that may not show up straightaway, a medical check-up is advisable.

WHAT TO BRING

Getting your gear together can be an expensive element of your preparations, but bite the bullet and spend up if you can – you won't regret having good-quality equipment once you're on the road. There are some ways to reduce your expenses, though. Common items such as clothing and toiletries can be bought cheaply in Asia, although big-ticket items such as cameras, personal stereos, binoculars and specialised camping equipment may not be any cheaper. Purchasing these hi-tech items duty-free might be a better option, depending on the country you fly out of (see Duty-Free Allowances in the Take-Off chapter for details).

This chapter contains suggestions for equipment and clothing to consider taking, plus some tips on packing and recording your trip.

EQUIPMENT

Backpacks

Your backpack will be your constant companion on the road and central to your comfort and convenience, so it's worth putting some time and effort into selecting an appropriate design. This is one item you should be prepared to spend some decent money on – after a few weeks hauling it around on your back, lifting it on and off buses and daily unpacking and repacking it, you won't regret the extra expense. A good-quality backpack will last you many years.

Thankfully, the days of external-framed, canvas rucksacks – desperately uncomfortable, heavy and cumbersome – are long gone. Modern backpacks are miracles of design; they can be customised to your back length and are constructed from highly durable fabrics. There are two principal designs: toploaders and travel packs.

Toploaders

Toploaders are essentially a fabric tube. They are generally more comfortable, hardwearing and watertight than travel packs (they have fewer seams), but are far less convenient because you have to haul everything out to reach the stuff at the bottom. If you plan to do a lot of mountain climbing or rafting, the comfort and waterproofing qualities will come to the fore. If, however, you're going to stay mostly in hostels or homestays, then you can't go past the travel pack.

Travel Packs

The chief advantage of the travel pack is the zip that runs all the way around the edge and top, allowing you to completely open up the main compartment. This means dead simple packing and access to your stuff (see the Packing section later in this chapter for some tips). Apart from the time and frustration it will save you, it has other advantages too. A zippered flap (which is stowed at the base of the back) can be used to hide and protect the harness when you put your pack on planes, buses, trains or taxis. A travel pack also has side handles and a detachable shoulder strap, making it easy to carry in crowds or other cramped spaces. It also looks more respectable if you have to deal with customs agents, police or other officialdom, and is easier to lock up.

Buying a Pack

It's sensible to go for a recognised brand; Macpac (www.macpac.co.nz), Karrimor (www.karrimor.co.uk) or REI (www.REI.com) are among a number of companies that offer ergonomic designs and use the latest synthetic blend fabrics. These will protect your stuff from showers (if not a downpour) and allow your skin to breathe during long-distance walks. Prices start at around US$150 and disappear into the stratosphere, but consider the following points as you check out the options:

- **Capacity** – Resist the temptation to buy the biggest pack in the shop. Apart from being cumbersome, you may not ever use all that space. Have a good idea of what you plan to take with you before you buy your pack, and then purchase the smallest pack for the job; you can always post things home and a smaller pack will compel you to travel light. We've found that a 60L pack generally allows enough space for equipment, clothes and purchases over a three month trip; if you're carrying a tent you might want to go for a slightly larger one.

- **Fabric and stitching** – Look for durable material and double stitching at weight-bearing places. Also ensure the zippers are strong. If the pack looks a little lightweight or flimsy, try for the more expensive model.

- **Straps and padding** – Good packs will be amply padded at the shoulders and hips, as well as lightly padded down the back. The hip pads are the most important as the bulk of the weight is carried there, not on the shoulders.

- **Fitting** – Always try on your pack before you purchase it. Most decent packs have an adjustable internal frame that you can fit to the length of your back. Also keep an eye on the shape of the pack. If it's too tall, your centre of gravity will be too high for stability; too wide and it will be extremely irritating to manoeuvre in tight spaces. Most companies now have gender-specific models which are designed to accommodate the different hip and spine shapes of women and men. These can add another dimension to your comfort level.

- **Versatility** – Look for packs with multiple compartments. A bottom section is ideal for your sleeping bag or dirty laundry and will also protect more fragile items in the main compartment, while front and side pockets are good for regularly needed items such as toiletries, waterproof gear, torch (flashlight), journal, novel, guidebook or map. Many packs include a zip-off daypack (see Daypacks later on). Loops are useful as tie-down straps for carrying a sleeping bag, sweater or tent outside your pack.

Securing Your Pack

Theft is a real risk in Asia, so make sure you can secure your pack effectively. Most packs have double zippers on the front and side sections that can be padlocked together. If not, find a strong place in the fabric above the zip where you can make a couple of holes; thread a small padlock through the holes and attach the zip fastener. If you're travelling long distances on trains, you might want to bring a light chain to attach your pack to the luggage rack so you can sleep with an easy mind. See Hazards & Safeguards in the Issues & Attitudes chapter for more on protecting your belongings from theft.

Daypacks

Your daypack will rarely leave your side, whether you're on a train, eating in a restaurant or seeing the sights. Most of your everyday items will be carried in it – camera, guidebook, map, water bottle, sunscreen etc – so comfort and quality are again the keys. Make sure the shoulder straps and back section are padded and that the fabric is strong and durable. External and internal pockets make smaller items easier to store and find; a side pocket for your water bottle is particularly useful.

Some backpacks have detachable daypacks, thus saving you the expense of buying a separate unit. However, these are often too small, so make sure it will be big enough to take all your bits and pieces. An overstuffed daypack is a pain to carry, as it lacks a solid frame and will end up digging into you and tiring your shoulders and back. One more thing: if you plan to reconnect your daypack to your main pack when travelling long distances, use padlocks and remember to remove fragile or valuable items.

THE TROJAN ALTERNATIVE

On my first solo trip to the UK and Europe, I disembarked at Gatwick airport proudly bearing the latest in boy scout-issue backpacks. However, it soon dawned on me that this was not going to be a happy relationship: the external frame rubbed cruelly against my back, the aluminium plumbing gouged into my shoulder blades, and carrying the whole cumbersome edifice engendered excruciating pain – and I'd only got as far as Victoria station. But there, in a small luggage accessory kiosk, I spied my salvation – a set of luggage wheels. To these, after handing over the requisite pounds, I lashed my pack.

There is hardly a moor in that green and fair land that myself and my trusty wheel-borne backpack didn't trundle over, nary a youth hostel up whose stairs we didn't rumble. Admittedly, I received some odd looks (ranging from astonishment to abject scorn) from some members of the backpacking community. A backpack on wheels is, I suppose, a contradiction in terms. Nevertheless, faced with a choice between multiple sessions of physiotherapy and the derision of my fellows (bowed under the weight of their well thumbed Penguin Classic editions of Camus and Nietzsche), I'd make the same choice again.

Years later, while working with the Tibetan community in northern India, I noted with interest a couple who disembarked from a dilapidated bus. This tall, sun-burnished, lean-limbed pair had definite traveller cred: long dreds, stylish grunge gear and a 'don't mess with us: we've crossed the Khyber Pass' attitude. I watched as they strode off up the road towards the Hotel Tibet, heads held high, eyes focused on the mountains, as with studied ease they pulled behind them their matching silver Samsonite suitcases on wheels – and I felt vindicated.

MICHELLE COXALL
LP AUTHOR, AUSTRALIA

Money Belt

Your money belt is a vital piece of equipment, as it's the safest way of carrying your cash, travellers cheques, credit/debit cards, passport, ticket and other important items. It is crucial to select a money belt that can be worn unobtrusively under beneath your clothing – keeping your valuables in a bumbag or otherwise exposed over your clothing is simply asking for trouble.

The most common types of money belts are worn either around the waist or the neck. Neither design is particularly easy to access, so don't keep your ready cash in it or you'll be fishing in it every five minutes and attracting attention. Think about the fabric too. Plastic sweats horribly and leather is heavy and retains perspiration. Cotton is probably the best bet as it's the most comfortable and can be washed, though it's less durable. If you use a cotton money belt, put your ticket, passport and other documents in a plastic bag so they don't deteriorate from your sweat.

Check out the belt's clasp or attachment. Your money belt is one item that you want to be secure at all times. Finally, consider taking a waterproof container for your documents and money which you can wear when swimming, diving or snorkelling.

Medical Kit

You can buy prepared kits (conventional, as well as homoeopathic) from many travel health clinics, mail order companies and homoeopathic practitioners, or you can make one up yourself. Use a container that's waterproof, rattle-proof and squash-proof; see-through plastic boxes or zip-up, pocketed plastic cases are good.

The following is a list of items you should consider including in your medical kit – consult your pharmacist for brands available in your country.

- **Antibiotics or any other regular medication** – Antibiotics are useful if you're travelling well off the beaten track, but they must be prescribed and you should carry the prescription of these (and any other regular medication you use) with you. If you are allergic to commonly prescribed antibiotics such as penicillin or sulfa drugs, carry this information with you when travelling.

- **Antifungal cream or powder** – For fungal skin infections and thrush.

- **Antihistamine** – Useful as a decongestant for colds; for allergies, such as hay fever; to ease the itch from insect bites or stings; and to prevent motion sickness. Antihistamines may cause sedation and interact with alcohol so take care when using them.

- **Antiseptic** – For cuts and grazes.

- **Aspirin or paracetamol** – For pain or fever (paracetamol is called acetaminophen in the US).

- **Bandages, Band-Aids (plasters) and other wound dressings** – For minor injuries.

- **Calamine lotion, sting relief spray or aloe vera** – To ease irritation from sunburn and insect bites or stings.

- **Insect repellent, sunscreen, lip balm and eye drops.**

- Cold and flu tablets, throat lozenges and nasal decongestant.

- **Loperamide or diphenoxylate** – These are 'blockers' for diarrhoea.

- **Prochlorperazine or metaclopramide** – For nausea and vomiting.

- **Multivitamins** – For long trips, when dietary vitamin intake may be inadequate.

- **Rehydration mixture** – To prevent dehydration, eg due to severe diarrhoea; particularly important when travelling with children, but is recommended for everyone.

- **Scissors, tweezers and a thermometer** – Note that mercury thermometers are prohibited by airlines.

- **Syringes and needles** – In case you need injections in remote parts of Asia, which may have medical hygiene problems. Ask your doctor for a note explaining why you have them.

- **Water purification tablets or iodine.**

Other Useful Equipment

The following items are pretty well essential:

- **Address book** – To keep in touch with friends and family, plus those you meet on the road.

- **Alarm clock** – You don't want to miss your flight/bus/train/other appointment. Travel alarm clocks are tough, light and cheap.

- **Batteries** – Bring spares for all your equipment (camera, personal stereo, alarm clock, torch etc) and put new batteries in each before you depart.

- **Contraception** – Condoms can be found in most Asian countries, but the quality is variable (always check the use-by date). It's easier to bring a supply with you. If you use the pill, then bring enough to cover your whole trip as it is difficult to obtain in many Asian countries.

- **Eye wear** – Sunglasses are indispensable for both comfort and protection of your eyes. If you wear prescription glasses or contact lenses, take the prescription with you, along with extras such as a case and contact lens solution.

- **Padlocks and a chain** – Apart from securing your backpack, you can use a padlock to fasten the door of your hotel room and give your belongings extra security. Chains are useful for attaching your backpack to the roof rack of a bus or the luggage rack on trains.

- **Pocketknife** – A Swiss army knife (or good-quality equivalent) has loads of useful tools, particularly scissors, bottle opener, can opener and straight blade.

- **Sunscreen** – You're likely to spend long hours in the sun and, apart from the long-term risk of melanoma, sunburn is painful. A moisturiser with sunscreen included will save some doubling up.

- **Tampons or pads** – These are available in most Asian cities, but keep a supply for when you're off the beaten track.

- **Toilet paper** – Never leave home without some! It won't be supplied in some public (and private) toilets in many Asian countries. Always keep a stash in your daypack.

- **Torch (flashlight)** – Most helpful to find stuff late at night in a dorm or in your hotel room, to avoid mishaps in outside toilets in the middle of the night, or if the electricity packs it in. It's handy, too, for exploring caves and ruins. The Penlite range is almost indestructible, but also consider a miner-style lamp which straps to your forehead and frees up both your hands.

- **Toiletries** – Most items are widely available across Asia, but take any specialty products with you.

- **Towel** – For swimming, as well as for showers in budget places (not all will supply one, or at least one you'd want to use). Don't take a beach towel as it'll take ages to dry, weigh a tonne and get very whiffy. A quick-drying travel towel (made from a chamois-like material or one of the new microfibres) is OK, as is the all-purpose sarong.

- **Travel guides, maps and phrasebooks** – For details, see those sections in the Planning chapter.

Nonessential Equipment

None of the gear listed here is really essential to your travels, but a selection will make life much more pleasant.

- **Binoculars** – Quite the luxury item really, but if you take a small light pair, you'll find them infinitely useful.

- **Books** – Take a couple of decent-sized books. You can swap them with other travellers or at bookshops, and they'll help while away idle hours when waiting for trains or planes, or late at night in your room.

- **Camping gear** – Only lug this around if you plan to do a lot of camping. Tents, stoves, sleeping mats and cooking gear are bulky and heavy. Remember that in some Asian countries (particularly China) it's almost impossible to camp anywhere, and in most others (Japan and Hong Kong excepted) accommodation is cheap and plentiful.

- **Candles** – Can lend a nice atmosphere to an otherwise dull room, and are also useful in a long-term blackout.

- **Earplugs** – You'll never regret these if you spend a lot of time in cities, are staying near a mosque or take a 10 hour ride in a bus with a blaring stereo.

- **Food** – It's nice to have a small stash of your favourite food from home, as long as it's a long-lasting product and properly contained.

- **Games** – Chess, backgammon, Scrabble, dominoes, Chinese chequers, snakes and ladders … whatever your favourite, it's likely there's a travel edition out there somewhere. Often magnetic and always small and light, these are excellent for alleviating boredom and a good way to meet fellow travellers. Also consider dice, playing cards and hand-held computer games.

- **Gifts** – For details on appropriate gifts for new friends and homestay families, see the boxed text 'It's Better To Give …' in the Accommodation section of the While You're There chapter.

- **Glue stick** – The glue on stamps and envelopes can be very dodgy. It's also useful to affix tickets and mementos in your journal.

- **Inflatable pillow** – This will allow you to sleep more comfortably on long trips.

- **Lighter/matches** – For campfires, mosquito coils, candles and cigarettes.

- **Mosquito net** – Malaria is no joke. Most hotels provide mosquito nets, but if you plan to sleep under the stars it's essential to have your own (also see Insect Bites in the Health chapter).

- **Personal stereo/radio** – Good for whiling away idle hours and, if you have a record function, you can send audio cassettes home. Short-wave radios can keep you in touch with news from home.

- **Plug** – These are rarely supplied in cheaper accommodation. Double-sided rubber or plastic plugs will fit most bath and basin plug holes.

- **Sewing kit** – Needle, thread, a few buttons and safety pins to mend clothing, mosquito net, tent or sunglasses.

- **Sleeping bag/sleeping sheet** – Only take a sleeping bag if you plan to camp a lot, as this is a bulky item. If you're going to need a bag in only one of the countries on your itinerary, then think about hiring one there. A sleeping sheet is a much better bet. Basically two sheets sewn together, it will give you some protection from insects and dodgy beds, and it's light and easily cleaned. Stick to natural fibres (cotton or silk).

- **Travel journal and pens** – See Recording Your Trip later in this chapter.

- **Washing line** – A piece of string will do the job, but there are relatively cheap lines on the market with suckers, hooks or both on each end, which make them much more versatile.

- **Washing detergent** – For cleaning your clothes in your room. In most Asian countries laundry services are very cheap, but the techniques can be pretty hard on your clothes.

- **Water bottle** – You can just refill a standard plastic bottle, but a more sturdy model will last a lot longer and be more suitable for purifying water on a regular basis.

Specialised Equipment

Diving, snorkelling, surfing, windsurfing, rafting or cycling equipment can be hired at recognised sites such as those in Bali and Lombok, at Puerto Galera in the Philippines and at Thailand's island resorts. If you prefer your own equipment, or will be heading off the beaten track, then bring everything with you (see the Air section in the Tickets & Insurance chapter for details on packing and taking your own equipment).

If you are a serious climber on a Himalayan adventure, you can get outfitted in Kathmandu. If you're into more esoteric activities such as caving, you'll have to bring everything with you. See also Thematic Trips in the Planning chapter for more on hiring equipment.

LESSONS FROM MARY POPPINS

On a sunny day in London or New York, it's rare to see anyone walking around with an open umbrella but up until the 1920s the parasol was a popular accessory. In fact, next to the spacesuit, the umbrella may be one of the greatest tools ever designed to protect the body from the elements, especially the rays of the sun. In many parts of Asia, women and (wise) elderly men have not yet abandoned the umbrella to the whims of progress. The informed traveller in these parts will find it indispensable while walking, waiting by the road side, riding in boats and even, for the acrobatically inclined, on bicycles. An umbrella is cooler than a hat and infinitely more elegant. Besides the obvious benefits of keeping out the heat and ultraviolet rays, walking in the sunshine with this ingenious device gives the bearer a semblance of dignity and poise (one of the umbrella's original functions, after all, was to designate rank for royalty), qualities that may otherwise be lacking in one's life on the road.

MARIE CAMBON
LP AUTHOR, CANADA

CLOTHING

Selecting your clothing is something of a balancing act. You want to bring a versatile range, particularly if you're travelling widely through Asia (ie from the chill of mountainous Nepal to the sunny beaches of Indonesia or Thailand), but too many items will simply weigh you down. Don't bring precious pieces of clothing as humid climates, rigorous hand-washing and the filth of the road will wear your clothes out. It's best to view most of your clothing as expendable. Remember that clothing is widely available and very cheap across Asia, so you can purchase items suitable to the climate of a particular country once you arrive. Even if you have a large build, tailors are easily found and their services generally affordable.

Day to Day

For regular pieces of clothing like trousers, skirts, shorts, shirts and underwear, natural fibres are definitely the go. While synthetics will dry faster and wrinkle less, they don't breathe very well, will stick to your skin and make you sweat horribly. The chances of contracting a fungal disease or yeast infection are also much higher with synthetic clothes. So look for cotton, silk and linen articles – either pure or blends – and steer clear of nylon, rayon and lycra.

Below are some suggestions for both warm and cool climates. No matter where you're headed, it's a good idea to have something presentable to wear at special occasions or when dealing with police, clearing customs or other officials. For some advice on culturally suitable clothing, see the boxed text 'Dressing Appropriately' in this chapter.

Keeping Cool

If you're travelling in predominantly hot climates then look for lightweight, loose-fitting clothes. Light colours will keep you cooler than dark ones, but are harder to keep clean. A sarong is a brilliantly versatile item as it can function as a full-length dress, skirt, sleeping sheet, beach towel, shade cloth or rope. Jeans, by contrast, are heavy, take up a lot of room and take ages to dry; drawstring or elastic-cotton trousers or long skirts are much lighter and will keep you cooler. Take a couple of short-sleeved shirts if you want, but long-sleeved shirts are more useful, as they will keep the sun off you, allow you easier access to religious sites and lessen your chances of offending local people. The same applies to shorts (see the boxed text 'Dressing Appropriately').

Another strong argument in favour of long clothing is that it lessens the risks of contracting malaria or dengue fever in south and South-East Asia. Malarial mosquitoes bite at night, and dengue carriers bite during the day, so there's really no safe time to wear shorts and a T-shirt in malarial zones.

Don't forget a wide-brimmed hat either – a cap is not adequate to protect your neck and ears.

Keeping Warm

If you're going to hit the heights, or spend any length of time in China, Japan, Korea or Mongolia, then you'll need to bring warmer clothes. Layers are the key here. Even in the heart of the Himalaya you'll experience sunny days, but the weather can quickly turn foul, so you need to be able to dress up or down quickly. Several layers of natural fibres, topped by a good-quality jacket, will give you the versatility you need. A good combination starts with thermal underwear (or a lightweight, cycling-style, thin silk T-shirt); then add a cotton T-shirt, long-sleeved cotton shirt, sweater and jacket. Also consider two pairs of socks – cotton under wool. If you get too hot you can ditch the woollies, while the cotton will absorb your sweat and prevent the irritation caused by damp wool on bare skin. Also bring waterproofs (a good-quality jacket might be adequate), gloves and a woolly hat. Don't forget your brimmed hat and sunscreen, as you can burn quickly in the thin air at high altitudes.

Specialised Clothing

If you're engaging in specialist activities such as trekking or cycling, this is where synthetics come into their own. Hi-tech fabrics such as Gore-Tex are light, pretty well waterproof and have a one-way design to their knit so your sweat

DRESSING APPROPRIATELY

In predominantly Muslim countries such as Indonesia, Malaysia, Brunei and Pakistan, immodesty in dress, particularly by women, is deeply frowned upon. In general terms, the further you get from the cities, the more conservative the dress codes are. In some parts of these countries, locals may take matters into their own hands if they feel sufficiently scandalised, by either making overt sexual advances or even becoming violent.

These attitudes are not just characteristic of Muslim countries. Across Asia, inappropriately clad men and women will be flouting local dress codes and may be perceived as demonstrating insufficient respect for prevailing religious and social codes. Women revealing too much leg, stomach or cleavage will be seen as promiscuous and fair game for any red-blooded man. As well as placing themselves in a potentially dangerous situation, they'll be doing future female travellers no favours by cementing the widely held opinion that all western women are 'easy'. Men who wear shorts in public simply won't be taken seriously, as shorts are the sole preserve of young boys in many countries. This is particularly the case when dealing with officialdom. In addition, men and women alike will be refused entry to many religious sites if sporting bare arms, legs or heads.

In short, it's easy to save yourself hassle, ignominy and possible hazard simply by dressing appropriately. Don't wear figure-hugging clothes, always cover your arms and legs, and keep the plunging necklines, bikinis and bare chests for westerner-friendly tourist towns and beaches. Apart from making good practical sense, you'll be showing a level of respect for local cultures that will make your trip more fulfilling and will go some way to lessening resentment against travellers as a whole. Never forget that you're a visitor in someone else's country.

can escape, while keeping you protected from external water. This makes them ideal cold-weather gear. Trousers of the same fabric will be useful if the weather turns really nasty, but mostly you can do without them.

Fleecy jackets don't have the waterproofing abilities of Gore-Tex, but are lighter and smaller to pack and are more suitable for use in lower altitudes.

Footwear

Rubber-soled sandals are the standard issue for most travellers in Asia. A good-quality pair will be comfortable, airy and hard-wearing, as useful when relaxing on the beach as on a long day hitting the pavement sightseeing in the city.

WHY BACKPACKERS WEAR HIKING BOOTS IN BARS?

I liked wearing boots. I thought they were cool, they made me look taller, and I could wear odd socks without anyone noticing. So naturally I took my boots with me – the brown ones for around town, the black ones for going out at night, and an expensive pair of lightweight brand-name hiking boots for serious walking. Then I added a few changes of jeans, some shirts, a thin sweater, two thick sweaters, a warm jacket, a waterproof jacket, a sleeping bag, camera, books and so on. I could barely walk with all this stuff in my backpack, but I knew that everything I had was essential.

In less than two weeks I was near crippled from walking the streets in leather-soled boots, and my pack was no lighter – in fact it was getting heavier. It was time to redefine my idea of 'essential'. By that stage my bag was filled mostly with unwashed clothing, and I realised I was travelling the world with 15kg of dirty laundry. Worse still, it was obvious that the few remaining clean garments were completely useless. Facing the fact that I was in little danger of eating in a fancy restaurant, I sent my good shirts home by surface mail.

A sweater has been defined as a garment a child wears when its mother feels chilly, and by extension it's something a traveller packs when they're going somewhere cold. But a thick sweater is not a great travel accessory – it's bulky, hard to wash, and just not versatile enough. If the weather is really cold, you should be wearing every garment you have, and your bag will be almost empty. But you can't wear two thick sweaters at once, or even a thick one and a thin one. Don't tell your mother, but one thin sweater is enough.

There's an important packing principle here – everything you carry should be mutually compatible. If you can't wear shirt A with jacket B, leave one of them at home. That's why the footwear is so problematic – you can only wear one pair at a time. But shoes and boots are bulky in your bag, and expensive to pack and post home, which is why my calf-length brown boots were ultimately abandoned on a lonely train station, standing straight but empty, as I walked away in my black boots, now too scuffed to wear in the classy nightspots I wasn't going to anyway. And what about the brand-name hiking boots? I'd bought them in Australia, but they were made in Taiwan for an American company. They didn't last a week.

So if you're planning a trip which includes trekking as well as some nightlife, or if you'll be walking city streets as well as strolling on beaches, you'll need something versatile from the ankles down. You'll have to decide which is more difficult – dancing in hiking boots or climbing a volcano in high heels.

JAMES LYON
LP AUTHOR, AUSTRALIA

However, they do not have either the strength or support required for long-distance trekking, and let in too much mud, twigs and water during forest or jungle treks. Sandals also leave you open to mosquito bites during the day, so if you're going to Malaysia or Indonesia (which have the highest risks of dengue fever) take shoes that will completely cover your feet. If you plan to do any trekking, get a decent pair of leather hiking boots and wear them in properly before you start any serious walking.

A compromise option is a pair of lightweight boots made from a synthetic material. These won't be as waterproof or hard-wearing as leather, but they'll be much more comfortable.

Shoes are quite heavy, so try to limit yourself to two pairs – preferably something sturdy enough for day-to-day use, plus a pair of thongs (flip flops) for relaxing, showering or hanging out on the beach.

PACKING

Backpack

When packing, it's important to realise that weight is just as important as bulk. Even if your pack is only half full, if you have many heavy items it will be just as uncomfortable to carry as one that's bursting at the seams. Also try to have plenty of spare room in your pack when you depart – you'll certainly pick up extra clothes, souvenirs and other material on the road. Here are a few tips for packing your backpack:

- Try not to leave your packing until the night before you depart. Have a trial run, and spend a couple of hours toting your backpack around your local area. If you can't maintain the load for any length of time, then rethink your selections.

- Pack your heaviest items as close to your spine as possible, preferably in the centre and top parts of the pack. This will prevent the pack pulling at your shoulders, maximise the strengths of the design and provide the most comfortable position for walking.

- Remember that your pack is unlikely to be treated with kid gloves by others, particularly when you're travelling by aircraft. Pack to protect your belongings.

CLOTHING CHECKLIST

- ❑ Light jacket
- ❑ Long pants/skirts/dress
- ❑ Long-sleeved shirts
- ❑ Sarong
- ❑ Shoes/boots/sandals/thongs (flip flops)
- ❑ Shorts (can double as swimwear)
- ❑ Short-sleeved shirt
- ❑ Socks/underpants/bras
- ❑ Something presentable
- ❑ Specialist clothing, such as hat, gloves, thermals, woollen socks
- ❑ Sweater
- ❑ Swim wear
- ❑ Waterproof jacket
- ❑ Wide-brimmed hat

- Make the most of any compartments. Putting your sleeping bag, dirty clothes or other soft items in the bottom compartment will provide a soft, protective layer for other more fragile items. These items are also relatively light, allowing you to store heavier items higher in the pack.

- Use plastic bags to prevent water damage and also to compartmentalise your belongings for easier access.

- Keep any items with hard points or angles away from your back. Wrap them in clothes for your comfort and their protection.

- Give some thought to which items you'll need most regularly. Place these near the access points (eg side pockets) of the pack if possible.

Daypack

After a few days sightseeing, you'll quickly work out what you want to regularly carry with you in your daypack. Here's a list to start with:

❑ book, journal, postcards, aerograms and pen

❑ camera and film

❑ guidebook

❑ hat

❑ personal stereo

❑ pocketknife

❑ sunscreen

❑ sweater

❑ water bottle

See Carry-On Luggage in the Take-Off chapter for a list of items to take with you on planes, buses or trains. For details on packing your bike or surfboard, see the Bikes & Surfboards section in the Tickets & Insurance chapter.

RECORDING YOUR TRIP

Cameras

Whether or not to take a camera is a thorny question. There's definitely a case to be made for not taking one. Firstly, a camera costs a lot of money, and secondly, it can be a hassle on the road if you're constantly worrying about whether it becomes stolen, lost or damaged. More importantly, a camera can come between you and the places you've travelled so far to enjoy. If you're constantly wondering if you should be taking a shot of a particular scene or are fumbling to get your camera out of your pack, you won't be able to enjoy the sights for yourself.

People who travel without cameras often remark on how free they feel. If you think a camera will only encumber you, there are many alternatives to taking your own pictures: postcards, photo books and your own memory. You could also arrange for people you meet on the road to send you copies of their pictures.

If you're travelling with a friend you could consider sharing a camera, especially since you're likely to be taking photos of the same scenes. You might have different ideas on what makes a good photo and who gets to take the shot, but a little diplomacy and plenty of film should alleviate most problems.

If you decide to take a camera (as most people do), the camera you choose will depend on the type of photos you want to take. If you plan to use your photos for professional purposes (see Work & Travel in the Planning chapter), or just want to take high-quality, creative shots, you'll need a single-lens reflex (SLR) camera. If, on the other hand, you just want to take decent shots to show your friends and remember your trip by, you'll do fine with an automatic, point-and-shoot camera. If you're torn between the quality of an SLR and the convenience of a point-and-shoot camera, you might consider buying a high-end compact with a built-in zoom; there are several varieties of these on the market.

Weight is another important consideration. SLRs and their lenses are heavy – usually several times the weight of point-and-shoot cameras – and take up a lot of luggage space. This can be a liability if you intend doing a lot of walking.

The more you spend on your camera, the more you'll worry about it on the road. A good SLR with a few decent lenses can cost upwards of US$1000. Having one along is almost like travelling with a child – when it's with you, you'll be worried about it; when it's not with you, you'll be twice as worried about it.

As well as the following information, check out the *Photo.net* web site (www.photo.net/photo) for information on all aspects of photography.

SLR Cameras

The main advantage of an SLR camera is it allows you to take creative shots by shooting with the camera on its manual setting (perhaps using the built-in light meter as a guide). Many SLRs also have automatic settings, which are handy for when you can't be bothered thinking about the details. SLRs also allow you to use different lenses, thus vastly increasing your creative range. It's possible to buy SLRs with lightweight plastic bodies, but these are significantly more fragile than those with metal bodies or frames. With an SLR, you'll also need the following:

- A couple of lenses – Zooms save space and weight. A 24-100mm and an 80-200mm should be sufficient for most situations. If you prefer fixed lenses, you'll need three or four to cover the same situations.

- Skylight (UV) filters for each of your lenses – These protect your lenses and screen out excess ultraviolet light (which makes pictures look dull).

- A camera case – This will protect your camera and can be used to keep it handily outside your backpack.

- A couple of spare camera batteries – These are hard to obtain in some parts of Asia (and impossible in rural areas).
- Lint-free lens paper – This may be hard to obtain in many parts of Asia.
- Silica gel packets – These will keep the moisture out of your film and equipment; an absolute necessity in many parts of Asia.

Point-and-Shoot Cameras

Point-and-shoot cameras take the worry out of travel photography. They also make shots or people easier since they focus almost instantaneously. Point-and-shoot cameras range from cheap disposables to top-of-the-range models with precision lenses and a range of features. Since there are so many models available, it makes sense to ask at a trustworthy camera shop for a recommendation. A case will protect your camera and some silica gel will keep it moisture-free. You'll also need spare batteries and lint-free paper to clean the lens.

Film

Good-quality film can be hard to find in some parts of Asia. Even if you do find what you're looking for, it may have been badly stored or be in poor condition. Thus, you may want to bring film from home. If you buy it on the road, buy in big cities before heading into rural areas.

Film comes as slide or print; colour or black and white; and fast or slow. If you have professional aspirations, take slide film. Otherwise consider print film, as it's easier to view and costs less. Some people like the artistic effects they can achieve with black and white film, while others like the realism of colour. You will achieve sharper results with slower films (around 100 ASA), but you may not be able to use these films in dark conditions. To solve this problem, bring 400 ASA film or films of several different speeds.

Treatment of film is an important consideration. The sooner you expose your film after purchase the better, because film slowly deteriorates over time. Heat can also damage your film – a day in the hot glove compartment of a car is usually enough to fry a roll. Store your film in as cool a place as possible, and always out of direct sunlight.

When flying, always carry your film on with you to protect it from the high-energy X-ray machines used in some airports to inspect baggage. The metal detectors used to check your carry-on baggage are usually film-safe. If you're concerned, simply take out your film and ask that it be hand-checked. To make this easier for the airport staff, you may want to store your film in a small bag or plastic container.

Developing Film You should have film developed as soon as possible after exposing it, to prevent deterioration. You can send process-paid slide film off to your home country for developing and request that the developed slides be sent to your home address. You can also have film developed on the road, but the results will vary widely, so ask other travellers for recommendations.

Alternatively, test a lab by putting in only one roll or wait until you arrive in a big city or a developed country. Once you have the film developed, consider sending the slides or prints back home, as they will probably be destroyed by a few months sitting in your pack.

Photo Etiquette

See Avoiding Offence in the Issues & Attitudes chapter for advice on etiquette when taking photos in Asia.

Video

Video cameras can give a fascinating record of your holiday and are an increasingly convenient option for travellers. Today's video cameras, while still relatively expensive, are small, lightweight and simple to use – a far cry from only five or so years ago where they resembled television cameras in size and weight. However, there are some downsides ... film is not always available and you'll need a range of plug converters, plus a transformer, to recharge the batteries. You also run the risk of becoming an observer of (rather than a participant in) the cultures you encounter during your travels. If you spend your time concentrating on the technical aspects of filming, you'll be limiting yourself to the visual medium, rather than using your fully array of senses to absorb the scenes before you. If you nonetheless decide that a video camera is worth having along, here are a few tips:

- As well as filming the obvious – sunsets, sights and spectacular views – remember to record some of the everyday details of life. Often the most interesting things occur when you're actually intent on filming something else.

- Remember that, unlike still photography, video 'flows'. This means you can shoot scenes of a winding road from the front window of a vehicle to give an overall impression that isn't possible with ordinary photos. Try to film in long takes, and don't move the camera around too much. If your camera has a stabiliser, you can use it to obtain good footage while travelling on bumpy roads.

- Video cameras have amazingly sensitive microphones, and you might be surprised by how much sound is picked up. This can be a problem if there is a lot of ambient noise – filming by the side of a busy road might seem OK when you do it, but viewing it back home might simply give you a deafening cacophony of traffic noise.

- Remember to follow the same rules regarding people's sensitivities as you would when taking photographs – having a video camera shoved in your face is probably even more annoying and offensive than a still camera. Always ask permission first. See also Photo Etiquette under Avoiding Offence in the Issues & Attitudes chapter.

Travel Journal

No matter the length of your journey, there are going to be experiences, stories, people, sights and events that will be worth recording. The beauty of a travel journal is that it's not only a record of a remarkable episode in your life, but it doubles as a time capsule of your thoughts, expectations and aspirations at a particular point in time. In years to come you can revisit the person that you were, in a way unmatched by photographs or videos. On a more practical level, there are always periods of unadulterated boredom when you're on the road, and a travel journal is an ideal way to keep yourself occupied. And, if you're blessed with particularly good writing skills, a journal can serve as a blueprint for professional travel articles or books (see Work & Travel in the Planning chapter for some advice on making journalism pay). There are plenty of good travel journals on the market, including a new one from Lonely Planet, but a lined notebook will do just as well at a fraction of the cost.

Cassette Recordings

Apart from being a great way to send a long letter to friends and family without cramping your wrist, cassettes can provide you with an audio record of your trip. Recording the bedlam of a Vietnamese street market, the sombre militarism of the changing of the guard in Tiananmen Square, or the chants at a Buddhist monastery in Nepal can evoke much stronger memories than a photograph or journal record. Now, if there was only a way to record smells!

NICHE TRAVELLERS

There are some groups of travellers who face particular issues when travelling, variously due to age, sexual preference, disability or family responsibilities. This section has a look at some of the issues each group faces and suggests some strategies to maximise the travel experiences.

SENIOR TRAVELLERS

If you're reasonably fit and have enjoyed travelling in other parts of the world, you could certainly give Asia a try. Brutal traffic conditions, unfamiliar foods,

TIPS FOR SENIOR TRAVELLERS

1. Travel as lightly as possible. You can buy almost anything you need on the road.

2. Research your trip thoroughly. A good guidebook will have a special section for senior travellers listing the difficulties and facilities of the country you intend to visit. The Internet is still a little short on information for seniors, but see what you can find.

3. Keep the weather in mind when planning your trip. The extremes of hot and cold you may encounter can be debilitating, so try to travel during a period of moderate weather.

4. Try to do most of your sightseeing and local travel during off-peak periods, as negotiating streets and public transport during busy times can be a nightmare.

5. Be prepared for long journeys. If you can, take trains (which are more comfortable and safer) instead of buses. Bring a pillow if you have a bad back and find out if there are toilets on board.

6. Bring any medications you need from home.

7. If you have bad knees or a bad back, you might want to bring a stool to help you deal with Asian squat toilets.

8. Be flexible. If you find that your original itinerary was too ambitious, don't be afraid to change it.

9. You may want to start your travels in a country that is easier to travel around, such as Japan or South Korea, before tackling a country like India.

10. Don't be afraid to give things a try. You'll be surprised what you can do in Asia, and a little effort and enthusiasm can go a long way.

extremes of weather and long train and bus journeys may make your trip unpleasant at times, but they will usually be offset by the friendliness of the people you meet along the way. The elderly in many Asian countries enjoy far more respect than they do in other parts of the world, and the same respect will more often than not be accorded to travelling seniors.

Discounts

Travelling seniors are eligible for a variety of discounts in Japan, Taiwan, Hong Kong, Malaysia and the Philippines. The cut-off point for these discounts is usually 65 years of age. Those countries that don't offer discounts are so cheap to begin with that not getting a discount isn't going to hurt much anyway. China is the only country that does not fit this pattern – it's rather expensive to travel in and few discounts are offered to travelling seniors, who will normally be expected to pay the usual 'foreigner's price'.

Health Considerations

Due to the taxing nature of travel in some parts of Asia, give some thought to your level of fitness and health before setting out. It's a good idea to get a full physical in your home country, and you may also want to ask your doctor for some advice on travelling in Asia. Unless you're joining a full-on organised tour, you'll do a lot of walking – so get some miles in before you depart to strengthen those leg muscles. As with any traveller, up-to-date immunisations are essential, as is a good travel/health insurance policy. If you are presently taking any medication, bring enough to last for your entire trip, as replacements may be difficult or impossible to obtain while on the road. (And be sure to bring the proper documentation, such as prescription slips, so you don't have any problems at customs.)

GAY & LESBIAN TRAVELLERS

On the whole, lesbian and gay people will find Asia fairly easy and safe to travel around. While some areas are notably tolerant and have well developed gay and lesbian scenes (such as Thailand and Indonesia), others are quite close-minded and have laws banning homosexuality (Pakistan, India and Singapore). Even in these more repressive countries, gay and lesbian travellers are unlikely to encounter difficulties. However, it is important to remember that regardless of your sexual orientation, public displays of affection are frowned upon in almost all parts of North and South-East Asia. If you abide by this convention, you are unlikely to run into trouble. Also, while hand-holding between men is a common display of friendship in many parts of Asia, women walking around hand in hand might draw puzzled stares. Wherever you go in Asia, you will find that gays are better represented than lesbians. Only the bigger cities appear to have anything resembling a lesbian scene.

Laws & Tolerance

Most countries in South-East Asia are very tolerant of lesbians and gays. Thailand is probably the most tolerant of the lot – all aspects of the lesbian and gay lifestyle find their expression here and travellers can easily mix among the home-grown scene. Similarly, Indonesia, Laos, Cambodia and the Philippines are all comfortable and popular destinations for gay and lesbian travellers.

In Singapore and in some states of Malaysia, homosexuality is illegal. In the more conservative north-east region of Peninsular Malaysia, Islamic fundamentalist groups regularly call for crackdowns on homosexuality. In this area, travellers could conceivably find themselves the targets of abuse or even blackmail threats from conservative hotel or guesthouse owners. Further south, small but confident gay scenes exist in Kuala Lumpur and Penang. In Singapore, homosexuality is illegal (punishable by up to 10 years in prison), but it tends to be tolerated and there is an active scene.

Countries in North-East Asia are generally quite tolerant of homosexuality. Japan and Taiwan both have well established lesbian and gay scenes, but Korea is significantly less tolerant. In China the government vacillates between repression and tacit acceptance; there are some recognised gay bars and clubs in China's bigger cities. You are unlikely to encounter any real problems in China, though the further you travel into the countryside, the more conservative the attitudes will be.

The most backward attitudes exist on the Indian subcontinent. In India, sex between males is punishable by up to life imprisonment (there's no perceived need for a similar law against lesbianism!). However, there are gay scenes in India's bigger cities, particularly in Mumbai (Bombay), and travellers are unlikely to have problems, although you should take care to avoid situations where locals could attempt to blackmail you. Neighbouring Bangladesh is fairly conservative as well, and local lesbians and gays are very much in the closet. Nepal and Bhutan are generally very tolerant, though there is little in the way of a gay scene in either country.

Lastly, Pakistan is the most conservative country in the region. Official penalties for homosexuality include flogging and imprisonment. However, hand-holding and other displays of affection are common between members of the same sex. Again, there is virtually no gay or lesbian scene in Pakistan, and you should be careful of prying locals attempting to blackmail you.

Some lesbian and gay travellers find it unpleasant to travel in countries where the local communities are repressed. If it violates your principles to travel in these countries, then there are plenty of more open-minded countries in Asia to visit.

Resources

Almost all the bigger cities of Asia have active gay and lesbian scenes. A good guidebook will have special listings of meeting places and tolerant hotels. The

Internet is also a great resource. Two excellent web sites which may be useful in planning your trip are *Utopia Asian Gay & Lesbian Resources* (www.utopia-asia. com) and *Rainbow* (www.rainbowquery.com/index.shtml). *Gay.com* has a travel section (content.gay.com/trcontent.html) that's a bit light on Asian destinations, but includes good lists of gay-friendly operators and plenty of links.

In the larger cities of Asia, some English-language newspapers and magazines carry listings for lesbian and gay organisations and meeting places.

TRAVELLERS WITH A DISABILITY

There's no question that travel in Asia for people with a disability can be extremely difficult. Even the more advanced countries lag behind their western counterparts in terms of facilities and infrastructure, while most of the developing countries have almost no infrastructure at all. Add to this the chaotic traffic in the cities and the rugged conditions in rural areas and you're facing a real challenge.

Fortunately, what most of Asia lacks in infrastructure, it makes up for with friendly people who are almost always willing to lend a hand. Whether you're boarding a train, trying to fit a wheelchair into the boot of a car or manoeuvring yourself into a restaurant, you'll almost always find someone nearby who can assist you. Of course, it does help to travel with a companion to help you in these situations as well.

Some travellers with disabilities take advantage of the favourable exchange rates in some Asian destinations and hire private cars and sometimes even private assistants to help them explore a country. You might be surprised at how affordable this can be in South-East Asia and on the subcontinent.

Recently, more and more people with disabilities are accepting the challenge of Asian travel and many have reported very positive experiences. If you've travelled in other parts of the world, there's no reason why you shouldn't give Asia a go – just know what to expect and be prepared.

Accessibility

As a rule, the wealthier the country, the better the infrastructure it will have for disabled travellers. You can expect some good facilities in Japan, Taiwan, Korea and Singapore – of these, Japan is probably the most accessible. China, on the other hand, makes few concessions to disabled travellers and there is little infrastructure outside Hong Kong.

In the developing countries of Asia, you will have to improvise quite a bit to get around. Public transportation will probably be the biggest challenge, followed by the squat toilets that are so prevalent (see the boxed text 'Tips for Travellers with Disabilities' in this section for some advice). On the plus side, these countries are usually so cheap that hiring an assistant or a private car is a realistic option.

Resources

Three US-based organisations which disseminate information on world travel for the mobility impaired are: Mobility International USA (☎ 1-541-343-1284; www.miusa.org), PO Box 10767, Eugene, OR 97440; Access Foundation (☎ 1-516-887-5798), PO Box 356, Malverne, NY 11565; and the Society for the Advancement of Travel for the Handicapped (SATH; ☎ 1-718-858-5483; sath.org/index.html), 26 Court St, Brooklyn, NY 11242.

Abilities magazine (☎ 1-416-766-9188; fax 762-8716), PO Box 527, Station P, Toronto, Ontario, Canada M5S 2T1, carries a column called 'Accessible Planet' which offers tips on foreign travel for people with disabilities. *Exotic Destinations for Wheelchair Travelers* by Ed Hansen & Bruce Gordon (Full Data Ltd, San Francisco) has some information on Asian travel.

The *Global Access* web site (www.geocities.com/Paris/1052) has lots of information for travellers with disabilities, as well as links to related sites.

TIPS FOR TRAVELLERS WITH A DISABILITY

1 Research the specific challenges and facilities for disabled travellers in the country you'd like to visit. A good guidebook will have a section on travel for people with disabilities and will give contact numbers for local organisations that can assist. The Internet is useful for researching your trip (see the Resources section above).

2 Consider travelling with a companion who can help with day-to-day affairs and arrange for assistance if necessary.

3 Consider travelling to one of Asia's more accessible countries, such as Japan or Singapore, before tackling a more challenging one like China.

4 Depending upon the nature of your disability, you may want to bring a folding stool to use in squat toilets.

5 Don't be afraid to ask locals for assistance. People are usually more than willing to help out. If someone is particularly helpful, give them a tip.

6 Don't be afraid to try new things. You'd be surprised what you can do with a little imagination and improvisation.

7 Don't feel that you have to travel as a part of a group tour. It is quite possible to travel independently and this can be far more rewarding.

8 Consider hiring a private car for sightseeing. You may want to hire a personal assistant for some parts of your travel.

9 Ask for ground floor rooms in hotels, as few Asian hotels have elevators.

Go For It...

I have visited India many times before, but never in a wheelchair as a disabled person. As India is so rewarding, it is worth the effort to see it despite the lack of facilities disabled people are used to in the west.

I have Multiple Sclerosis (MS). I can walk two or three steps with support, which does help, but I was carried up and down steps very willingly many times. I have enough money to use mid-range hotels with ground floor rooms and to take taxis when necessary. Even a car and driver for a few days isn't too expensive and Indians are experts at getting wheelchairs into the boots of cars. Such a trip would, however, be almost impossible without a willing companion, not only for the pushing and pulling (pavements are never smooth) but to see if a restaurant, shop, hotel or temple is feasible. That saves a lot of time.

There is always plenty of manpower available if people are shown what to do, and paying for the assistance or tipping is obviously appreciated. You can also hire a nurse for relatively little cost. Bathrooms in the modest hotels are actually better than those in the expensive ones. They are big, have western toilets and marble or cement floors, and the shower taps are about 1m from the ground with a tap at that level too. Using toilets while I was sightseeing was the biggest problem. I solved this by taking a fold-up stool and a 'slipper' potty to slot underneath, so I could get into a toilet (often they are squat toilets) and balance somewhat precariously.

Every disabled person is different and I find that thinking through every eventuality beforehand and taking whatever equipment is essential is important. It would be difficult to buy tools for disabilities but Indians are very good at making do and mending. You may be very surprised at how you can survive and enjoy a holiday in India.

Margaret Wilson
UK

In the UK, the Royal Association for Disability & Rehabilitation (RADAR; ☎ 020-7250 3222; fax 7250 0212; www.radar.org.uk), 12 City Forum, 250 City Rd, London EC1V 8AF, produces three holiday fact packs (costing UK£2 each) which cover planning, insurance and useful organisations; transport and equipment; and specialised accommodation.

Australians and New Zealanders can contact the National Information Communication Awareness Network (NICAN; ☎ 02-6285 3713; fax 6285 3714; www.nican.com.au), PO Box 407, Curtin, ACT 2605.

TRAVELLING WITH CHILDREN

Travel with children can be difficult in any part of the world. It can also be tremendously rewarding, both for you and your children. The difficulties you will encounter in Asia are pretty similar to those you would encounter anywhere else: boredom on long journeys, trouble with local foods, inadequate facilities for children and the need to keep your children constantly entertained. In Asia you'll also worry about disease, the lack of good supplies like nappies (diapers) and baby food and, in certain parts of Asia, potentially dangerous animals.

These worries aside, you will find that travelling with children is a great introduction into Asian society. Most Asian people love children and will constantly shower them with affection. While this may grow tiresome, it is nonetheless a great ice-breaker. Furthermore, your children will almost never want for playmates and will probably enjoy the experience of meeting their counterparts in foreign countries.

Child-Friendly Countries

Japan, Singapore and Taiwan have plenty of parks, game centres and amusement parks. In contrast, Nepal and Mongolia have very few attractions that children will enjoy (unless your kids are crazy about the great outdoors). The rest of the countries in Asia fall somewhere between these two extremes. Thailand and Indonesia have few specifically child-oriented attractions, but you

TIPS FOR TRAVELLING WITH CHILDREN

1. Consider travelling in an easier country like Thailand before heading to a difficult one like India. This will give you an idea of how your kids (and you!) hold up to the stresses.

2. In some countries, you may need to bring your own supplies of nappies (diapers), baby bottles and baby food.

3. Bring your children's favourite toys and games to keep them amused.

4. While clothes are readily available, good-quality shoes in your children's sizes may not be, so bring these from home.

5. Travel on buses is not recommended, as children quickly grow restless with no room to move about. Take trains or private cars instead.

6. Be careful about what your children eat as they are particularly vulnerable to food-borne illnesses.

7. Bring plenty of sunscreen, and wide-brimmed hats.

8. Make sure your child is fully immunised for the countries you plan to visit.

9. If your children are old enough, get them international student ID cards so you can take advantage of student benefits (see Other Paperwork in the Passports & Visas chapter for details on cards).

can while away endless hours just playing on the beaches. In contrast, India and China are likely to be tough, as most of their attractions are cultural and may well bore the kids silly.

Resources

Most web sites relating to children deal with health on the road. Check out the good Travellers Medical and Vaccination Centre site (www.tmvc.com.au/info7.html) or the Travel Health Information Service (www.travelhealth.com/kids.htm). For an in-depth look at the issues, Lonely Planet publishes *Travel with Children* by Maureen Wheeler. Good guidebooks also have specific sections on travelling with children.

TAKE-OFF

You've saved the money, researched your route, packed your bags, said goodbye to your friends and family; now you're ready for the best part – the trip itself. Before you start making tracks across Asia, however, there is one last hurdle to clear: the long flight there. This chapter provides useful travel pointers both for seasoned travellers and those with less experience of international travel. We also offer some tips for dealing with the organised chaos of airports, the formalities of reconfirming your ticket and the intricacies of customs and immigration.

BEFORE YOU FLY
Ideally, the following should be taken care of well before the day of your flight.

Special Needs & Requests
If you have special needs of any sort – you've broken a leg, you're vegetarian, travelling in a wheelchair, taking the baby, terrified of flying – you should let the airline know as soon as possible so they can make arrangements. Remind the airline when you reconfirm your booking, and again when you check in at the airport. It may be worth ringing several airlines to find out how each can handle your particular needs. Airports and airlines can be extremely helpful with a little advance notice.

Most international airports will have ramps and lifts, and accessible toilets and phones for wheelchair-bound passengers. Most will also provide an escort from the check-in desk to the plane if needed. Aircraft toilets, however, are likely to present a problem; you should discuss this with the airline at an early stage and, if necessary, with its doctor.

Guide dogs will often be required to travel away from their owner in a specially pressurised baggage compartment with other animals, although smaller guide dogs may be admitted to the cabin. All guide dogs will be subject to quarantine laws (such as six months in isolation) when entering or returning to countries currently free of rabies, including the UK, Japan and Australia. Deaf travellers can ask for airport and in-flight announcements to be written down.

Children under two generally travel for 10% of the standard fare (free of charge on some airlines) if they don't occupy a seat, but they do not get a baggage allowance. Skycots, which will take a child up to about 10kg, should be provided if requested in advance. Children aged between two and 12 can usually occupy a seat for half to two-thirds of the full fare, and do get a baggage allowance. Pushchairs can often be taken aboard as hand luggage.

Reconfirming Your Flight

Most airlines require that you reconfirm your flight at least 72 hours prior to departure, though to be on the safe side it's worth reconfirming between three and five days beforehand, and even reconfirming twice. Some airlines or travel agents may tell you there's no need to worry about reconfirming, but you should do it anyway.

Some airlines will give you a number when you reconfirm. This is proof that you reconfirmed, and will be useful for getting a refund or a new ticket if for some reason you are bumped from your flight (see the Glossary at the end of this this book for details on this and other air travel terminology). A few airlines will allow you to make a seat selection when you reconfirm, so ask if this is possible. If you have any dietary restrictions or preferences, this is the best time to remind the airline.

Carry-On Luggage

Your carry-on luggage should contain all your breakable and valuable belongings – luggage handlers are not generally known for their care and attention. A 5kg weight limit is enforced by many airlines, but most daypacks will meet this criteria. If you exceed the limit, you will probably have to transfer some items to your main luggage. The following is a list of standard items to consider carrying with you on the plane.

- Passport, tickets, insurance papers, identification and money should be with you at all times, preferably in your money belt.
- Fragile electronic equipment such as camera, personal stereo, alarm clock or binoculars.
- Exposed and unexposed film, because your main luggage may receive a higher dose of X-rays, which could spoil your film.
- A change of clothes appropriate for the climate of your destination, plus simple toiletries.
- A bottle of water, as the air in the cabin can be very dry and you can't always rely on cabin crew to keep you supplied with drinks. Moisturiser is also a good idea.
- Something warm for your torso and feet, as the cabin can get quite cool.
- Any medication you take regularly, plus aspirin or paracetamol for headaches, and cough drops.
- Earplugs in case you have difficulty sleeping.
- Games, novel, guidebook, travel journal or whatever else you need to keep yourself entertained.
- A pen for filling in immigration and customs forms.

Duty-Free Allowances

Most countries allow you to import 200 cigarettes (or an equivalent amount of other tobacco products) and 1L of liquor without paying duty (import tax), although some countries allow twice this amount. You will have to pay duty on arrival on anything that exceeds these limits; or the items may be confiscated.

All countries in Asia prohibit the import of firearms and ammunition, narcotics, pornography and fireworks. Asian countries are deadly serious about keeping drugs out of their countries. If you attempt to bring forbidden items into a country, you will probably be arrested on suspicion of smuggling – and no one wants to see the inside of an Asian jail as part of their trip.

If you have to bring medication with you, be sure to have a note from your doctor explaining why you need it, and the original prescription slip. Some countries, such as Japan, will confiscate items not accompanied by such documentation.

Some countries, such as China, prohibit the import of fresh fruit, while Indonesia prohibits the import of anything written in Chinese characters! Several Asian countries (including India, Vietnam and Myanmar) require that you declare expensive items such as cameras, stereos and calculators upon entry, to prevent the illegal import and sale of such items. You will be given a form listing these items, which you must produce upon leaving the country. You may also be asked to declare how much currency you are carrying. For more details on customs formalities upon arrival, see Customs in the Touchdown chapter.

Buying Duty-Free

Once you've cleared customs and immigration, you'll have the chance to indulge in some last-minute buying in the duty-free shops. Possible purchases include liquor, cigarettes, perfume, beauty products and electronic goods, but you'll usually find that only cigarettes and liquor are good value. You can also do some duty-free shopping on board the plane, though the prices on most airlines are nothing special. Watch that you don't exceed the duty-free allowances of the country to which you're heading.

DEPARTURE DAY

A lot of the following may seem obvious, but you'd be surprised what you can forget in the frenzied moments leading up to departure. You could even use these sections as a predeparture checklist.

Dressing for Your Destination

There's nothing quite like arriving in a tropical airport decked out in full winter kit. Before you can even get to your backpack and summer clothes, you'll be drowning in sweat and feeling miserably self-conscious. Arriving in the cold of a Beijing winter wearing little more than shorts and T-shirt can be even more uncomfortable. If you're flying from a cold to a warm climate, it's easy enough to discard some of your warm clothes just before check-in on arrival (but keep something warm for the cool cabin). Alternatively, if you're heading to a cold destination, bring extra clothes and change in the airplane bathroom before landing.

Being on Time

You'd be surprised how many people somehow contrive to be late for their flight, often from being stuck on the freeway in a traffic jam. Some cities seem to organise nonstop traffic jams around their airports just for this purpose. If at all possible, take a train, or if you're travelling by road, leave plenty of extra time.

The airline will probably to tell you to arrive at least two hours prior to departure. Even if you are still reeling from the previous night's going-away party, it's worth heeding this advice. Dashing around with heavy bags with little time to board the plane is highly stressful. Having all your bags packed the night before will make things easier.

FLIGHT DAY CHECKLIST

- ❏ Turn off the gas and electricity in your home
- ❏ Make sure you've reconfirmed your flight (better late than never)
- ❏ Make sure you have your house key for when you return

Also ensure that you have the following essentials:

- ❏ Plane ticket
- ❏ Passport
- ❏ Money belt (with all your credit cards, travellers cheques, cash)
- ❏ Wallet/purse
- ❏ Medications you might need
- ❏ Camera
- ❏ Address book
- ❏ Visas you've already received
- ❏ Backpack
- ❏ Daypack

Navigating the Airport

Packed with people and cluttered with luggage, airports can be confusing places. Luckily, most display plenty of signs indicating which direction to go for the check-in counter and pointing you on to immigration and your departure gate. If you do get lost, don't waste time trying to figure things out – ask someone. Many large airports have information desks where you can pick up a map of the airport.

Ready Money

If you can purchase the currency of your destination at home before you depart (not all Asian currencies are readily available overseas), it's a good idea to change some money, so you don't have to worry about exchange booths being open on your arrival. You can do this at a local bank, or at the airport on the day of your flight, but the bank is likely to have better rates. Change just enough to get you to your hotel and to pay for the first night's accommodation and dinner.

Check-In

Once you've arrived at the airport, you need to make your way to the departure terminal and the check-in counter of your airline. Make sure you've tagged your backpack with your name, address, telephone number, airline and flight number. You may want to add a contact address in the country you're headed to. Prepare your backpack for the baggage handlers by tying all pieces of loose webbing, closing all pockets securely, placing all liquids (like shampoo) in plastic bags and making sure your film and camera are in your daypack. If your pack is in bad shape, ask the airline to place it in a large plastic bag.

You'll need both your passport and ticket on hand for check-in. At this time, you'll be asked to make your seat selection (see Best Seats below) and you should remind the airline of any dietary preferences. The agent will then issue your boarding pass.

Also make sure the agent places the appropriate destination tag on each piece of luggage. If you are changing flights en route, ask whether you must collect and recheck your bags yourself. Finally, take your baggage claim slip (this may be attached to your ticket) and you're off.

Best Seats

Unless you're flying business or 1st class, you'll have to fight it out in economy with the rest of us. To make your flight a little more comfortable, try asking for an exit row seat. These seats are usually above the wing and have twice the legroom of normal economy class seats, though they are often next to the service area, so they can be noisy.

The next best choices are aisle seats (which give you room to stretch your legs) or window seats (if you like to view the scenery). Often, however, these seats will be taken, and you'll find yourself in the middle of a row between a hyperactive child and a talkative insurance salesman. In this case, there's nothing left but the philosophical approach – consider it practice for those long-distance bus rides in Asia.

Inspection & Immigration

Inspections for departing passengers are usually brief. Your bag will be X-rayed and you will have to walk through a metal detector (ask for film to be hand-checked). In addition to weapons, you cannot take spray cans, explosives and other flammable substances on the plane. Anything that looks like a weapon will be given close scrutiny, so stow your pocketknife in your checked-in baggage.

Immigration formalities are similarly brief when leaving your home country. Usually, the inspector will simply look at your passport and wave you through, and possibly place a departure stamp in your passport.

SURVIVING THE FLIGHT

While many people look on flying as a necessary evil of travel, your flight need not be totally boring or an endurance test. This section outlines some ways to help the time pass a little more quickly and comfortably. For a list of items to bring with you on the flight, see Carry-On Luggage earlier in this chapter.

Alcohol

International flights are a little like wedding receptions – the booze is usually free and plentiful. However, having more than one or two drinks during the flight can be a very bad idea. The atmosphere inside the cabin will be very dry, and consuming alcohol will hasten the dehydration you are already suffering just by breathing. Worse still, you may end up with a raging hangover halfway through the flight.

Sleep

The world is made up of two kinds of people: those who can sleep on airplanes and those who can't. If you're one of the lucky ones, you may even arrive at your destination feeling refreshed. If you're among the unlucky, and have no hope of catching even a wink, you'll need plenty of distractions to help you through the long hours ahead – a good book, your language tapes, the in-flight magazine, the latest Bruce Willis flick ... whatever it takes.

Sleeping pills or tranquillisers aren't a good way to help you sleep on a flight, as they may leave you feeling groggy at the other end and thus make negotiating your way around a strange city very difficult.

The Best Meals

Airplane food is a favourite subject of ridicule among travellers. Still, you can generally get a decent meal if you know what to ask for. Many travellers request vegetarian or vegan meals because these are often better prepared than regular meals (though there are some glaring exceptions to this). Some travellers go one step further and request Hindu meals, which are often delicious. You will have to request special meals when you book your flight, and again when you reconfirm. If you just can't face airplane food, take along your own.

Transit Breaks

Many airports have facilities to assist you to pass lengthy transit breaks as agreeably as possible. There may be a day room where you can take a nap or shower, and decent restaurants or cafes offering a civilised bite to eat. Ask at the airport information counter; probably anything's better than sitting on the floor surrounded by your packs and watching the minute hand slowly moving around.

Picture this: you've been awake for the last 36 hours, endured three Bruce Willis films and eaten several questionable meals. Your plane banks beneath the clouds and you take a hesitant peek out the window to see an Asia city roiling under a blanket of haze, with chaotic streets spreading in every direction. What you really need is a hot shower and 12 hours in your own bed. What awaits you is immigration, customs, and a sea of touts and taxi drivers outside the airport.

Arriving in Asia for the first time can be unnerving, but it is also a special time. Your first impressions will last a lifetime, and you should make every attempt to savour them. Although you're exhausted, the jet lag and confusion will probably sharpen your perceptions and deepen your memories.

Again, it's all a matter of being prepared. Remember, all those touts and con artists outside the arrivals gate are simply the demons guarding the gates of the temple – make your way past them and you'll be rewarded with the wonders on the other side.

Immigration

At most Asian airports, you'll have to take care of passport formalities before collecting your baggage and proceeding through customs. Usually you'll be given an embarkation/disembarkation card and a customs form to fill out on the plane, or you can pick these forms up in the immigration hall. The disembarkation card goes to the immigration officer upon arrival. For information on items you may have to declare on your customs form, see Duty-Free Allowances in the Take-Off chapter.

Some countries also require that you fill out a health form upon arrival. Don't report minor health complaints (or risk being examined for several hours or even being quarantined), but do report any serious problem.

Immigration formalities usually take very little time, as long as your passport is in order and contains any visas you were required to get before arrival. Immigration inspectors are not known for their flexibility and you can be put on the next flight home if your passport and visas are not up-to-date. To avoid such nightmares, research the visa requirements of the countries you intend to visit (see the Passports & Visas chapter, and the country profiles later in this book). Many countries issue visas on arrival (called landing stamps), but those that don't won't make an exception if you turn up without a visa.

Also ensure that your passport is not due to expire before the visa itself expires. A passport that is in bad condition can also be a source of problems. If either of these is the case, it's worth getting a new passport before you leave home.

After handing over your passport to immigration, you may be asked a few simple questions, such as how long you intend to stay in the country, and what is the purpose of your visit. Whatever you do, don't lie. Some countries, such as Japan and China, can be very strict about these matters and will not hesitate to throw you out for small inconsistencies in your story. Other countries, such as Thailand, may also require that you show an ongoing ticket (see the country profiles for details).

It also helps to dress neatly to facilitate a smooth passage through immigration and customs. Many seasoned travellers carry one smart outfit with them for just these occasions. Sure, you can't do much about those luxuriant dreadlocks or the bone through your nose, but you can at least put on a clean shirt.

Baggage Collection

Once you've passed through immigration, you're free to collect your baggage from the luggage conveyor. Your bag may take a while to appear: be patient and don't panic. If the worst happens, and your baggage does not materialise, report the problem to the baggage office. Fortunately, baggage loss is fairly rare, even in Asia's less developed countries.

Customs

At customs you will probably have to choose the green channel (no goods to declare) or the red channel (goods to declare). On presenting your customs declaration form and passport, you may be asked to open your bags. This is generally routine, though if the customs officer is suspicious they may perform a more detailed search of your bags, and even your body.

Remember that Asian countries are deadly serious about keeping drugs out, and if you are carrying even the smallest amount you run the risk of jail and being tried for drug smuggling (in Malaysia and Singapore the harshest penalty for drug smuggling is death). If you have any doubts about what may be tucked away in some hidden pocket of your bag, be sure to check your bag carefully before leaving home.

ON YOUR WAY

If you didn't change money before setting out, you can do this once you have cleared immigration and customs. There will probably be an exchange booth or bank in the arrivals lobby (while changing money, be wary of pickpockets). In many countries, you get a poor exchange rate at the airport, so try to change just enough to get into town and pay for your first night's accommodation and food. You can change more money in town the next day at a better exchange rate. If you change money at the airport, be sure to get some small bills (useful for taxi fares). Remember to keep your foreign exchange receipts in case you are asked to produce them when leaving the country. For more details, see Changing Money in the Money Matters chapter.

Now it's time to walk out the arrivals gate and wade through the sea of touts and taxi drivers. Make sure all your valuables are in your money belt, your wallet is safely in your front pocket and that your pack is securely closed. You are very vulnerable to pickpockets at this point.

You'll probably be besieged by touts offering you cheap taxis and accommodation. A purposeful look is usually enough to deter them, though you may have to be a little more insistent.

Left-Luggage

The left-luggage facilities at the airport will allow you to leave your bags in safe storage to pick up when you depart. This can be very useful if, for example, you land in Bangkok and plan to explore the Thai islands before flying out to Kathmandu to trek in the Himalaya. You can leave your mountaineering gear at the airport and pick it up on the way to Nepal. Left-luggage can be fairly expensive, so you might be better off leaving your extra baggage at the left-luggage facility of a trustworthy guesthouse, which will be either free or very cheap.

Getting into Town

If you need information on how to get from the airport to your hotel, or to a part of town where you can look for accommodation, try the information counter in the arrivals lobby. Be aware that some information counters are private concerns that will try to steer you towards their own overpriced buses, limousines or taxis, and to accommodation from which they receive a commission. It is best to research local transport options in your guidebook before setting out, so that you have a good idea of the cost of taxis or buses.

Many travellers, even those on a tight budget, take a taxi to their accommodation when they arrive in Asia. When you're tired and disoriented, figuring out which bus to take and where to get off can be a real nightmare. A taxi will drop you at your hotel and you won't have to worry about pickpockets on the buses.

Note that taxi drivers in almost all countries in Asia will try to extract as much money as possible from you (Manila and Bangkok are notorious for this, although Seoul and Tokyo are blissful exceptions). Many taxi drivers will simply refuse to use the meter, so you must bargain for a reasonable fare. Don't get too hung up on the price – this is your first day in Asia, and your main goal is to get yourself to a clean, comfortable room as soon as possible (see Bargaining in the Money Matters chapter for some useful tips).

In some cities, such as Tokyo and Seoul, catching a bus or train from the airport is the best option. Public transport in these cities is generally excellent, is vastly less expensive than taxis and may take you very close to your destination. A good guidebook will have details on options for getting from the airport to the city centre.

YOUR FIRST NIGHT

Ideally, you already know where you want to spend your first night in Asia – if not the exact hotel or guesthouse, at least the general area. If you haven't prebooked your first night's accommodation (see Your First Night in the Tickets & Insurance chapter), it's handy to head to one of the so-called 'travellers ghettos' for your first night, where there will be plenty of other options should your first choice of accommodation be full or closed down. Some well known backpackers areas are Khao San Rd in Bangkok, Thamel in Kathmandu, Paharganj in Delhi, and Pham Ngu Lao in Ho Chi Minh City. Once you arrive in the area, it's simply a matter of walking into a few places and asking to see a room. If you're travelling with a friend, one of you can mind the bags while the other searches for a room.

OPENING NIGHT

It was just after midnight on Christmas night when our plane touched down in Bombay (as it was then). My friend and I each had an open return ticket and some travellers cheques, and I had a brand-new Lonely Planet guidebook in my rucksack. India lay before us – no bookings; no fixed itinerary. The air was richly scented, the cyclone-wire tunnel that led through the airport and out into the night was lined with staring faces, and the suburbs of Melbourne had never been further away. We got chatting to a German backpacker who seemed to know what she was doing, and followed her onto a bus bound for Colaba, which carried us through ever narrower, more crowded streets and eventually deposited us outside the Taj Mahal Intercontinental. Undeterred by my guidebook's grim predictions, we set off up the street in search of a cheap place to see out the night. Like scruffy moths we wandered towards a patch of incongruously bright light. Across the road from a floodlit colonnade was a film crew – megaphone-wielding director, cameramen, grips and all – piled high on the back of a battered old truck. The penny dropped: we had walked onto a Bollywood movie shoot. Before we could retreat into the night, an assistant jumped down from the truck, ran towards us and motioned us to stay, and we loitered in the light, a crowd scene of three, while a few moments of celluloid action were consigned to the can. By now it must have been 2 am. My journal records that we abandoned our budding film careers and resumed the search for a hotel only to end up, defeated, back at the Taj, very slowly sipping expensive coffee. Some time before dawn, on a whim, the three of us piled into a taxi and made our way to the docks, where we bought tickets for the steamer to Goa and joined the crowd sweating at the barriers. The sky was lightening when at last the gates opened. We stumbled forward with the throng, found the porter we'd offered a few rupees to secure us benches on the upper deck, and leaned back on our rucksacks. As the sun rose on day one, we reflected on an opening night that no amount of planning could have bought.

NICK TAPP
LP AUSTRALIA

When you find a likely place, always ask to see the room, and don't be afraid to refuse a room that looks unappealing. You can ask for a better room, or simply head to the next guesthouse. See the Accommodation section in the While You're There chapter for more advice on finding a room and checking that it's OK.

Once you find a room you like, you may want to negotiate the price. If there are other travellers about, ask them what they're paying so you have an idea of what's a fair price. Once again, don't be too concerned about getting a bargain or being ripped off on your first night – you can always find a cheaper place the next day.

If you arrive in the city with absolutely no idea of where to stay, don't panic. Many airports have accommodation counters which can book you into a room, though you'll be paying mid-range prices and a commission to boot.

You could also try asking other travellers at the airport if they know of a decent place to stay (they may even offer to share a cab into town with you), or try a taxi driver (who will more than likely take you to a dump from which he receives a commission).

If the worst comes to the worst and you find yourself in a strange city, late at night and without a clue as to where to stay, you can either stay in the airport until morning, or use your credit card for a room at the airport hotel. This last option may dent your budget, but it can be preferable to the potential dangers of blundering around an unknown city at night.

COPING WITH JET LAG

What day is it today? Did I leave home this morning or yesterday morning? Why am I wide awake at 3 am? These are the sorts of questions you might be asking yourself the night you arrive and for your first few days in Asia. For some travellers, jet lag is a mild inconvenience, but for others it can be quite unpleasant and disorienting.

Jet lag is caused by the discrepancy between your body clock (which is in tune with the day/night cycle of your home country) and the day/night cycle of the country in which you've just landed. Within a few days of arrival, your body clock will fall into sync with the local day/night cycle. Until this occurs, you may find yourself prowling your room in the wee hours and feeling groggy at high noon.

There's not a lot you can do to prevent jet lag. Try to get your body into its new time cycle by going to bed in the evening and waking up in the morning, just as locals do. The longer you stick to napping during the afternoon and staying up all night, the longer you'll suffer from jet lag.

Some travellers use sleeping tablets to help them sleep on their first night. Other travellers report that melatonin works (available from health-food shops). Still others rely on the tried-and-true method of a glass of warm milk and a good book. Following are a few more tips for dealing with jet lag:

- Avoid drinking alcohol while you're on the plane and during your first few days in the country. Hungover and jet lagged is a pretty wretched way to spend your first days in Asia.
- Try to rest as much as possible before your departure.
- Try to select a flight that minimises sleep deprivation. If you arrive late in the day, you'll be able to go straight to bed and you'll get into sync with local time a lot sooner.
- Avoid overeating, especially fatty foods, as these will make you feel bloated and slow you down, thus adding to the feeling of jet lag.

ISSUES & ATTITUDES

Packing your brain is as important as packing your bag. In this chapter, we give you some tips on dealing with culture shock, avoiding offence, and protecting yourself and your gear from scam artists and thieves. We also cover the contentious issue of ecotourism, which is currently booming in many parts of Asia. Used wisely, the information in this chapter will come in handier than your Swiss army pocketknife and will ensure that your trip is a good and safe one.

CULTURE SHOCK

Most first-time travellers, and even many experienced travellers, suffer some form of culture shock when they set foot in Asia. First encounters with the new and unfamiliar are a kind of traveller's growing pains, but to let culture shock get the better of you would be to miss out on all the wonderful opportunities that Asian travel offers.

Culture shock describes the confusion and disorientation travellers feel when exposed to new environments. You will find everything in Asia to be vastly different to your known experiences, from the heat, the noise levels, the crowds and the shocking poverty so evident in some countries, to the language, food and even the way you have to fight it out to board the bus. Although these

TIPS ON DEALING WITH CULTURE SHOCK

1. Travel from 'easy' countries (eg Malaysia, Singapore, Thailand or Japan) to more 'challenging' ones (eg India, China, Bangladesh or Pakistan).

2. Read up on your destination before you get there so you know what to expect.

3. Consider travelling with a friend who can lend moral support in unfamiliar circumstances.

4. Call home regularly. Familiar voices will help keep you on an even keel.

5. Talk to other travellers and expats, to help you put your thoughts and feelings into perspective.

6. Try not to compare the country you're in to your home country; accept that it's different and simply observe and analyse the differences.

7. If you find yourself getting too stressed or depressed by an unfamiliar culture, find one in which you feel more comfortable. This might involve heading, say, from India to Thailand or Malaysia. After all, you didn't come to Asia to torture yourself – if you aren't having a good time, find a place where you can.

stresses can be quite overwhelming, the best approach is to regard culture shock as an inevitable period of adjustment. Your preconceived values, notions and world-view are all being challenged, but gradually you will adapt as you become more familiar with the world you are travelling in.

The impact of culture shock will vary, depending on your previous cross-cultural experiences, your language proficiency and your pre-arrival knowledge of the new culture. Culture shock is not the same as homesickness, although homesickness is often one of its symptoms. It's natural to yearn for the familiar when everything seems strange.

Other typical symptoms of culture shock are anxiety, depression, insomnia, feelings of helplessness, an acute sense of isolation and withdrawal, and apathy

CULTURE SHOCK AND THE BOMBAY TO GORAKHPUR EXPRESS

I had all these great ideas of travelling from Bombay (now Mumbai) to Jalgaon about 300km to the north-east, before heading off to the 'must-sees' of Delhi, Agra and Jaipur. But I was homesick, lovesick and broke – and suffered severe culture shock within three minutes of leaving the airport.

Dumped in the middle of Bombay, I paid too much for a bad room in a dingy hotel and contracted stomach cramps that night. Two days later I had recovered enough to buy a ticket on the Bombay to Gorakhpur Express to Jalgaon. My inexperience was appalling: I didn't bother finding out which was the quickest train to my destination; I didn't think about what time I would arrive; and I bought the cheapest ticket available – 2nd class. My diary for that day reads: 'I severely underestimated the Indian railways system ... the train trip has exterminated my travel bug, possibly forever'.

I waited on the platform and watched in horror as the train pulled alongside, already impossibly full: people hung out the windows, sat on the roof and perched on steps between carriages. I precariously balanced on some steps before someone hurriedly pulled me into the doorway as the huge signal box loomed ahead. I later counted 35 seats in the carriage, and lost count of the passengers at 180. Someone noticed my total confusion and disorientation, and created a prime piece of space for me to sit: a section of a steel luggage rack less than half a metre wide and about 1.5m above the carriage floor. I had to sit with my knees to my chest for 10 hours; my legs couldn't dangle as there was simply no room.

I couldn't read, write or look out the window, and my backpack was used as a cushion by about 12 fellow passengers. The pain in my body, and the general culture shock in my mind, was indescribable. At Jalgaon, I jumped off my 'seat' (landing on several people), somehow retrieved my bag, placed it on my head and steamrolled my way through the wall of passengers.

I found a hotel (which leaked, was full of voracious mosquitoes and home to many inquisitive guests) in Jalgaon and slept for about 20 hours. I later changed some money (another test in patience) and then booked a 1st class ticket for the 36 hour trip directly to Calcutta (from where my next flight departed).

In hindsight I realise I had prematurely curtailed my trip, as travelling by 1st class train around India is a real pleasure. I now regularly travel to India, but still suffer culture shock among the seething mass of humanity and ubiquitous poverty. But I minimise this by allowing plenty of time to travel and choosing a decent hotel room to escape to when it all gets too much.

PAUL GREENWAY
LP AUTHOR, AUSTRALIA

and lethargy. When you can't speak a word of the language, or even read the city map, the sense of loss can be overpowering, and it can be difficult to keep things in perspective. Take time to ease yourself into the travel experience; catch up on your sleep (on top of everything else, you're probably jet lagged as well) and don't try to cram in too much sightseeing in your first few days.

There are several stages of culture shock, though people do experience it differently. The first is the honeymoon stage, characterised by a sense of euphoria and excitement, when everything new seems extraordinary. Inevitably, the novelty wears off – welcome to the disintegration stage. Instead of being thrilled to be thrust into the midst of this new environment, you find yourself disliking and rejecting many aspects of the culture you have come so far to see. To keep yourself out of 'the pits', it's important to stay motivated by setting yourself realistic goals. Keep an open mind and avoid focusing entirely on the negative.

Soon enough you'll hit the reintegration stage, when you'll be gritting your teeth and getting on with things. You might still feel defensive, vulnerable or hostile, and be tempted to blame every little problem or setback on your host culture, but your survival instinct will have kicked in. By the autonomous stage, you have new goals and objectives based on a more realistic assessment of travel. With more self-confidence, you can relax and be more sensitive to the people around you.

Finally, the interdependence stage arrives, when an emotional bond develops between you and the new culture. This may take some time and effort, but it will happen. To help yourself along, try to do some research before you leave home: read travel and history books, look up the place in an atlas, search the web, and hone up on the country's art and literature (see Researching Your Trip in the Planning chapter for some specific pointers). Soon enough, time runs out, funds dry up and travel comes to an end – leading to a shock of an altogether different variety on your return home.

Poverty & Begging

Almost inevitably you are going to be distressed by the extreme poverty that is plainly evident in many Asian countries. Unless you stick to wealthy countries like Japan and Singapore, you'll probably find it hard to avoid scenes of poverty, particularly on the subcontinent and in South-East Asia where you will be confronted by poverty almost daily. To cope with this, it helps to formulate a consistent policy towards the poor people you will meet, and towards beggars.

There are several scams involving beggars in Asia. Some beggars are controlled by local 'operators' who pocket most of what is collected. In other situations, parents may force their children to beg, knowing that children elicit far more sympathy than adults. You will probably hear stories of adults mutilating children and putting them on the streets to beg – all this aside, many of the beggars you will see in Asia are simply poor individuals trying to survive.

Obviously, whether or not you end up giving to beggars is a purely personal decision. Some travellers feel that giving to beggars only encourages them to hassle future travellers. Others feel it is a superficial interaction with no long-lasting benefit. In contrast, you may feel that giving away a little of your money is the least you can do, especially considering that your spare change is probably more than enough to feed a person in Asia for an entire day.

If you want to give to beggars, one way of avoiding scams is to observe wealthy locals, who will probably know who is genuinely begging. Alternatively, you could give food or other goods instead of money, thus ensuring the person will at least have some of their needs met.

Donations

A different solution if you are troubled by the plight of beggars is to donate money to local aid organisations or schools, where you can be sure the money will be put to good use. You could also make a donation to an international aid organisation, such as Oxfam International (www.oxfaminternational.org).

As well as the beggars you will encounter in many Asian cities, you will probably be hassled by children in rural areas of Nepal and Pakistan, who ask foreigners for pens, balloons or sweets. Instead of encouraging these children to beg from every traveller they see by giving them these small gifts, bring along pens, pencils, books or notebooks that you can donate to the local school.

The dire poverty you will encounter in Asia won't yield to quick solutions. Rather than turning away or consoling yourself with easy rationalisations, consider that having the money to travel places you on an economic level that most people in Asia can only dream about. If this really bothers you, you could consider the opportunities for voluntary work discussed in the Work & Travel section of the Planning chapter.

AVOIDING OFFENCE

When travelling in foreign countries, it's only natural that you worry about committing some dreadful *faux pas* that will go down as the most monumental blunder of all time. Fortunately, this is a lot easier said than done. You'll find in Asia that if you abide by the rules of common decency and good manners that apply in your own country, you will almost never go wrong. There are, however, some fundamental cultural differences between Asia and the west which you need to be aware of. In this section, we advise you on some simple rules of behaviour that should guarantee you stay on the right side of your hosts and make a good impression wherever you go.

For country-specific dos and don'ts, see the society and conduct sections of your guidebooks.

Buddhist Sensibilities

In Buddhist countries, images of the Buddha, monks and religious structures are all held as sacred, though the degree of reverence varies from country to country – Thais are very devout Buddhists and are very strict about behaviour and dress at *wats* (Buddhist temple-monasteries), while the Japanese take a remarkably casual attitude towards religion. The following rules generally apply when visiting a Buddhist religious site:

- Remove your shoes before entering the main hall. At some temples and wats, you can tour part of the structure with your shoes on.
- Dress respectfully. This usually means long trousers for men and long skirts for women. You may be required to remove your hat.
- Do not point at Buddha images, especially with your feet. If you sit in front of a Buddha image, sit with your feet pointing away (in the 'mermaid pose').
- Women should avoid touching monks, especially in South-East Asia.
- Before taking pictures, make sure photography is permitted. You cannot take photos of Buddha images in many Buddhist temples.

Muslim Sensibilities

In Muslim countries fairly rigid rules apply to dress and behaviour, both in mosques and on the street, and these rules are infinitely more strict for women than for men. The Muslim regions of Pakistan, Bangladesh and India are stricter than those in Indonesia, the Philippines and Malaysia. Nonetheless, it's a good idea to adhere to the following rules when visiting a mosque in any Asian country:

- Remove your shoes before entering. If you really want to show respect, wash your hands, feet and face at the washing basins provided.
- Dress respectfully. Men should wear trousers and shirts, women long skirts or trousers and loose, long-sleeved blouses, with their hair covered by a scarf. In many mosques, robes and scarves are available if you need them.
- Women cannot enter the main prayer hall.
- Non-Muslims of either sex may not be permitted to enter some mosques, especially during prayer times.
- Never walk between a Muslim and Mecca when they are praying.
- Always ask for permission before taking photos and do not take pictures during prayer times.

Hindu Sensibilities

Hindus are generally less strict than Muslims and South-East Asian Buddhists, though there are some general rules you should conform to in a Hindu temple (if you're actually permitted entry).

The most important is that the cow is sacred in Hinduism and must be treated with respect; cow products are not acceptable in Hindu temples, so you may have to remove leather items such as belts when entering, and leave leather backpacks outside. As in a Buddhist temple, you should dress respectfully, remove shoes before entering and ask before taking pictures. You generally cannot take pictures of the sanctum.

Face

The concept of 'face', a notion similar to western ideas of pride and reputation, is extremely important in Asia. Face can be gained by having and displaying wealth, particularly in the form of extravagant wedding celebrations and funerals. Face can also be lost, through defeat in an argument or by being out-bargained or outdone in any transaction.

When travelling in Asia, you do not want to cause someone to lose face. This means you should avoid driving too hard a bargain, bettering people in arguments or causing anyone embarrassment. Mostly this is common sense, but you can get carried away in the heat of the moment. Try to keep your cool in all your dealings. Even if you feel you are obviously right in an argument, leave your opponent an easy way out. It is especially important to avoid emphasising any obvious distinctions in wealth between yourself and others. Remember, you are just passing through, but your actions and words can have lasting repercussions.

Photo Etiquette

There's no doubt about it: some of the people and places you encounter in Asia make for superb photographs. However, you shouldn't let the temptation to take a great picture get the better of you; treat locals with respect when taking pictures. The following are some basics tips to make sure that both you and your subject come away happy from your interaction:

- If you are taking a picture of a person at close range, ask their permission. Do not treat people like zoo animals. Some people enjoy having their picture taken and some do not – just as in the west. Obviously, you lose some spontaneity by asking permission. There are ways around this however: bring a long lens and take photos from a distance; take two pictures – the first posed and the second when your subject has relaxed; or use humour to relax your subject.

WHAT'S IN A SMILE?

My wife and I were on Flores in Indonesia and decided to travel from Ende to Moni by boat (via Nggela) rather than by bus. After a 45 minute trip the captain pointed to a cove at the bottom of high and steep cliffs where fishing boats were beached by a river. 'Nggela,' he said. When asked where the village was, he pointed upwards and explained that a trail led to the village at the top. 'Where's the trail?' I asked, seeing only thick forest. The captain assured us that we couldn't miss it, it was 'over there', on this side of the river. He was smiling – I should have remembered that smiling in Indonesia often means 'I don't know' and that most locals won't admit to ignorance for fear of being rude.

It took us almost two hours of beating the bush, sweating, cursing and a close encounter with two huge water buffalo before we admitted we weren't taking the scenic route and didn't know where that trail was. We backtracked and found a fisherman fixing his nets. The man (bless him for 10 generations) led us across the river (sigh) to a steep goat path we never would have found on our own ...

FRANÇOIS LASALLE
CANADA

PAN-ASIAN DOs & DON'Ts

The following rules generally apply throughout Asia. While you will find exceptions to every rule, you'll never go wrong by being too cautious:

DOs

1. Dress discreetly. This is the most important rule to observe (see the boxed text 'Dressing Appropriately' in the What to Bring chapter for details).

2. Remove your shoes before entering a home. There are some exceptions to this, and your host will tell you if it's all right to leave them on.

3. Observe proper etiquette in religious structures such as temples, shrines, mosques, monasteries and wats.

4. Bring a gift if invited to someone's home. This is particularly important if you're at a homestay.

5. Ask for permission before taking someone's photo.

6. When beckoning to someone, wave to them with your palm down, almost as if you were waving goodbye. The western way of doing this, with the palm up, is considered rude by most Asian people.

7. Use two hands when giving or receiving important documents and business cards. Many Asian cultures are very sensitive about how such items are handled.

DON'Ts

1. Don't engage in public displays of affection.

2. Don't lose your temper, especially when dealing with authority figures. This will generally get you nowhere and may lead to serious problems.

3. Don't point your feet at people or objects. Using your feet in this manner is considered extremely rude throughout Asia.

4. Don't use your left hand for eating or shaking hands. In many Asian countries, the left hand is used for cleaning oneself after going to the bathroom.

5. Don't leave your chopsticks sticking straight up in a bowl of rice. This is part of a Buddhist funeral rite and is considered a very bad omen in many parts of Asia.

6. Don't attempt to shake hands with members of the opposite sex. If a handshake is acceptable, the other person will offer their hand.

7. Don't wear thongs (flip-flops) anywhere except in your hotel room and around the beach, as they are considered too 'low' for public wear in most parts of Asia. Oddly, fixed-heel sandals, such as Tevas, are usually quite acceptable.

8. Don't openly criticise the political leaders or royalty of the country you're in. Even if you're on friendly terms with the locals, you can easily land yourself in hot water with a few ill-considered remarks.

- Do not take photos of private or sacred events unless you are absolutely sure it is OK to do so (by asking permission). Just imagine if a stranger burst in on a wake in your home country and started taking pictures. Crazy as it sounds, this is pretty much what lots of foreign travellers do at the ritual cremations performed on the banks of the Ganges in Varanasi.

- If you are photographing a religious ceremony or similar event, take care not to bother the participants and onlookers with the sound of your camera or the light of your flash.

- Do not take photographs inside religious structures, such as temples or shrines, unless you are sure it is OK to do so.

- People whose pictures you take may sometimes ask you to send them copies; do not promise to do so unless you really intend to follow through.

ECOTOURISM

Ecologically sound tourism is one of the most contentious issues in the travel industry. While some see it as merely a marketing ploy to fleece gullible travellers of cash while easing their consciences, others feel it is a valuable practice that minimises the impact travellers have on world ecosystems and cultures.

Ecotourism is usually defined as travel that conserves the natural environment, while benefiting the wellbeing of local people in a sustainable way. It was born as a backlash against destructive travel practices, particularly in the more remote regions of the world. In Nepal, for example, the growth of the trekking industry has accelerated the pace of deforestation as more and more trees are cut down to provide fuel for foreign trekkers. Worse still are the plastic water bottles which travellers discard all across Asia.

A number of organisations have developed useful guidelines for ecotourism, including Conservation International's Ecotravel Center (www.ecotour.org/eco tour.htm) and the Ecotourism Association of Australia (www.wttc.org). For more information on ecotourism and lists of reliable ecotour operators, check out their web sites.

Ecotourism Guidelines

- Leave only footprints and take only photographs. This one is almost a cliché, but it sums up the most important tenet of ecotourism: do not leave garbage in the places you visit and do not take any natural souvenirs (especially coral and plants).

- Learn about the culture and environment of the places you plan to visit, so you are familiar with the specific problems facing a region.

- Respect the people and cultures of the places you visit. This means encouraging people in their efforts towards sustainable tourism and not disrupting the fabric of their daily lives.

- Learn about local and international conservation groups working in the area and support their efforts.

- Patronise environmentally friendly and locally owned businesses, and buy locally produced goods.

- Never buy products made from endangered species.

HOLIDAY ROMANCES

If you've seen Julie Delpy and Ethan Hawke killing time in Vienna in the film *Before Sunrise*, you might well be planning a holiday romance yourself. And while losing yourself in the arms of a mysterious lover at the same time as losing yourself on the streets of a strange city has enormous romantic appeal, there are a few things to consider. If you're going to be spontaneous these days, it's important to plan. And there's more to consider than just the price of a bottle of red wine and the easy spread of sexually transmitted diseases.

Lots of travellers, and especially those travelling alone, set out with the intention of seeing a bit of love action while away from home. But few contemplate the variety of motivations and enormous list of repercussions such play might carry with it.

Many travellers find part-time love with other travellers. This is hardly surprising; you're unlikely to find a native Frenchman in a Paris youth hostel. You might even hook up with someone you've just met in order to cut costs on a day trip or taxi fare, then end up beginning a beautiful – if necessarily short – friendship. People travel with different itineraries, and after a couple of days in the City of Lights, you'll be off to the French Riviera to catch a tan and he'll be heading to Somalia to unload grain for the Red Cross. Now if you never really liked him anyway – maybe you've just always wanted to kiss a Welsh guy – there's no problems. Unless he likes you. Or unless you start to miss him. Or unless he's stolen your daypack. The liberation of travel is quickly eclipsed by affairs of the heart, and where that troublesome organ is concerned, all other cares can fly out the bus window.

Breaking up is hard to do. It's almost inevitable, though, when travelling. And the longer you drag out travel together, the harder the parting is likely to be. It's important to remember that although you may share intimate secrets with your new pal, you probably won't tell them everything, and they'll keep things from you too. They might have a partner they're planning to return to, they might be homesick for the Vladivostok coast or they might simply be after some quick, disposable sex. If you're just after sexual experience and conquest too, you might be in luck. But all can end in disaster if the people you meet have more serious intentions, attach stronger cultural importance to physical relationships or if you plunge headlong into love. If anyone's going to get hurt, the best advice is to skip the encounter and head to Hong Kong as you'd planned.

If you're looking to hook up with a local in a new country, many of the same pleasures and risks can be expected. Again, discovering your intended partner's expectations is the first step to carnal bliss. Are they aware of your travel plans? Are they aware that you need to marry a local in order to stay? Are you aware of local customs and expectations of a sexual partner? A night of passion is all well and good, but you don't want to wake up the next morning buried to your waist and being force-fed raw lobster in the first of a 12 step marriage ceremony. As with new relationships at home, establishing the ground rules is the best way to avoid nasty or upsetting confusion.

If sex (always safe sex) is one of the reasons you're travelling, remember that it carries different connotations in different cultures. Learn a little about where you are before heading for someone's pants. There are plenty of girls on the road looking for a little short-term affection and plenty of guys at their local bar who'd love to show a traveller their etchings, which means there's no need to take advantage of someone who is playing by different rules.

There is, of course, a chance that you may find the love of your life on the road. My parents met while my mother was on holidays. But their blossoming relationship meant that my father-to-be had to pack his bags, leave his job, family and friends and chase her halfway around the world. Not everyone is happy to throw it all away to give it a go with someone they've just met. Are you?

JOHN RYAN
LP AUSTRALIA

- If possible, use environmentally friendly methods of transportation or walk from place to place.
- Stick to designated trails and camping spots.
- Avoid polluting water sources. Use established toilets, or go at least 50m from rivers or lakes.
- Try to minimise all aspects of your energy consumption.
- Produce as little garbage as possible by using recyclable containers. If your garbage won't be disposed of properly, carry it out yourself.

These guidelines will not always be easy to follow, but they will make your travel more rewarding.

Be wary, however, of tour operators who use the banner of ecotourism simply to attract customers. You can search for trustworthy ecotour operators through the web sites listed earlier in this section.

Potential ecotourists should also be wary also of unintentionally damaging indigenous cultures and environments, a real danger on trips that take you to visit groups living in remote areas. Your mere presence can be enough to destabilise their way of life, and makes it easier for other travellers to visit. If you think you will be paving the way for less responsible tourists, don't be afraid to change your plans.

And finally, the most important point to make about ecotourism is this: true ecotourism begins at home. Try to carry some of the spirit and concepts of ecotourism over to your daily life and you'll find the experience a lot more meaningful.

HAZARDS & SAFEGUARDS

It's easy to become paranoid about the dangers of travelling in Asia, but in fact it's probably at least as safe as travelling in your home country. Indeed, in some places you may even be safer. Most crimes committed against foreigners are opportunistic thefts; if you use your common sense, you will have very little to worry about. The same is true of other potential hazards in Asia. Natural disasters, political unrest, wild animals, unexploded landmines and terrorism are generally far less a danger than you might think from reading the news. If you heed the warnings and do not deliberately expose yourself to danger, you'll have little to fear except random acts of fate. (To be on the safe side, do not travel without adequate travel insurance covering both medical expenses and loss of baggage – see the Tickets & Insurance chapter for details.)

Also do some research before you go, so that you are well informed about the countries you intend to visit. A good guidebook will have a detailed section on the hazards particular to each country and how to avoid them. Update your information through newspapers, magazines and the Internet just before visiting a country. The Researching Your Trip section in the Planning chapter lists useful web sites, or see the Internet Addresses appendix at the back of the book.

Theft

Theft is a definite danger in most countries of Asia, with the possible exceptions of Japan, Korea and Bhutan. However, you will almost never be the victim of theft unless you are careless or foolish. Try to keep your wits about you all the time. If your money belt is stolen, it may spell the end of your trip, or at least several days wasted replacing your passport and travellers cheques, and cancelling your credit cards. The following tips should help you have a theft-free trip.

- Always keep your passport, plane tickets, travellers cheques, most of your cash and important travel documents in your money belt. The only time you shouldn't be wearing your money belt is when it's in a secure hotel or guesthouse safety deposit box or when you're sleeping (in which case it should be under your pillow). For more details, see Carrying Your Money in the Money Matters chapter.

- Keep photocopies of all your important travel documents in a separate place from your money belt.

- When swimming, diving or snorkelling, bring your important documents and money with you in a waterproof container, or leave them in the safety deposit box of your hotel or guesthouse (if you're confident it's safe).

- When you're in a restaurant or bar, secure your pack with a lock or strap or lean it against you so that you'll know if someone is trying take it.

- Have a small padlock to secure your hotel or guesthouse room door, and to lock your luggage to overhead racks on long-distance buses or trains.

- Keep an eye on your backpack when on long bus trips. If it is placed on the roof or in a luggage compartment, make sure it's secure (add your own lock if possible). During rest stops, make sure no one tries to walk off with it.

- Don't flash your cash, valuables or camera around. If possible, do not let people see that you are wearing a money belt.

- Think twice before accepting drinks or food from strangers. In some countries in Asia, thieves have been known to put drugs in drinks or food and then rob the unconscious victim.

- Don't give the name of your hotel or room number to strangers, as they might follow you back and try to rob you.

- Pickpockets usually work in teams. If you feel that people are jostling or crowding you for no reason, stand back and check discreetly to see that your valuables are still on you.

- It's difficult to keep your wits about you when you're drinking. If you know you're going to have a big night out, try to store your valuables and most of your cash in a secure hotel or guesthouse safety deposit box.

- Be careful of your valuables while you're taking a shower. If you're not sure that your room is safe, bring them into the bathroom with you.

- Don't walk alone at night or in unfamiliar areas. If you find yourself in an unsavoury spot, flag down a taxi or tuk-tuk.

- Be especially careful when boarding and riding buses and trains. You're at your most vulnerable to pickpockets at these times. If the bus or train is really crowded, try to keep your hands unobtrusively over your wallet and money belt.

- Be careful of unregistered taxis and never fall asleep in the back of a taxi.
- Don't close the door of a taxi or pay the driver until your baggage has been unloaded.
- Remember that it's not just locals who may steal your belongings – there are quite a few travellers around who pay for their trips by ripping off other travellers.

Scams

Every year we get hundreds of letters from hapless travellers reporting that they've joined the long list of victims of Asia's many scams. In many cases, there are two culprits involved: a shrewd scam artist and the traveller's own greed. If someone offers you a deal that seems to good to be true, then it almost certainly is. The only get-rich-quick schemes that have any chance of paying off in Asia are the lottery and the horse races. The more common scams are listed below. There are myriad others which prey on a traveller's gullibility or carelessness.

GEM SCAMS – Most common in Thailand and India, these involve a tout luring you into a gem shop and suggesting you can buy some gems cheaply to sell back home for many times the price. He may even have some contacts for you in your home country and may offer to post the gems for you. Invariably, if you get the gems at all, you'll find they're almost completely worthless. People often lose hundreds of dollars this way. Even if you go back to the store where you bought the gems, you won't be able to get a refund as the stores are usually protected by the police. The key point here is: don't buy any gems unless you're a professional.

A GEM OF A SCAM

The Indian city of Agra is famous for the Taj Mahal and infamous for tourist cons. We knew this, yet were feeling at ease when an apparently innocent invitation found us having breakfast at the colonial home of an Indian family. However, one of us was to learn a hard lesson in deception.

We were introduced to a man named 'Prince' and conversation was gently guided onto the subject of the family gem-export business. As a matter of fact, we were informed, tourists often bought gems at a good price to resell to an importer at home. Two winners: the business pays no export duties and the tourist doubles their money. We were nibbling the bait, and a disinterested 'yes' drew us further out. Soon we were in the next door office, where authentic invoices from European businesses nurtured our confidence. I backed out at the asking price of UK£300. But one of my friends bought in.

The gems, which could have been anything, were packaged in front of us. A letter was drawn up asking his bank not to honour the transaction until authorisation was given on receipt of the gems. We took both to the post office and handed them to the clerk, our driver standing behind us.

The gems were never sent, and his money was as good as gone as soon as Prince swiped the card. Later there were frantic phone calls from Australia – 'Prince make many people angry, he's gone to Bombay,' we heard, and the line went dead.

GARETH MCCORMACK
NORTHERN IRELAND

CARPET SCAMS – This works pretty much like the gem scam; someone (usually a shop owner) convinces you that if you buy his carpets, you can resell them for a huge profit in your home country. Of course, if this was true, he wouldn't be cutting you in on the deal, he'd be sending them to his cousin who lives in your country. Unless you are a carpet expert (and do you know many of these?), steer clear of these deals.

CARD SCAMS – The drill here is that you're invited by a very friendly local to visit his relative's house. Once you get there, you find that a card game is under way. Your friend may coach you on how to win big and you'll be invited to join the game. Invariably, you'll be allowed to win a few hands, then you'll start losing until you have no more money to play with. At this point, your friend or another player will offer to lend you some cash. Needless to say, you'll quickly lose this and then find yourself in debt to a complete stranger. Of course, the game was rigged from the start. Bang – time to go cash some travellers cheques.

CREDIT CARD SCAMS – There are various credit card scams out there, and most are pretty simple. For example, a shop owner takes your card out the back of the shop and runs off three or four purchase slips with it and then uses the one you sign to forge the signature on the others. Never let your credit card out of your sight and carefully watch what is done with it. Likewise, while you are trekking be wary of leaving your valuables in a guesthouse safe. More than a few travellers have returned home to find their cards have been charged to the limit. If you find charges on your card that don't belong there, call the credit card company to have them removed.

SMUGGLING SCAMS – You may be approached in some countries to carry drugs, gold or electronic items to another country in exchange for cash (to be paid by a contact on the other end). Never accept these offers – you run the risk of being busted by customs officers at the other end, and may not be paid for the goods anyway.

FAKE POLICE OR IMMIGRATION OFFICIAL SCAMS – These involve men in official-looking outfits who demand to see your passport and then order you to pay a fee to stay in the city. Never hand over your passport, and demand to see their ID. If they are adamant, tell them you'll be happy to cooperate at the local police station.

Natural Disasters & Wild Animals

It's not just thieves and con artists who can make your life miserable in Asia – the forces of nature also can conspire to ruin your trip. Asia suffers from a vast array of natural disasters – earthquakes, volcanoes, typhoons, floods and land-slides, to name a few. In addition there are reptiles, large mammals, biting insects and sea creatures to contend with. However, careful research and keeping abreast of the news regarding weather conditions will keep you safe. Although natural disasters such as floods in Bangladesh or earthquakes in Japan will make headline news, these are rare and isolated events. You have far more to worry about from Asia's crazy bus drivers. Here are some basic safety pointers:

TYPHOONS – These occur in Japan, Korea, Taiwan, parts of China, and the Philippines, usually in late summer and in autumn. Most South-East Asian countries are hit also by the occasional severe tropical storm. Usually you'll have ample warning of approaching typhoons and storms from newspapers, television and radio. In such cases, move away from coastal areas and onto higher ground, or at least try to get into the most secure lodgings available. You may want to stockpile some food and water in case things shut down for a while. Never go out in a storm – pieces of flying metal and wood can be lethal.

VOLCANOES — There are active volcanoes in the Philippines, Indonesia and Japan. Check with local people or authorities before going anywhere near them and leave the area at the first sign of an eruption.

EARTHQUAKES — These are a danger in many Asian countries, particularly Japan and China. If one strikes while you're indoors, take shelter in a doorway or under a strong table. Do not run outside as this exposes you to falling debris. If you're outside, get away from buildings or other things that can collapse on you. Fires and tidal waves often follow earthquakes, so don't let down your guard just because the shaking has stopped.

FLOODS — Depending upon the season, floods can strike almost anywhere in Asia. Often you will be forewarned, in which case you should get to high ground as soon as possible. Be very careful when crossing flooded streams and so on. If you're camping near a river and heavy rain sets in, move to higher ground even if you must do so in the middle of the night (better yet, do not camp in areas that can be reached by rising waters).

DANGEROUS ANIMALS — In some parts of Asia, you'll have to beware of dangerous animals when trekking in wilderness areas. These include crocodiles in Indonesia, tigers in India, bears in northern Japan and various poisonous snakes in most countries. While swimming, diving or snorkelling, look out for sharks, stonefish, sea snakes and the like (though the risk of being attacked in the water is infinitesimally small). Also keep an eye out for dogs, cats, bats and monkeys that could be carrying rabies. Read up on the hazards in each country and take the appropriate precautions.

Drugs

The times they are a'changing in Asia. In the past, people flocked to India, Nepal and Thailand to indulge in drugs in an open-party atmosphere. These days, the party is pretty much over and the penalties for drug possession or smuggling are so strict that even the most cavalier party animals think twice before indulging. To get involved in drugs is to potentially invite a long jail

LEND ME YOUR EARS

Asia is an assault on the ears. Unless you pack industrial-strength earmuffs, not much can completely block out the symphony of snoring that emanates from the hard-bed class of a train in China. Earplugs do soften the blow, however, and they are also useful for communal televisions in guesthouse lobbies, karaoke going full blast, calls to prayer in Muslim regions and music blaring from speakers in trains and buses. Sometimes the music is fun, but often the decibel level is so high your nerves get as tight as the skin stretched across you ear drum, especially after hearing the theme song from *Titanic* over and over again, which is enough to drive even the most tolerant traveller crazy.

Often drivers will let you put your music into the tape machine, though don't be offended if they toss it back unceremoniously after a couple of tunes. So the man at the wheel isn't ready for Joni Mitchell? Try the Propellerheads. There are few drivers in the world who can resist throbbing bass lines. Hang on to your seat! Of course, some of the machines might end up eating your tape. If you really want a challenge, try getting your music played on a Chinese train, though in some cases that might entail packing some old vinyl albums.

MARIE CAMBON
LP AUTHOR, CANADA

sentence or, in some places, the death penalty. There are enough foreign travellers lingering in Asian jails as it is; don't add to their numbers.

The dangers involved in attempting to buy drugs are that the dealer may be the police or a police informer, or may simply rip you off. You will be lucky to bribe your way out of the hands of the police (for several hundred dollars), and it's just as likely that you'll be prosecuted for possession or even smuggling.

Also, be careful of other travellers or local criminals using you as a mule to smuggle drugs by placing them in your pack. It's a good idea to check your pack carefully before any border crossing or plane flight; never accept gifts from strangers, however charming they may be. Lastly, do not fall victim to the temptation to buy cheap drugs in Asia to sell at home – the customs people in your home country will probably inspect your gear closely when they see that you've spent time in South-East Asia or on the Indian subcontinent.

For information on the potential health risks of drug use, see Alcohol & Drugs in the Health chapter.

Sexual Harassment

For the most part, travelling by yourself is a richly rewarding and usually safe experience. As a woman you face subtle discrimination in your everyday life anyway, and are likely to be perfectly familiar with the behaviour you encounter on the road. This won't necessarily make it any easier to deal with, especially if you're feeling lonely or homesick. As with all travel, care and precautions are essential. If you're a lone female, or a woman travelling with a female friend, consider how to deal with the most common forms of harassment – lewd looks, touching and unwanted advances. Researching the culture you're planning to travel in can help you avoid much of this.

Attitudes towards women vary across Asia. In South-East Asia, women play an active role in day-to-day public life. Provided you dress appropriately and treat people with respect, you are unlikely to encounter problems. Nevertheless, women can experience some difficulties in Sumatra, along the east coast of Malaysia and in the southern Philippines – all Muslim areas – so extra care should be taken in these places.

In other countries you may encounter more severe problems. In India, for example, you will probably be the butt of provocative comments, or groping and inappropriate body contact in crowded places. Travel in Pakistan can be particularly hard work for women, though even here serious harassment or sexual assault are rare. Following local practices – such as wearing a light scarf to cover the hair and chest in conservative company and in mosques, not shaking hands with a new male friend and keeping eye contact to a minimum – can smooth your interactions with locals.

Dress is an especially important aspect of travel in Asia. Clothes that expose the thighs, shoulders or breasts are considered improper, and beach wear should be reserved for the beach. While it may appear unfair to tailor your dress according to the perceptions of others, a little sensitivity can not only protect you from harassment, but will show respect to the people of the country you are visiting. For more advice on culturally suitable clothing, see the Avoiding Offence section earlier in this chapter and the boxed text 'Dressing Appropriately' in the What to Bring chapter.

Women should also take extra care not to find themselves alone on empty beaches, alone in dark streets or in any other situation where help might not be

YOU CAN BE TOO CAREFUL ...

One day as I was walking along a busy road in Agra, home of the Taj Mahal, I happened upon two young girls playing badminton. They invited me to join them in their game, and we were soon chatting and laughing. Inevitably, they invited me into their home to meet their family. A chair was quickly found for me, and a glass of steaming chai placed in my hand. They told me they were a Christian family, and when I told them I had been brought up as a Christian (albeit a somewhat lapsed one), they warmly took my hands and declared that I was their 'daughter' and 'sister'. Would I do them the honour of sharing their evening meal with them? Of course I would love to! The father of the household arrived, and I was introduced to him. I told him I was staying at the Hotel Ashok, and he said that he knew the brother of the manager there. Meanwhile, the neighbours appeared in the doorway, anxious to meet the Australian visitor.

I told the family I was leaving on the train that evening for Varanasi, and would return to my guesthouse to pick up my backpack, then rejoin the family for the evening meal before walking to the train station. The son of the household offered to drive me back to my guesthouse. While checking out, the manager, who knew I wasn't due to leave until that evening, asked where I was going. I explained I had been invited to dine with a family. He looked suspiciously over at the Indian youth and his idling motorbike. I explained that it was OK, as the boy's father knew the manager's brother, whereupon the manager informed me he didn't have a brother.

I was thrown into great confusion. It seemed impossible that this generous and warm family could be lying. The manager explained that new visitors to India were often fooled by these elaborate scams, and that I definitely shouldn't get back on the motorbike. Feeling terrible, I told the son that I couldn't return with him to his home, and to please apologise to his family.

Resolutely I walked away. I knew that the family was genuine, that there had been a terrible misunderstanding. But I was a woman travelling alone in India. And I'd read and absorbed all the warnings in the guidebooks. I spent a miserable evening alone in my room, and at midnight, made my way to the train station. And there, waiting on the platform, was the entire family. They thrust gifts at me, forced bangles over my wrists, and necklaces into my hands. The youngest daughter, crying, asked me for my address so that she could write to me. For years I received letters addressed to 'my Australian sister'. Later I learnt that there are two Hotel Ashoks in Agra, and the father of the household evidently knew the brother of the manager at the other hotel.

It *is* important to be on your guard when travelling. It is true that there are people whose main objective in life is to separate you from your possessions. However, while constructing a wall of suspicion between yourself and the people of your host country may protect you from thieves, it can also, as I learnt at that station, rob you of genuine opportunities for interaction and friendship.

MICHELLE COXALL
LP AUTHOR, AUSTRALIA

available. Keep some cash on you at all times, in case you want to take a taxi back to your hotel or guesthouse. Above all, try to stick to your own moral code. As an outsider, some people may feel that it's OK to touch or bully you. Assertive behaviour is often the best reaction – don't allow yourself to be pushed around or made to feel like a victim. If you are clear about your rules, others will soon get the message.

Remember, you're travelling to see and experience new cultures, and you can't do that if you're entirely protected and afraid to meet people's eyes.

Other Hazards

There are a host of other hazards to be aware of in Asia, almost all of which you can avoid through careful research and by taking the proper precautions.

LANDMINES – In Cambodia, Vietnam, Laos, Myanmar and Sri Lanka, unexploded landmines are a grim reminder of past wars and ongoing military conflicts. Fortunately, most landmines are in areas off-limits to travellers. Avoid restricted areas and never trek into an area about which you are unsure.

ROAD AMBUSHES AND INSURGENT ACTIVITY – Political instability and/or extreme poverty mean the possibility of attacks by insurgent groups in Cambodia, Myanmar, Indonesia, Pakistan, Kashmir in northern India, the Philippines and in Sri Lanka. Keep abreast of the news and stay well clear of trouble zones.

RIOTS – In the period leading up to elections in some countries (most commonly India and Indonesia) there may be street riots. Likewise, occasional antiwestern or anti-American riots occur in Pakistan.

PACKS OF WILD OR STRAY DOGS – These are a danger in many parts of Asia, including some cities (such as Kathmandu). Be especially careful when walking at night and avoid venturing out alone. If followed by dogs, shelter in a building as soon as possible.

MACHO POSTURING – In Vietnam and Korea local men may take offence at seeing a western man with an Asian woman (even if the woman is western born or raised), and may make rude comments or even try to pick a fight. Avoid holding hands and stay away from local drinking spots.

COAL FIRES – Several travellers have died from suffocation or carbon monoxide poisoning in poorly ventilated guesthouses where coal fires are used for heating. If you cannot avoid a coal fire, make sure the room is adequately ventilated by leaving a window partly open.

UNSAFE DRIVERS – Don't ever let the compulsion to 'just get there' get in the way of your better instincts. And it's not simply the drivers of vehicles in which you travel that you must be wary of; take care when crossing roads, walking around cities and riding bicycles.

Annoyances

There are myriad day-to-day annoyances that can make your trip unpleasant if you can't handle them. These range from the hoards of touts who besiege you in India, to the staring squads in China who ogle you as though you were a zoo exhibit. Since there's little you can do to change people's behaviour, the best solution is to steel yourself to the inevitable.

NOISE — Many Asian people seem able to tolerate a lot more noise than westerners, and you may find noise levels uncomfortable in many cities. The Asian habit of listening to the TV or radio at full blast can also be extremely annoying. One of the best defences against the onslaught is a good pair of earplugs (cigarette filters will do in a pinch).

TOUTS — Although they may occasionally help you find a decent place to stay, touts are more often than not a pain in the neck. They're particularly active in South-East Asia and on the subcontinent. The best way to deal with touts is to tell them politely but firmly that you don't need their help, or that you have a reservation elsewhere.

STARING SQUADS — In China and India and a few other countries, the locals have no compunction about staring at you for hours on end. They may even call friends and relatives over to join in the fun. You'll find the problem much worse in rural areas than in cities. There's little you can do but ignore them. If this really gets to you, head to Thailand or Japan where things aren't so bad.

BEGGAR FATIGUE — You may become very depressed by the constant stream of beggars asking for money or goods in Asia's poorer countries. See the Poverty & Begging section earlier in this chapter for some advice on how to deal with begging.

SPITTING — In China, you'll have to get used to the Chinese habit of spitting. Not only is it disgusting, but it can pass on diseases like the bronchitis and flu endemic to the country.

LACK OF QUEUES — In many countries, instead of forming a nice even line, people form a huge mass and elbow their way to the front. Either join the fray or use foreigners' queues where they're available.

POLLUTION — Air pollution can be almost unbearable in some Asian cities, especially in India, Bangladesh, China and the Philippines. Air pollution can aggravate asthma, coughs, colds, sinus problems and cause eye irritation. If you suffer from any of these, consider wearing a surgical mask, as is the custom in some countries.

If You Do Get Into Trouble ...

If the worst happens and you're the victim of a crime or some other disaster, try to take decisive steps to set things right as quickly as possible. As long as you are physically in one piece, the simple fact that you are taking action will go a long way towards making you feel better. You can always enlist the assistance of another traveller or trustworthy local, and you may be surprised how helpful others can be when you're in need.

If something has been stolen or you've been the victim of any other crime, immediately report it to the police, or in China the Public Security Bureau (PSB). Even if you've lost your passport, you will need a police report so you can get a new passport. A report may also be necessary for replacing travellers cheques or claiming on insurance.

In the case of lost or stolen passports, you should also go to your country's embassy or consulate, which can issue you a new passport, advise you about local laws, put you in touch with English-speaking lawyers or doctors, and contact friends or relatives back home in the case of an emergency. They will not, however, lend you money, get you out of jail or pay to fly you home (except in extraordinary circumstances).

Dealing with the day-to-day realities of accommodation, transportation, and even getting a decent meal can be a hassle while you're on the road. However, since there's no escaping these daily tasks, it's a good idea to arm yourself with a little knowledge to make them as painless as possible. In this section, we provide some basic tips on finding good accommodation and a tasty meal, and moving around as safely and as comfortably as possible. Once you get these things sorted out, you can concentrate on having a great time experiencing the incredible people and places of Asia.

ACCOMMODATION

Accommodation will be your greatest day-to-day concern. Without question, there are a lot of really horrid places out there – the kind that make for great drinking stories, but tortured, sleepless nights. Luckily, there is plenty of clean, cheap and comfortable accommodation right across Asia. In this section, we outline the types of accommodation available, and provide tips on discerning the good from the bad and on keeping your valuables secure.

Types of Accommodation

Accommodation ranges from five-star hotels in Hong Kong to *ger* (traditional tents) on the Mongolian steppes. You could stay in a maharaja's palace in Rajasthan, an atmospheric wooden *ryokan* (traditional inn) in Japan, a mountain teahouse in Nepal or a bamboo beach hut in Thailand. At the less salubrious end of the scale, you could also sample a sweaty concrete box with broken plumbing in China or a flea-infested, overpriced dormitory in Malaysia. Shelling out just a little more cash will often mean the difference between holing up in a rat-trap or relaxing in a cleaner place with some amenities. For example, in Indian cities you can find single rooms for about US$3, but you'll often have to put up with pretty dire conditions. However, if you're willing to pay twice this amount, you can get a clean, quiet room, sometimes with air-conditioning and attached bath. Likewise, in Vietnam US$8 or perhaps less will get you a room in a dubious hotel, while US$12 is often enough to get a clean room in a decent hotel.

When weighing up your options for where to stay, a little imagination and effort can transform a necessity into an adventure. It's always easy to settle for the characterless hotel next door to the train station, but a little research and initiative might see you bedding down in atmospheric traditional lodgings. Of course, it's not always practical to search for such places, and they may not even exist in some countries, but where they do you can count on a memorable experience.

Guesthouses

You'll probably spend more nights in guesthouses than in any other type of accommodation. Whole neighbourhoods of guesthouses exist in the cities of India, Indonesia, Malaysia, Nepal, the Philippines, Thailand and Vietnam. These include private homes with a few converted rooms, and large purpose-built structures with extensive facilities. Guesthouses usually cater specifically to foreign budget travellers, so they tend to be inexpensive, at ease with the ways of foreigners, fairly comfortable and good places to meet fellow travellers. Often they'll have a range of convenient services like left-luggage, fax, Internet, post restante, notice boards, laundry and perhaps even a travel agency. They almost always have a restaurant and common area.

Rooms in guesthouses tend to be quite simple, usually with little more than a bed, a ceiling fan and maybe a sink. Shared toilet and bath facilities are often the rule, but in some places a little extra money can get you a room with an en suite toilet and bath. Guesthouse rooms can be depressingly character-less, but as you'll be using them mainly for sleeping and stowing your luggage, you'll probably find them quite adequate. A typical room costs from US$2 to US$5 per night, though prices vary widely across Asia. You can save money by sharing a double or staying in a guesthouse dormitory.

A drawback to guesthouse accommodation is that you'll be surrounded by other travellers and largely cut off from the everyday life of the country you're visiting. This is especially true in the backpacker ghettos of Ho Chi Minh City, Bangkok, Kathmandu, Denpasar and Delhi. Such places tend to be almost interchangeable, with the same types of restaurants serving similar food (you'll start to wonder if backpackers subsist entirely on muesli and banana pancakes) and providing similar services to an amorphous clientele. If this gets you down, search for accommodation in a different neighbourhood. You can always check into a guesthouse for your first night in a city and use it as a base while you look for something preferable.

Hotels

Hotels in Asia range from Bangkok's luxurious Oriental Hotel to truly shocking dives complete with bedbugs, dirty sheets and filthy toilets. Unlike guesthouses, hotels usually cater to local or international business travellers and may not be used to backpackers. Nonetheless, hotels are usually a dependable option and may be the only accommodation available in some areas.

Most hotels have a variety of rooms. The cheaper rooms usually have fans and shared bathrooms, while the more expensive have air-conditioners and en suite bathrooms, and possibly a TV. The cheaper fan rooms are usually adequate (except when the heat is truly oppressive). You will often also have the choice of single, double and twin rooms. A single is usually a room with one single bed, but it can also be a room with one double bed (this is often the case in cheap Chinese hotels, where a couple can sometimes economise by asking for a single). A double usually means a room with one large double bed, but can also be a room with two single beds (again, especially in Chinese hotels). A twin is almost always a room with two single beds, and is usually more expensive than a single or double room. Many hotels also have a few large rooms which can hold three or more people for a very reasonable price.

Hotels vary as much in price as they do in quality. You can easily fork out US$1000 for a night in one of the swanky hotels in Tokyo, Hong Kong or Singapore, although there are plenty of hotel rooms in these cities for less than US$100. In the cheaper countries of Asia (such as Thailand, Indonesia and Vietnam), plan on spending from US$7 to US$20 for a room in a modest hotel, though cheaper places do exist. Wherever you are, it pays to compare different hotels. The cheapest place in town might be truly horrific, while its slightly more expensive neighbour is fine. Likewise, a hotel will often have different grades of rooms. A good tactic is simply to ask, 'Do you have a nicer room?' Often you'll be shown a significantly better room that costs only slightly more.

Some hotels in Vietnam and China are not legally permitted to accept

'REAL' TRAVELLERS

Spend enough time on the road and you'll definitely run into a few 'real travellers'. These are people who think they've been everywhere there is to go, done everything there is to do, and seen everything there is to see. More importantly, they like to think they did it the right way (read: the hard way). The problem with 'real travellers' (who invariably are men) is that not only do they insist on boring you with their tales of derring-do, but they tend to look down their noses at other travellers.

If you tell them you're going, say, to Ko Tao in Thailand, they'll tell you shouldn't bother — the place was good 10 years ago, but it's a total bust today. They know a better island in Indonesia that you can only get to by swimming. Of course they won't tell you where it is, because that would ruin the spot. Likewise, if you say you're staying near Kuta in Bali, they'll tell you the place is strictly for tourists, a 'real traveller' wouldn't go near the place. They know a much better place in an uninhabited part of the island where the rent is free, everyone plays an instrument and the vibes are *shanti* (peaceful). Again, they can't tell you where it is since that would attract the wrong sort of people.

You'll find that 'real travellers' like to think of themselves as Stanley or Livingston types pushing out alone into untrammelled wilderness, where no westerner has been before (an unlikely situation these days). Oddly enough, the only place you seem to meet 'real travellers' is in the travellers ghettos, like Bangkok's Khao San Rd or Kathmandu's Thamel. Of course, they're only passing through — they wouldn't dream of spending too much time in such places.

The point is that your trip need not be a gruelling test of survival. Nor is it a competition to find the last untouched spot in the country. If that's what you're after, fine. But there's nothing wrong with seeing the famous sights of a region (along with everyone else) or treating yourself to some luxury. And don't let yourself be intimidated or belittled by these people; if you find that you can't stand the company of a 'real traveller' any longer, try telling them that you eat mostly at McDonald's, insist on air-con wherever you stay and wouldn't dream of travelling anything but 1st class. More than likely they'll quickly lose interest in you.

CHRIS ROWTHORN
LP AUTHOR, JAPAN

foreign guests and may refuse to take you. Other places, such as some top-end hotels in India, may not want to accept backpackers. If you really want to stay at one of these places, try calling ahead for a reservation, or leave your luggage elsewhere and smarten up before you approach reception.

Some cheap hotels in Asia double as brothels, although it can be difficult to tell at first look. The facilities are often acceptable enough, but women may feel uncomfortable staying in them and could be harassed. If you have any doubts about a particular place, ask at the local tourist office.

Hostels

Hostels aren't nearly as popular in Asia as they are in the west because there is so much other cheap accommodation. Fortunately, the more expensive countries (Japan, Korea, Hong Kong, Singapore and Taiwan) all have decent youth hostel systems. There are also some good youth hostels in India.

Hostels usually offer both private and dormitory rooms (the latter can be very noisy). If you're travelling alone, you'll pay quite a bit for a private room, but if you can get a group of two or three together to share a room, you may pay no more than for a spot in the dormitory. Some hostels include breakfast and sometimes even dinner in the price of accommodation. If you'd rather eat elsewhere, try for a reduced price for the room only. Be very careful with your belongings in hostels – particularly in dormitories – as theft can be a problem. See Other Paperwork in the Passports & Visas chapter for information on the Hostelling International (HI) card.

Homestays

Staying in the home of a local family is one of the best antidotes to guesthouse fatigue. It is also a great opening into the local culture. Depending upon the country, homestays are organised either through official agencies (usually in the more wealthy countries) or on an impromptu basis simply by asking to stay or by being invited (as in rural areas of the Philippines and Indonesia). However,

IT'S BETTER TO GIVE ...

It's common practice to offer a gift when staying with a local family (a homestay) during your travels. After all, you're basically receiving a free – or very cheap – room and board, simply because the family is eager to meet foreign visitors. A thoughtful gift will go a long way towards showing your gratitude and will make your stay more rewarding and memorable for both you and your hosts. The best gift is something special to your own country which is difficult or impossible to obtain in your host's country. Unfortunately, the things which best fit this description are often heavy or bulky – just imagine carting several bottles of your country's best wine around Asia in your backpack.So consider lighter, more compact items such as postage stamps, phonecards, picture books or even coins. Of course, these go over best with the kids. In most parts of Asia, adults (particularly men) are more eager for western alcohol and cigarettes. Although you may have mixed feelings about such gifts, this may be a good time to put aside your scruples and think pragmatically.

homestay accommodation isn't perfect. You will have very little privacy and must always be on your best behaviour, which can be tiresome when you just want to be left alone. On the other hand, you will gain an insight into the daily lives and routines of ordinary people. And in remote places, this may be the only accommodation available. The best way to locate homestays is to check in guidebooks or ask at local tourist offices.

Beach Bungalows

If you spend any time on the popular beaches of Thailand, Indonesia, Malaysia or the Philippines, you'll probably stay in bungalows. These are similar to guesthouses in operation, but instead of everyone being clustered together under one roof, each guest or group of guests has a private bungalow. Bungalows are usually simple affairs of wood, bamboo or thatch, although some newer ones may be concrete or brick. Amenities may include fan, air-con, en suite bathrooms and mosquito netting on the windows (as opposed to nets which hang over the beds, or none at all). You may find that you need very few amenities – probably the most important features are a nice balcony, a comfortable hammock and a waterfront location.

Bungalows tend to be very inexpensive, although prices can skyrocket during the tourist season. Expect to pay from US$2 to US$5 in the low season and from US$5 to US$20 in the high season.

Camping

Camping is a great way to save money while you're travelling in Asia. It also allows you to explore remote areas and is just about a necessity if you head off the beaten track in Nepal, Mongolia, Indonesia or Malaysia. Surprisingly, camping is also possible in such urban areas as Singapore and Hong Kong (though they are not the most beautiful places you'll ever pitch a tent). The downside to camping is that you have to lug your tent everywhere you go, and this can be a real burden in hot weather. Consider carefully whether you will need a tent, and make sure you use a lightweight backpacker model. For more information on tents, see Nonessential Equipment in the What to Bring chapter.

Other Types of Accommodation

The standard types of accommodation only scratch the surface of where you can stay in Asia. Some other options are:

RAILWAY RETIRING ROOMS – These are small hotels or dormitories in train buildings in India and Pakistan, which are often cheap and sometimes quite comfortable. You are supposed to have a rail pass or ticket to stay in these rooms, but you can sometimes get around this. The main problem is that the rooms are almost always full.

GOVERNMENT RESTHOUSES – Remnants of the Raj era, these large and often comfortable lodgings can be found in India, Pakistan, Bangladesh, Malaysia and Sri Lanka, often in stunning, if slightly remote, spots. While many are supposed to be for government use only, you can often stay if they are vacant or you have booked (call ahead or check with the local tourist office).

SAUNAS – In Japan, Korea and Taiwan, it may be possible to stay in an all-night sauna. You pay an all-inclusive admission price and are free to stay as long as you want (which means crashing out on a vacant reclining chair until morning, as many locals do). Most saunas cater to men only.

TEAHOUSES – These combination restaurant/guesthouses are found in the mountains of Nepal. Many specialise in serving foreign trekkers, particularly on the more popular treks like the Annapurna Circuit and the Everest Base Camp trek. In Nepal's more remote areas, you'll have the pleasure of sampling teahouses that still cater primarily to Tibetan and Nepali traders, and these are often just open rooms with a central fire and a few mats for sleeping.

MOUNTAIN HUTS – Both Japan and Korea have excellent hut systems for mountain trekkers. In Korea, these tend to be simple, inexpensive affairs, while in Japan they can be quite elaborate and cost up to US$70 per night, including two meals.

YOGWAN (OR YOINSUK) – These simple, traditional guesthouses in Korea cater primarily to low-budget Korean travellers. Most places will accept foreigners, but almost certainly no English will be spoken. You'll find them around train and bus stations, but be warned that some are used as brothels.

RYOKAN & MINSHUKU – These traditional Japanese inns are infinitely more atmospheric than hotels or youth hostels. While minshuku are simple, inexpensive places, often converted from private homes, ryokan are grand old buildings where a stay can cost up to US$500 a night. At both, breakfast and dinner are usually included in the price.

GER – A stay in a traditional Mongolian tent-house may well qualify as your most exotic night on the road. There is a distinct etiquette to staying in a ger, so read up in the appropriate guidebooks before heading out to the steppes. If you want a slightly less traditional experience, try spending a night in a tourist ger.

Finding the Right Place

Finding a place for the night is a tiresome task, especially if you've just travelled for 12 hours on a bumpy road or tramped all morning around a hot, crowded city. Nonetheless, since a good night's sleep is essential to maintaining your health and sanity while on the road, it's worth mustering up the energy to locate a clean, comfortable room.

Use an accurate, up-to-date guidebook and talk to fellow travellers to find the best budget accommodation. A decent guidebook will have listings of several kinds of accommodation in different parts of town. You'll soon discover if these write-ups are accurate and if they cater to your personal taste.

You can also ask at tourist offices and at airport accommodation counters. In some countries – such as Japan, Singapore and Korea – these sources will provide reliable, unbiased information. In many others – such as Thailand, the Philippines and Vietnam – staff will send you to places that pay them a commission, and these can be both expensive and of dubious quality. Finally, taxi and rickshaw drivers may give you information or take you directly to a place to stay, but they also will probably be receiving a commission. Try to clarify with the driver exactly what you are willing to pay and the type of place you're looking for before he takes you anywhere. Generally, you should only rely on these sources as a last resort.

In most towns in Asia, you'll find accommodation clustered around train and bus stations, which can be very convenient when you first arrive. Other options are the backpacker ghettos of larger cities (see Guesthouses earlier in this chapter). When searching for accommodation, it pays to be choosy. If there is a range of options, check out a few before making up your mind. This is easiest when you have a travelling partner; one of you can stay with the bags while the other searches for a room.

Also, try to time your arrival for before noon, or even earlier, when there will probably still be some rooms available. If all the rooms are taken, you can ask to be put on a waiting list, or try a different part of town. If you cannot find the accommodation you want, you may have to shell out for something in a different price bracket, if only for one night.

Inspecting the Room

Before paying for a room you should definitely ask to inspect it. Failing to do so is a sure way to end up in truly horrific surroundings. If the first room you see is not to your liking, ask to see another – this will often yield good results. When you inspect a room, you should check the following:

CLEANLINESS – Have a close look at the toilet, under the bed and between the sheets. In particular, look for any evidence of insect infestation (looking at the mattress itself is a good idea).

FACILITIES – Does everything work? Check the lights, the fan or air-con, the hot and cold water taps, the toilet and shower. If you are near the sea, make sure the taps run fresh water.

SAFETY & SECURITY – Can you escape in the event of fire? Check for fire exits, ladders, and windows and doors that open and close properly. Does it have a good lock on the door, or a place to mount your own padlock? Make sure the windows are barred or lockable and that any other doors leading into the room are locked or sealed.

NOISE LEVEL – There may be a busy street, market, mosque or bar nearby. Usually, you'll find that the rooms on the upper floors near the back of the hotel are the quietest.

PEEPHOLES – Are there any holes in the walls or ceilings? In some cheaper guesthouses and hotels, you'll find holes in some rooms or bathrooms that are used to spy on guests. If possible, move to another place, or plug the holes with toilet paper.

MOSQUITO PREVENTION – Are there any holes in the screens on the windows or in the mosquito net over the bed? Check also for other ways mosquitoes can enter the room, like spaces under the doors and holes in the ceiling.

COMFORT – Give the bed a try. Pace the floors. Imagine spending time in the room. If it passes this final test, then you're ready to check in (or at least to start haggling over the price).

Negotiating a Rate

When you decide on a room, double-check the price and ask about any hidden costs, such as taxes and service charges. In many countries, cheaper places do not levy additional fees, but in others you may have to pay tax, service charges and perhaps even a few other 'adjustment charges' (Vietnam is notorious for this). Ask for the total price, and even ask for it to be written down in case of later discrepancies.

Depending upon the country, the type of accommodation and the season, you may be able to negotiate the price of your room. High and low tourist season pricing policies apply to many countries in Asia, not only in the tourist hotspots like Bali and Ko Samui, but in tiny guesthouses across the continent. In the high season, guesthouse owners may not be willing to negotiate at all. In most budget places, especially in South-East Asia and on the subcontinent, when business is slow you have a good chance of a reduction (for some tips on bargaining see the Money Matters chapter). One of the best opening gambits is to simply ask, 'Is that your best price?' and then wait patiently for an answer. If there are other options nearby and you're getting nowhere, try walking slowly to the door – more often than not, you'll be called back with a better offer.

Checking In

In most Asian countries, you'll have to fill in a form upon checking in. Forms are generally straightforward, though in China they might call for more detail than a university application. In Vietnam, you may also be asked to leave your passport and visa at reception to ensure you pay your bill and in case it is required by government or police officials. This policy varies from region to region, so check in your guidebook.

If at all possible, do not hand over your passport or visa, as these may be misplaced, lost or stolen. Instead, leave a photocopy of your passport, or another form of identification such as a student ID card or an expired passport. If the passport is being asked for as security against your bill, offer a cash deposit instead and get a signed receipt. If you absolutely must leave your passport, get a signed receipt listing both the passport and whatever visas it contains. You should also be given a receipt if you are asked to pay upon check-in for that night's lodgings.

Security

It is always risky to leave valuables like your passport, visas, credit cards, cash, travellers cheques and camera in your room when you go out. If you don't want to carry your valuables around, you could leave them in a safety deposit box at the hotel. Ask other travellers or check in your guidebook to be sure the hotel can be trusted. You should get a signed receipt detailing the contents and value of everything you put in the safety deposit box.

If you're unsure about the security of your room, use your own lock. If the security of the room is really questionable, it might be time to find a better place to stay.

Lastly, we recommend that you lock your room from the inside when you're in it, especially before you go to sleep (provided you can easily unlock it in the case of fire). This prevents thieves from sneaking in and thwarts surprise intrusions by hotel staff or guests (Chinese hotel employees are particularly notorious for this).

Bathrooms & Toilets

As with most other aspects of Asian life, you'll find that the 'facilities' in Asia range from breathtakingly modern to downright primitive (with most places a lot closer to the latter).

Bathrooms

While most mid-range and upper-end hotels have showers and baths similar to those in hotels back home, backpacker places are much more likely to have only shared showers or other communal bathing facilities, such as baths or the Indonesian *mandi* (large cisterns of water from which you scoop water over your body). In many parts of Asia, you'll also find public washing places outside your guesthouse. These range from the public bathhouses of Korea and Japan to the rivers and streams which are used as washrooms by villagers across the

ON THE THRONE IN JAPAN

You can tell a lot about a culture by its toilets and nowhere is this more the case than in Japan. Just as Japanese communities range from the thatched-roof villages of Hokkaido to the ultramodern metropolis of Tokyo, so too Japanese toilets run the gamut from stone-age primitive to space-age hi-tech.

I remember visiting my Japanese teacher's house long before I had any real grasp of the written language. After dinner, I begged off to do some business in the bathroom. On opening the bathroom door, I was greeted by a futuristic toilet the likes of which I'd never seen. Instead of the simple flush handle that we're used to in the west, this toilet had a control panel with an alarming range of functions. Needless to say, everything was written in Japanese. Daunting as it was, nature was calling and I figured I could work out these intricacies, so I sat down and did what I had to do.

As I was seated, I noticed that one of the buttons on the control panel had a little picture on it resembling a fountain. 'Ahah,' I thought, 'that must be the bidet function'. Never having tried a bidet, I thought I'd give it a whirl. So, I hit the button and was immediately hit by a rather surprising jet of hot water. I figured this thing ran on some kind of timer and would soon turn itself off, but it showed no signs of tiring. I searched the control panel frantically for some sort of 'stop the bidet' button but was met by an incomprehensible array of squirls and scribbles. I was well and truly trapped – if I stood up to flee the maniacal bidet, I feared it would reach all the way to the ceiling and soak the bathroom. Calling for help wasn't really an option here. What could my teacher do, short of invading the bathroom to rescue me?

Finally, in desperation, I decided to take a chance on a likely looking button near the bidet button. To my great relief, the stream stopped and I was free. When I finally made it back to the table, my teacher looked at me a little quizzically. After a few minutes of small talk I asked, 'Just out of interest, how do you write 'stop' in Japanese?' She's a smart woman, and I think she got the picture.

CHRIS ROWTHORN
LP AUTHOR, JAPAN

continent. A visit to a communal bathing place can be a great cultural experience, but be sure to respect local customs; while nudity is accepted in Korea and Japan, it is strictly forbidden on the subcontinent and in South-East Asia. Also keep in mind the following:

- The public baths of Japan and Korea are a great way to relax after a day of travelling, but there is a definite etiquette to bathing at these places. Most importantly, since the water in the tub is used by everyone, it is important to wash and rinse your body thoroughly before climbing into the tub (there are taps nearby where you can wash yourself, otherwise you can pour buckets of water from the tub over yourself). Likewise, when visiting a hot-spring bath in these countries, remember to wash yourself before entering the tub. The same holds true for baths in guesthouses, inns, youth hostels and private homes.

- If you insist on bathing in the nude while in rural areas, make sure you are out of sight of any locals. If this is not possible, then wash yourself without removing all your clothes. For men, boxer shorts will do; for women, a sarong will come in handy. You can always dry off in your tent.

- Avoid the temptation to take too many hot showers while trekking in the Himalaya. Most places in the mountains heat their water with wood and this contributes to deforestation.

- Check the walls and ceiling of the bathroom in the guesthouse or hotel in which you plan to stay. Peeping Toms are not unknown, and suspicious holes in the ceiling or walls are usually an indication that you should find another place to stay.

Toilets

Outside the wealthier countries like Singapore, Japan, Taiwan, Korea and Malaysia, you'll be looking at fairly simple and often rather grim toilets. In particular, you'll find some truly apocalyptic bogs in countries like India, Nepal and China. While western-style toilets prevail in mid-range and upper-end hotels across the continent, simple squat toilets (often no more than holes in the floor) are the rule in most parts of Asia. While these take some getting used to, you'll certainly appreciate the fact that squat toilets are significantly more hygienic than western-style toilets.

Most Asian people do not use toilet paper, but instead use water and their hands. Thus, you will undoubtedly come across many toilets which are not supplied with toilet paper. Instead, you'll usually find a cistern and a bowl for scooping the water out. The drill here is to hold the bowl underneath you and then use your left hand to splash some water onto your behind (this explains the general prohibition against eating or shaking hands with your left hand in much of Asia). If you find this practice distasteful, bring your own toilet paper with you, as many travellers do. Keep in mind, though, that many Asian plumbing systems are not designed to cope with toilet paper. For this reason, guesthouses often have a separate bin for used paper; otherwise, you can put it in a bag to dispose of later. Women should deal with sanitary products in the same way.

A few other things to keep in mind are:

- Wherever you travel, you'll find that toilets are much better in hotels and guesthouses than in public places like train stations and on the trains themselves. It's a good idea to take advantage of good facilities when you have the chance. In big cities, the toilets in fast-food restaurants are often a good solution when you can't find anything better.

- When trekking in rural or wilderness areas, try to use established toilet facilities. If you must go to the bathroom out in the open, be sure to go at least 50m from streams or rivers and make sure to bury or burn both your waste and your paper.

- In some countries, like Japan and Korea, you'll find that common slippers are provided for wearing in bathrooms. Try to avoid the all-too-common gaff of forgetting to remove them and wandering around with them on.

- Although public urination is common in some parts of Asia, you'd be a fool to give it a whirl in Singapore where you'll be slapped with a heavy fine.

FOOD

A major highlight of Asian travel is sampling the wonderful and diverse foods. Whether it be spicy *tom yam kung* (prawn, lemongrass and mushroom soup) in Bangkok, fresh *sushi* in Tokyo, steamed *dim sum* in Hong Kong, or banana leaf curry in Kerala in south-west India, you could travel around Asia with your eyes closed and have a marvellous time just breathing in the aromas of cooking. A stroll through any South-East Asian market will reveal a myriad of fruits and vegetables you may never have heard of, let alone tasted, from the bearded rambutan to the pungent durian.

This isn't to say that all your meals in Asia will be delicious. No doubt you'll have plenty that are memorably bad. The diet in rural areas can be excruciatingly monotonous (infinite variations on fried rice and noodles). Worse, it's possible to become sick from eating improperly stored or prepared foods or by drinking contaminated liquids (see Everyday Health in the Health chapter for details of food and waterborne illnesses and how to avoid them). Don't get too paranoid, though; most foods and drinks are perfectly safe. It pays to be adventurous and try some exotic foods, even when you don't speak a word of the local language. There'll times when you're served up pigeon giblets when you thought you were ordering Beijing duck, but usually you will be rewarded with a tasty meal.

Local Food

We're assuming that you didn't travel all the way to Asia to dine every night on hamburgers and chips. Eating local dishes is not always as easy as ordering a burger at McDonald's (you may not be able to read the menu to start with), but it is far more enjoyable than relying on western standards, and infinitely cheaper.

A good guidebook will contain details of the food and drinks of the country in which you are travelling, plus a section explaining proper eating etiquette and types of eating places. Most important is a section listing the names of some common dishes, written in both English and that country's language, which you can point to when ordering in restaurants. It should also have a language section with useful phrases for ordering food, such as 'What do you recommend?' and 'I don't eat meat'. It will also list specific places to eat. If a restaurant appears in a guidebook, the staff will be comfortable with foreigners and may even speak a word or two of English. See the Ordering Meals entry later in this chapter for more details.

The staff at your hotel or guesthouse may be able to recommend a good place, though they may simply send you somewhere that serves western food, believing that you cannot eat local food. Another option is to eat where the locals do. If everyone in town crowds into a particular spot at lunchtime, then it's a pretty sure sign that the food is good. Just follow them in, point at what they're having and dig in. Alternatively, ask at the local tourist office. Expats also can be excellent sources of information on the good places to eat and drink in town.

Types of Eating Places

Eating places in Asia are as varied as the countries themselves. One night may find you in an automatic sushi diner in Tokyo, while later in your trip you may be sitting around a campfire in Pakistan eating grilled goat. A real delight of Asian dining is that much of it is done outdoors. Just try the famous hawker centres of Singapore for an experience of inexpensive and delicious outside dining. Listed below are some of the most common types of eating places in Asia:

HAWKER CENTRES AND NIGHT MARKETS – Most common in South-East Asia, these are places where food sellers with carts or stalls gather around a common seating area. Most of these are outdoor, but you'll find upscale hawker centres in department stores and shopping malls in some of the more affluent countries. It's hard to beat hawker centres and night markets for their variety of tasty dishes and reasonable prices.

RESTAURANTS – An Asian restaurant could be a giant dim sum hall in Hong Kong or a roadside shack in the Philippines. Crowds of diners usually indicate that the food is both safe to eat and tasty.

STREET VENDORS – You'll seldom be far from a street vendor in the cities. Vendors sell all manner of snacks, fruits and vegetables and sometimes even full meals, all at very low prices. Treat them with caution, however, as goods sold on the street have been the source of more than a few cases of 'Delhi Belly'.

COFFEESHOPS – Often run by Chinese, these places serve coffee and tea and a limited range of foods, eg fried rice and noodle dishes. You'll find them throughout South-East Asia and China.

HOTELS – Both western-style and local restaurants can be found in Asian hotels. Surprisingly, hotels are often the best places to look for well prepared local cuisine. Many offer cheap lunchtime buffets or Sunday brunches.

DEPARTMENT STORES – These sometimes have floors set aside for restaurants, and are often cheap and clean places to eat. There may also be a grocery floor where you can buy food to prepare yourself.

Markets & Self-Catering

Wherever you are in Asia, visit the food markets. The sheer variety of exotic goods makes for excellent sightseeing, and you can buy fresh fruit, vegetables and other foodstuffs to prepare your own meals, thus saving on daily expenses. Asia's more affluent countries have supermarkets, corner grocers and even the occasional convenience store (though the latter, at least, are vastly more expensive than the markets). If you're planning to cook for yourself, bring a backpacker's stove and some cookware with you, or you can pick up cheap pots and pans in the markets.

Vegetarians in Asia

Being mostly Buddhist and Hindu, you might expect Asia to be a vegetarian paradise. In reality, it is very much a mixed bag. In some countries, like India and Thailand, there are plenty of vegetarian restaurants, and most other places are also used to catering to vegetarians. However, in countries like China and Mongolia, you will find the pickings awfully slim if you don't eat meat or foods containing meat-based broths. If you don't eat fish either, finding a decent meal can be even more complicated. Many Asian countries have some non-meat source of protein, like tofu or lentils, but these may not always be available. And while good fruit is generally available, fresh vegetables are far less plentiful. Research the vegetarian possibilities in the country you plan to visit, and bring supplies from home if you think you'll be unable to meet your dietary needs.

Ordering Meals

Although it is possible to eat in backpackers cafes, and to find eating establishments with English-language menus, sooner or later you will find yourself in a restaurant with an incomprehensible menu, or standing in front of a food cart facing someone who doesn't speak a word of English. Fortunately, you needn't starve to death or enrol in an intensive language course. Here are a few tips:

- Point at the food on display – Pretty obvious, but also pretty useful. A lot of restaurants in Asia prepare their food in advance so it's simply a matter of pointing at whatever appeals to you.

- Point at what another diner is eating – Again, fairly obvious. Don't be shy; stroll around the restaurant and see what others are eating.

- Use your guidebook – A good guidebook will have a section with common dishes written in both English and the local language.

- Learn a few key phrases from your guidebook – eg 'What do you recommend?,' 'I'll have that' or 'Do you have any set meals?' are useful ones. Also memorise the names of some common dishes.

Western Food

Inevitably there will be times when you can't face the thought of another meal of fried rice or noodle soup. In many parts of Asia, particularly rural areas, the food can be quite monotonous. In Nepal, for example, if you trek into a remote area you will eat nothing but *dal bhat* (rice and lentils) three times a day for weeks on end. It won't be long before you're fantasising about demolishing some tasty western food. Strangely enough, many travellers feel ashamed to crave western food, as if they are violating some kind of traveller's code – walk into the Pizza Hut near Khao San Rd in Bangkok and you'll see some pretty sheepish-looking foreign diners. But if you're wishing you were one of them, don't be too hard on yourself. If you lose your appetite for local dishes or they don't satisfy you, then seek out a place that serves western food – it's not a sin (and you'll have the opportunity to use a western toilet!).

The most common western food in Asia is fast food, with (you guessed it) McDonald's leading the way. You'll also find plenty of KFC outlets (absurdly popular in Malaysia), a few Pizza Huts and a smattering of lesser known fast-food chains. A meal in one of these restaurants will almost always cost two or three times the price of a meal in a simple local place.

The larger cities have restaurants specialising in international cuisine, serving everything from French food to Mexican. Hong Kong, Singapore and Tokyo in particular can rival any western city for the quality of their international food, so make the most of a visit to these cities.

Many guesthouses along the backpackers trail serve western favourites like toast and eggs, muesli, hamburgers, sandwiches and chips. You can even get pizza at a guesthouse in Nepal's Annapurna Sanctuary, but it won't taste like the pizza you're used to eating back home. In general, these places serve reasonable breakfasts, but their attempts at lunch and dinner dishes often miss the mark. Still, what can you expect when the same cook is churning out everything from spaghetti to tom yam kung? A savvy traveller might start the day with breakfast at the guesthouse, but eat in local restaurants for lunch and dinner.

DRINKS

Drinks in Asia run the gamut from delicious fresh fruit shakes in tropical countries to decidedly dodgy *chai* (tea) across much of the subcontinent. Perhaps the most common drink of all is Coca-Cola, and you'll find bottles of the stuff from huts high in the Himalaya to isolated Indonesian islands. Almost every country also produces its own carbonated drinks; these are generally a fraction of the price of western brands, although they tend towards the sickly sweet. Of course, you'll probably be drinking a lot of bottled water and you may find yourself troubled by the amount of empties you see piling up across much of Asia. If you don't want to contribute to this problem, consider investing in a good water filter before setting out (and perhaps a bottle of iodine as a backup).

As for alcoholic beverages, most countries produce their own local beers. The popular ones include Singha (Thailand), Tiger (Singapore), San Miguel (Philippines), Bintang (Indonesia), Tsingtao (or Qingdao, China) and anything from Japan. These are often quite acceptable and usually a good bit cheaper than their imported counterparts. Most countries also produce a variety of home-grown brews. These include Japanese *sake*, Tibetan *chang*, Chinese *lao shu* and Nepali *rakshi*. Although these local brews are often remarkably cheap, you may find them a little hard on the palate and even harder on the head if you overindulge.

Whatever you drink in Asia, be sure to follow the advice contained in the Everyday Health section of the Health chapter. In particular, be wary of ice, improperly sealed bottles, drinks from unknown sources and anything that looks like it has been sitting around for a while. Remember, if you have any doubts about the safety of a drink, it's better to forgo it and skip any potential stomach troubles. If there's no other option, adding some iodine is a cheap insurance policy.

SIGHTSEEING

Some days it will be a chore to motivate yourself to get out there and see the sights. The heat in South-East Asia and on the Indian subcontinent can seriously sap your energy, and you may have just put in hours or days of tough travelling. If you are starting to feel a bit travelled out, relax around the pool with a cool drink or doze on your bed with a good book for the day; it might be all you need to restore your enthusiasm.

Alternatively, if the prospect of negotiating another day's sightseeing is simply too overwhelming, try working out the following day's schedule over dinner or drinks. Peruse your guidebook, chat to travellers and helpful locals, and create an itinerary that caters to your interests and your own pace. Many local travel agencies, tourist offices and even the occasional guesthouse offer day tours of various sights. While some might be designed for package tourists and will bore the socks off you, others can be quite worthwhile if led by a knowledgeable guide, and will make organising your sightseeing far less strenuous.

In the cheaper countries of South-East Asia and the subcontinent, it can be quite economical to hire a private guide for the day. This can usually be arranged through tourist offices, or some hotels or guesthouses. Tourist offices may also be able to arrange tours with volunteer guides (usually local students keen to practise their English). These tours are generally free, but you should cover the guide's entrance fees, transport and lunch. They can be a great way to meet the locals and get an insider's perspective on the country you are visiting.

Sightseeing doesn't necessarily mean covering every last one of the famous spots listed in your guidebook. Simply strolling around, stopping now and then for a drink in a local cafe and soaking up the atmosphere can be a pleasant change to dashing madly about town trying to squeeze in just one more tourist sight before sundown. As an independent traveller, you can take whichever approach suits you from day to day.

Off the Beaten Track

You'll soon realise that there's a definite backpackers trail blazed across Asia. Major points along this trail include Bangkok and Chang Mai (Thailand), Kathmandu (Nepal), Kuta and Yogyakarta (Indonesia), and Goa and Varanasi (India). Spend any time in these cities and you'll discover that many of the guesthouses, restaurants and even the backpackers are almost interchangeable.

There's no doubt that these backpackers ghettos are convenient, but they don't give you much real sense of being in a foreign country. If you begin to feel as though you're trapped in a transit zone where everyone eats the same banana pancakes, drinks the same beer and listens to the same music, it's time to step off the backpackers trail for a while.

An excellent way to escape the scene is to head somewhere not accessible by road or air. In other words, try going on foot or by river boat or ferry. You might visit remote Himalayan villages, longhouses along Borneo's rivers, isolated islands in the Indonesian archipelago, or ger settlements on the Mongolian steppes. Few other tourists make it to these spots. The lack of roads has also ensured that the people living in these areas are largely unaffected by modern technology. In some isolated parts of Asia you can observe simple, agrarian life as it was lived hundreds of years ago. There won't be much in the way of tourist amenities either, and this can be a welcome challenge after the ease of hanging out in the backpackers ghettos.

If you're really keen to strike off on your own, head for a place which isn't listed in the guidebooks. Literally venturing into the unknown like this is especially exciting – there might be transport and accommodation, but then again there might not. More importantly, you guarantee that the people you meet will be unused to foreigners, and possibly more genuine and welcoming than the jaded locals you meet in the travellers centres. On the Everest Base

DOWN (BUT NOT OUT) ON KUTA BEACH

At the end of my first big overseas trip – three months in the UK and Europe – I decided to break my journey on my way back to Australia with a two week stop-off in Bali. I only had A$100 left, but figured I could make it stretch at a pinch.

The lack of ready cash imposed on me a not unwelcome enforced leisure: I didn't have enough money to tear around visiting temples and sights, so I slipped into a routine of walking along the beach in the early morning, spending a good part of the day lying on the beach, and reading in the evening after buying my supper from a roadside trolley. On one occasion, as I was sitting on the beach, I was invited to join a group of Balinese women who were engaged in a thanksgiving ritual beneath a makeshift bamboo shelter. Before them was spread a sumptuous feast – fresh fruit, seafood and rice. On another evening I watched as an entire village walked to the water's edge, brightly dressed in ceremonial sarongs, and the male elders carried offerings into the sea.

I have travelled quite a bit since that first trip, both independently and as an author for LP, but some of my best travel memories are of that quiet two weeks in Bali. There are as many different types of travellers and reasons for travelling as there are destinations: there are those who feel they've let themselves down if they don't visit every single sight mentioned in their guidebook, those who revel in the camaraderie of 'the road', and those who simply want to get a great suntan. All of these 'ways' of travelling are legitimate. As for me, I learned during that two weeks in Bali that a culture reveals itself in subtle, unexpected ways, and if you sit back quietly, often you'll find that it will unfold without any concerted effort on your part.

MICHELLE COXALL
LP AUTHOR, AUSTRALIA

Camp trek, the locals are so used to foreigners that they hardly offer the cus-tomary greeting of 'Namaste'; but try trekking in one of Nepal's more remote areas and you'll be sharing a heartfelt 'Namaste' with every person you pass (including those who dash across the field to offer the greeting).

Visiting a less travelled country such as Myanmar (Burma), Bhutan (if you can afford it), Mongolia or Bangladesh can be a good way to escape the back-packers scene. Tourism in these countries is a relatively new concept and the backpackers trail hasn't had time to develop. Eventually it will, but for now these places can be explored in relative isolation from other tourists.

You can also avoid the backpacking hordes by travelling outside of the high season. Though this will mean often putting up with the worst weather – India during the monsoon, the Himalaya or North-East Asia in winter – you will see the side of a country that other travellers rarely experience and, as the only traveller around, you'll have ample bargaining power.

Finally, if you're not tempted to head into the wild blue yonder, but do want to escape the city crowds, catch a bus out to the suburbs, where you'll see everyday life first-hand.

Hazards

It pays to be cautious when venturing off the beaten track, especially when your destination is not covered in a guidebook. For a trip into real wilderness, be sure you have the skills and equipment to deal with any likely challenges; when-ever possible, take a guide with you. A particular danger in Cambodia, Vietnam, Laos, Myanmar and Sri Lanka is unexploded landmines – do not venture into restricted areas for any reason. Likewise, avoid areas of political instability, or out-right battle zones. Several travellers have been caught in the crossfire or taken hostage in recent years. For more information on these and other dangers in remote areas, see Hazards & Safeguards in the Issues & Attitudes chapter.

SHOPPING

Few places in the world can match Asia for the astonishing variety of its hand-crafts, clothing and souvenirs. Indeed, with some planning and imagination, you can return home with some exceptional souvenirs and gifts.

There are generally two main choices for shopping: items that are made expressly for sale to tourists and those made for local consumption. With few exceptions, goods made for tourists will cost several times more than the local product. To save money and ensure you are purchasing authentic goods, try shopping at local markets and small shops, rather than in the souvenir empori-ums. You will need to bargain quite hard for a good price, but with a little practice you may find this to be all part of the fun of shopping in Asia (see Bargaining in the Money Matters chapter for some useful tips).

To avoid being ripped off and ending up with nothing more than a collec-tion of junk, you'll need to take the time to shop around. Don't try to make quick money from your Asian purchases, in particular gemstones and carpets (see Hazards & Safeguards in the Issues & Attitudes chapter for details of some common scams). Similarly, be especially wary when buying antiques or artworks; only an expert will be able to assess the authenticity of such items. You'll probably be much safer with lower-priced handcrafts, clothing and folk art.

Keep in mind that as a backpacker you don't want to be lugging tonnes of souvenirs across Asia, so try to do most of your shopping shortly before returning home. By this time you'll have a good idea of what a reasonable price is, and you won't risk blowing your budget. Alternatively, consider shipping your purchases home. This can be a safe, reliable and cheap option (see the Staying in Touch chapter for more details). If you're planning to return to the same place later in your trip, you could store your goods at a reliable guesthouse or at the airport (although the latter can be quite expensive).

Some countries are better for shopping than others. For a wide range of inexpensive and interesting souvenirs, it's hard to beat India, Nepal, Thailand and Indonesia (especially Bali and Yogyakarta). You could plan your trip so that you leave from one of these countries, and really go to town just before heading home. A few more tips for good shopping in Asia include:

- Look around to get a feel for the typical price of an item. In India and China, try checking the prices in the state-owned shops. You can also ask other travellers what they have been paying. Try to avoid uninformed impulse purchases.

- Be wary of promises to ship goods straight to your house. In India, in particular, some stores claim that door-to-door

GOOD SOUVENIRS

Bangladesh – carpets, rickshaw art, clothing, jewellery

Bhutan – thangkas, textiles

Brunei – Malay-produced handcrafts

Cambodia – textiles, handcrafts

China – stamps and coins, paintings and scrolls

Hong Kong – appliances, electronics, cameras, tailor-made suits

India – carpets, papier mache, jewellery, metalwork, textiles

Indonesia – woodcarvings, batik, *ikat* (dyed woven cloth), coffee, ceramics, Balinese paintings

Japan – photographic equipment, *washi* (Japanese paper), wood-block prints, ceramics, bamboo crafts

Laos – textiles, carvings

Malaysia – traditional kites, *kris* (knives), *songket* (gold thread) weaving, batik

Mongolia – Mongolian clothing and boots, stamps

Myanmar – lacquerware, clothing and textiles, tapestries

Nepal – thangkas, Tibetan carpets, woollen items

Pakistan – camel-skin lamps, textiles, jewellery, carpets

Philippines – cane work, baskets, woodcarvings, shell jewellery

Singapore – electronics, tailor-made clothes, handcrafts from all over Asia

South Korea – sporting goods and clothing, lacquerware, ceramics, ginseng

Sri Lanka – wooden masks, batik, leather goods

Taiwan – motorcycle goods, electronics

Thailand – Thai silk and other textiles, tailor-made clothes, shoulder bags, hill-tribe crafts, jewellery

Vietnam – clothing, handcrafts

shipping is included in the purchase price – quite often, they'll ship it to the nearest port in your country, and you'll have to pick it up and pay the often considerable duties.

- Many countries (including China, Thailand, Vietnam and Laos) prohibit the export of antiquities. This is aimed at preventing the wholesale looting of important cultural properties. If you purchase anything that even resembles an antique, be prepared for some probing questions at customs.

- Beware of 'instant antiques'. Some vendors use smoke or other means to make brand-new items look ancient, and then charge customers high prices for 'valuable antiquities'.

- When buying electronics items, watches, cameras and the like, always get a manu-facturer's warranty. Make sure that it's valid outside the country of purchase and that it's properly filled in by the dealer. Also, check that the voltage and plug design on electronics items are compatible with those of your home country.

- Use good judgement when buying tailor-made clothes, especially suits. In countries like Thailand and India you'll see unbelievably low prices advertised for tailor-made suits. Unfortunately, often these garments are poorly made. Ask a local or an expat to recommend a good shop.

- Be sensible about what can be carried on a plane and keep in mind that if your luggage exceeds the specified weight limits, you'll have to pay a fee. Also, unwieldy items can be difficult to manoeuvre through airports.

GETTING AROUND

Transport in Asia is extraordinarily diverse, ranging from bicycle-rickshaws to Japanese bullet trains, and with everything from elephants to hovercraft in between. In the less wealthy countries, the types of transport can take some getting used to. If you make it back home without one 'bus ride from hell' story, consider yourself very lucky.

There's no doubt that Asian travel can be difficult, frustrating and at times even dangerous, but it's all part of the Asian experience, and as such can even be enjoyable. (At least it never seems too bad in retrospect.) The most difficult journeys will be offset by the special experiences – you'll never forget watching the moon rise over the rice paddies from the comfort of a sleeper berth on a Thai train, or floating down the Ganges at dawn in a small rowboat while the sun appears above the hills.

Transportation varies considerably from country to country, and your memories of Asia may be coloured by the way you travelled around. In moun-tainous Nepal, walking is often the only option; in the Philippines and parts of Indonesia, boats are commonly used; while in relatively flat India and much of South-East Asia, buses and trains are the rule.

You will generally, however, have a choice of plane, train, bus and perhaps even long-distance taxi to make a particular journey. As well as safety, you'll need to take into account the price, travel time, comfort and sightseeing potential. In some countries, such as China, people avoid flying because of poor airline safety records and the lack of instrument landing facilities at some airports. Likewise, trains are almost always safer than buses in the majority of countries.

Apart from the more developed countries (Japan, Taiwan, Korea, Malaysia and Singapore), you should leave yourself plenty of time when travelling long distance. Schedules seldom run on time and there may be delays of several hours, or even days, due to human incompetence, mechanical breakdown or uncontrollable weather conditions (or some combination of the three) . Having a little extra time built into your schedule will save you some frustration, as will a few good books and a personal stereo.

It's worth researching the transport options of the countries you intend to visit through a good guidebook and the Internet (see Researching Your Trip in the Planning chapter for a list of resources) and by talking to other travellers. You might find you can take a pleasant journey instead of a horrific one simply by using a different mode of transport, or by paying a little more for a better class of train carriage or bus.

Air

Air travel is surprisingly affordable within Asia and shouldn't be overlooked even if you're trying to budget. Domestic air networks are generally reliable, safe and often quite extensive, and air travel between countries in Asia is also fairly cheap. Bangkok, Hong Kong and Penang are probably the three cheapest places to buy international tickets.

Asian Air Fares
Some typical discount one-way air fares from four Asian air hubs to destinations in the region are:

Bangkok to	Delhi	4100B (US$110)
	Hong Kong	3150B (US$85)
	Kathmandu	3900B (US$105)
	Singapore	1850B (US$50)
	Tokyo	4800B (US$130)
Hong Kong to	Kathmandu	HK$2000 (US$255)
	Kuala Lumpur	HK$1400 (US$180)
	Manila	HK$950 (US$120)
	Yangon (Rangoon)	HK$800 (US$105)
Penang to	Bangkok	440R (US$115)
	Jakarta	350R (US$90)
	Mumbai (Bombay)	700R (US$185)
Tokyo to	Bangkok	¥40,000 (US$330)
	Beijing	¥35,000 (US$290)
	Singapore	¥42,000 (US$345)
	Taiwan	¥34,000 (US$280)
	Jakarta	¥51,000 (US$420)

Some typical one-way air fares on common routes within three of Asia's larger countries are:

Beijing to	Hong Kong	Y2000 (US$240)
	Ürümqi	Y2550 (US$310)
	Shanghai	Y1100 (US$135)
	Shenzhen	Y1790 (US$215)
	Xi'an	Y980 (US$120)
Delhi to	Calcutta	Rs 6850 (US$160)
	Goa	Rs 8130 (US$190)
	Chennai (Madras)	Rs 8990 (US$210)
	Mumbai (Bombay)	Rs 8350 (US$195)
Jakarta to	Denpasar	727,000 rp (US$89)
	Pontianak	525,000 rp (US$65)
	Ujung Pandang	1,085,000 rp (US$134)

Air travel obviously saves you from having to deal with long and difficult journeys by ground transport. This is an important consideration when you're looking at a 30 hour bus ride across western China in the dead of winter. And if you're facing a particularly long journey – such as travelling the length of Indonesia – it may be a fair bit cheaper to fly than to take surface transport when you take into account the cost of bus and ferry tickets, guesthouses and food along the way.

Air travel also allows you to get into the wilderness in very little time. For example, the one hour flight from Kathmandu to Lukla, at the start of the Everest Base Camp trek, can save you five days of difficult trekking. Likewise, flying into the more remote villages of Indonesian and Malaysian Borneo can save you days of exhausting river travel and jungle trekking, as well as the cost of hiring guides. Some isolated islands in eastern Indonesia are so rarely served by boats that flying is your only option.

However, for the gains in time-saving and ease of travel, you'll be sacrificing scenic views and the experience of surface transport. If you have all the time in the world and have the fortitude for plenty of difficult bus and train journeys, then you'll gain a far greater insight into the local culture if you travel overland. On the other hand, if you find that you're becoming run-down by too many exhausting bus and train trips, don't be afraid to give yourself a break by flying from time to time.

Air Travel Tips

- You can often tack cheap internal flights onto your international ticket. For example, if you fly Garuda from your home country to Indonesia, you can qualify for a 'Visit Indonesia Decade Air Pass', which allows you to make three internal flights in Indonesia for US$300. Check with Malaysia Airlines and Philippine Airlines for similar deals.

- Some airlines offer cheap internal passes even if you haven't flown with them internationally. However, you will generally have to take several long flights to get your money's worth.

- Check with travel agencies, airlines and in guidebooks for any special discounts available on air tickets. Many airlines offer student, group and senior discounts. You may also get a discount for night flights or for flying from slightly less convenient airports.

- When you buy an air ticket, ask about the airline's cancellation policy. Also, ask if it's possible to change your reservation without charge.

- In some countries, such as China and Laos, you have to pay an inflated foreigners' price for air tickets.

- Asian airlines, particularly those in less developed countries, are notorious for 'losing' your reservation, so confirm and reconfirm.

- Often it's cheaper to buy your ticket from a travel agent than directly from an airline, but be wary of shady operators. Many countries have a licensing board for travel agents, so check that the one you're dealing with is licensed. Try not to part with your money before having the ticket in hand. If you must pay in advance, make sure you get a receipt and the name of the person who sold you the ticket.

- Be at the airport several hours before you have to depart, especially in out-of-the-way places. Boarding passes may be given out on a first-come, first-served basis. Also, some airlines may ignore posted schedules and your plane might depart early (though the opposite is usually the case).

- Expect delays or cancellations. This isn't always the airline's fault – weather is sometimes to blame and, in more than a few Asian countries, local bigwigs can just show up and commandeer a plane for their own use.

- Some airfields don't have facilities for instrument landings. If the weather looks bad, you may want to try for a seat on a later flight.

- Some great aerial sightseeing is possible in Asia, especially on internal flights in Nepal. Likewise, the sensational Islamabad to Gilgit route in Pakistan affords great views of the Himalayan giant, Nanga Parbat, and perhaps even K2 (for only US$20!).

- If possible, keep an eye on your luggage and make sure that it's loaded onto your flight. Also, stow any knives or other dangerous items in your backpack.

- Finally, expect a mad rush to the door when the plane lands, especially in China. Wait until everyone has disembarked before following suit. Invariably, you'll meet the same fools who rushed off the plane waiting sad-faced around the luggage carousel.

Bus

You can expect to spend a lot of time on buses while you're in Asia. Long-distance buses can be clean, ultramodern coaches like those in Japan, or rusting rattle-traps like those plying the roads of Mongolia. Although bus travel in Asia can be unpleasant – you'll have to contend with bad roads, crazy drivers, cramped conditions, cigarette smoke and blaring music – buses are often the cheapest, and sometimes the only, way to travel. As a general rule, a regular highway bus costs about the same as a 3rd class train ticket over the same distance, and will often be far more comfortable than a 3rd class carriage. Furthermore, buses tend to leave far more frequently than trains, thus giving you greater flexibility.

However, due to the relative dangers and discomfort of bus travel, if you have a choice between bus and train it may be better to pay a little extra for the comfort and safety of a better class train carriage.

There are often several classes of bus plying a particular route. (In India up to five different classes of bus will be running.) There may also be a choice of express, semi-express and local buses – the main difference being how often

BUS RIDE FROM HELL

I bought a ticket on a private tourist bus running from Bangkok to Krabi, in the south of Thailand. It was my first bus ride in Asia and I didn't know what to expect. After a long wait on the street, we were finally allowed to board the bus, and I grabbed a seat a few rows back. I figured the ride would be smoothest up near the front and I'd have a nice view of the road. Just after I sat down, a wild-eyed man sat down next to me and it seemed pretty clear that he was out of his mind on speed; he immediately went into a frantic routine of unpacking and repacking his small backpack. Before we had even left the parking lot he must have gone through it about 20 times. Needless to say, I quickly looked around for another seat but they were all taken. 'Great,' I thought, 'I'm not gonna get a wink of sleep with this nutcase next to me all night.' But as the bus lumbered through the crowded streets of Bangkok towards the highway, I had no idea of what was to come.

When we hit the highway, I couldn't help but notice that our driver was driving a little fast for the conditions. Actually, he was driving like a complete lunatic. Since the highway was nothing but a two lane road, each time the driver went to pass a slower vehicle, I was treated to a bird's-eye view of the headlights of the trucks hurtling towards us. Every time, just as it seemed that we were sure to perish in a flaming head-on collision, the driver somehow managed to pull back into his lane. I couldn't watch but I couldn't force myself to look away, either.

For hour after hour the driver continued his high-speed game of chicken, egged on by three underlings who were crowded into the front next to him. Even the sight of a freshly crashed bus surrounded by rescue vehicles did nothing to dampen his spirits.

Long after midnight, the second movie *(Robin Hood)* came to an end. One of the assistants must have liked the theme song because he cranked it up to ear-splitting volume as the credits rolled. The noise was too much for my speed-addled seat mate. He called out in a thick French accent, 'What is this? Rock and roll concert?' At this, the assistant came charging down the aisle, grabbed him by the shirt and hurled a string of Thai and English profanities at him. I was pretty sure that fists were going to fly, but the assistant finally calmed down and returned to his post. However, to punish my seat mate for his belligerence, he turned on the light immediately over our row. This caused my seat mate to burst out indignantly, 'What is this? Lightshow?' Luckily, the assistant decided to ignore him.

So, for the rest of the night, as other travellers snored contentedly around me in the dark, I sat there wide awake under the glare of the light, imprisoned between the horrors visible out the front of the bus and the antics of the speeding Frenchman to my side. Just as dawn was breaking, he fell into a tortured sleep. I seized the chance to grab some sleep of my own. I dozed for about five minutes before the bus pulled into Krabi and we were ordered to disembark. I grabbed my bag and blundered down the streets to the first guesthouse I could find and installed myself for a very long nap.

Two years later I discovered my mistake: I had taken a cheap tourist bus instead of going to the public bus station and paying just a little extra for an infinitely safer government bus. It's a mistake I don't intend to repeat.

CHRIS ROWTHORN
LP AUTHOR, JAPAN

the bus stops. On longer journeys, express or semi-express buses are preferable as these are faster and usually more comfortable than local buses. You may also have other choices, such as whether or not the bus has air-con, reclining seats or video.

And the numerous choices don't end there. There may be public/government buses and private/tourist buses running the same routes. In some countries, such as Vietnam, tourist buses (or minibuses) are safer, faster and less crowded than public buses. In others countries, such as Thailand, the public buses are safer because the tourist bus drivers often take stimulants and drive like madmen to make their runs in as little time as possible.

A peculiarity of Asian bus travel is that one town will often harbour several bus stations. There will be a bus station for local buses and another for long-distance buses, while bigger cities will have several long-distance bus stations, divided according to the areas which the buses serve. When you buy your ticket be sure to check which station your bus departs from.

Bus Travel Tips

- If tickets are hard to get at the bus station, try booking through an agent or your hotel.

- If a travel agent shows you pictures of a fleet of brand-new, gleaming tourist buses, you can usually be sure the buses are actually ageing rust buckets.

- In less developed countries, buses sometimes leave long before or after scheduled departure times, so show up early to avoid being left behind.

- If seats are unreserved and lots of people are waiting to get on, try to 'reserve' a seat by reaching through the window and placing an item on a seat. You might be able to pay a small boy to climb through a window and hold a seat for you (a fairly common practice in India). If you're travelling as a pair, delegate one person to board the bus and hold two seats while the other takes care of the luggage.

- Buy some snacks and drinks for your trip. Toilet paper is also a good idea.

- Take some warm clothes out of your pack in case they crank up the air-conditioning (very common).

- Bring earplugs in case you're bombarded with loud music or videos (again, very common).

- Watch carefully as your baggage is placed on the roof or in a luggage compartment. You may want to chain your bag in place. Carry all valuable items on board with you.

- Choose your seats carefully. Back seats tend to be bumpiest and furthest from the video and stereo speakers. Those at the front are less bumpy, but you may find yourself face to face with a bad Bollywood movie, or worse, looking out the front window as the driver practises his Grand Prix technique. Avoid riding on the roof – you could fall off or be hit by low branches.

- If you're a woman, be careful to avoid physical contact with monks while on buses in South-East Asia. In Pakistan, sit near the front of the bus and next to other women.

- Always keep your money belt on you and well covered, even while sleeping. Keep your daypack or camera safe, preferably on your lap, with a strap wrapped round your arm or leg.

- When the bus stops keep an eye on your luggage.

- Enjoy the video!

Train

Some countries in Asia – such as India, China and Japan – boast well developed train systems. Many people prefer trains to buses because they tend to be more comfortable and safer, although they do vary in comfort. You could take a plush express, or find yourself packed into a rolling cattle car along with screaming kids, smoking adults, mountains of luggage and a few farm animals to boot. Often a little extra cash would have bought you some legroom in a better class carriage.

Three main variables determine the price of your ticket and the comfort of your journey: the speed of the train, the class of the carriage and the type of seat or berth you choose. Most train lines run express, semi-express and local trains. Express trains stop only at major cities while local trains stop at every hamlet and roadhead on the line. Local trains are fine for short journeys, but if you're going long-distance, opt for express or semi-express. You'll pay more for the service, but the difference in journey time is usually worth it.

The usual classes are first, second and third, but there are many variations, depending upon the type of seat (hard or soft, reclining or nonreclining), the presence or absence of air-conditioning, and whether the train has individual compartments. Third-class carriages in many countries, including India and China (where 3rd class is known as 'hard seat'), are often filthy and packed to

GREAT TRAINS & TRAIN JOURNEYS

Asia has some memorable trains and train journeys. Train enthusiasts could spend a lifetime in India alone exploring the classic railways there. Here are some of the continent's rail highlights:

- Japan's bullet train – The *shinkansen* claims the title as the world's fastest train, reaching speeds of up to 285km/h. It's worth riding at least once if you visit Japan, even if you can only afford a quick hop from one stop to the next. In particular, have a look at the new 700 series, the front of which looks like a giant duckbill.

- The Kuala Lumpur to Bangkok International Express – Book yourself a 2nd class sleeper, open a good book and enjoy train travel the way it ought to be.

- The Blue Mountain Railway – Running from Mettupalayam to Ooty, in Tamil Nadu, India, this quaint miniature railway offers great views of the rainforest-covered Nilgiri Mountains. The grade is so steep in parts that the line has toothed cogs onto which the locomotive locks while climbing. Some scenes from *A Passage to India* were filmed on this train.

- The Palace on Wheels – For those with money to burn, a great way to tour Rajasthan is aboard this very plush hotel on wheels, which features carriages modelled on those used by Indian maharajas. A one week tour costs US$300 per person and includes all admission fees and food.

- Steam trains – India is home to some of the world's last working steam trains. Enthusiasts can track them down in Assam, Bihar, Rajasthan and Gujarat, among other places.

the rafters. However, they're usually unreserved which means that you can get tickets for them when all others are sold out. Travelling 3rd class is an exercise in fortitude, but it's a fantastic way to experience the lives of the locals. First and 2nd class carriages are much more comfortable for longer journeys, particularly overnight ones. Usually you must reserve or purchase 1st and 2nd class tickets several days in advance.

On overnight journeys you may be able to choose between a regular seat and a sleeping berth. Some seats recline, but you'll get a much better night's rest in a berth. Sleeping berths are available only in 1st and 2nd class and cost significantly more than regular seats, though remember you are saving money on a hotel or guesthouse. Inquire as to whether bedding comes with the price of a sleeper or whether it must be rented.

Buying tickets can be quite a hassle. In some countries, you can purchase tickets through a travel agent, but in others you must buy them at the train station. In China and India this often involves waiting in long queues, dealing with insane bureaucracy and generally wasting several hours. If tourist queues are available, use them; in India, women can save time by using the women's queues. Your hotel or a local travel agency can sometimes buy tickets for you for a small fee (it's usually well worth it). For local trips, you can sometimes purchase tickets on board the train. Some travellers try to do this on longer trips as well, but there's the risk of simply being thrown off the train.

Rail passes are available in Japan, India, Thailand and Malaysia, although only the Japan (JR) Rail Pass is particularly good value. Check the purchase information in your guidebook as some passes, including the JR Rail Pass, can only be purchased overseas.

Long-Distance Taxi

Taxis are an option for long-distance travel in some countries, but only in Malaysia is this truly affordable. Long-distance taxis can be found at specially designated taxi stands near major train and bus stations. You could be sharing the taxi with up to three other passengers, and often the driver won't depart until he has four passengers. If you're in a hurry and insist on going with less people, you'll still have to pay for the whole car (four individual fares).

Although the rates of long-distance taxis are supposed to be fixed, make sure you negotiate an agreed price before you depart – many drivers will attempt to overcharge foreign travellers. Long-distance taxi drivers are also notorious for driving like madmen, so you might prefer to take a bus.

Car & Motorcycle

Renting

Car or motorcycle rental is possible in most Asian countries though in some, such as Vietnam and Bangladesh, road and traffic conditions are so bad that only the most fearless drivers would want to consider it. In other countries, particularly Japan and Malaysia, conditions are very similar to most western countries.

Most countries will require an International Driving Permit, but some will let you drive for a limited time on your home-country licence. Some rental companies also have age restrictions (usually 25 years), and you may find that even though you have a licence, you're unable to rent a car. If you don't have a credit card, you may be asked to leave a significant cash deposit or even your passport – both fairly risky propositions in less developed countries. You should also get vehicle insurance, and most rental places will provide this for an additional fee (carefully check what is covered).

The major car rental chains like Hertz, Avis and Budget can be found in many of Asia's larger cities. There may also be local operators, which are usually cheaper. Motorcycles are most commonly rented from small local shops, and these are numerous in tourist areas like Bali and Phuket.

A popular option if you can't face the dangers and annoyances of driving yourself, is to hire a driver. This is an affordable option in South-East Asia and on the Indian subcontinent. You'll be able to enjoy the scenery, you'll have a guide/translator/navigator on hand, and you won't be responsible for any accidents. Agree on the cost beforehand, and on multiday trips be prepared to pay for your driver's food and accommodation. Car rental places can recommend drivers, or ask at your hotel or guesthouse reception. You could simply negotiate an all-day or longer fare with a regular taxi driver, and this may be cheaper than bothering with car rental. A few points to keep in mind are:

- If you plan to rent a car or motorcycle, make sure you get an International Driving Permit in your home country.

- Before leaving the rental place, go over the car thoroughly for any dents, scratches and other defects with the owner of the shop. Make sure you get a signed list of all damages, or you may be charged for pre-existing defects. Check that everything in the car works and that there is a good spare tyre and a jack.

- Learn the rules of the road before setting out. Good guidebooks usually list the major road rules for each country. The rental place may be able to give you a list of common road signs with English translations. It may also supply you with road maps.

- Be careful where you park at night. The ideal spot is in a fenced-in parking lot at a hotel or guesthouse. You can park your car in the lot of the local police station if you have any doubts about the safety of an area.

- Be suspicious of the gasoline for sale in some rural areas, particularly in Vietnam where it's sometimes cut with kerosene.

- Keep the rental papers in the car along with a list of the rental company's regional offices, in case you break down. Most of the bigger companies have 24-hour emergency numbers.

- Try to get a spare key. There's nothing worse than locking yourself out of a rental car when you're in the middle of nowhere.

- If you're renting a motorcycle, wear a helmet and protective clothing.

- If you have little motorcycle riding experience, start with a smaller bike.

Buying

Buying a car or motorcycle is a good option for those wanting to spend a long time exploring a particular country. If you intend to take the vehicle over an international border, however, be prepared for a mountain of paperwork (see the boxed text 'Across Asia on Your Own Wheels' in the Planning chapter). Buying a motorcycle is popular in some parts of Asia, especially India, where the vehicle of choice is an Indian-made Enfield (but many riders say you'll do better with a Japanese model). Carefully research the road and traffic conditions in the country you intend to visit. Don't underestimate the dangers involved, particularly on a motorcycle. See the pointers listed above for car and motorcycle rental, and also take into account the following:

- Research the types of motorcycles or cars available. Travellers with experience in buying cars or motorcycles are your best reference. They may also be able to recommend a trustworthy dealer.
- Make sure all the paperwork is in order. You may want to get a local lawyer to check all the documents.
- Make sure you have adequate third-party insurance.
- If you're heading out into rural areas, take some tools and spare parts with you.
- Learn a little about repairing a car or motorcycle before setting out.

Bicycle Touring

Bicycle touring is an increasingly popular way to see Asia. Most of South-East Asia and the Indian plains, especially, are ideal, and hardy riders have taken bicycles across every country in Asia, including the Karakoram Highway. Due to the generally poor conditions of Asian roads, you'll probably need a mountain bike or at least a hybrid. You can buy high-quality bikes in Japan, Singapore and Taiwan, but in most other countries you'll be looking at cumbersome local or Chinese-made bikes. For this reason, many riders bring their bike with them from home. If you plan to do so, check carefully the import regulations of the country you intend to visit. Border crossings on a bicycle are usually easier than with a car or motorcycle. A useful book on bicycle touring is the Sierra Club's *The Bike Touring Manual* by Rob van de Plas (Bicycle Books, 1993). A few points to keep in mind are:

- Good spare parts aren't always available in Asia, so bring plenty from home, including lots of extra inner tubes.
- Have a working knowledge of bike repair. Bring a manual if you're a little shaky.
- Get bike bags (panniers) that are easy to remove from the bike, as you'll often be taking them into hotels and guesthouses.
- Be aware that in most Asian countries drivers will never grant you the right of way and will run you off the road, cut you off and generally make your life miserable.
- You can take your bike on most forms of public and private transport. This is a good option if you are exhausted or sick, or want to bypass a difficult or dangerous area.

Hitching

Hitching is possible in most of Asia, even if the locals themselves don't do it. Hitching, however, is never entirely safe in any country and we don't recommend it. Those who decide to hitch should realise that they are taking a small but potentially serious risk. Women, particularly those travelling alone, are at greatest risk of attack. Thus, we strongly advise against women hitching in Asia, even in seemingly safe countries like Japan (where several foreign women hitchers are molested or raped each year). If you do choose to hitch, you should do so in pairs and let someone know where you're planning to go and what time you expect to arrive there.

Hitching in Asia is quite different from hitching in other parts of the world. In many countries, the driver will expect to be paid or at least offered a gift, such as alcohol or cigarettes. You'll also find that the standard thumbs-up signal is not widely understood, so simply flag down an oncoming car or truck. And you may find your driver takes you on several out-of-the-way errands before delivering you to your destination.

Walking

Every country in Asia has been traversed at one time or another by travellers on foot, and there are some who wouldn't do it any other way. Even if you don't undertake a long-distance trek while you're in Asia, walking may be the only means of reaching some places – especially in most Himalayan villages and the upland villages of Borneo, Irian Jaya and other parts of South-East Asia.

For serious walking, you'll need the best boots you can afford and a very comfortable pack. Packing light is also a good idea (see Equipment in the What to Bring chapter). If you're planning some extended treks, get into shape before arriving in Asia and keep in mind that trekking in tropical climates is a lot more difficult than in temperate ones.

Sea Travel

In Indonesia and the Philippines (which together contain over 20,000 islands) you'll do a lot of your travelling by boat. Even in other parts of Asia, there are lots of opportunities to travel by boat, and this can be a distinct pleasure after you've spent any time bouncing around on Asia's treacherous roads. Possibilities include short ferry hops to the Thai islands, or multiday trips like the journey from Kobe to Shanghai across the Sea of Japan.

Sea travel is usually cheaper than air travel. It allows you to enjoy the scenery that you miss by plane, and is great way to mix with the locals. It can also be significantly more dangerous than air travel and you should pay close attention to weather forecasts, as well as to the condition of the vessel. Check out the safety features on board, including life jackets and lifeboats, and never board a vessel that's overcrowded (the cause of several boat disasters each

THE TEMPEST

One year while updating LP's *Indonesia* guide, I decided get out to Krakatau, site of the largest volcanic eruption in human history. An Aussie I bumped into on Carita Beach suggested hiring a local fishing boat for the 100km return voyage. We found a boatman willing to do the trip, and gathered together nine other backpackers to split the hire fee. It was supposed to take four hours each way, but once outside the sheltered waters of the bay, the chop provided quite a challenge for the 7m diesel-powered craft and it took seven hours to reach Krakatau.

On the way back the engine gave out completely, just as a tropical storm burst, and we pitched and rolled in a strong south-western current – away from Java and towards India – all night. It was hellish – everyone, including the Indonesian crew of three, was puking and howling and preparing to meet their maker. Twenty-six hours after we left Carita the storm subsided, the crew managed to get the engine running and we made it back to Java's safe shores. I learned upon our return that we were the third craft to run adrift on such a trip. I vowed then and there never to set foot on a boat without first asking the captain some serious questions as to the boat's seaworthiness and previous track record.

JOE CUMMINGS
LP AUTHOR, USA

year in Asia). It's always better to wait for the next boat or cancel your trip entirely than to risk your life on an unsafe vessel.

Here are a few tips for boat travel in Asia:

- On longer trips, bring your own food and drinks as the offerings on board can be pretty grim.
- Arrive at the dock well before sailing time as the boat might depart early.
- If you're travelling on deck, bring warm clothes, something to lie on and plenty of sunscreen.
- If you're travelling below deck, make sure all exits are open and working. In Thailand, ferry operators might lock all the exits to prevent passengers from milling about on deck.
- Watch you luggage carefully and, if possible, keep it with you.

River Travel

Spectacular river trips can be made all through Asia. In Bangladesh, river travel is often the only way to get around, while in the uplands of Borneo it is an excellent alternative to expensive air travel (plus a great way to experience the jungle).

Other great river journeys are the three day trip down the Yangzi, and trips through the backwaters of Kerala. And for boating experiences that may be right at hand, don't overlook urban services like Bangkok's *khlong* (canal) boats, which ply the waters of the 'Venice of the East', or the Star ferries which cross Hong Kong's Victoria Harbour (providing stunning views of the skyline, particularly at night).

Local Transport

At first glance, Asian cities appear to be chaotic snarls of traffic, people and indecipherable billboards, and you may despair of ever being able to find your way around. But there's usually some kind of method to the madness, and with a little familiarity you'll find navigation far less daunting (though you will still be dealing with crowds and extremely high levels of air and noise pollution). In your favour is that public transport costs next to nothing, and if you can't decipher the routes and symbols, private transport is generally a very affordable alternative.

Private transport will usually include taxi, auto-rickshaw, bicycle-rickshaw, motorcycle taxi and even the occasional bullock-drawn cart. When using any of this transport, you must negotiate the fare before starting your journey. To get anything close to the proper price, you will have to bargain hard (see Bargaining in the Money Matters chapter for some tips).

Bus

If you can figure out the local bus system, you'll be able to travel around most Asian cities very cheaply. Unfortunately, this is often easier said than done, as route maps are not always available and are not always written in English. Bus destinations are sometimes written in local script and it may be difficult to tell where to catch the bus you want. More importantly, local buses are often hideously crowded – many travellers avoid them altogether. With a little initiative, however, it is possible to take local buses to destinations you might not otherwise reach. In the more advanced countries, the local bus system may be as good as, or better than, the one you use at home.

Minibuses, most of which operate like regular buses, are very common on Asia's streets, as are fleets of smaller vehicles that go under various names depending on the country: *bemos* in Indonesia, *jeepneys* in the Philippines, and *tempos* in Nepal. These usually ply regular routes, but may not leave until the vehicle is full, or may cruise around town trying to pick up passengers before setting out on their proper route. There's usually a fixed fare on these vehicles, but drivers often try to overcharge foreigners. Ask the price before you board, or ask another passenger after boarding. Make sure that the driver doesn't speed off with only you on board (after which he'll charge you an exorbitant rate for a 'special private tour').

Guard your belongings carefully from thieves and pickpockets on local buses (see Theft under Hazards & Safeguards in the Issues & Attitudes chapter for some helpful advice). Here are some other useful hints for local travel:

- Try to get a route map. These are often available at local tourist offices or guesthouses.

- Bring plenty of small change as it's often impossible to change money aboard the bus.

- Watch local riders to figure out how you pay. Sometimes, a fare collector will collect your fare, or you put the fare into a fare box.

- Have your stop or destination written in local script by the owner of your hotel or guest-house, to show to a local passenger so they can tell you when to get off.
- Try not to take a local bus during morning or evening rush hours, when they are unbelievably crowded.

Taxi

Even if you never take taxis in your home country, you'll probably take quite a few in Asia where they are usually quite cheap. The catch is getting a fair price. In South-East Asia, on the Indian subcontinent and in China, you'll find it very difficult to get the driver to use the meter, if one exists at all. Sometimes the driver will claim that the meter is broken, or he may simply refuse to use it. You might achieve results by threatening to find another driver (this will often result in the meter magically fixing itself). Otherwise, you will have to negotiate the fare. Make sure you agree on a price before setting out, and that the driver understands the price is for the whole car, not per person. After some time in a country, you'll get a feel for what a fair price is, and your negotiating skills will improve. A few more tips for successful taxi travel include:

- Fares often increase faster than meters can be reset. For this reason, some drivers carry fare adjustment cards. These are very easy to tamper with, so if you're shown a fare adjustment card, it's probably better to negotiate the price.
- Watch for taxis with fast-running meters. Having an idea of how often the meter should change will help you avoid rip-offs.
- Taxis that wait outside hotels and tourist attractions often expect more money than regular ones. You may want to walk a block or two further and hail a regular cab.
- Try to have an approximate idea of the route to your destination.
- In some countries, taxi fares are higher at night.
- If you're going to take a lot of taxi rides in one day, it may be cheaper to negotiate a day rate.
- Do not pay before the driver has unloaded your bag.
- Many cities have complaint numbers you can call if you feel you've been ripped off.

Subway, Tram & Local Train

A few cities in Asia have subways or light-rail lines which are invariably cheap, easy and comfortable to use. These cities include Tokyo, Osaka, Mumbai, Seoul, Singapore and Kuala Lumpur. Prices are fixed, routes are posted and there are no traffic jams, so train and subway travel is a joy compared to urban bus travel (though if you board a Tokyo subway during peak hour, you may not think so). If you intend to use the subway or light rail frequently, check if there are any special deals like day passes or tourist passes.

Motorcycle Taxi

A motorcycle taxi is simply a regular motorcycle on which you ride pillion. For thrill seekers, this is a great way to get around crowded Asian cities in a hurry.

You'll often find motorcycle taxis on street corners or near bus and train stations. Sometimes, the drivers wear coloured vests to set them apart from normal motorcyclists.

In general, a motorcycle taxi costs half to one-third of the price of a regular taxi. You should wear a helmet (sometimes provided) and long pants and a shirt when riding in a motorcycle taxi. Motorcycle taxis do not have meters and you must fix the price before you set out.

Auto-Rickshaw

Auto-rickshaws (known as *bajaj* in Indonesia, *tuk-tuk* or *samlor* in Thailand, and *auto* in India) are three-wheeled vehicles with an enclosed or covered area at the back for holding two or more passengers (or freight). Powered by noisy, two-stroke engines, and outfitted with the most rudimentary suspension, auto-rickshaws seem purposely designed to loosen the teeth in your head. Worse still, because they're partially open to the elements, you'll be breathing in fumes for the whole trip – if you find it unpleasant just put yourself in the driver's shoes!

A ride in an auto-rickshaw can be thrilling and you won't soon forget the experience of whizzing through the Bangkok night in the back of a smelly, screaming tuk-tuk. In many places, auto-rickshaws are half the price of taxis, but in some places you might do better to get a metered taxi (this is usually the case in Bangkok). Although some auto-rickshaws have meters, you'll almost never find a driver who's willing to use it, and auto-rickshaw drivers have a nasty habit of quoting absurdly high prices. You'll have to work hard to get a reasonable price; make sure it's understood that the price is for the vehicle, not per person, and that an extra fee is not going to be charged for luggage.

It pays to be careful when riding auto and bicycle-rickshaws at night as there have been cases of drivers turning down dark alleys and robbing passengers. See also the warnings listed earlier under Taxi.

Bicycle-Rickshaw

Bicycle-rickshaws are bicycles outfitted to carry passengers. You'll find different designs all over Asia; sometimes the passengers sit in front of the driver, or they may sit behind. In Malaysia and the Philippines some bicycle-rickshaws have a side car beside the driver for taking a single passenger. From an environmental and aesthetic standpoint, bicycle-rickshaws are a great improvement on most other forms of transport in Asia.

Again, you'll have to fix the price before setting out. In China, India and Vietnam, bicycle-rickshaw drivers are notorious for agreeing on a price and then asking for a higher one when you arrive at your destination.

Some travellers feel guilty about using bicycle-rickshaws – the driver sweats horribly in the hot sun while you sit comfortably in the cushioned seat.

However, the driver probably has few other work options and might face star-vation if he can't find customers for his rickshaw. To ease your conscience make sure you pay a fair (but not inflated) price, do not overload the rickshaw and don't just sit there if you get to a big hill – get out and walk!

STAYING IN TOUCH

While you're having a great time on the road, it's all too easy to forget about your friends and family back home. All the same, your parents may well be worried sick about you, and the occasional phone call or postcard will go a long way towards easing their minds. And don't underestimate the extent to which hearing familiar voices will cheer you up when you're in an unfamiliar place. With the advent of the Internet, keeping in touch has become so much easier, and you can send and receive emails all through Asia (except Laos and Bhutan).

It does cost some money to keep in touch with home, so factor it into your budget. You may want to keep a regular schedule of correspondence, because it's easy to forget when you last wrote or phoned home when you're caught up in the nitty-gritty of daily travel.

If there's been a natural disaster, plane crash or military conflict in Asia while you're travelling, try calling home as soon as possible to assure your folks that you're all right. Some tips on staying in touch include:

- Give those at home a general itinerary, so they'll have an idea when you'll be in a place from which you can call.

- Call friends and family before heading out on long treks or trips into remote areas to let them know that you'll be out of touch for a while.

- Ask someone at home to save the letters you send them. This is almost as good as keeping a diary and they make great reading when you get home.

- You may want to make a regular schedule for calling home so that people know when to expect your calls.

- Even if you hate writing letters, it's easy enough to scribble off a few quick postcards.

- If you get tired of writing the same news to everyone, write up one good, detailed letter and send copies to everyone, with some personalised information at the end.

- If your personal stereo has a record function, you can send back detailed audio letters on cassette tapes without getting wrist cramp.

- Include a few photos that you've had developed on the road to add spice to your letters and help people visualise what you're experiencing.

TELEPHONE

Unless you're in the wilds of Mongolia or trekking in the Himalaya, you'll probably be within easy reach of a phone. In some countries, making a call is as simple as walking to the nearest pay phone and dialling the number. In others, you may have to use a telephone or communication centre. Phoning home can be relatively expensive, although phone rates do vary considerably across the continent.

When calling other Asian countries, remember that engaged signals and ringing tones may sound very different from those at home. For details on telephone services in specific countries, see the Post & Communications sections of the country profiles later in this book.

Where to Call From

In the more advanced Asian countries (such as Malaysia, Japan, Hong Kong and Singapore) you can make international calls from some pay phones (usually marked as international phones). You can often find these in hotel lobbies and airports. In rural areas it may be impossible to find an international pay phone. International calls can also be made from hotel room phones, though most hotels will tack a 30% service charge onto these calls.

In the less developed countries (such as Vietnam, Nepal, Pakistan and Mongolia) you'll have to go to communication centres, telephone centres or post offices to make international calls. Communication centres are private affairs in tourist areas, processing calls, faxes and possibly email. At these places, you place the call yourself and pay when you've finished. Usually, the first minute costs more and there may be a charge even if you get a busy signal at the other end. Reverse-charge (collect) and credit card calls can also be made from these places, for a small fee. Telephone offices and telephone booths in post offices operate in a similar way, although you must usually pay a deposit. In some countries, you may also have to fill out various forms.

In India, international calls can be made from small stores which have International Subscriber Dialing (ISD) phones. The procedure is quite similar to that of a communication centre, except that the phone issues a print-out indicating the cost of the call.

Note that there may be reduced rates for telephone calls on weekends, in the evenings and at night. Sunday is often the cheapest time of all. Check in your guidebook, local phonebooks or with the phone company. If you're calling from a communication centre, these savings will almost never apply.

International Phonecards

There is a wide range of local and international phonecards on the market. Lonely Planet's eKno Communication Card (see the insert at the back of this book) is designed specifically for travellers and provides cheap international calls from more than 40 countries, a range of messaging services and free email (for local calls, you're usually better off with a local card). eKno does not yet cover all the countries in this book, although new countries are being added all the time.

As we go to print, you can access the eKno service from the following places in Asia – China, Hong Kong, Indonesia, Japan, the Philippines, Taiwan and Thailand. You can join eKno online (www.ekno.lonelyplanet.com) or from the above countries. To do so, dial the relevant registration number. Once you have joined, to use eKno dial the access number.

Country	Join Number	Access Number
China	10800-180-0073	10800-180-0072
Hong Kong	800-90-3362	800-90-3361
Indonesia	008-800-103-114	008-800-103-111
Japan	00531-21-2039	00531-21-2036
Philippines	1-800-1-119-0015	1-800-1-119-0014
Taiwan	0080-15-1013	0080-15-1010
Thailand	001-800-13-288-7648	001-800-13-286-9029

Types of Calls

Prices differ significantly between the types of calls available. Don't be surprised if you can't make certain types of calls in some countries, particularly the less developed nations.

DIRECT (PERSON-TO-PERSON) – This is the easiest and usually the cheapest way to call. Direct calls can be made from international pay phones and private phones in countries that have International Direct Dialing (IDD) facilities. You first dial the IDD number, then the country code, then the area code and number of the party you want to reach. If you're dialling from a pay phone, a phonecard will be more practical than lots of small change. Prepaid phonecards, in a variety of denominations, are usually sold in small shops, telephone offices and some post offices.

OPERATOR ASSISTED – In some Asian countries you must make international calls through an operator. They can normally be made from private phones, hotel phones and telephone offices.

REVERSE CHARGE (COLLECT) – The operator will place these calls for you. They can be pretty expensive, so ensure the other party understands how much their bill is likely to be. These calls can be made from some pay phones, hotel phones and telephone offices.

HOME COUNTRY DIRECT – By dialling a specific number you can bypass local operators entirely and speak directly to an operator in your home country, who can then arrange a credit card or reverse-charge call. The Home Country Direct service is available in most Asian countries and the service is rapidly expanding. Home Country Direct numbers will be listed in most guidebooks, or call the telephone company. Calls can be made from hotel and pay phones, or from communication centres for a small charge. Telephone offices may allow these calls, but may charge a fee. Some airports have phones which allow one-touch Home Country Direct calls.

CREDIT CARD – Credit card calls can be made from some Asian countries (particularly at airports) if you know the local access number for your card. These may be listed in local phonebooks, or you can get a list of the numbers from the card-issuer before leaving home. Credit card calls can be made from the same places as Home Country Direct calls. Some airports have specialised credit card phones which allow one-touch calls to your credit card access number.

POST

In Japan, post offices are bastions of efficiency, but in most of South-East Asia and the subcontinent they are crowded, chaotic affairs. Nonetheless, letters, packages and postcards make it to their intended destinations, although the time this takes varies significantly from country to country. An airmail letter sent from one of Asia's more developed countries will reach Europe, North America or Australia in five to seven days, but if it's sent from a less developed country it may take twice as long. The real mystery is how letters sent on the same day from the same post office can arrive in your home country several days, or even weeks, apart.

Post offices in big cities are usually the most efficient, offer the biggest range of services and are more likely to have English-speaking staff. Some countries have specialised international post offices and these are your best bet for good, reliable service. The larger post offices will have several different windows, each allocated to a different service, and you'll often have to wait in long queues before being served. In rural areas, the post office could be just a shack with a postal worker who doesn't speak a word of English. Furthermore, items sent from rural post offices usually take much longer to reach their intended destinations.

Some countries, such as Indonesia, also have private post offices offering many of the same services as public post offices for a slightly higher price. These are often less crowded and more efficient than public post offices. Also, if you don't want to waste time dealing with the post office, you can often send letters and postcards from your guesthouse or hotel. For country-specific details of postal services see the Post & Communications sections in the country profiles.

Receiving Mail

There are three ways to receive mail while you're travelling. The best and most common way is to have it sent post restante. If you have an American Express card or American Express travellers cheques, you can also have your mail sent to American Express offices along your route. Some hotels and guesthouses will hold mail for you, though letters are often misfiled or simply thrown away. To receive mail this way, you should warn the hotel or guesthouse that someone is going to send mail there, and try to have it addressed to a specific person who will then take care of it.

Post Restante

Post restante is a good way to receive letters while you're on the road, provided those back home have a rough idea of your itinerary. You simply ask people to send letters to the general post office in a city along your route, with your name and the words post restante written clearly on the envelope.

Post restante letters are filed under your surname, which should be written clearly in capital, block letters and underlined. Letters are sometimes filed under your given name, so search under that too.

To collect post restante mail, you'll need to show your passport and you may have to fill out a form. Keep in mind that small, rural post offices may be unfamiliar with the concept of post restante, so ask people to send mail only to general post offices in large cities. Most post offices will only hold mail for a month or so before either discarding it or returning it to the sender. If you're not entirely sure of your itinerary, ask people to send copies of the same letter to two or three different post offices along your route.

You can also receive packages by post restante, although these seem to go astray more often than letters. Don't have important goods sent this way. You'll usually be notified of the arrival of a package via a slip of paper in the letter box corresponding to your last name. In some countries, the package will be inspected before being turned over to you. You'll probably have to fill out some forms and you may have to pay import duties. Any prohibited items will be confiscated and you could get into serious trouble if someone sends you drugs, pornography or any other prohibited item.

For important or valuable items, or if you need something in a hurry, you can use an international courier service like Federal Express or DHL (generally for a hefty fee).

Sending Mail

Provided that letters and postcards are addressed clearly, there should no problems mailing them (in rural areas it can be useful to have the country of the letter's destination written in local script, in case the postmaster can't read English). If you want the letters or postcards sent airmail, you should write 'airmail' or 'par avion' clearly somewhere near the address. Some post offices will have stickers or special envelopes that can be used. In some countries, dishonest postal workers have been known to steam uncancelled stamps off letters and resell them. If you have any doubts, have the stamps cancelled in front of you, or use a franking machine if the post office has one.

You can save money by sending letters by sea mail, in which case they will take several months to reach their destination. Sea mail is far less reliable than airmail and the item may simply vanish en route. For important items, you can use registered mail, which is available at most general post offices for a slightly higher fee than regular airmail. You can also insure the item for an additional fee.

For photographs or books you can get a printed matter discount, but you can't include a letter (don't seal the envelope until you arrive at the post office so that postal workers can inspect the contents). Some countries also offer EMS (express mail service) from larger post offices; items sent this way usually reach their destination in two or three days.

Shipping Items

Shipping items home can be a much bigger hassle than sending normal letters, but it's an excellent way to keep the weight of your backpack to manageable proportions. In Asia's more developed countries, it's a relatively painless procedure, but in India and China, be prepared to spend several hours on the paperwork and getting things properly packaged.

You can send packages by airmail or surface mail from post offices. Sending heavy items by airmail will eat up your budget pretty quickly, so surface mail is usually the best choice. Items sent by sea mail usually arrive at their destination four to six months after being sent, but may take even longer. Surface mail is far less reliable than airmail and items do go missing, so use a courier for anything valuable.

In most Asian countries, you will have to package the item yourself before sending it. There may be a packing service in the post office or nearby. The item may have to be inspected before shipping, so don't seal the package. In India, it must be sealed for you (a tailor will stitch in cheap linen for a small fee). In Nepal, there are usually men working on the street outside the post office who will do this for you. There may also be some time-consuming forms to fill out. The procedures for mailing packages are quite complex, so check in your guidebook for country-specific details.

If you have a number of items to ship, or even just one very heavy item, you might save some money by using a shipping agent. Unlike the post office, which charges by weight, shipping agents usually charge by space (one cubic metre is the minimum amount). In many countries, shipping agents offer door-to-door service and will pick up the goods from your hotel or guesthouse. Goods sent by shipping agents take several months to reach their destinations. In theory, they should be shipped to your home address, though in practice you may have to pick them up from the nearest port.

At the other end the goods will be inspected by customs and you may have to pay import duties, in some cases before you can pick up the goods.

Address Books

Whatever you do, don't leave home without your address book and make sure that all the addresses in it are current. Since this may be lost or damaged during your travels, you should copy the entire book before setting out and leave the copy at home. An address book is important not just for sending mail home but also for collecting the addresses of people you meet along the way. If your address book isn't particularly rugged, you may want to keep it inside a holder of some sort, or buy a durable address book for your trip.

CASSETTE RECORDINGS

Cassette recordings are a great way to record your thoughts while you're on the road. A detailed letter can take a great deal of time to write, while a cassette recorder enables you to chat away for a good half-hour or so, and allows friends and family to hear your voice. However, for the sake of your listeners, take the time to write down a list of topics you plan to discuss, so you keep your audience entertained, and ensure that the tape doesn't degenerate into a boring series of umms and errs …

FAX

It's possible to send faxes from every country in Asia, but this is definitely more of a headache than making phone calls, even in Asia's more advanced countries. Communication centres, some telephone and post offices, and most upmarket hotels have fax machines. Since fax charges are based on the phone charge used to send the fax, it may be cheaper to send the fax on a weekend or at night, if that's possible. You'll also have to pay to receive a fax, although this is much cheaper than sending one.

EMAIL

Email is by far the cheapest, easiest and most convenient way to keep in touch while you're on the road. At the time of writing, Bhutan and Laos were the only two countries in Asia from which it is impossible to send and receive email (although you could theoretically use a laptop computer and private phone line to access an Internet Service Provider in another country). In most Asian countries you'll be able to log onto the Net at Internet cafes, communication centres and even the occasional computer-equipped guesthouse. In others, you can use facilities in post offices and airports. In Vietnam, you cannot access the Internet (due to government paranoia), so the only way to send and receive email is by setting up an email account at a local post office (US$20 to sign up plus US$7 per month). Out of the big cities, you probably won't be able to check your email, although it's probably only a matter of time before you can log on from teahouses high in the Himalaya.

There are three ways to receive email while you're on the road. Lonely Planet's new eKno communication card offers a free email service (see Telephone earlier in this chapter), as do services like Yahoo and Hotmail. You can also use your existing account if your Internet Service Provider (ISP) has dial-ups in Asia. Or you can have people send email to various Internet cafes along your route, using them as a kind of electronic post restante.

Free Email Services

Free email services are so easy and convenient to use that it's difficult to imagine why anyone wouldn't want one. You can set up an account on any Internet-capable computer back home; if you don't have a computer, do this at a local Internet cafe. You don't even have to be particularly computer literate, as the staff will assist you. If you don't manage to set up an account before leaving home, you can do so from any Internet facility in Asia.

With a free email service, you register and receive an email address (and password), to which people can send emails. The emails are stored on the service's computer, and you can access them from anywhere in the world. Most Internet cafes and communication centres will have popular free email services listed on the Bookmarks or Favourites menus of Internet programs. This means you don't even have to type in the address of your service, but simply pull down the menu, select your service and read your messages. You can also send emails with these services. They often have other handy features, such as address books. Microsoft's Hotmail service is popular with travellers, while LP's new eKno Communications Card includes a free email service.

If you already have an account with an ISP at home, you can configure your free email service to access that account, so you can read emails sent to your regular address. Look under the Options menu of the free email service for instructions on how to do this. You can also configure your existing account to forward your emails to your free email service account.

Using Your Existing Account

Some of the larger ISPs, such as AOL and IBM, have dial-ups in most major Asian cities. If you have an account with one of these providers, you can access your email with a local call. In rural areas, you'll have to make a long-distance call to reach the dial-up, but the poor quality of phone lines could make this a pretty dicey affair; it's probably only a good option if you have your own computer and modem, and there is no Internet cafe nearby.

Using Internet Cafes

To have email sent to Internet cafes along your route, you'll need to find Internet cafes willing to hold email for travellers in the cities you plan to visit. Try *The Internet Cafe Guide* (www.netcafeguide.com) to search for such Internet cafes. Most commercial Internet cafes operate like post restante services – they will only hold messages for a certain period of time (generally three or four weeks) before deleting them.

When you're giving your address to family and friends, make sure that they put your name in the subject box (last name in capital letters) of the message so that it can be filed properly. Just like regular post restante, you should check under your first name as well, in case your message was misfiled. Of course, you have very little security with this method, so tell people not to send sensitive or private information.

MEDIA

When you're on the road, it's very easy to lose track of events in the world at large. For some people this is a blessing (and one of the reasons they're travelling in the first place), but for others it is downright unsettling. It's really not too difficult to keep abreast of the news, though if you're trekking in the Himalaya or staying on a remote Indonesian island, you might have to be satisfied with local gossip.

Radio

With a radio, you may be able to tune into world news services like BBC World Service, Radio Australia or Radio America (although even Americans may find the latter a little overbearingly patriotic). In some countries, such as India and Malaysia, you'll be able to listen to direct broadcasts from local BBC or Radio America stations. More likely, you'll be able to catch rebroadcasts of some of their programming on other local stations. Check their respective web sites for the frequencies of local stations and for scheduling information (www.bbc.co.uk/worldservice; www.abc.net.au/ra; www.voa.gov). These services often also broadcast features and music, and can be valuable sources of information about potential trouble spots in Asia.

Television

Some hotels and guesthouses in Asia have televisions on which you can watch local programming, some of which may be in English. If they have a satellite dish or cable TV, you'll also be able to watch CNN or BBC world news. Sports fans may be able to catch some sporting events – anyone who's been in Asia during the World Cup soccer or cricket knows just how serious the locals are about their sport.

Some countries (such as India, Malaysia and Singapore) have full-time English-language stations broadcasting a full range of programming, including international news. Unfortunately, many of the guesthouses on the backpackers trail use their TVs for showing videos, so you'll have a better chance of viewing the latest Hollywood blockbuster than catching up on the news.

Newspapers & Magazines

Most Asian countries have locally produced English-language newspapers, although the quality varies from excellent to almost laughably poor. Still, they're all perfectly adequate for checking on exchange rates, weather forecasts, and national and international news (coverage of the latter may be heavily biased for domestic political reasons).

In the bigger cities you'll find copies of the *International Herald Tribune* and international editions of some of the world's larger newspapers, most commonly the *New York Times* and *USA Today*, plus Asian editions of magazines such as *Time* and *Newsweek*. Copies of some western newspapers – such as the *Sydney Morning Herald*, *New York Times*, *Le Monde* or *The Times* – may be available in the larger cities, but you'll pay a huge premium to get your hands on them. Airports are the best places to find newspapers and magazines, followed by large bookshops and top-end hotels.

The Internet

The Internet may the single best source for up-to-date news while you're on the road. Most major newspapers maintain web pages on which they post the day's top stories. See the appendix 'Internet Addresses' at the back of this book for online news service addresses.

COMING HOME

This is the part of your trip that no one wants to talk about. Coming home can certainly be an anticlimax after you've spent the previous few months living footloose and fancy-free in exotic lands and are confronted with the realities of normal life. It's enough to make you want to turn right around and get on the next plane to anywhere. But it doesn't have to be that bad. If you approach your homecoming in the right frame of mind, your travel experiences can be the springboard to a positive new stage of your life.

POST-HOLIDAY BLUES

One of the hardest aspects of returning home is that your friends and family may not be particularly interested in hearing about your experiences. So what if you've trekked to the Everest Base Camp? Though this was an incredible experience for you, when you try to relate it, their eyes glaze over and they cut you off with the latest gossip about your friends. Try not to let this lack of appreciation get you down – the reality is that the world you experienced in Asia is so far removed from their daily lives that it's difficult for them to really comprehend your stories. Plus, there may be an element of jealousy floating around about the good times you've had. Maybe you need to exercise some restraint and not wave your good luck in the faces of those who stayed at home slogging out their usual routine. You'll soon learn who really wants to hear your stories.

Even worse than the inability to communicate is the simple realisation that the good times are over and now you're back to the daily grind. Life on the road is challenging, exciting and fulfilling while life back home can appear bleak, boring and dreadfully lacking in meaning. The best way to fight the depression caused by this disparity is to be realistic – you cannot travel all the time, so you are going to have to get on with your regular life. Don't be tempted by the notion of perpetual travel as a way of escaping from 'real' life, as this can be a trap in the long run. Eventually, everyone has to return home, and the longer you put off your re-entry, the harder it will be.

There may in fact be a physiological component to your post-holiday blues. You may feel depressed, tired, emotionally unbalanced or even unable to sleep. Many of these symptoms may be chemical in nature and are quite similar to Seasonal Affective Disorder (SAD). This disorder affects millions of people each year during autumn and winter, and is thought to result from physiological changes caused by lack of sunlight. A very simple way to combat your post-holiday blues may be to do as the SAD people do, and get out in the sunshine and do some exercise. Some people also recommend a good daily intake of vitamins B and C, and still others prescribe the herbal remedy St John's wort (thought to act as a natural antidepressant). Whatever you do, it's best not to sit around moping and wishing you were back on the road.

If you are suffering from deep or long-lasting depression, don't try to fight it, but see a doctor. Likewise, if you're suffering from any physical symptoms such as loose bowels, chronic fatigue or skin inflammations, seek medical attention as soon as possible, as there's every chance you've picked up a bug in Asia.

MAKING THE TRANSITION

To ease yourself into life back home, it helps to give the end of your trip some serious thought while you're still on the road. You'll have a lot of free time while travelling to think about what you want to do when you get back. Ideally, your time away will recharge your batteries, give you a new perspective on the world and realign your priorities. If you simply avoid thoughts of home while you're on the road, you'll be in for a big shock when you arrive back at the airport.

When you do arrive home, you may find that you are suffering from post-holiday blues, or you may find that your are infused with a kind of manic energy. Either way, you'll want to get started on your new life as quickly as possible, and implement the changes you've decided to make. Most of all, try to apply some of what you've learned to your daily life. By doing so, you'll feel that your travel was not just a fleeting holiday, but a meaningful step in your life.

REMEMBERING YOUR TRIP

Within a few days of coming home, your trip can seem as though it never happened at all. To prevent the memories from sliding into oblivion, try some of the following techniques:

- Make a photo album with prints from your trip. Choose the best ones and put them in chronological order. If you've taken slides, put them in the proper order if you wish to inflict slide shows on people.

- Keep in touch with the people you met along the way – both locals and fellow travellers. If you've promised anyone copies of your pictures, then send them as soon as you can – if you let a few months go by, you'll never get around to it. You can also send thank-you letters to some of the local people who went out of their way to help you, whether guesthouse owners, tour guides, porters or just people you met on the street.

- Deepen your interest in some of the countries you visited. Take a course at your local university or search out some books at the library. Even if it's just one small facet of that country, like Thai cooking or Indian yoga, you'll find your study is much more meaningful once you've encountered the real thing.

- Study the language of a country that particularly interested you. Whether it's just for your own interest or because you'd like to go back some day, studying a language is one of the best ways to become better acquainted with another culture.

- Read the journal you kept during your trip. Even more than pictures, the words you wrote can bring your trip alive again months, or even years later. And if you find that your journal reads like the a great travel novel, you could always write up some of the better passages and send them off to magazines or newspapers ... it may be the start of a career as a travel writer.

Images of
ASIA & INDIA

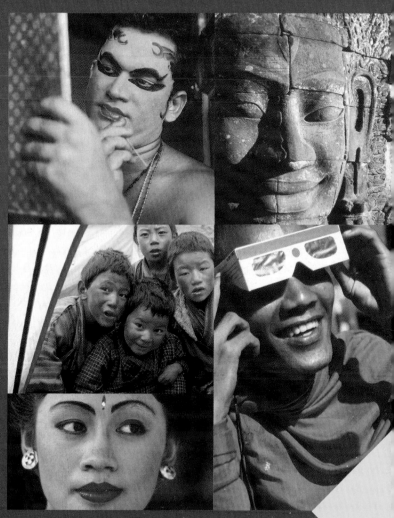

1. Kathakali dancer before a show in Kerala, India 2. Face of
Angkor Wat, Cambodia 3. Khmer monk watching a solar eclipse,
Cambodia 4. Balinese dancer 5. Boys at a trekking camp, Bhutan

1. Portuguese mission-style architecture. Macau 2. Peak-hour arrival at dusk, Chennai (Madras), India 3. Filigree gold-decorated carved doors guard the entrance to That Luang Pagoda in Vientiane, Laos

Wandering in the cool pavilion at Amber Palace, Rajasthan, India 2. Masjid egara mosque provides quiet refuge from a mid-afternoon tropical downpour, uala Lumpur, Malaysia 3. 'Jaws' in Bollywood, Chennai (Madras), India

The tastes and sights of South-East Asian street cuisine 1. Whipping up an oyster omlette, a Melakan speciality, Malaysia 2&3. The contrasting flavours of fresh steamed greens and fiery chillies 4. Roti chanai dotted with egg yolk

...eing prepared at an indoor hawker centre, Singapore 5. Street chef cooking ...p for diners at a night market in Johor Bahru, Malaysia 6. Tofu sizzling in a ...aming wok, Guangzhou, China.

 1&2. Amid the speed and concrete of modern Tokyo, old-style trolley transport still has a place at the city's Tsukiji Fish Market. Japan 3. The undulating pattern of Asia's ubiquitous rice terraces. Guangxi Province, China

. An elegantly attired resident keeps her cool in Ho Chi Minh City's chaotic
traffic. Vietnam 2. The lush Cameron Highlands hill station is popular for its
refreshing climate, tea plantations and colourful Buddhist temple, Malaysia

1. Hanoi street sign, Vietnam 2. Temple offerings, Vientiane, Laos 3. Mosaic face of a god decorating a Thai wat 4. Muslim women chatting, Malaysia 5. Racks of coloured silk, Thailand

BANGLADESH

Reading the world's press you could be forgiven for thinking that Bangladesh is more a disaster zone than a travel destination. However, hiding behind the images of cyclones and floods is a strikingly lush and beautiful land with a rich history and a variety of attractions unusual for such a small country. You can see archaeological sites dating back over 2000 years, check out the longest beach and largest littoral mangrove forest in the world and visit the decaying mansions of 19th century maharajas.

Despite being the world's most crowded country, rural Bangladesh feels relaxed, spacious and friendly: travellers from India have been agreeably surprised to find border officials offering them cups of tea rather than reams of forms to fill in. Facilities are limited, but if you have an independent streak it's definitely worth avoiding the crowds in India and Nepal and following the old slogan of Bangladesh's tourist body – 'Come to Bangladesh before the tourists'.

When to Go

Tropical Bangladesh can be visited year-round; each seasonal phase offers a different quality to the warm climate. It's hottest during the premonsoon spring from April to mid-June, when both temperature and humidity are uncomfortable. With the monsoon, the weather cools off slightly as the whole country begins to fill with water, mostly from the rivers in the Himalaya. This is a fascinating time for travel, although not without its difficulties. As the rivers swell, most low-lying land around the major river systems becomes inundated. In some rural areas only the elevated highway is above the flood line, along with clusters of raised settlements that become islands in vast expanses of water. By October, things have begun to cool off and dry up, and between November and

AT A GLANCE

Full Country Name: The People's Republic of Bangladesh

Area: 143,998 sq km

Population: 130 million

Capital City: Dhaka (pop six million)

People: 98% Bengali, 1% Bihari and 1% tribal

Languages: Bangla (Bengali) and some English

Religion: 87% Islam, 12% Hindu, 0.6% Buddhist and 0.4% Christian

Government: Constitutional Republic

Currency: Bangladeshi taka (Tk)

Time Zone: Six hours ahead of GMT/UTC

International Telephone Code: 890

Electricity: 220V AC; power outlets feature two-pronged, round-pin connections

February the weather is at its best, especially in December and January when it gets rather chilly in the evenings.

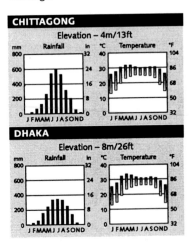

CHITTAGONG
Elevation – 4m/13ft

DHAKA
Elevation – 8m/26ft

Highlights

Bangladesh has a rich cultural heritage and is full of ancient mosques and temples, as well as the mansions of the *zamindars* (landlords). This mainly rural country is crisscrossed by innumerable rivers, so boat travel will feature in your stay, particularly if you are into wetlands and birdlife. A limited budget will take you a long way – this is one country where a touch of luxury is very affordable.

Dhaka

Dhaka is Bangladesh's most modern city and offers luxuries, goods and services unavailable elsewhere in the country. The Old City holds many of the attractions; running along the northern bank of the Buriganga River, it's a fascinating area crowded with people and watercraft. It also features the baroque-style palace of Ahsan Manzil, Lalbagh Fort and a couple of attractive mosques, including Hussain Dalan and Sat Gumbad. The National Museum is well worth a visit, while the upmarket Gulshan-Banani-Baridhara area has some excellent and very affordable shopping and restaurants. The ancient capital of Sonargaon is a day trip away and shouldn't be missed.

Sundarbans National Park

This park is the largest littoral mangrove belt in the world, stretching 80km into the Bangladeshi hinterland from the coast. These forests also include some of the last surviving stands of the mighty jungles which covered the Gangetic plain. This has been a wildlife sanctuary since 1966 and it is estimated that there are now 400 royal Bengal tigers and about 30,000 spotted deer in the area, as well as reptiles, monkeys and more than 250 species of birds. You will need a permit and guide to see the park – access is normally by air to Jessore and then a bus to the park. Also in the area is Bagerhat with its excellent collection of 15th century Muslim monuments.

Temples & Ruins

Puthia in Rajshahi has the largest collection of historically important Hindu structures in Bangladesh, including the intricate Govinda Temple, the 16th century Jagannath Temple and the five spired Siva Temple. Buddhist architecture fans should visit the Mainimati ruins south-east of Dhaka. Famed as a centre of Buddhist culture from the 7th to 12th centuries, the ruins include more than 50 scattered sites, with Salban Vihara, Kotila Mura and Charpatra Mura considered the most important. The 8th century Somapuri Vihara at

Paharpur covers 11 hectares and was once the biggest Buddhist monastery south of the Himalaya; it's one of the most impressive archaeological sites in the country.

Chittagong Hill Tracts

The Chittagong Hill Tracts form a contrasting landscape of tropical jungles on rolling hills, populated by the colourfully dressed people of Buddhist tribes. Visit Rangamati, in its lush setting on the shores of Kaptai Lake, and meet the people of the Chakma tribe. A boat trip on the lake is the highlight of any visit and will enable you to view beautiful scenery and many species of birds.

Islands & Beaches

Just off the easternmost tip of the country, St Martin's Island is almost a tropical cliche, with coconut palm-fringed beaches and bountiful marine life. There's nothing more strenuous to do here than soak up the rays, and it's a clean and peaceful place without even a mosquito to disrupt your serenity. Just to the north, Cox's Bazar is Bangladesh's only beach resort. It has a Burmese Buddhist flavour and few amenities to service the visitors attracted by its enormous expanse of shark-free beach. South of Cox's Bazar are more secluded beaches, including Himachari and Inani.

Itineraries

Bangladesh is small, but travel can be time-consuming, so don't try to do too much. No matter how long you have, make sure you travel by rocket (steamer) at least once to see the changing panorama and village life along the river banks – one of the enduring images of this riverine country.

ONE WEEK

Start with a couple of days exploring Dhaka by rickshaw and boat, then take a day trip to the ancient capital of Sonargaon or the National Martyrs Memorial in Savar. Fly to Cox's Bazar for a couple of days on the beaches and for walking in the tropical rainforests of the Chittagong Hill Tracts. Alternatively, travel by road or train to Srimangal in Sylhet and explore the beautiful scenery in the tea estates, the Jaflang area (close to Tamabil and the Indian border) and the Madhabkunda Waterfalls (south-east of Sylhet). Finally, if time permits, go back to Dhaka for an organised tour to the Sundarbans in Khulna.

TWO WEEKS

With an extra week you can follow the one week itinerary more slowly, or add some side trips along the way. From Cox's Bazar, you could travel to Teknaf to take a boat trip to St Martin's Island for some serious relaxation. You could also explore Chittagong, the second largest city in Bangladesh and visit the Mainimati ruins on your way back to Dhaka. The Sylhet route can be extended by taking a trip to the Jaintiapur ruins or to the wetlands of Sunamganj for some excellent birdwatching. On the way to Khulna stop at Jessore for a look at some world-famous aid projects or see the ancient architecture at Bagerhat. All of the above will take three weeks or more, so follow your interests.

ONE MONTH

If you have four weeks, you could spend a couple more days in Dhaka before seeing all the sights in the two week itinerary at your leisure. If you have the time, head north to the less touristed regions of Mymensingh and Rajshahi. The latter features marvellous historic architecture at Mahasthangarh, the Somapuri Vihara at Paharpur, Sura Mosque at Rangpur and the many temples at Puthia. The latter also features the country's finest Raj-era palace.

BANGLADESH HIGHLIGHTS & ITINERARIES

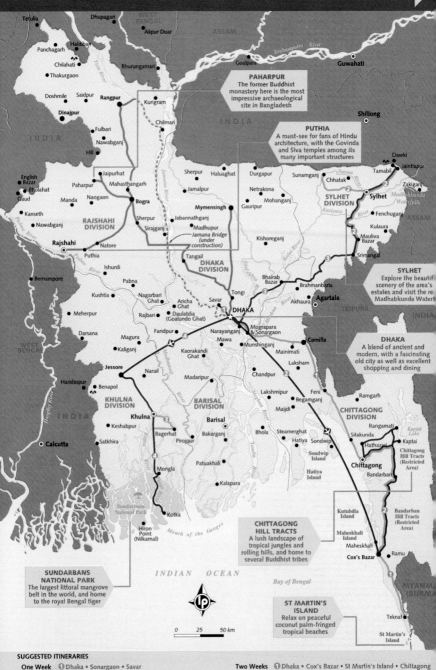

PAHARPUR
The former Buddhist monastery here is the most impressive archaeological site in Bangladesh

PUTHIA
A must-see for fans of Hindu architecture, with the Govinda and Siva temples among its many important structures

SYLHET
Explore the beautiful scenery of the area's estates and visit the re[...] Madhabkunda Waterf[...]

DHAKA
A blend of ancient and modern, with a fascinating old city as well as excellent shopping and dining

CHITTAGONG HILL TRACTS
A lush landscape of tropical jungles and rolling hills, and home to several Buddhist tribes

SUNDARBANS NATIONAL PARK
The largest littoral mangrove belt in the world, and home to the royal Bengal tiger

ST MARTIN'S ISLAND
Relax on peaceful coconut palm-fringed tropical beaches

0   25   50 km

SUGGESTED ITINERARIES

One Week
1. Dhaka • Sonargaon • Savar
2. Dhaka • Cox's Bazar • Chittagong Hill Tracts
3. Dhaka • Srimangal • Jaflang • Madhabkunda Waterfalls
4. Dhaka • Khulna • Sundarbans

Two Weeks
1. Dhaka • Cox's Bazar • St Martin's Island • Chittagong
2. Dhaka • Srimangal • Sylhet • Jaintiapur Ruins • Sunam[...]
3. Dhaka • Jessore • Khulna • Bagerhat

One Month
Dhaka • Mymensingh • Rajshahi • Mahasthangarh • Paharpur • Rangpur

Visa Requirements

All visitors to Bangladesh must have a visa. If you're arriving by air and your stay will not exceed 15 days, there's no real reason to get one before arriving because visas are issued at the airport. The fee varies according to nationality, but they are relatively expensive, ranging from US$20 to US$60. Extensions are easily obtained. If you arrive overland or plan to stay for more than 15 days, you'd be better off getting a visa at home. The fees are the same as those issued at the airport, but these visas are valid for six months and allow a stay of up to three months.

Bangladeshi Embassies & High Commissions

AUSTRALIA
(☎ 02-6295 3328) 35 Endeavour Street, Red Hill, ACT 2603

CANADA
(☎ 613-236-0138/9) 85 Range Rd, Suite No 402, Ottawa, Ontario KIN 8J6

UK
(☎ 020-7584 0081) 28 Queen's Gate, London SW7 5JA; (☎ 021-643 2386) 31-33 Guildhall Building, 12 Navigation St, Birmingham 42 4NT; (☎ 061-236 4853, 236 1064) 28-32 Princess St, 3rd floor, Manchester MI 4LB

USA
(☎ 202-342-8373; fax 333-4971) 2201 Wisconsin Ave NW, Suite 300, Washington, DC 20007; (☎ 212-599-6767, 599-6850) 211 East 43rd St, Suite 502, New York, NY 10017

Tourist Offices Overseas

Bangladesh has no tourist offices abroad. Check out some of the web sites listed under Online Services and see your travel agent.

Health

Food and waterborne diseases (eg typhoid, dysentery and hepatitis) are the most likely health problems. Drink only boiled or purified water (most bottled water and soft drinks are OK) and in particular avoid shellfish, fish and meat. Freshly cooked street food is good and generally healthy, but steer clear of dishes, such as curries, which may have been reheated many times during the day. Malaria exists in all parts of Bangladesh, especially in the Sylhet and Chittagong areas, but does not occur in Dhaka. Outbreaks of dengue fever occur and filariasis is common, so take precautions against these diseases. Leishmaniasis, a disease transmitted by sandflies, is on the increase in Bangladesh, so avoid sandfly bites. Medical services are poor or nonexistent in Bangladesh. If you need a doctor, go to Dhaka, but for serious medical treatment, leave Bangladesh.

Post & Communications

Bangladesh's postal system is reasonably reliable, but extremely slow. You'd be better off sending and receiving goods in Thailand or India. There is a post restante service in Dhaka, but it's of little use, unless you're spending three months in the country. International calls can be made at hotels and at private business centres in the main cities, but they can be expensive and the quality of the line dubious. Email and Internet services are still uncommon in Bangladesh. Dhaka and Chittagong are your best bets.

Money

Costs

Bangladesh is a very cheap country to travel in, but the quality of budget food, accommodation and travel is poor. It's possible to average US$4 a day if you travel 2nd class on trains, travel on local buses, stay in the cheapest hotels with shared bath and no air-con and eat at the very cheapest restaurants. However, for US$10 to US$15 a day you'll get a decent hotel room with its own bathroom, a couple of good meals a day and 1st class train travel. There isn't a huge range of top-end accommodation or restaurants outside Dhaka.

Changing Money
Cash and travellers cheques in US dollars are preferred by banks to pounds sterling. Outside Dhaka and Chittagong you'll have problems changing pounds. Credit cards are widely accepted at hotels, guest-houses and restaurants in Dhaka and Chittagong, but virtually nowhere else. American Express users can get a cash advance with their card.

Online Services
Lonely Planet's *Destination Bangladesh* page is at www.lonelyplanet.com/dest /ind/ban.htm.

The Pacific Asia Travel Association (www.pata.org/nations/bang .html) provides a succinct snapshot for travellers, while *Tour Bangladesh* (venus .gsu.edu/~mir/bangla) does the same job from a local perspective. Get all your daily news from the *Dhaka-Bangladesh* site (www.dhaka-bangladesh.com).

Books
Bangladesh: Reflections on the Water by James J Novak is the best all-round introduction to the country. *A Quiet Violence* by Betsy Hartmann & James Boyce is the account of two Americans who lived for nine months in a small rural village.

Taslima Nasreen's *Lajja* (Shame) is set during the 1992 Ayodhya stoush in India. The book is banned in Bangladesh and Nasreen is hiding in exile.

The Rickshaws of Bangladesh by Robert Gallagher is a fascinating study of the ubiquitous rickshaw and its impact on the economy and society, while *A Tale of Millions* by Rafiqul Islam is the story of Bangladesh's War of Liberation told by a senior army officer.

Films
The great majority of films shown in cinemas are imports from India, with the usual themes of romance or personal triumph accompanied by lots of singing and dancing. Around 50 films are produced locally each year, though most are little more than copies of Indian films. The country's most acclaimed film is *Surjo Dighal Bari* (The House Along the Sun).

Entering & Leaving Bangladesh
Although Dhaka international airport is far from being a major Asian cross-roads, there are plenty of international flights. Indeed, many travellers use Dhaka as the gateway to the Indian subcontinent to take advantage of cheap fares from Europe. Bangkok and Calcutta are the main destinations for flights in and out of Bangladesh. The departure tax for international flights is US$7.50.

The situation regarding overland crossings to/from India is vague, but the principal crossings are at Benapol-Haridaspur, Chilahati-Haldibari and Tamabil-Dawki. Overland border crossings between Bangladesh and Myanmar (Burma) have been closed for more than 40 years.

Bhutan is an extraordinary place hardly touched by the hands of time. Nestled in the heart of the great Himalaya, it remained in self-imposed isolation for centuries. Since its doors were cautiously opened in 1974, visitors have been mesmerised: the environment is pristine, the scenery and architecture are awesome, the people are hospitable and charming and the culture unique in its purity.

Despite the huge potential of its natural resources, Bhutan emerged as one of Asia's poorest countries, shunning the 'profit at all costs' mentality of the rest of the world. With one foot in the past and one in the future, it strolls confidently towards modernisation on its own terms, fiercely protecting its ancient culture, its natural resources and its deeply Buddhist way of life.

Special Conditions

The Bhutan government insists that foreign visitors travel as package tourists with a pre-planned itinerary. A tariff of US$200 per day is imposed, which covers all accommodation, food, land transport within Bhutan (there is no domestic air service), guides and porters, the supply of pack animals and some cultural programs. The tariff drops to US$165 during the monsoon (June to September) and winter (December to February).

For group travel, Bhutan's system is convenient, efficient and generally comfortable. If you want to travel independently, you will have to accept a certain degree of regimentation, but there are ways to retain your freedom and avoid the drawbacks associated with an organised tour – for example, you can design your own itinerary according to dates that are convenient for you.

AT A GLANCE

Full Country Name: Kingdom of Bhutan

Area: 46,620 sq km

Population: 600,000

Capital City: Thimphu (pop 20,000)

People: Sharchops, Ngalong, Lhotshampa (ethnic Nepalis) and numerous small ethnic groups

Languages: Dzongkha (related to Tibetan), Sharchop, English, plus several regional languages and dialects

Religion: 70% Mahayana Buddhist, 25% Hindu and 5% Muslim

Government: Hereditary monarchy

Currency: Ngultrum (Nu); the Indian rupee is also widely accepted

Time Zone: Six hours ahead of GMT/UTC

International Telephone Code: 975

Electricity: 230V, 50AC; power outlets most commonly feature two-prong round sockets

When to Go

The best time to visit is October and November when the major festivals are being held. These colourful events offer a first-hand glimpse of Bhutanese life and often provide the only opportunity to see inside the great *dzongs* (fort-monasteries). It's possible to work at least one festival into a tour or trek program. The largest festivals – at Paro and Thimphu – take place during the time of the best weather and flights become hopelessly over-booked. The climate is best in autumn (late September to late November), when skies are clear and the mountain peaks are visible. This is the ideal time for trekking and for travelling throughout the country. You're likely to get wet no matter the season, but avoid the heavy monsoon period (June to September).

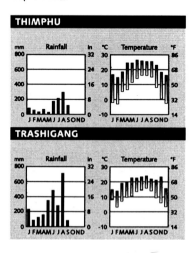

Highlights

Everywhere in Bhutan you will find spectacular scenery, deep forests, high Himalayan peaks, and a traditional Buddhist culture with amazing architecture and the massive dzongs that dominate the countryside. Almost everything in Bhutan is different from the rest of Asia, and probably unlike anything you may have imagined.

Trekking

Bhutan offers a true wilderness experience while retaining some comforts of a traditional Himalayan trek, as all your food and accommodation needs are met by the touring company and trekking staff. Along the trekking routes there are no hotels, few villages and even fewer trekkers, but the scenery is both remarkable and spectacular – you couldn't be further from the 'apple pie' trails of Nepal.

Dzongs

Bhutan's extraordinary architecture is best represented by the massive white fort-monasteries that dominate the major valleys. It's sometimes possible to enter the dzongs for a close view of the impressive artwork and traditional construction techniques. Even from a distance, the dzongs are among the most photogenic of Bhutan's highlights.

Festivals

There are festivals *(tsechu)* throughout the year, and crowds of Bhutanese and foreign tourists descend on monasteries and dzongs to witness ceremonies and lama dances that continue for several days. The festivals are colourful pageants and important social occasions, with locals dressed in their finest traditional attire.

Bhutanese Hospitality

The Bhutanese are extraordinarily friendly and hospitable. In the towns almost everyone speaks English and you will make friends easily during your travels. All Bhutanese, whether government officials, drivers, guides or policemen, will treat you with a deference and politeness that can verge on the embarrassing.

Textiles

The traditional handloom weaving is so exotic and varied that a number of museums in the west have permanent exhibitions of Bhutanese textiles. While it's traditionally used for clothing, you can purchase lengths of colourful material to turn into curtains, bedspreads or clothing of a more western design.

Itineraries

ONE WEEK

Start with three days visiting the dzongs and museums in Thimphu and Paro and then take a trip into the mountains, staying in Punakha or Wangdue Phodrang. If you can, allow an extra day in Paro to climb to the point overlooking Taktshang, the famous 'Tiger's Nest' monastery that burned down in 1998. There are plans to faithfully rebuild it, but in the meantime the view is still worthwhile.

TWO WEEKS

A longer program will allow an overnight trip from Thimphu to Paro, before heading east to Bumthang. On the way, spend a night in Punakha and Wangdue Phodrang before detouring to the Phobjikha Valley to see Gangte Goemba (monastery) and, in late autumn, the rare and endangered blacknecked cranes. Continue east to Trongsa, with its impressive dzong, and then spend a couple of days in Bumthang for some beautiful architecture and hiking, before taking the long road back to Thimphu.

Alternatively, you could miss Paro and go further east from Bumthang to Mongar and Trashigang (possibly making the long detour to Lhuentse if you're into dzongs).

This trip involves lots of driving, but you can save yourself the long (546km) drive back to Thimphu by exiting Bhutan via Samdrup Jongkhar into India (you'll need to organise a permit in advance).

TREKS

Allow at least three days, and preferably a week, for trekking in Bhutan. The Druk Path from Paro to Thimphu is a short trek and not too difficult. The Jhomolhari Trek offers some of the best high-mountain scenery in Bhutan, and crosses two very high passes (4500m). An excellent alternative is to do only the first three days of this trek to Jhomolhari Base Camp (Jangothang), spend a day exploring, then return to Paro via a variation of the upward route. This avoids the high passes and still provides spectacular mountain views, as well as visits to highland villages and yak pastures. The 23 day remote and gruelling Snowman Trek to the Lunana district is said to be the most difficult in the world – certainly the price of US$4600 will deter most aspirants, but it's a remarkable journey.

Visa Requirements

The visa process is a little complicated, but generally runs quite efficiently. Rather than go to an embassy (Bhutan maintains very few anyway), you must apply for a visa in advance through a Bhutan tour operator, who will then submit it to the Tourism Authority in Thimphu. The authority will approve the visa only after your trip is completely paid for. The application then goes to the Ministry of Foreign Affairs, which takes about a week to issue a visa clearance. The clearance is sent to the tour operator and Bhutan's national carrier, Druk Air (which will not issue plane tickets until clearance has been granted). The actual visa endorsement is stamped in your passport once you have arrived in the country, pay a fee of US$20 and provide one passport photo with your passport number written on the back. Your visa will be current for the exact period you've paid for, up to a maximum of 15 days. Extensions are possible (really only necessary if you're going on a lengthy trek) and can be arranged by your tour operator.

Tourist Offices Overseas

Bhutan has no overseas tourist offices, but travel agents will be able to supply you with most information. Also check out the web sites listed under Online Services.

Health

The main health concerns in Bhutan are food and waterborne diseases (such as dysentery, hepatitis and typhoid) and respiratory infections. Tap water is not safe to drink; avoid unwashed vegetables and fruit, ice cream and meat dishes. If you are doing some trekking in Bhutan, be aware of the risks associated with accidents or altitude illness. Malaria is nonexistent in tourist areas, but is present in lowland areas year-round. Hospital facilities are limited, but treatment is free. If you are seriously ill or injured, go to Bangkok or Singapore.

Post & Communications

Bhutan's postal system is inexpensive and fairly reliable, although it can be slow. The most reliable method of receiving mail is to have it sent to the office of your tour operator (if you'll be in the country for any length of time). The telephone system is modern, sophisticated and reasonably expensive, although facilities for international calls are scarce outside the main towns. A national public email service and an international Internet service should be up and running by the time you read this, although the rates are not likely to be cheap.

Money

Costs

Apart from the daily tariff of US$200, there's a daily surcharge for lone travellers and people travelling in pairs (US$40 and US$30 each respectively). This covers all costs apart from drinks, laundry and cultural splurges such as a traditional Bhutanese hot-stone bath. The daily tariff is discounted by 10% for days 11 to 20 of your stay, and by 20% from day 21 onwards (for which you would need a visa extension).

Changing Money

Bhutan has two banks, with branches throughout the country. You can cash travellers cheques at any bank and most hotels but you should only carry well known brands such as American Express. Don't plan to use your credit card in Bhutan. Also, there are no ATMs for debit cards.

Online Services

Lonely Planet's *Destination Bhutan* page can be found at www.lonelyplanet.com/dest/ind/bhu.htm. You can keep up to date at *Kuensel*, Bhutan's national newspaper (www.kuensel.com).

Druk Yul (www.bhutan.org/index 2.html) has numerous links, and this very useful site is still growing. Another good site with plenty of tourism information, including the latest tourist regulations, a yeti watch and a Bhutan chat, is *Bootan* (www.bootan.com). You can find even more tourism information (the official version this time) at *Kingdom of Bhutan* (www.kingdomofbhutan.com).

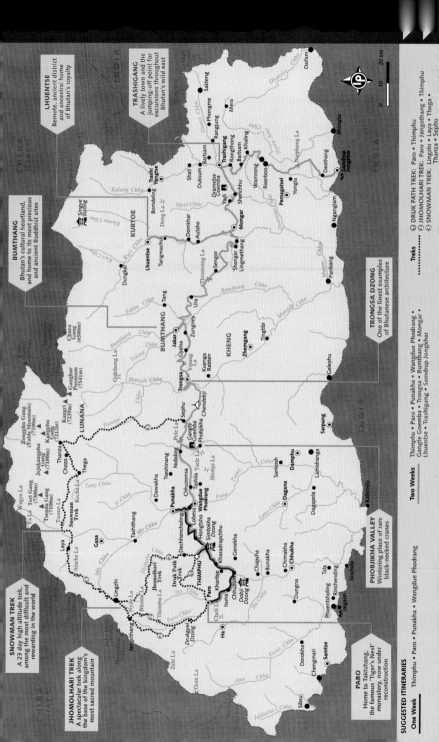

SNOWMAN TREK
A 23 day high altitude trek, among the most difficult and rewarding in the world

JHOMOLHARI TREK
A spectacular trek along the base of the kingdom's most sacred mountain

LHUENTSE
Remote ancient district and ancestral home of Bhutan's royalty

TRASHIGANG
A lively town and the jumping-off point for excursions throughout Bhutan's wild east

BUMTHANG
Bhutan's cultural heartland, and home to its most precious and ancient Buddhist sites

TRONGSA DZONG
One of the finest examples of Bhutanese architecture

Treks

① DRUK PATH TREK: Paro • Thimphu

② JHOMOLHARI TREK: Paro • Jangothang • Thimphu

③ SNOWMAN TREK: Lingzhi • Laya • Thega •
Thanza • Sephu

PHOBJIKHA VALLEY
Wintering place of rare black-necked cranes

PARO
Home to Taktshang, the famous 'Tiger's Nest' monastery, now under reconstruction

SUGGESTED ITINERARIES

One Week   Thimphu • Paro • Punakha • Wangdue Phodrang

Two Weeks   Thimphu • Paro • Punakha • Wangdue Phodrang •
Gangte Goemba • Trongsa • Bumthang • Mongar •
Lhuentse • Trashigang • Thega • Mongar •
Samdrup Jongkhar

0   10   20 km

A discussion on the exodus of Nepali-speakers from Bhutan in the early 1990s can be found at Amnesty International's site (www.amnesty.org) or at www.geocities.com/HotSprings/Resort/6327. The Bhutan government's perspective can be found at www.bhutan-info.org/bhutancon.htm.

Books

So Close to Heaven, The Vanishing Buddhist Kingdoms of the Himalayas by Barbara Crossette is an excellent account of Bhutan's history and culture. Published in 1995, it discusses some of the current development and political problems facing Bhutan.

Dreams of the Peaceful Dragon is a traveller's account of a walk across Bhutan in the 1970s, before the road between Bumthang and Mongar was completed, and provides a good picture of trekking in Bhutan. *The Raven Crown* by Michael Aris is a lavishly illustrated history of Bhutan's monarchy.

The Tibetan Book of Living and Dying by Sogyal Rimpoche is a translation of Guru Rimpoche's *Tibet-an Book of the Dead*. It's quite a sophisticated Himalayan Buddhist text, but it's well worth a look if you are interested in Bhutan's religious foundations.

Bhutan – Mountain Fortress of the Gods is a coffee-table book and provides documentation of a 1998 Bhutanese exhibition in Vienna. Edited by Christian Schicklgruber & Françoise Pommaret, it has extensive illustrations and excellent information.

Films

There are a few documentary films about Bhutan, the most recent being the BBC TV special *Joanna Lumley in the Kingdom of the Thunder Dragon*. The Royal Society for the Protection of Nature has produced a video about the black-necked cranes, but it is not easily available. Much of the film *Little Buddha* was shot in Bhutan, and

PROBLEMS IN THE SOUTH

Bhutanese citizens of Nepali descent dominate the southern part of the country. A government policy of integration in the 1950s resulted in them gaining political representation and admission to the bureaucracy, as well as the teaching of Nepali in schools and permission to practise cultural customs. In the late 1980s, however, the government introduced *driglam namzha* (traditional values and etiquette) under which the Nepali language was eliminated from primary schools, and a census system introduced which required citizens to produce documentation proving they had resided in Bhutan before 1958. Thousands of ethnic Nepalis lacked proper documentation, and violence in the south led to an exodus of Bhutanese citizens of Nepali descent.

By the end of 1992, some 80,000 Nepali-speakers were housed in refugee camps in southeastern Nepal. Since 1993, Bhutan and Nepal have held several rounds of talks to try to identify which refugees are legitimate citizens of Bhutan, but little progress has been made. The status of the refugees is protected by the UN High Commissioner for Refugees. If this support disappears, and the deadlock on how to resolve the crisis continues, those in the camps will probably enter the larger diaspora of landless Nepali-speakers in south Asia.

Bhutanese boys played the role of the Dalai Lama at various ages in the 1997 movie *Seven Years in Tibet*. Nomad Films in Australia has produced a number of award-winning documentaries that you can order through its web site at www.ekidna.com/nomad or from Nomad Films International (☎ 03-9819 3350), PO Box 176, Prahran, Vic 3181. The films are *Tiger's Nest*, *Mountain of the Goddess*, *Man of the People* and *Man of the Forest*.

Entering & Leaving Bhutan

There are only two entry points to Bhutan: most travellers arrive by air at Paro, while some arrive by road at Phuentsholing (Jaigaon on the Indian side) on Bhutan's southern border with India. In any event you have to fly by Druk Air, either in or out. Druk Air has no interline agreements with other carriers so you will need to arrange your own ticket to and from wherever you connect with them.

BRUNEI

This tiny oil-rich Islamic sultanate lying on the north-western coast of Borneo is known chiefly for the astounding wealth of its sultan, its tax-free, subsidised society, and the fact that (statistically at least) its people enjoy one of the highest per capita incomes in the world. Despite the ostentatious modern public buildings in the capital, most of Brunei is undeveloped and virtually untouched by the outside world. Brunei is a little slice of Islamic heaven – alcohol is difficult to obtain (although tolerated if you're circumspect), there's no nightlife to speak of, and the political culture encourages quiet acquiescence to the edicts of the sultan. The folk of Brunei are amply rewarded for their conformist ways with free health care and education, free sporting centres, cheap loans and high, tax-free wages. There are a few attractions, but generally a few days is enough to satisfy visitors.

When to Go
Weather is not much of a consideration when heading for Brunei – whenever you go it's going to be warm and wet. Rainfall occurs throughout the year, but is heaviest between September and January. Temperatures are consistently between 24°C and 31°C. Average humidity is 79%, making it a pretty warm and sticky place. Things tend to close down during Ramadan (around March).

AT A GLANCE

Full Country Name: Negara Brunei Darussalam

Area: 5765 sq km

Population: 305,000

Capital City: Bandar Seri Begawan (pop 80,000)

People: 69% Malay, 18% Chinese and 13% Indians, indigenous tribes and expatriate workers

Languages: Malay, English and Chinese

Religion: 65% Muslim, 15% Buddhist, 11% indigenous religions and 9% Christian

Government: Constitutional monarchy

Currency: Brunei dollar (B$); the Singapore dollar is also accepted

Time Zone: Eight hours ahead of GMT/UTC

International Telephone Code: 673

Electricity: 220V to 240V, 50 AC; plugs are of the three square-pin type also used in Malaysia

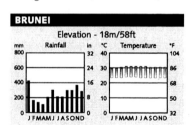

BRUNEI

Elevation - 18m/58ft

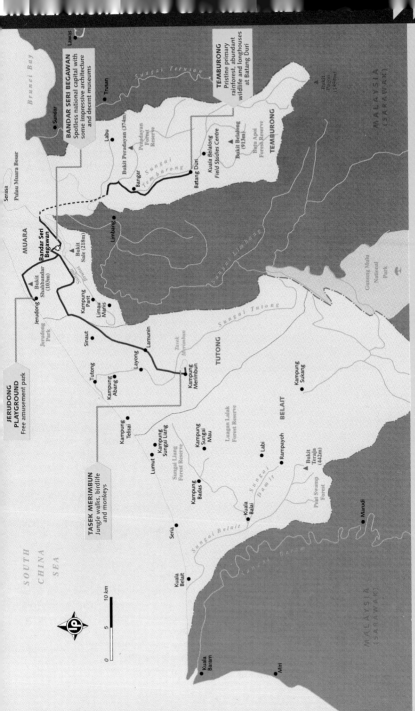

JERUDONG PLAYGROUND
Free amusement park

TASEK MERIMBUN
Jungle walks, birdlife and monkeys

BANDAR SERI BEGAWAN
Spotless national capital with some impressive architecture and decent museums

TEMBURONG
Pristine primary rainforest, abundant wildlife and longhouses at Batang Duri

Brunei Bay

SOUTH CHINA SEA

MALAYSIA (SARAWAK)

Gunung Mulu National Park

Bandar Seri Begawan

MUARA

TUTONG

BELAIT

TEMBURONG

0   5   10 km

SUGGESTED ITINERARIES

One Week   Bandar Seri Begawan • Jerudong Playground • Tasek Merimbun • Batang Duri • Temburong

Highlights & Itineraries

Brunei's list of highlights is a short one, but all are within easy reach of Bandar Seri Begawan (BSB). In BSB, take a look at Omar Ali Saifuddien Mosque (a massive tribute to both Brunei's wealth and its devotion to Islam), Brunei Museum and the nearby Malay Technology Museum. Along the Brunei Sungai, Kampung Ayer is a reminder of the days before Brunei struck it rich – a photogenic collection of stilt villages beside the river.

On the northern coast, Jerudong Playground is an enormous, free amusement park that's worth devoting an evening to, while further south Brunei's largest lake, Tasik Merimbun, features some good birdlife and lots of monkeys. Brunei's eastern territory, Temburong, makes a good day trip from BSB for walks in primary rainforest (Batu Apoi Forest Reserve) and a look at a longhouse of the Iban ethnic people at Batang Duri.

Visa Requirements

Citizens of Canada and New Zealand can stay for 14 days without a visa, while Brits get 30 days and Americans 90 days. Australians can get a 14 day visa on arrival. Transit passengers arriving by air are issued a 72 hour visa at Brunei international airport. If you intend to make a short trip to Brunei it could be worth taking advantage of this visa, as three days is enough to see most of the sights.

Brunei Embassies

AUSTRALIA
(☎ 02-6290 1801) 16 Bulwarra Close, O'Malley, ACT 2606

CANADA
(☎ 613-234-5656) 395 Laurier Ave East, Ottawa, Ontario K1N 6R4

UK
(☎ 020-7581 0521) 19/20 Belgrave Square, London SW1X 8PG

USA
(☎ 202-342-0159) Watergate Suite 300, 2600 Virginia Ave NW, Washington, DC 20037

Tourist Offices Overseas

Brunei has no overseas tourist offices, but travel agents will be able to supply you with most information. Also check out the web sites listed under Online Services.

Health

Brunei has high standards of hygiene, but the usual precautions should be taken to avoid heat exhaustion and dehydration. Tap water is safe to drink and malaria has been eliminated. The smoke haze is another matter and, when at its worst, face masks are *de rigueur* in downtown BSB. Seek information before you arrive, especially if you're taking young children with you; it's probably as well to avoid Brunei altogether if the situation is bad. There is a very good modern hospital in BSB.

Post & Communications

The postal service is reliable and reasonably priced and there's a post restante service in BSB. The telephone infrastructure is equally modern and there are plenty of public phones with international call facilities. There is an Internet cafe on the outskirts of BSB, but rates are fairly high.

Money

Costs

Accommodation in Brunei tends to be fiercely expensive. There is only one budget accommodation option in the country (around US$7 a bed), but it may well be full. Brunei's mid-range accommodation (US$35 to US$50) is a bit of a disaster, but most top-end hotels (US$100-plus) aren't that much more expensive than the equivalent in Malaysia. Transport and food are more expensive than in Peninsular Malaysia, but not outrageously so; a budget meal will cost around US$2 or US$3, and top-end meals start from US$10.

Changing Money
Although the official currency is the Brunei dollar, Singapore dollars are accepted almost everywhere. It's comparatively easy to change both cash and travellers cheques, but banks will give you a better rate (around 10% more) for travellers cheques.

Online Services
Lonely Planet's *Destination Brunei* page is at www.lonelyplanet.com/dest/sea/brunei.htm.

The Official Web Page of Brunei Darussalam (jtb.brunet.bn/index.htm) has the bland stamp of authority, but also hosts daily news bulletins, and has tourist information and lots of useful phone numbers.

A mop-up list of the few sites devoted to Brunei is at *Microstate* (www.microstate.net/cgiwin/msnet.exe/show micro,110). There isn't a great deal more around at the moment, apart from commercial travel sites.

Books
Books on Brunei are scarce, but there are a few useful titles for travellers and glossy publications which are nice to look at and make good mementos, such as *Explore Brunei*, the free government tourist guide.

Brunei Darussalam, A Guide is an informative, glossy book with beautiful photos. It outlines a host of day trips and sights around the country, although it's a bit out of date. Few bookshops stock it, but it can be purchased at the publications office of Brunei Shell in BSB, opposite the Hongkong Bank. *By God's Will – A Portrait of the Sultan of Brunei* by Lord Chalfont is a measured look at the sultan and Brunei.

If you're thinking of exploring the hinterland by car, the *Road Map and Street Index of Brunei Darus-salam*, published by Shell, has detailed maps of all built-up areas, plus information on where to go and what to see.

Entering & Leaving Brunei
Most visitors fly into and out of Bandar Seri Begawan. Brunei has direct air connections to 10 Asian cities and to Australia. Because of the difference in exchange rates, it's almost 40% cheaper to fly to Brunei from Malaysia than vice versa. Departure tax is US$3.50 to Malaysia and Singapore and US$8.50 to all other destinations. There are express boats between Bandar Seri Begawan and Lawas and Limbang in Sarawak, and the duty-free island of Labuan off Sabah. The main overland route into Brunei is from Miri in Sarawak to Bandar Seri Begawan.

CAMBODIA

Cambodia is the successor-state of the mighty Khmer Empire, which once ruled much of what is now Vietnam, Laos and Thailand. Foremost among the achievements of Khmer civilisation are the magisterial temples of Angkor – there are few historical sites in South-East Asia that can match the grandeur of this ancient complex. Cambodia has a rich and proud culture, a charming French-era capital (if a little weather-beaten these days) and some impressive natural scenery.

Today, Cambodia is bloodied and bowed after two decades of internecine war and the 1997 collapse of the shaky UN-sponsored democratic reforms. Despite Prime Minister Hun Sen's violent assumption of power, travel opportunities have improved substantially in recent times. The road and rail systems are now considered generally safe, and if you stay within the confines of Phnom Penh, its surrounding attractions and Angkor, you should be fine. If you're planning to head further afield, check with your embassy on the latest situation.

When to Go

Cambodia is a relatively small country, but travel is complicated by the complete lack of infrastructure in the provinces. As ever, what you can expect to see depends mainly on how much time and money you have available and, if travelling by road, a little bit of luck – breakdowns are common and can wipe a day or so out of a schedule. During the wet season, many roads become much harder to navigate and this can slow you down considerably.

That said, Cambodia can be visited any time of year. The ideal months are December and January. At this time of year the humidity levels are relatively low and there's little

---

AT A GLANCE

Full Country Name: Kingdom of Cambodia

Area: 181,035 sq km

Population: 10.5 million

Capital City: Phnom Penh (pop one million)

People: 90% to 95% ethnic Khmers, plus ethnic Chinese and Vietnamese minorities

Languages: Khmer, French and English

Religion: 95% Buddhist, 2.5% Muslim, 2% animist and 0.5% Christian

Government: Transitional democracy

Currency: Cambodian riel (r), and US dollars are accepted throughout the country

Time Zone: Seven hours ahead of GMT/UTC

International Telephone Code: 855

Electricity: 220V, 50 AC; electric power sockets are generally of the round two-pin variety

likelihood of rain. From early February, temperatures start to rise until the hottest month, April, in which temperatures can reach 38°C. The wet season, which lasts from April to October, is not necessarily a bad time to visit Cambodia. Angkor, for example, is surrounded by lush foliage and the moats are full of water at this time of year. If you are planning to visit the hill-tribe regions of the north-east, however, the wet season should be avoided.

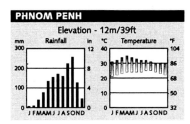

Highlights

Temples
The celebrated temples of Angkor are Cambodia's greatest tourist attraction. These 100 or so temples are the sacred remains of what was once a much larger administrative and religious centre. They were built between the 9th and 13th centuries to glorify a succession of Khmer kings. Most of Angkor was abandoned in the 15th century and the temples became cloaked by forest. The site was rediscovered in the late 19th century and restoration continues today. Two other magnificent temples are the Bayon and Ta Prohm; like Angkor Wat, these are both near the town of Siem Reap.

Phnom Penh
The capital retains an undeniable charm despite its tumultuous and often violent past. It boasts several impressive *wats* (temple-monasteries) such as Wat Ounalom, Wat Phnom and Wat Lang Ka. It is also home to the spectacular Khmer Silver Pagoda. There are displays of Khmer crafts in the National Museum and the Royal Palace. Other attractions include the Central Market and the School of Fine Arts. Just 15km south-west of the city centre, the Killing Fields of Choeung Ek are a grisly reminder of the atrocities committed by the Khmer Rouge under Pol Pot.

Sihanoukville
Sihanoukville (also known as Kompong Som) is Cambodia's only port. It's currently being redeveloped as a tourist attraction, with a casino planned for Naga Island. For the moment, Sihanoukville's chief attraction is the great snorkelling and diving that can be found around the nearby islands. The best of the beaches around the town is probably Ochatial Beach.

Festivals
The Bon Om Tuk (Water Festival) begins in late October or early November when the Tonlé Sap River reverses its flow and begins to empty into the Mekong River. Pirogue races are held in Phnom Penh at this time. Chaul Chnam, held in mid-April, is a three day celebration of the Khmer New Year. Ethnic Chinese and Vietnamese celebrate Lunar New Year in late January or early February.

Ratanakiri
Mountainous Ratanakiri Province is best known for its isolated hill tribes. The province is free of both landmines and Khmer Rouge activity, which means it's fairly safe to explore the surrounding countryside and visit some

of the hill tribes. It is, however, best to avoid travelling here in the wet season, when the roads are impassable and the risks of malaria and dengue fever are high. Just 4km east of the provincial capital of Ban Lung is Yak Lom Volcanic Lake, a major attraction of the region. It forms a near circle and is surrounded by forest. There are also waterfalls west of Ban Lung.

Udong

Udong, 40km north of Phnom Penh, was the capital of Cambodia from 1618 to 1866. It's generally very quiet, and you'll often have the town's *stupas* (religious structures housing relics) to yourself. The ruins are sprinkled across two ridges – the smaller has two ruined buildings, several stupas and the remains of Ta San Mosque. Surrounding the ruins are some intact smaller *viharas* (Buddhist religious buildings), stupas and Buddhas. At the base of the ridge is a memorial to victims of Pol Pot, containing the bones of people buried in the 100 or so mass graves found in the area.

Itineraries

ONE WEEK TO 10 DAYS

Visitors with only a week will realistically find themselves restricted to Phnom Penh and Angkor's temples. Angkor is accessible by plane, fast boat (up the Tonlé Sap River) and, more recently, by bus. Those with 10 days might like to include more time at the temples and attempt a visit to the holy mountain of Phnom Kulen, make a trip to the beaches at Sihanoukville or take a boat journey up the Mekong River to Kratie or Kompong Cham.

TWO WEEKS

An extra week will allow you to consider a more ambitious trip into the provinces. It is possible to do a loop around the attractions of the south coast, taking in Sihanoukville, Kampot, Kep, beautiful Bokor National Park (home to wild elephants and with accommodation at the summit), the ruined temples around Takeo and the attractions along National Highway 2, including Phnom Chisor or Tonlé Bati. Another option would be to stop in some of the provincial towns around Tonlé Sap (Great Lake) between Phnom Penh and Siem Reap. Battambang has a relaxed atmosphere and Kompong Thom offers a chance to break the long and uncomfortable journey on National Highway 6. By road, it's fairly straightforward to get to Mondulkiri, an isolated forested province in the north-east, and back in just one week with enough time to get a feel for the area's elevated lifestyle (the average altitude is 800m). However, nearby Ratanakiri can only be considered as part of a two week trip if you are willing to factor in a return flight, as it is generally a three day journey in each direction.

ONE MONTH

In one month, you can see almost all of the country's attractions, although in the wet season road conditions may limit access to some places. It is not unrealistic to include all the places listed above, although you may find yourself choosing between Mondulkiri and Ratanakiri, unless you want to shell out on a flight to the latter. Those feeling adventurous might want to try an overland trip to the mountain temple of Preah Vihear, in the north on the Thai border, although in the foreseeable future this will remain more accessible from the Thai side.

Visa Requirements

Most nationalities receive a one month visa on arrival at Pochentong airport. The cost is US$20 and you will need one passport photo. Travellers arriving overland from Ho Chi Minh City (Saigon) will have to obtain a visa before they arrive, but these are easy to get in Vietnam.

CAMBODIA HIGHLIGHTS & ITINERARIES

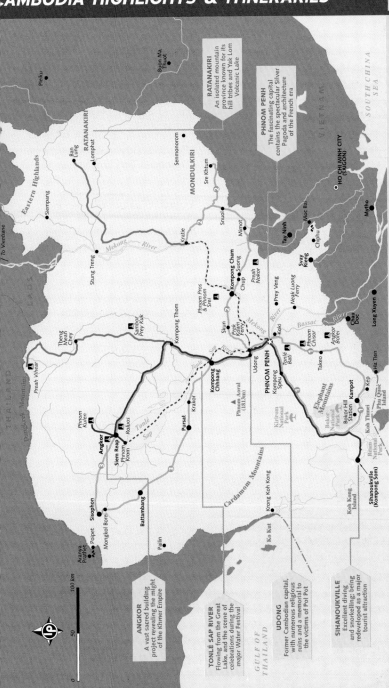

RATANAKIRI
An isolated mountain province known for its hill tribes and Yak Lom Volcanic Lake

PHNOM PENH
The fascinating capital contains the spectacular Silver Pagoda and architecture of the French era

ANGKOR
A vast sacred building project revealing the might of the Khmer Empire

TONLÉ SAP RIVER
Flowing from the Great Lake, and the scene of celebrations during the major Water Festival

UDONG
Former Cambodian capital, with numerous religious ruins and a memorial to the victims of Pol Pot

SIHANOUKVILLE
Excellent diving and snorkelling; being redeveloped as a major tourist attraction

SUGGESTED ITINERARIES

One Week
❶ Phnom Penh • Tonlé Sap • Angkor • Phnom Kulen •
to 10 Days Mekong River • Kompong Cham • Kratie • Sihanoukville

Two Weeks ❶ Phnom Penh • Tonlé Bati • Phnom Chisor • Takeo •
Kampot • Kep • Bokor National Park • Sihanoukville
❷ Phnom Penh • Battambang • Siem Reap
❸ Phnom Penh • Kompong Cham • Mondulkiri

One Month Phnom Penh • Mondulkiri • Ratanakiri • Preah Vihear

Cambodian Embassies

AUSTRALIA
(☎/fax 02-6273 1053) 5 Canterbury Crt, Deakin, ACT 2600

CHINA
(☎ 10-532 2101; fax 532 3507) 9 Dongzhimenwai Dajie, Beijing 100600

LAOS
(☎ /fax 21-314951) Thanon Saphan Thong Neua, Vientiane

THAILAND
(☎ 02-254 6630; fax 253 9859) 185 Rajadamri Rd, Bangkok 10330

USA
(☎ 202-726-7742; fax 726-8381) 4500 16th St NW, Washington, DC 20011

VIETNAM
(☎ 4-253 789; fax 265 225) 71 Tran Hung Dao St, Hanoi. Consulate: Ho Chi Minh City

Tourist Offices Overseas

Cambodia maintains no tourist offices abroad and it is unlikely that Cambodian embassies will be of much help in planning a trip, besides providing visas. Check out some of the web sites listed under Online Services and see your travel agent.

Health

Malaria exists year-round everywhere except in Phnom Penh. There have been recent large outbreaks of dengue fever. You should take appropriate precautions against both these serious diseases. Schistosomiasis (bilharzia) occurs in the Mekong Delta, so avoid swimming or paddling here. Food and waterborne diseases, including dysentery, hepatitis and liver flukes occur, so pay particular attention to basic food and water hygiene. Note that although liver flukes are generally contracted through eating raw fish, you can also get them by swimming in the southern reaches of the Mekong River.

Medical services are poor for the most part. In the event of a medical emergency, you will probably need to get to Bangkok or, at the very least, to Phnom Penh.

Post & Communications

Cambodia's mail is now routed by air through Bangkok, which makes it much more reliable but delays are still common, particularly for incoming items. The rates remain low by regional standards and the Phnom Penh main post office has a poste restante service. Telephone connections with the outside world have also improved, but they are not cheap. Phonecards have become more common for international calls from public phones. Phnom Penh and Siem Reap have business centres which offer email access but, again, this is not cheap.

Money

Costs

For the most part, Cambodia is a pretty cheap place to travel. Rock-bottom budget travellers can probably get by in Phnom Penh on US$10 a day – accommodation can be as cheap as US$2 or US$3 in the capital, though you'll pay about US$5 elsewhere, and you can eat for US$2 or US$3. To travel around, you'll need to spend more, as transport is a major expense. Entrance fees (particularly for Angkor Wat – currently around US$20 a day) can also set you back. Mid-range travel is very reasonable, with excellent accommodation from US$15 to US$25 and good meals for around US$5.

Changing Money

If you have cash US dollars, you won't need to change money in Cambodia and you'll pay much the same as you would with riel. Thai baht are also widely accepted. Both US dollars and baht are easy to change, as are most other major currencies. It can be difficult to change travellers cheques (in fact, it's pretty much impossible outside Phnom Penh and Siem Reap), and credit cards are rarely accepted. To make life as simple as possible, organise a supply of US dollars before you arrive in Cambodia.

Online Services

Lonely Planet's *Destination Cambodia* page can be found at www.lonelyplanet. com/dest/sea/camb.htm.

The Internet Travel Guide (www. datacomm.ch/pmgeiser/cambodia) provides a no-nonsense introduction to Cambodia for travellers.

The Cambodian Information Center (www.cambodia.org) lives up to its name with a comprehensive list of sites relating to Cambodia.

Beauty and Darkness: Cambodia in Modern History (members.aol.com/ cambodia/index.htm) concentrates on the Khmer Rouge period.

Itis (www.itisnet.com/english/ asia/cambodia/e-cam-top.htm) is an interesting travel site with up-to-date information on important issues like border crossings and the price of toilet paper.

The Royal Embassy of Cambodia to Japan (www.iac.co.jp/~kpnarin/ index.htm) has basic information and a royal message for those who can read French.

Books

The best, widely available history is David P Chandler's *A History of Cambodia*. Keep an eye out for Milton Osbourne's *Sihanouk – Prince of Light, Prince of Darkness*, a no-holds-barred look at the man who has played such a crucial role in the shifting fortunes of Cambodia's modern history.

For information on Angkor Wat, try *Angkor – An Introduction to the Temples* by Dawn Rooney. This book is packed with illustrations and makes for fascinating reading. Also recommended are the pocket-size *Angkor – Heart of an Empire* by Bruno Dagens; *Angkor: An Introduction* by George Coedès; and *Angkor, Guide Henri Parmentier* by Henri Parmentier.

For an insight into Cambodia's darker, more recent history, try William Shawcross' *Sideshow: Kissinger, Nixon & the Destruction of Cambodia*; Ben

WARNING

Over the past 15 years, travelling in Cambodia has been no picnic, and remains so to a certain extent. Although road and train travel is now considered safe; all visitors are advised to register with their embassy and seek advice on the current security situation. Although the danger of being kidnapped and murdered by the Khmer Rouge may have waned with the organisation's collapse, banditry is still prevalent in the more remote regions and foreigners continue to be targeted. Visitors should not attempt to enter Cambodia by land, except from Moc Bai in Vietnam. There is tension along the Vietnamese-Cambodian border following Cambodian accusations that the Vietnamese are extending their territory several hundred metres onto Cambodian soil. The amount of smuggling that takes place across the border also means that strangers are often considered intruders.

223

Kiernan's *How Pol Pot Came to Power*; François Ponchaud's *Cambodia: Year Zero*; Jon Swain's *River of Time*; and Pol Pot's biography *Brother Number One*, also by David P Chandler.

Films

The best known western film about Cambodia, *The Killing Fields* (1984), is a stark, gut-wrenching portrayal of life under the Khmer Rouge during the 1970s, shown from both American and Cambodian perspectives. This haunting and powerful film was directed by Roland Joffé.

Other films and documentaries to look for include *Swimming to Cambodia* (1987) starring and directed by Jonathan Demme; *Cambodia: Living in the Killing Fields* (1996) by Scott Shaw; *Intrusion Cambodia* (1981) by Jun Gallardo; *Angkor: Cambodia Express* (1985) by Lek Kitaparaporn; and *Samsara: Death and Rebirth in Cambodia* (1989) by Ellen Bruno.

French-language films and documentaries include *Cambodia, entre guerre et paix* (1991), *Un soir après la guerre* (1998) and *Neak sre* (1993), all by Rithy Panh.

Entering & Leaving Cambodia

Commercial flights to Phnom Penh were suspended following the July 1997 coup d'état. Limited flights have since recommenced to Bangkok, Kuala Lumpur and Ho Chi Minh City, but connections are not reliable. Phnom Penh's Pochentong airport terminal was destroyed in the fighting, so don't expect to wait in an executive lounge. There is a land connection from Ho Chi Minh City to Phnom Penh, via the Moc Bai border crossing: buses take five to six hours. It is also possible to rent both a car and driver in Vietnam for trips into Cambodia. You can enter Thailand at Poipet (Aranya Prathet on the Thai side).

CHINA ▶▶

China is not a country – it's a whole different world, from its shop-till-you-drop metropolises to the epic grasslands of Inner Mongolia, with deserts, sacred peaks, astounding caves and imperial ruins in-between. Thankfully, temples are no longer being destroyed – now they are ripping down mountains and poisoning rivers instead. But there's still plenty to see once you've mastered the art of bulldozing your way through the crowds and avoiding the ever-present phlegm that decorates footpaths and the floors of buses and restaurants. China is possibly the region's most challenging travel destination, but it's well worth the effort. You will need at least four weeks to properly explore any region of China; if you want to see more, you could spend up to a year travelling through this huge country.

When to Go

Spring (March to April) and autumn (September to October) are the best times to visit. Daytime temperatures range from 20°C to 30°C in these seasons, but nights can be freezing, and it can be wet and miserable. Major public holidays, in particular Chinese New Year, are best avoided as it's difficult to get around and find accommodation. Temperatures in the north can drop to -40°C in winter (December to March) and rise to 38°C in summer (May to August). The central Yangzi River valley area also experiences extreme temperature ranges. In the far south, the hot and humid summer lasts from April to September

AT A GLANCE

Full Country Name: People's Republic of China (PRC)

Area: 9,596,960 sq km

Population: 1.2 billion

Capital City: Beijing (pop 11 million)

People: 93% Han Chinese, plus more than 50 minority groups including the Tibetan, Mongol Zhuang, Manchu and Uighur

Languages: Putonghua (Beijing dialect Mandarin), Cantonese, Tibetan, Mongolian, Russian, Mien, Hmong (Miao), Lisu, Akha (Aini), Lahu, Uighur, Uzbek, Kyrgyz, Kazakh and Tajik

Religion: Officially atheist, but Confucianism, Buddhism, Taoism, Islam, Christianity, ancestor worship and animism are all practised

Government: Communist People's Republic

Currency: Renminbi (RMB); the basic unit is the yuan

Time Zone: Eight hours ahead of GMT/UTC (the whole of China is set to Beijing time)

International Telephone Code: 86

Electricity: 220V, 50 AC; plugs can be three-pronged angled, three-pronged round, two flat pins or two narrow round pins

and, as in northern China, coincides with the rainy season. Typhoons can hit the south-east coast between July and September. The north-west region has dry, hot summers, with China's hottest place – Turpan in Xinjiang – reaching maximums of 47°C.

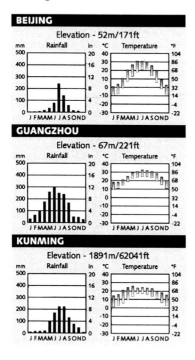

BEIJING
Elevation - 52m/171ft

GUANGZHOU
Elevation - 67m/221ft

KUNMING
Elevation - 1891m/62041ft

Highlights

With the exception of good beaches, China has something of everything: sacred mountains, deserts, grasslands, forests, imperial remains, crumbling city walls and temples galore.

Imperial Splendour

Dynasties have risen and fallen for millennia in China, but there's not as much imperial debris as you might expect. Between rampaging peasant uprisings, pillaging armies, the Cultural Revolution and rapid urbanisation, it's a wonder there's anything left at all.

China's imperial jewel is Beijing. Capital city for around 500 years, its highlights are the Forbidden City and the Summer Palace, and it's also the jumping-off point for the Great Wall. Of China's various other former capitals, Nanjing is the best preserved, with some surviving city walls and the tomb of the first Ming emperor. Xi'an, headquarters of the Qin and Tang dynasties, is the most impressive of the remaining walled cities, and nearby are the famous entombed warriors.

Minority Regions

China's ethnic and cultural minorities are mostly scattered around the edges of the country, particularly in the south-west. Yunnan alone is home to around 20 different minority groups, including the Dai (Xishuangbanna), Bai (Dali) and Naxi (Lijiang). Numbering more than five million people, Tibetans are one of China's largest minorities and there are populations in Gansu and Qinghai provinces, as well as in Tibet. Another visible minority is the Muslim Uighur people of Xinjiang in the west, while Hainan Island to the south has almost 40 different cultural groups, mostly dwelling in the mountainous centre of the island.

Backpacker Getaways

There are few recognised traveller retreats in China, but two places that remain very popular are Yangshuo (in Guangxi Province) and Dali (in Yunnan). Yangshuo is set amid the famous karst scenery of Guilin and the surrounding countryside alone, which can be explored by bicycle, makes it worth a stay. Dali is more exotic, but a similar deal to Yangshuo. The old walled town, home to the Bai minority, nestles beside Erhai Lake. Dali is a superb place to rest up for a few days.

Sacred Mountains

Eulogised through the centuries in countless paintings and poems, the sacred mountains of China were once places of pilgrimage, but are now mostly major tourist attractions packed with people, souvenir sellers and cable cars, and demanding extortionate entrance fees. They can be worth the effort, but you'll experience few contemplative moments.

The sacred mountains have well marked trails to the summits. Usually there are stairways carved into the rockfaces; sights en route can include poems, inscriptions and temples, many with accommodation (often off limits to foreigners). The most popular with travellers are Huangshan (in eastern China), Taishan (coastal China) and Emeishan (south-western China).

Cave Art

The Mogao Caves, set in desert cliffs above a river valley about 25km south-east of Dunhuang in Gansu Province, are the most impressive and best preserved examples of Buddhist cave art in China. Some 492 grottoes are still standing. The Yungang Buddhist Caves (Shanxi Province) are cut into the southern cliffs of Wuzhoushan, near Datong, and contain more than 50,000 statues, while the Grand Buddha at Leshan (Sichuan Province) is the largest buddha in the world at 71m tall. It's carved into a cliff face overlooking the confluence of the Dadu and Min rivers.

Foreign Concessions

By the late 19th century the weakness of the Qing government allowed various European powers to grab a large number of 'foreign concessions'. The best known collection of European architecture faces the sea on the Bund in Shanghai. The city's French Concession, mostly derelict and falling in swathes to modern building projects, also turns up some delightful architectural surprises. Guangzhou has an unexpectedly peaceful enclave of European buildings on Shamian Island, as does Xiamen (Fujian) on Gulangyu Island. Qingdao (Shandong) has a strong German influence.

Itineraries

Unless you have a couple of years up your sleeve, oodles of patience and inexhaustible funds, you'll be able to see only a small part of China on any one trip. It's a good idea to follow a loose itinerary. These suggestions assume you have a minimum four weeks in China.

HONG KONG TO KUNMING VIA GUILIN

This has long been China's most favoured backpacker trail. The standard routine is a brief stay in Guangzhou, followed by a ferry to Wuzhou and direct bus to Yangshuo. Many travellers end up being seduced by Yangshuo and spend much longer there than planned. Onward travel to Kunming can be made by train or plane. From Kunming, there is a wide range of choices – south to Xishuangbanna and Dehong or north-west to Dali and Lijiang (or both). Other possibilities include flights from Kunming to Chiang Mai or Bangkok (Thailand), or a train to Hanoi (Vietnam).

BEIJING TO HONG KONG VIA THE SOUTH-WEST

There are many variations on this route, depending on how much time you have

CHINA HIGHLIGHTS & ITINERARIES

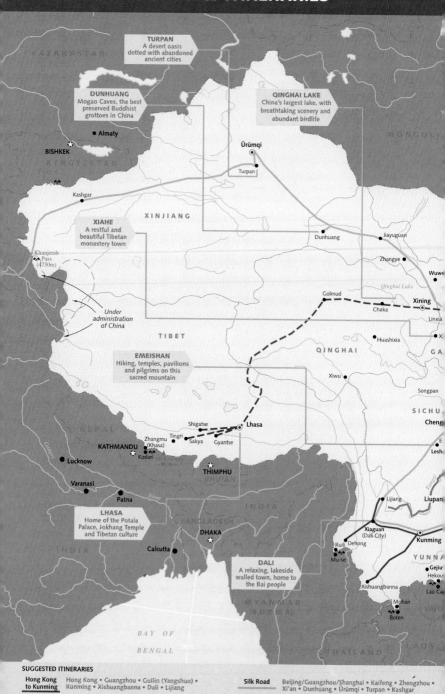

TURPAN
A desert oasis dotted with abandoned ancient cities

DUNHUANG
Mogao Caves, the best preserved Buddhist grottoes in China

QINGHAI LAKE
China's largest lake, with breathtaking scenery and abundant birdlife

XIAHE
A restful and beautiful Tibetan monastery town

EMEISHAN
Hiking, temples, pavilions and pilgrims on this sacred mountain

LHASA
Home of the Potala Palace, Jokhang Temple and Tibetan culture

DALI
A relaxing, lakeside walled town, home to the Bai people

KAZAKHSTAN

Almaty

BISHKEK

KYRGYZSTAN

Ürümqi

Turpan

Kashgar

XINJIANG

Khunjerab
Pass
(4730m)

Under
administration
of China

TIBET

Dunhuang

Jiayuguan

Zhangye

Wuwe

Golmud

Chaka

Xining

Linxia

X

Huashixia

GA

Xiwu

QINGHAI

Songpan

SICHU

Cheng

MONGOLI

Qinghai Lake

Shigatse

Tingri

Zhangmu
(Khasa)

Sakya

Gyantse

Lhasa

KATHMANDU

Kodari

NEPAL

Lucknow

Varanasi

Patna

THIMPHU

BHUTAN

BANGLADESH

DHAKA

INDIA

Calcutta

Lesh

Lijiang

Liupan

Xiaguan
(Dali City)

Kunming

Dehong

Ruili

Mu-se

YUNNA

Gejiu

Hekou

Lao Ca

Xishuangbanna

Mohan

Boten

MYANMAR
(BURMA)

BAY OF
BENGAL

THAILAND

LAOS

SUGGESTED ITINERARIES

Hong Kong to Kunming Hong Kong • Guangzhou • Guilin (Yangshuo) • Kunming • Xishuangbanna • Dali • Lijiang

Silk Road Beijing/Guangzhou/Shanghai • Kaifeng • Zhengzhou • Xi'an • Dunhuang • Ürümqi • Turpan • Kashgar

Yangzi River Yangzi River (Three Gorges • Chongqing • Wuhan)

and how much you enjoy Chinese trains. A stopover in Kunming allows exploration of Yunnan, rich in ethnic colour and with excellent scenery. From Kunming, many travellers trek on to Chengdu (via Dali and Lijiang). From Chengdu options include: onward to Chongqing and from there to Wuhan or Shanghai down the Yangzi River, or onward to Guizhou, Guilin and Hong Kong. You can speed things up a bit on this route with a flight or two.

BEIJING TO TIBET VIA XI'AN

This route is very popular, particularly with travellers overlanding from Europe by train and heading for Nepal and India via Tibet. The route gives you the best of China's historical sights, plus the opportunity to travel out into the remote and sparsely populated western regions. Beijing, Xi'an and Lhasa are the main attractions. Further west, Xining is worth a day or so, mainly for the nearby lamasery of Ta'ersi, but the less time spent in Golmud, the better. From Lhasa, it is possible to travel to Kathmandu via the Tibetan temple towns of Gyantse, Shigatse and Sakya, a once-in-a-lifetime trip.

COASTAL ROUTES

The obvious route up (or down) the east of China between Guangzhou and Beijing will actually take you through some of the most densely populated regions in the country. China's coastal cities are little more than a blur of smog, grey housing estates and factories. There is also intense competition for train tickets, so you may spend days bouncing around on crowded buses. If you opt for this route, start with Beijing, travel to Shandong and from there make a beeline south via Shanghai to Guangzhou.

YANGZI RIVER ROUTES

Cruises on the Yangzi have long been touted as one of China's premier attractions. In reality, some travellers have found even the Three Gorges (the whole reason for the cruise) overrated, and in any event the area will soon be submerged by the controversial Three Gorges Dam project. The best part of the Yangzi is the section between Chongqing (Sichuan) and Wuhan.

SILK ROAD ROUTE

Kashgar and the Karakoram Highway (to Pakistan) can be approached directly from Beijing, but a fascinating trip is the overland route once used for transporting silk to Europe. It covers little travelled parts of central China (eg Kaifeng) and passes through the archaeological treasure houses of Xi'an and Dunhuang, before heading into the deserts of Xinjiang (you could detour to spectacular Qinghai Lake, west of Xining, where the rare black-necked crane breeds from March to early June). From Ürümqi you must go by bus to Turpan and Kashgar. Onward travel to Pakistan and India is an option.

NORTH-EAST ROUTE

Visit the former treaty port of Dalian and then head north to what was once Manchuria, and the cities of Shenyang, Harbin and Changchun. This region feels less Chinese and more a combination of Canadian prairies, rust-belt heavy industry, leftover traces of Japanese colonialism and undeniably Russian influences. It's also possible to try and commune with nature (always an elusive prospect in China) in the reserves of Changbaishan (thousands of hectares of dense virgin forest) and Zhalong (home to several rare species of crane). The northeast offers a true winter experience, including skiing and -30°C weather, and during summer is a good place to escape the heat. You could keep heading north to the grasslands of Mongolia at Manzhouli and on to Siberia or Europe on the Trans-Manchurian Railway.

Visa Requirements

Visas are required by all foreigners entering mainland China. Standard tourist visas are valid for 30 days and are activated on arrival. Single-entry visas of 60 or 90 days are possible, but are normally available only from the

China Travel Service (CTS) office in Hong Kong (see the PRC Embassies section below). Multiple-entry visas are expensive and rarely issued for more than 30 days, but extensions are normally straightforward and can be arranged at Public Security Bureaus (PSBs). If you overstay your visa you could be fined up to US$50 per day. If you're entering or leaving China by land, ensure you have arranged the appropriate visas in advance.

PRC Embassies

AUSTRALIA
(☎ 02-6273 4780, 6273 4781) 15 Coronation Drive, Yarralumla, ACT 2600. Consulates: Melbourne, Perth and Sydney

CANADA
(☎ 613-789-3509) 515 St Patrick St, Ottawa, Ontario K1N 5H3. Consulates: Toronto and Vancouver

HONG KONG
(☎ 852-2585-1794, 2585-1700) Visa Office, Ministry of Foreign Affairs, 5th floor, Low Block, China Resources Building, 26 Harbour Rd, Wan Chai

NEW ZEALAND
(☎ 04-587 0407) 104A Korokoro Rd, Petone, Wellington. Consulate: Auckland

UK
(☎ 020-7636 9756) 31 Portland Place, London W1N 5AG

USA
(☎ 202-328-2517) 2300 Connecticut Ave NW, Washington, DC 20008. Consulates: Chicago, Houston, Los Angeles, New York and San Francisco

Tourist Offices Overseas

CITS

The China International Travel Service (CITS) deals mainly with group tours. Still, it can be useful for hard-to-get-hold-of train tickets, or tickets for entertainment events. Outside China, CITS is usually known as the China

National Tourist Office (CNTO). Representatives include:

AUSTRALIA
(☎ 02-9299 4057; fax 9290 1958) 19th floor, 44 Market St, Sydney, NSW 2000

UK
(☎ 020-7935 9787; fax 7487 5842) 4 Glenworth St, London NW1

USA
(☎ 818-545-7504; fax 545-7506) Los Angeles Branch, 333 West Broadway, Suite 201, Glendale, CA 91204;
(☎ 212-760-9700; fax 760-8809) New York Branch, 350 Fifth Ave, Suite 6413, Empire State Building, New York, NY 10118

CTS

The China Travel Service (CTS), originally set up to deal with Overseas Chinese tourists, is now a keen competitor with CITS. Offices include:

AUSTRALIA
(☎ 02-9211 2633; fax 9281 3595) Ground floor, 757-9 George St, Sydney, NSW 2000

CANADA
(☎ 800-663-1126, 604-872-8787; fax 604-873-2823) 556 West Broadway, Vancouver, BC V5Z 1E9;
(☎ 800-387-6622, 416-979-8993; fax 416-979-8220) Suite 306, 438 University Ave, Box 28, Toronto, Ontario M5G 2K8

UK
(☎ 020-7836 9911; fax 7836 3121) CTS House, 7 Upper St, Martins Lane, London WC2H 9DL

USA
(☎ 800-332-2831, 415-398-6627; fax 415-398-6669) Main Office, L/F, 575 Sutter St, San Francisco, CA 94102;
(☎ 818-457-8668; fax 457-8955) Los Angeles Branch, Suite 303, US CTS Building, 119 South Atlantic Blvd, Monterey Park, CA 91754

Health

China is generally a fairly healthy place to travel in. Respiratory infections are the most common ailment to afflict visitors. Malaria is not generally a risk in the main tourist routes, and is found predominantly in rural areas in the south-west. Dengue fever occurs in parts of southern China. Food and waterborne diseases, eg dysentery, hepatitis and liver flukes, also occur in parts of China, and tap water should not be drunk anywhere. China is one of the world's great reservoirs of hepatitis B, and hepatitis A is also common. Schistosomiasis (bilharzia) is found in the central Yangzi River basin, so avoid swimming or bathing there.

Large cities such as Beijing and Shanghai have good and very cheap medical facilities, but in the backwaters of Inner Mongolia, Tibet or Xinjiang facilities are primitive.

Post & Communications

Domestic post is very fast and quite cheap, but international mail is costlier and takes longer – allow at least eight to 10 days. There are poste restante services in just about every city and town, and they seem to work reasonably well. The telephone system is being constantly upgraded and is quite reliable. Again, local and interstate calls are relatively cheap compared with international services. For long-distance calls, buy a phonecard and use a public phone or go with an overseas call-back provider. Internet services are still in their infancy so email is problematic, but most major cities and tourist destinations are establishing services.

Money

Costs

Generally, eastern China is much more expensive than western China. In eastern China, you could budget on around US$35 to US$40 a day, but it would be a challenge. Budget travellers in western China should be able to keep costs down to US$20 per day. Food is cheap everywhere; the main drain on savings tends to be long train journeys. The bottom line is that you will often be charged 'tourist prices', despite official government policy to dissuade the practice.

Changing Money

You can change travellers cheques and foreign currency at the main branches of the Bank of China, tourist hotels, Friendship Stores and some department stores. Hotels generally charge the official rate. Keep all your exchange receipts in case you need to change any remaining RMB at the end of your trip. Travellers cheques are useful as the exchange rate is normally more favourable than for cash; Thomas Cook, American Express and Bank of America are the most commonly accepted travellers cheques.

Credit cards are gaining ground, with Visa, MasterCard, American Express (branches in Guangzhou, Beijing, Shanghai and Xiamen), JCB and Diners Club the most common. Cards can be used in most mid-range to top-end hotels, and Friendship and department stores, but cannot be used to pay for transport. Cash advances can be made at head branches of the Bank of China (4% commission).

Online Services

Officially distrustful of the bourgeois web-surfing lifestyle, China comes over a tad shy on the Internet – except in the business arena, where it's all systems go. Note that many Chinese web sites require you to have a Chinese-enabled web browser to see the Chinese characters, but look for an icon on which you can click to change the display to English.

For the overall Chinese whisper, check out Lonely Planet's *Destination China* (www.lonelyplanet.com/dest/nea/chi.htm). You'll also find pages on Northern China, Beijing, Eastern China, North-Eastern China, Southern China, South-Western China, Shanghai, Tibet & Qinghai and Hong Kong.

China News Digest (www.cnd.org:8001) is an large regularly updated collection of history, politics and culture, while *Chinapages* (www.chinapages.com), the heavyweight in the facts and figures division, places an emphasis on business travellers and investors. *China the Beautiful* (www.ChinaPage.com) makes a refreshing change, with pages on art, poetry and language that are both stunning and informative.

Chinese Character Genealogy (www.zhongwen.com) is an interesting guide to the history of Chinese characters and also has information on pronunciation.

Gate of Heavenly Peace (www.nmis.org/gate) is a chilling look at the 1989 Tiananmen Square massacre, and includes excellent background information and a gallery of stills.

Tibet Online Resource Gathering (www.tibet.org) covers the sadness, the scandal and the solidarity that surrounds this disputed holy land.

Some Hong Kong-specific sites include *Hong Kong WWW Starting Point* (user.hk.linkage.net/~nckwan/hkwww/hk/hongkong.html), which has a comprehensive set of links. The Hong Kong Tourist Association's *Wonder Net* (www.hkta.org) is a flashy yet friendly site which will tailor tours to Hong Kong's attractions according to your interests.

Books

Jung Chang's mega-seller *Wild Swans* is a fascinating family saga spanning three generations against the backdrop of China's turbulent 20th century history. Other survival titles include Nien Cheng's *Life and Death in Shanghai*, *Son of the Revolution* by Liang Heng and Judith Shapiro, and *Bitter Winds: A Memoir of My Years in China's Gulag* by Harry Wu.

Western views of contemporary Chinese politics are offered by Nicholas D Kristof and Sheryl Wudunn in *China Wakes*, Orville Schell's *Mandate of Heaven* and the highly recommended *Evening Chats in Beijing* by Perry Link.

For a spot of biography to enlighten your trip there's *The Private Life of Chairman Mao*, written by the man's private physician, Zhisui Li. Books on other Chinese personalities include *Deng Xiaoping and the Making of Modern China* by Richard Evans, *The White Boned Demon: A Biography of Madame Mao Zedong* by Ross Terrill and *Eldest Son: Zhou Enlai and the Making of Modern China, 1898-1976* by Han Suyin.

Colin Thubron's *Behind the Wall* and Paul Theroux's *Riding the Iron Rooster* remain the best two recent travel books written about China.

Films

Hong Kong produces many times more films than the rest of China put together, although this traditionally little censored industry could suffer a major setback as a result of the handover to China. Some well known Hong

233

Kong directors include John Woo, Eric Tsang, Tsui Hark, Wong Jing, Wong Kar Wai and Ringo Lam, while Jackie Chan has directed some of his own films.

The Hong Kong film industry excels in comedies (*Aces Go Places 1, 2, 3, 4* and *5*; *God of Gamblers 1, 2* and *3*; *Golden Girls, Haunted Cop Shop 2; Love on Delivery*; and *Mack the Knife*), but is best known for its action-packed kungfu films (*Chinese Connection, Fist of Legend*; *Licence to Steal*; *Police Story* and *The Twin Dragons*).

Mainland Chinese films have traditionally been fairly clumsy propaganda efforts, but in recent years independent directors have been more prominent and some Chinese films have received excellent reviews in the west (although the response from the Chinese government has often been less enthusiastic). Two outstanding films are *Raise the Red Lantern* and *Farewell My Concubine*.

Movies produced by westerners and filmed in China include the definitive classic, *The Last Emperor*, directed by Bernardo Bertolucci. Documentaries about China are numerous – *The Gate of Heavenly Peace* by Carma Hinton & Richard Gordon is a well balanced video about the democracy protests and bloodshed at Tiananmen Square.

If nature documentaries are your interest, have a look at *The Amazing Panda Adventure* (1995) or check out one of the many excellent videos on China produced by the National Geographic Society. Lonely Planet has also produced a video on travel in South-West China.

Entering & Leaving China

Despite China's 115 ports of entry and exit, most visitors arrive and depart via Hong Kong. The national carrier is the Civil Aviation Administration of China (CAAC, known on international routes as Air China), which also operates the Dragonair airline as a joint venture with Cathay Pacific. There is a departure tax of Y105, which is payable only in local currency.

Exotic overland routes into and out of China include Vietnam-China, the Trans-Siberian Railway, Tibet-Nepal and Xinjiang-Pakistan. However, don't even think about bringing your own car, as foreigners are rarely allowed to drive in China. China has land borders with Vietnam, Laos, Myanmar, India, Bhutan, Nepal, Pakistan, Kyrgyzstan, Afghanistan, Tajikistan, Kazakhstan, Russia, Mongolia and North Korea. It is not possible to cross the border into (or enter from) Bhutan, Afghanistan or Russia, while the Indian border area remains in dispute and should not be considered. Border crossings include:

KAZAKHSTAN – Almaty to Ürümqi services go via Khorgas-Zharkent by bus and Dostyq by train

PAKISTAN – Sust-Kashkurgan on the Karakoram Highway (open 1 May to 30 November only)

KYRGYZSTAN – Bishkek-Kashgar via the Turugart Pass

VIETNAM – Pingxiang-Dong Dang and Hekou-Lao Cai

LAOS – Mohan-Boten

MYANMAR – Ruili-Mu-se, but you may only be issued a day pass into the Myanmar town

NEPAL – Nyalam-Kodari are on either side of the Friendship Pass, but there's lots of bureaucracy each way

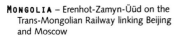

- **MONGOLIA** – Erenhot-Zamyn-Üüd on the Trans-Mongolian Railway linking Beijing and Moscow
- **NORTH KOREA** – Dandong-Sinuiju, but visas will take the best part of a month, are very expensive and you'll probably only get a sanitised tour of Pyongyang

You can take a slow boat to China from Japan. There are ferries from Osaka, Kobe and Nagasaki to Shanghai; there's also a weekly ferry from Kobe to Tanggu (near Tianjin). Some other popular places to sail to include Xiamen (opposite Taiwan), Macau and Hong Kong. From Inch'on (near Seoul) in South Korea, ferries sail regularly to Weihai and Qingdao, both in Shandong Province.

INDIA

No matter how willing you are to step outside logic-based western thinking and give up the joys of using toilet paper, India will still manage to side-swipe you with its size, clamour and diversity. India is a litmus test for many travellers and some visitors are only too happy to get on an airplane and fly away, but if you enjoy delving into convoluted cosmologies, thrive on sensual overload and have a firm grasp of the absurd, then India provides some of the most intricate, fascinating and rewarding dramas unfolding on the planet.

When to Go

India has such a wide range of climatic factors that it's impossible to pin down the best time to visit, although broadly speaking October to March tends to be the most pleasant period around much of the country. In the far south, the monsoonal weather pattern makes January to September more pleasant, Sikkim and north-eastern India tend to be more palatable between March and August, while Kashmir and the mountainous regions of Himachal Pradesh are most accessible between May and September. The deserts of Rajasthan and the north-western Indian Himalayan region are at their best during the monsoon.

The trekking season in the Indian Himalaya runs roughly from April to November, though this varies widely depending on the trek, altitude and region. The ski season occurs between January and March. For the dates of particular festivals and holidays, see Festivals & Events under Itineraries.

Highlights

India can offer beaches, forts, amazing travel experiences, fantastic spectacles or even a search for yourself. Listed here are a few of the possibilities.

AT A GLANCE

Full Country Name: Republic of India

Area: 3,287,000 sq km (India has several disputed international borders)

Population: 968 million

Capital City: New Delhi (pop 10.1 million)

People: 72% Indo-Aryan, 25% Dravidian and 3% Mongoloid

Languages: Hindi and English, plus 15 other languages and more than 700 dialects

Religion: 82% Hindu, 11% Muslim, 2% Christian, 2% Sikh, 2% Buddhist and 1% Jain

Government: Constitutional democracy

Currency: Indian rupee (Rs)

Time Zone: Five-and-a-half hours ahead of GMT/UTC

International Telephone Code: 91

Electricity: 230V to 240V, 50 AC; sockets take plugs with three round pins, similar to European sockets

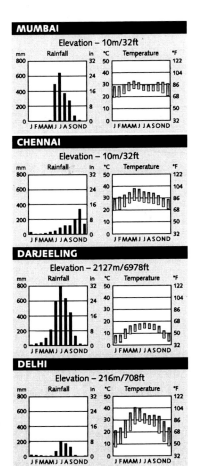

Beaches

India boasts some superb beaches. On the west coast, at the southern end of Kerala, are Kovalam and Varkala; further north, Goa has a collection of beautiful beaches complete with soft white sand, lapping waves and swaying palms; or head for the tiny island of Diu off the southern coast of Saurashtra (Gujarat).

On the east coast you could try the beaches at Mamallapuram in Tamil Nadu or at Gopalpur-on-Sea in Orissa. Out in the Bay of Bengal, the Andaman Islands have beaches straight out of a tourist brochure – white-coral sand, crystal-clear water and multi-coloured fish and coral.

Faded Touches of the Raj

Although the British left India 50 years ago, there are many places where you'd hardly know it. Relax in true British style with afternoon tea at Glenary's Tea Rooms in Darjeeling, and then retire for a preprandial cocktail in the lounge of the Windamere Hotel.

If you prefer fading Edwardian splendour, you can stay at the Hotel Metropole in Mysore, while the twee Home Counties rural atmosphere of the Woodlands or Fernhill Palace hotels in Udhagamandalam (Ooty) is very Raj. Other particularly British institutions include the Victoria Terminus train station in Mumbai (Bombay), the secretariat buildings in Delhi, the Naini Tal Boat Club, the Gymkhana Club in Darjeeling and St Paul's Cathedral in Calcutta.

Freak Centres

To some extent, India remains the on-the-road hippie dream. Goa has always been a great freak centre – the beaches are an attraction at any time of year and every full moon is the occasion for a great gathering of the clans. Further south the fine beaches at Kovalam also attract a steady clientele. The holy lake of Pushkar in Rajasthan has a smaller and semi-permanent freak population drawn by the quiet, spiritual atmosphere of this holy town. The technicolour Tibetan outlook on life has found its place in Dharamsala and Manali, both in Himachal Pradesh. Finally, Puri (Orissa), near Konark, and Mamallapuram both offer temples and beaches – a sure-fire freak combination.

Festivals & Events

India is a country of festivals and there are a number that should not be missed. They start with the Republic Day Festival in Delhi in January – elephants, a procession and military might with Indian princely splendour. In January/February is the three day Desert Festival in Jaisalmer, Rajasthan, while June/July sees the great Car Festival (Rath Yatra) held in Puri, a superb spectacle as the gigantic temple car of Lord Jagannath makes its annual journey, pulled by thousands of eager devotees. In Kerala, a major event is the Nehru Cup Snake Boat Races held in August on the backwaters at Alappuzha (Alleppey). September/October is the time to head for the hills for the delightful Festival of the Gods in Kullu. November is the time for the huge and colourful Camel Festival at Pushkar in Rajasthan. Finally, at Christmas the only place to be is the Christian enclave of Goa.

Deserted Cities

There are a number of places in crowded India where great cities of the past have been deserted.

Fatehpur Sikri, near Agra, is the most famous – Akbar founded, built and left this impressive centre in less than 20 years. Hampi, the centre of the Vijayanagar Empire, is equally impressive. Not far away are the ancient centres of Aihole and Badami.

Great Forts

India has more than its share of great forts – many of them now deserted – to tell of its tumultuous history. The Red Fort in Delhi is one of the most impressive, but Agra Fort is an equally massive reminder of Mughal power at its height. A short distance south is the huge, impregnable-looking Gwalior Fort. The Rajputs could build forts like nobody else – theirs include Chittorgarh, Bundi, Kota, Jodhpur, Amber and Jaisalmer. Way out west in Gujarat are the impressive forts of Junagadh and Bhuj built by the princely rulers of Saurashtra. Further south there are forts at Mandu, Daulatabad (near Aurangabad), Bijapur and Golconda (Hyderabad).

Naturally the European invaders left their forts too. You can see Portuguese forts in Goa, Bassein (outside Mumbai), Daman and Diu, while the British Fort St George in Chennai (Madras) is open to the public. The forts built by the French, Dutch and Danes are, unfortunately, largely in ruins, though the ruins have a certain appeal.

Itineraries

There is a mind-boggling array of amazing sights and places to visit in India. The following itineraries assume you have a month available. They take in the highlights of a region and should help you make the most of your time. They also assume that you don't want to spend the greater part of your visit travelling between places – many first-time visitors to India try to see too much in too short a time, and end up tired and frustrated.

RAJASTHANI COLOUR

This route gives you a taste of just about everything: Mughal architecture, including the Taj Mahal (Agra); wildlife; the desert; Hindu temples; hippie hang-outs; Rajput exuberance; unusual Islamic architecture; and the superb Buddhist paintings and sculptures of the Ajanta and Ellora caves. You could happily spend a week in Mumbai and Delhi, although a couple of days in each is usually all there's time for. Travel is by bus and train, except for the Udaipur to Aurangabad leg, which can be flown.

MUGHALS, JAINS & THE PORTUGUESE – WEST INDIA

The state of Gujarat offers the chance to get off the well beaten tourist circuit. The route takes in Rajasthan and the best of Gujarat: the tribal cultures of the Rann of Kutch in the far west; the fortified town of Junagadh with the magnificent Jain temples atop Girnar Hill; Sasan Gir, the last home of the Asian lion; Diu, the old Portuguese enclave and its beaches; Palitana, also with hilltop Jain temples; and Ahmedabad, the busy city which has the Gandhi Ashram. Travel is by bus and train.

HINDU & MUGHAL HEARTLANDS

Madhya Pradesh, the geographical heartland of India, is largely untouristed, but a visit is certainly worthwhile. The Hindu temples at Khajuraho are the big attraction, but Sanchi and Mandu between them boast very fine examples of Buddhist, Hindu and Afghan architecture.

Varanasi, one of the holiest places in the country; Agra, with the incomparable Taj Mahal; and the caves of Ajanta and Ellora are other attractions on this route.

HILL STATIONS & THE HIMALAYA

The hill stations of Shimla and Dalhousie hark back to an era that is rapidly being consigned to history; Dharamsala is a fascinating cultural centre, being the home of the exiled Tibetan leader His Holiness the Dalai Lama; Manali in the Kullu Valley is simply one of the most beautiful places in the country; while the two day bus trip from Manali to Leh, high on the Tibetan plateau, is incredibly rough but equally memorable – it's one of the highest motorable roads in the world. Leh is the centre for another unique Himalayan culture. There are direct flights from Leh back to Delhi.

From Manali there are dozens of treks, ranging from a couple of days to a couple of weeks, into places such as the remote Zanskar Valley. Leh, too, is a centre for trekkers, and the Markha Valley is a popular trip. Trekking agencies in Manali and Leh can arrange everything, or you can strike out on your own.

Travel in this part of the country is generally by bus and, because of the terrain, is slow. This is a good route to follow during summer, when the heat on the plains becomes unbearable, and in fact the Manali-Leh road is only open for a couple of months each year when the snow melts.

PALACES, TEMPLES & HOLY CITIES

Starting from Delhi, this route gives you a taste of Rajasthan and includes the Taj Mahal. Jhansi is the station for the bus journey to the famous temples of Khajuraho, but it's worth stopping at Orchha, 18km from Jhansi, to see this well preserved old city of palaces and temples. From Khajuraho, a three hour bus journey brings you to Satna for trains to Jabalpur. A boat trip through the Marble Rocks is the main attraction here. Next stop is Kanha National Park where the chances of seeing a tiger are good, and then it's back to Jabalpur to pick up a train to Varanasi. There are direct trains from here to Calcutta, one of the most fascinating cities in the country.

FLIGHT-PASS ROUTE

For US$500/750 you can buy a flight pass on Indian Airlines for two/three weeks. Distance becomes no object and you can visit as many places as you like within the time limit. This itinerary links a number of the more exotic and distant places as well as 'must-sees' like the Taj Mahal. From Delhi fly to Agra, on to Khajuraho the next day and continue to Varanasi two days later. Next stop is the temple city of Bhubaneswar before taking the flight to Calcutta. An early morning departure brings you to Port Blair, capital of the Andaman & Nicobar Islands, for a few days at this rarely visited tropical paradise. With a three week pass you could also nip up to Darjeeling, changing planes in Calcutta en route to Delhi.

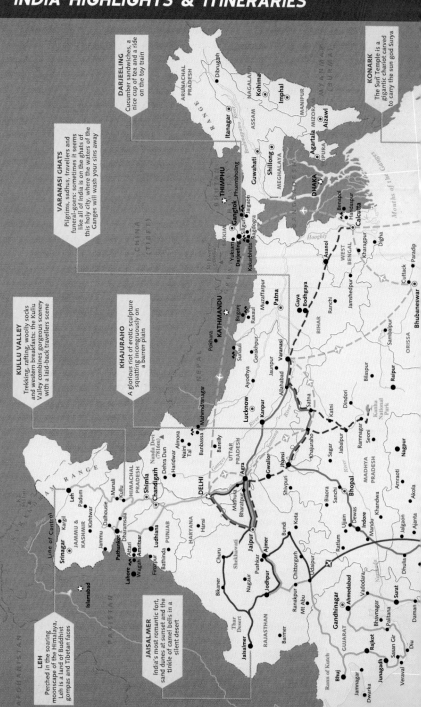

INDIA HIGHLIGHTS & ITINERARIES

DARJEELING
Cucumber sandwiches, a nice cup of tea and a ride on the toy train

KONARK
The Sun Temple is a gigantic chariot carved to carry the sun god Surya

VARANASI GHATS
Pilgrims, sadhus, travellers and funeral-goers: sometimes it seems like all of India is on the ghats of this holy city, where the waters of the Ganges will wash your sins away

KULU VALLEY
Trekking, rafting, woolly socks and western breakfasts: the Kullu Valley combines gorgeous scenery with a laid-back travellers scene

KHAJURAHO
A glorious riot of erotic sculpture squatting incongruously on a barren plain

LEH
Perched in the soaring moonscape of the Himalaya, Leh is a land of Buddhist gompas and Tibetan faces

JAISALMER
India's most romantic fort, sand dunes at sunset and the tinkle of camel bells in a silent desert

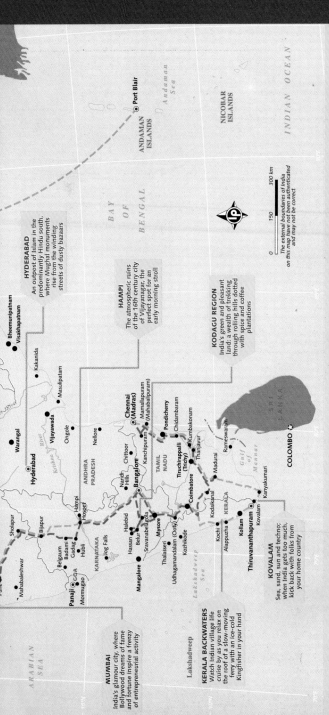

MUMBAI
India's glamour city, where Bollywood dreams of fame and fortune inspire a frenzy of entrepreneurial activity

HYDERABAD
An outpost of Islam in the predominantly Hindu south, where Mughal monuments rise from the winding streets of dusty bazaars

HAMPI
The atmospheric ruins of the 16th century city of Vijayanagar, the perfect spot for an early morning stroll

KODAGU REGION
India's green and pleasant land: a wealth of trekking through rolling hills dotted with spice and coffee plantations

KERALA BACKWATERS
Watch Indian village life cruise by as you relax on the roof of a slow-moving ferry with an ice-cold Kingfisher in your hand

KOVALAM
Sea, sand, sun and techno; when India gets too much, kick back with folks from your home country

The external boundaries of India on this map have not been authenticated and may not be correct

| 0 | 150 | 300 km |

SUGGESTED ITINERARIES

Rajasthani Colour
Delhi • Agra • Bharatpur • Jaipur • Shekhawati • Bikaner • Jaisalmer • Jodhpur • Pushkar • Bundi • Chittorgarh • Udaipur • Aurangabad (Ajanta and Ellora Caves) • Mumbai (Bombay)

Mughals, Jains and the Portuguese
Delhi • Agra • Jaipur • Pushkar • Jodhpur • Ranakpur • Udaipur • Bhuj • Rajkot • Junagadh • Sasan Gir • Diu • Palitana • Ahmedabad • Mumbai (Bombay)

Hindu and Mughal Heartlands
Delhi • Jaipur • Agra • Varanasi • Khajuraho • Jhansi • Sanchi • Mandu • Aurangabad • Mumbai (Bombay)

Hill Stations and the Himalaya
Delhi • Dalhousie • Dharamsala • Shimla • Manali • Leh • Delhi

Palaces, Temples and Holy Cities
Delhi • Jaipur • Agra • Jhansi • Khajuraho • Jabalpur • Kanha • Varanasi • Calcutta

Flight-Pass Route
Delhi • Agra • Khajuraho • Varanasi • Bhubaneswar • Calcutta • Andaman and Nicobar Islands • Darjeeling (Bagdogra) • Delhi

Temples and Ancient Monuments
Chennai (Madras) • Kanchipuram • Mamallapuram (Mahabalipuram) • Pondicherry • Kumbakonam • Thanjavur • Tiruchirappalli • Madurai • Kodaikanal • Udhagamandalam (Ooty) • Mysore • Bangalore • Belur/Halebid/Sravanabelagola • Hampi • Badami • Bijapur • Mumbai (Bombay)

Temples and Beaches South India
Chennai (Madras) • Mamallapuram • Pondicherry • Thanjavur • Tiruchirappalli • Madurai • Kanyakumari • Kovalam Beach • Thiruvananthapuram • Kollam • Alappuzha • Kochi • Mysore and Bangalore • Hampi • Bijapur • Mumbai (Bombay)

TEMPLES & ANCIENT MONUMENTS – CENTRAL & SOUTH INDIA

This route takes in a small slice of modern India plus the popular travellers beach resort of Kovalam, a glimpse of ex-French India at Pondicherry, and several days in the mountains bordering Tamil Nadu and Kerala. Transport is by train and bus plus the use of a one day Indian Tourism Development Corporation (ITDC) bus from Mysore or Bangalore to the temple towns of Belur, Halebid and Sravanabelagola.

TEMPLES & BEACHES – SOUTH INDIA

This route, a variation of the Central & South India route, provides a much broader perspective of southern India. It takes you through the tropical paradise of Kerala with its beaches, Kathakali dance-dramas and historical Indo-European associations. It also includes some of the major temple complexes of Tamil Nadu, the palaces of Mysore, the Vijayanagar ruins of Hampi and the Muslim splendour of Bijapur (its Golgumbaz monument is said to have the world's second largest dome). Transport is by train, bus and boat, but flights are available from Bangalore to Mumbai.

Visa Requirements

Virtually everybody needs a visa to visit India. Tourist visas are issued for six months and are valid from the date of issue of the visa, not the date you enter India. Tourist visas are not extendable. Those travellers wishing to stay in India for longer than six months will have to travel to a neighbouring country and re-enter.

Indian Embassies & High Commissions

AUSTRALIA
(☎ 02-6273 3999) 3-5 Moonah Place, Yarralumla, ACT 2600. Consulates: Perth, Melbourne and Sydney

BANGLADESH
(☎ 02-503 606) 120 Road 2, Dhamondi, Dhaka

CANADA
(☎ 613-744-3751) 10 Springfield Rd, Ottawa, Ontario K1M 1C9

NEW ZEALAND
(☎ 04-473 6390) 180 Molesworth St, Wellington

THAILAND
(☎ 02-258 0300) 46 Soi 23 (Prasarn Mitr), Sukhumvit Rd, Bangkok 10110

UK
(☎ 020-7836 8484) India House, Aldwych, London WC2B 4NA. Consulate: Birmingham

USA
(☎ 202-939-7000) 2107 Massachusetts Ave NW, Washington, DC 20008. Consulates: New York and San Francisco

Tourist Offices Overseas

The Government of India Department of Tourism maintains a string of tourist offices in other countries where you can get brochures, leaflets and some information about India. There are also smaller promotion offices in Osaka, Dallas, Miami, Washington, DC and San Francisco.

AUSTRALIA
(☎ 02-9264 4855) Level 2, Piccadilly, 210 Pitt St, Sydney, NSW 2000

CANADA
(☎ 416-962-3787) 60 Bloor St West, Suite No 1003, Toronto, Ontario M4W 3B8

UK
(☎ 020-7437 3677) 7 Cork St, London W1X 2LN

USA
(☎ 212-586-4901) 30 Rockefeller Plaza, 15 North Mezzanine, New York, NY 10112; (☎ 213-380-8855) 3550 Wilshire Blvd, Suite 204, Los Angeles, CA 90010

Health

Malaria exists throughout most of India (anywhere below 2000m) but is not a risk in parts of Himachal Pradesh, Jammu and Kashmir, and Sikkim. Filariasis exists, as does Japanese encephalitis, and outbreaks of dengue fever occur mainly in large, urban areas. Take preventive measures against all these diseases and avoid mosquito bites. Recurring outbreaks of meningococcal meningitis occur in northern India. Leishmaniasis is on the increase, so avoid sandfly bites. Rabies also exists, and is carried by dogs, monkeys and bats. Food and waterborne diseases (including dysentery, typhoid and hepatitis) are common, and though not a major risk for travellers, cholera also occurs. Drink only boiled or purified water throughout the country, and avoid shellfish and meat, unpeeled fruit and vegetables.

There are excellent hospitals in some of the larger cities but elsewhere medical services are limited. Hospitals run by western missionaries usually have better facilities than the government hospitals. If you require serious medical care or hospitalisation, go to Bangkok or Singapore.

Post & Communications

India's postal service is reliable, if a little slow at times, and local and international rates are very reasonable. There are post restante services in every major city. The telephone network is also very good, with public offices offering domestic and international call facilities in even the smallest towns. Domestic rates are relatively cheap, but international rates are less of a bargain.

India is developing an email network, but services are still mainly restricted to large cities and towns popular with travellers.

Money

Costs

If you stay in cheap hotels, always travel 2nd class on trains, and learn to subsist on dhal and rice, you could see India on just US$10 a day. If you prefer a few more creature comforts, like a simple private room with bathroom, a varied diet, and occasional 1st class rail travel on long journeys, count on around US$20 to US$25 a day. Staying in mid-range hotels, eating in decent restaurants, and occasionally hiring a car and driver will cost around US$30 to US$35 a day. If you don't want to trespass beyond converted maharaja's palaces and five-star hotels, budget as if you were travelling comfortably in the west.

Changing Money

You are not allowed to bring Indian currency into the country, or take it with you when you leave. The rupee is fully convertible so there's not much of a black market. In cities you can change most major foreign currencies and brands of travellers cheques, but you'll widen your options if you stick to US dollars or pounds sterling, and Thomas Cook or American Express travellers cheques.

Changing money is a long and complex process – try to change large amounts as infrequently as possible (preferably in big banks in big cities). You are supposed to be given an encashment certificate when you change money at a bank or an official moneychanger. Some hotels insist you show this before they will accept payment in rupees.

Credit cards are widely accepted in Indian cities and larger towns, particularly American Express, Diners Club, MasterCard and Visa. Credit cards can also be used to get cash advances in rupees. The Bank of Baroda seems to be the most efficient at handling such transactions.

Online Services

Lonely Planet's *Destination India* page is at www.lonelyplanet.com/dest/ind/ind.htm.

For mainstream Indian news, check out the *Times of India* (www.timesofindia.com), *The Hindu* (www.webpage.com/hindu/index.html) and the *India Express* (www.indiaexpress.com). You can get your pics fix and regular travel articles at the Indian Tourism Development Corporation's monthly *Discover India* magazine (www.pugmarks.com/d-india).

You'd better hope half the fun is getting there. Take a long ride with *Indian Railways* (www.indianrailway.com) – timetables, tourist information, special trains and more.

The *West Bengal Home Page* (www.gl.umbc.edu/achatt1/wbengal.html) has information on the state's language, culture and attractions, and the *Calcutta Home Page* (www.gl.umbc.edu/achatt1/calcutta.html) does a similar job on the state capital. The *Madhya Pradesh tourism corporation* (www.mptourism.com) will tell you about tours, events, hand-crafts and places you mustn't miss.

The Global Hindu Electronic Network's introduction to *The Hindu Universe* (www.hindunet.org) is an all-you-ever-wanted-to-know guide to Hinduism, and includes the entire texts of the *Ramayana*, *Mahabharata* and other scriptures.

If you're keen to do something useful while you're in the sub-continent, check out *Project India* (emol.org/emol/projectindia).

Books

Colonial literature includes Rudyard Kipling's *Kim* and *Plain Tales from the Hills*, and EM Forster's *A Passage to India*. The postcolonial Indian novel par excellence is Salman Rushdie's *Midnight's Children*, though Vikram Seth's suitcase-sized *A Suitable Boy* runs a close second. Over the past decade, a swag of Indian authors writing in English have achieved international recognition. They include Rohinton Mistry, Shashi Tharoor and Arundhati Roy. The delightful novels of RK Narayan are evidence that Indian literary talent in English is not particularly new.

Worthy travelogues covering India include seminal texts such as Eric Newby's *Slowly Down the Ganges*, Paul Theroux's *The Great Railway Bazaar* and Alexander Frater's delightful *Chasing the Monsoon*. William Dalrymple explored Delhi in *City of Djinns,* while Geoffrey Moorhouse took the plunge in *Calcutta – a city revealed.*

Commentaries on India can provide travellers with some of the best insights. They include VS Naipaul's acerbic *An Area of Darkness*, *India – A Wounded Civilisation* and the more mature *A Million Mutinies Now;* James Cameron's insightful *An Indian Summer;* Mark Tully's *No Full Stops In India;* and John Keay's *Into India.*

The two volume *Pelican History of India* is a dry but comprehensive historical treatment. More readable accounts include Christopher Hibbert's

The Great Mutiny – India 1857; Plain Tales from the Raj edited by Charles Allen; Tariq Ali's *The Nehrus & the Gandhis;* and the potboiler *Freedom at Midnight* by Larry Collins & Dominique Lapierre.

Both the Hindu holy books, *The Upanishads* and *The Bhagavad Gita* are available in English translations. *Hinduism* by KM Sen is a blissfully brief and succinct introduction to India's major religion. *A Classical Dictionary of Hindu Mythology & Religion* will help unravel who's who in the Hindu cosmology. And anyone tempted to search for spiritual salvation should read Gita Mehta's witty *Karma Kola*.

Films

Indian Films

The Indian film industry is the largest in the world in purely volume terms. The vast proportion of what is produced is your average Bollywood 'masala movies' – cheap melodramas based on romance, violence and music. India has also produced some wonderful films from brilliant directors, foremost among them being Satyajit Ray. His best films include *Pather Panchali*, *Apur Sansar*, *Ashani Sanket* and *Jana Aranya*.

Shot on the streets of Mumbai is the excellent *Salaam Bombay* by Mira Nair. It concentrates on the plight of the street children in Mumbai, and won the Golden Camera Prize at Cannes in 1989. Also directed by Nair is *Kama Sutra*. Its theme of sensuality and sexuality in 16th century India shocked the Bollywood establishment. Also controversial in India was *Bandit Queen*, directed by Shekhar Kapur, and based on the life of the female outlaw, Phoolan Devi. Other notable

Indian directors include Mrinal Sen, Ritwik Ghatak, Shaji N Karuns and Adoor Gopalakrishnan.

Foreign Films

Keep your eyes open for a showing of Louis Malle's two part *Phantom India*. Running to about seven hours in all, this is a fascinating in-depth look at contemporary India. Though somewhat dated, as an overall view it can't be beaten – it has been banned in India. The Australian ABC TV has produced two excellent documentary series: *Journey into India* and *Journey into the Himalayas*.

Of course the epic *Gandhi* was a major film. *Heat & Dust* has also been made into an excellent film, as have *A Passage to India* and *Far Pavilions*. The film version of Lapierre's *City of Joy* was filmed in Calcutta in 1992 at a purpose-built slum. It attracted a lot of flak from the West Bengal government which felt it was yet another condescending look at India's poor.

Entering & Leaving India

India's major international airports are Mumbai (Bombay) and Delhi, though there are plenty of international flights arriving in Calcutta and Chennai (Madras). Flights from Europe tend to arrive in the early hours of the morning, which can be most inconvenient if you haven't arranged accommodation in advance, or don't like tramping around unfamiliar cities in the dark. Delhi is the cheapest place in India to buy air tickets, followed by Calcutta and Mumbai. The departure tax on flights to Pakistan, Sri Lanka, Bangladesh and Nepal is approximately US$3, but to other countries it's about US$10.

The most popular overland routes between India and Nepal are

Birganj-Raxaul, Sunauli-Gorakhpur and Kakarbhitta-Siliguri. There is also a less frequently used crossing from Banbassa to Mahendranagar, in Nepal's extreme west. From Kathmandu or Pokhara to Delhi or elsewhere in north-western India, Sunauli is the most convenient entry point; to reach Calcutta or most of eastern India, Birganj is the best place to cross; and for Darjeeling, it's easiest to go via Kakarbhitta. It's fairly easy to travel overland from Calcutta to Dhaka, Bangladesh via Haridaspur-Benapol. The only border crossing currently open between India and Pakistan is at Wagah (Attari on the India side), between Lahore and Amritsar, and this can be crossed by rail and road.

The only entry point to Bhutan is at Jaigaon (Phuentsholing on the Bhutanese side), but you will have to fly either in or out of Bhutan by the national carrier, Druk Air.

INDONESIA

The islands of the Indonesian archipelago stretch almost 5000km from the Asian mainland into the Pacific Ocean. Richly endowed with natural resources and hosting a phenomenal array of distinct cultures, they have been a magnet to Chinese and Indian traders, European colonisers, proselytising wayward adventurers, mining companies, missionaries, intrepid travellers and package tourists.

Despite the national motto 'unity in diversity', the many cultures of the islands are threatened by gradual unification under centralised Javanese rule. Economic, nationalist and religious-based riots – particularly in Java, East Timor and Ambon – have put a dampener on the tourist trade, but there are still plenty of safe places to visit (check with your embassy before you go) and travel is even cheaper than normal.

When to Go

Straddling the equator, Indonesia tends to have a fairly even climate year-round. It has two seasons – wet and dry – and there are no extremes of winter and summer as in some northern parts of Asia. In most parts of Indonesia the wet season falls between October and April, and the dry season between May and September. This means that, in general, the best time to visit is between May and October.

The Christmas holiday period until the end of January brings a wave of migratory Australians to Bali, as do the shorter school breaks during the year. There is an even bigger tourist wave during the European summer holidays, bringing crowds to Bali, Java, Sumatra and Sulawesi in July and August. The main Indonesian holiday period is the end of Ramadan (normally January/February) when some resorts are packed to overflowing and prices skyrocket. Other important holidays include Christmas and the end of the school year (from mid-June to mid-July).

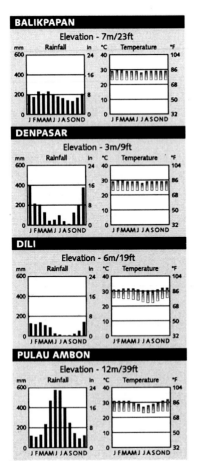

BALIKPAPAN
Elevation - 7m/23ft

DENPASAR
Elevation - 3m/9ft

DILI
Elevation - 6m/19ft

PULAU AMBON
Elevation - 12m/39ft

That leaves May/June and September/October as the pick of the months to travel to Indonesia, though even during the peak tourist months you can always find a place away from the crowds. Always allow yourself some extra time. Travel can be hard and you may need to recuperate, or you may find yourself side-tracked by some wonderful place that you never knew existed. Remember that schedules in Indonesia are flexible, and you may be forced to bend yours.

Highlights

Indonesia has beaches, volcanoes, ancient cultures, magnificent wilderness, vibrant cities and archaeological ruins – it is impossible to see all of Indonesia in the 60 days allowed by a tourist pass.

Beaches, Surfing & Snorkelling

The Bali beach resorts at Kuta/Legian, Sanur, Nusa Dua, Lovina and Candidasa have great tourist facilities and excellent surfing and diving, while nearby Lombok has a number of rapidly developing resorts and quiet islands. The Bandas islands are remote, but boast some magnificent beaches and reefs, as do Manado and the Tongian islands in Sulawesi and spots along the northern coast of Irian Jaya.

Traditional Culture

Ubud in Bali's central mountains is the centre for traditional Balinese art and culture and makes a good base for exploring the 'real Bali'. In Sulawesi, Tanatoraja's communal funerals are among Indonesia's most colourful events and showcase a unique culture. The central islands of Nusa Tenggara (notably Sumba and Sumbawa) offer a fascinating insight into village-based life, as does the Baliem Valley in Irian Jaya, with the added bonus of some excellent trekking.

Architecture

The Buddhist pyramid of Borobudur in Java is one of the world's modern wonders and nearby Yogyakarta is a centre for Javanese culture. Banda Aceh in northern Sumatra is notable for its mosque architecture. There's also plenty of evidence of Indonesia's colonial past, particularly the Dutch and Portuguese forts and public buildings in Maluku and Timor.

Lakes & Volcanoes

Indonesia has some of the most beautiful scenery in the region. High levels of volcanic activity have created the famous coloured lakes of Keli Mutu (Nusa Tenggara), the spectacular crater lake of Danau Toba (Sumatra) and the nascent island emerging within the shattered rim of Krakatau volcano off Java's north-western tip. Other volcanoes (not all of them dormant) also offer excellent trekking, particularly at Gunung Bromo (Java), Gunung Batur (Bali), Gunung Agung (Bali) and at Gunung Rinjani (Nusa Tenggara).

Wildlife

The best known beast in Indonesia is the Komodo dragon, which is also found on the neighbouring island of Rinca, but there's much more to see than this. The Orang-utan Rehabilitation Centre at Bukit Lawang (Sumatra) is justly world-famous, while along the Sungai Mahakam river, Kalimantan retains tracts of virgin jungle which support a huge variety of unusual and rare species, including bear-cats, hornbills, dolphins, proboscis monkeys and gibbons. The renowned Sea Gardens of Manado are a marine paradise, while ornithologists flock to north-east Irian Jaya hoping to glimpse the elusive and gorgeous bird of paradise.

Arts & Crafts

Shadow puppets, ikat weaving, masks, statues, wood-carvings, basketwork, beadwork, painting, ceramics, jewellery, knife-making ... you name it and you'll probably find it somewhere on the archipelago. Java, Bali and the islands of Nusa Tenggara are the best known for their arts and crafts, but who could go past a penis sheath from the Irian Jayan highlands?

Itineraries

Most visitors to Indonesia have one month or less to travel the vast archipelago, and it pays to choose only one, two or a maximum of three regions to explore. Many travellers pass through Indonesia on their way from Thailand or Malaysia to Australia, so the most visited islands tend to be Bali, Java and Sumatra. It's possible to see the main highlights of these three islands in one month, but that doesn't leave much time for relaxation. Sulawesi is a growing tourist destination, and can be comfortably combined with a trip to another region. More visitors are heading out through Nusa Tenggara, but Maluku, Irian Jaya and Kalimantan are still unexplored territory for the vast majority of visitors.

TWO WEEKS — SUMATRA

Sumatra's big attractions are in the north from Medan to Padang. Between Medan and the beautiful lake of Danau Toba, popular stops are the mountain town of Berastagi and the Orang-utan Rehabilitation Centre at Bukit Lawang. Pulau Samosir in the centre of Danau Toba is a comfortable travellers centre and there's lots to do around the area. Of the many side trips, Banda Aceh in the far north is increasingly popular – Pulau We is the main

INDONESIA HIGHLIGHTS & ITINERARIES

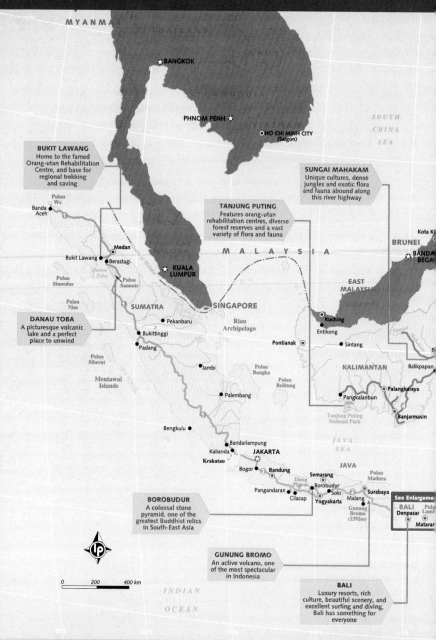

BUKIT LAWANG
Home to the famed Orang-utan Rehabilitation Centre, and base for regional trekking and caving

SUNGAI MAHAKAM
Unique cultures, dense jungles and exotic flora and fauna abound along this river highway

TANJUNG PUTING
Features orang-utan rehabilitation centres, diverse forest reserves and a vast variety of flora and fauna

DANAU TOBA
A picturesque volcanic lake and a perfect place to unwind

BOROBUDUR
A colossal stone pyramid, one of the greatest Buddhist relics in South-East Asia

GUNUNG BROMO
An active volcano, one of the most spectacular in Indonesia

BALI
Luxury resorts, rich culture, beautiful scenery, and excellent surfing and diving, Bali has something for everyone

SUGGESTED ITINERARIES

TWO WEEKS

SUMATRA ① Medan • Banda Aceh • Pulau We • Berastagi • Bukit Lawang • Pulau Samosir • Danau Toba • Bukittinggi • Padang • Krakatau • Jakarta

JAVA ② Jakarta • Bogor • Bandung • Pangandaran • Dieng Plateau • Yogyakarta • Borobudur • Prambanan • Surabaya • Gunung

BALI & LOMBOK ③ Kuta/Legian • Tanah Lot • Ubud • Danau Bratan • Lovina • Gunung Batur • Gunung Agung • Pura Besakih • Panangba Lembar • Kuta • Senggigi • Gili Islands • Gunung Rinjani

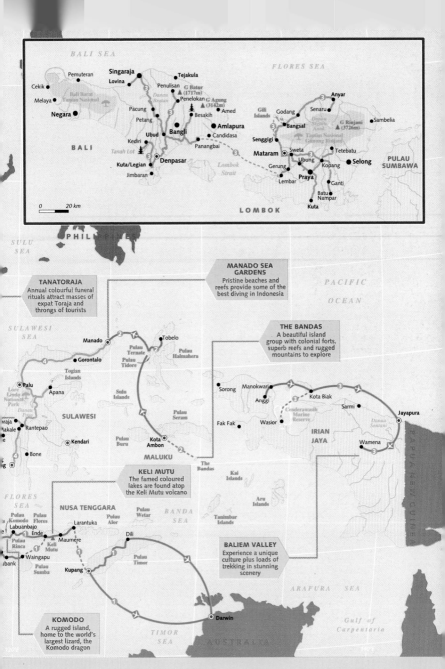

attraction. From Danau Toba it's a long bus trip to Padang, with a side trip to the mountain town of Bukittinggi, a cultural centre for the Minangkabau people. Most travellers skip southern Sumatra and take a bus, boat or plane directly to Jakarta – there's little to see in the southern part of the island other than remnants of Krakatau, accessible by boat from the small port of Kalianda. This entire route can be done in two weeks, but three is less gruelling.

TWO WEEKS — JAVA

From Sumatra, the typical route is to spend a day or so in Jakarta (with maybe a day trip to Bogor) before heading to Yogyakarta, the cultural heartland of Java and main base for visiting Borobudur and Prambanan. On the way, you could stop at Bandung, the beach resort of Pangandaran or the Dieng Plateau. From Yogya, continue to Surabaya and head south to see the impressive volcanic landscapes of Gunung Bromo. Try to squeeze in two days in north-western Bali before returning to Jakarta.

TWO WEEKS — BALI & LOMBOK

Compact Bali, with its good infrastructure and travel services, is an easy island to explore, while Lombok has many attractions but is less developed. You could easily spend a month here, but if you only have a fortnight then start with a couple of days in Kuta/Legian, including a day trip to the Tanah Lot temple, and then head for Ubud in central Bali. After two days exploring the surrounding villages – taking in some dance and fine food – consider day trips to attractions in the north, such as Danau Bratan, Gunung Batur and Gunung Agung (with a visit to Bali's main temple, Pura Besakih) or some lazing on the beach at Lovina. Make your way to Panangbai for the boat to Lembar on Lombok, where you can trek up Gunung Rinjani (a three day trip), relax and snorkel at Senggigi or on the Gili islands, or explore the villages to the west and south (Lombok's Kuta area has superb surfing). Then head back to Bali for your flight out.

TWO WEEKS — SULAWESI

From the main city of Ujung Pandang, most people head straight to Rantepao in Tanatoraja, Sulawesi's main attraction. Some don't get beyond it, but you can head up through Central Sulawesi via Danau Poso to the Lore Lindu National Park or detour to the magnificent Togian islands. Sulawesi has other good wildlife reserves, but is more famous for its beaches and coral, such as the sea gardens at Pulau Bunaken near Manado, which offer some of the finest diving and snorkelling in South-East Asia.

ONE MONTH — NUSA TENGGARA

Spend a week on Lombok seeing the major sights (see the Bali & Lombok itinerary), as well as soaking up some sun and surf on the southern coast, before making your way to Labuhan Lombok for a boat to Pulau Sumbawa. This island has some fine surf beaches, but is usually just a transit stop on the way to the dragons of Komodo and Rinca. Flores is home to the coloured lakes of Keli Mutu, and also has beaches and traditional villages between Labuanbajo and Maumere to break the tiring bus trips. From Maumere, you can fly back to Bali or head to Timor's Kupang and Dili (if it's safe – check the latest political situation) and on to Darwin in Australia. Sumba's fascinating traditional culture is an insightful detour if you have the time.

ONE MONTH — MALUKU

The main island, Pulau Ambon, has some good beaches and reefs, and is easy to reach by air from Bali, Sulawesi or Irian Jaya, but religious riots and killings have turned it into a no-go area. Check with your embassy if you want to travel there. Maluku's main attraction is the Bandas islands, but flights from Ambon are not always reliable, so allow at least a week and consider using the Pelni boats which travel through the islands every week or so. Northern Maluku boasts the interesting islands of Ternate and Tidore (the original spice islands), and wonderful beaches, diving and trekking on Pulau Halmahera (Tobelo is the transport hub here). It will take you a long time to get anywhere, but you won't see many other travellers.

ONE MONTH — IRIAN JAYA

Jayapura is easily reached by air from the rest of Indonesia. Nearby Danau Sentani is worth exploring but the Baliem Valley, reached only by air from Jayapura, is the major tourist attraction. Cancellations and overbooking occur so allow another week or more for Baliem. Pulau Biak, with regular air and boat connections, is popular for diving, beaches and WWII remnants. Other areas of interest – such as the Cenderawasih Marine Reserve and the Anggi Lakes – also require time-consuming air or boat travel, so allow at least a month.

ONE MONTH — KALIMANTAN

This vast island has relatively few roads and, unless you fly, sea and river travel takes time. Banjarmasin and its river life is one of the main attractions, and is a good starting point. From Banjarmasin you can head to Tanjung Puting National Park, famous for its orang-utan centres. A road runs from Banjarmasin to Balikpapan, the main air hub on the west coast, and further north is Samarinda, where boats go up the Sungai Mahakam into the interior.

TWO MONTHS — SUMATRA TO TIMOR

This is the classic route from South-East Asia to Australia. Mix and match the above itineraries to suit your interests, but beware of running out of time – the Nusa Tenggara islands can take a long time to travel through and they also contain some wonderful sights that would be disappointing to miss if time's running short. In addition, visa extensions are generally not issued and there are very steep fines or jail terms for overstaying.

Visa Requirements

For many nationalities, a visa is not necessary for entry and a stay of up to 60 days; these include Australia, Canada, New Zealand, UK and USA. A 60 day tourist pass (which is a stamp in your passport) is issued on arrival, as long as you enter and exit through recognised entry ports. Officially (but not always in practice) you must have a ticket out of the country when you arrive. Officially (and almost certainly) you cannot extend your visa beyond

60 days. If you're really intending to explore Indonesia in some depth, 60 days is inadequate and you will have to exit the country and re-enter.

For citizens of countries not on the visa free list, visitor visas can be obtained from Indonesian embassies or consulates, although they are not always keen to do this ... persevere. Visitor visas are only valid for one month and can only be extended for two weeks.

Indonesian Embassies

AUSTRALIA
(☎ 02-6273 3222) 8 Darwin Ave, Yarralumla, ACT 2600. Consulates: Adelaide, Darwin, Melbourne, Perth and Sydney

CANADA
(☎ 613-236-7403/5) 287 Maclaren St, Ottawa, Ontario K2P OL9. Consulates: Vancouver and Toronto

NEW ZEALAND
(☎ 04-475 8697) 70 Glen Rd, Kelburn, Wellington

UK
(☎ 020-7499 7661) 38 Grosvenor Square, London W1X 9AD

USA
(☎ 202-775-5200) 2020 Massachusetts Ave NW, Washington, DC 20036. Consulates: Chicago, Honolulu, Houston, Los Angeles, New York and San Francisco

Tourist Offices Overseas

Most Indonesian Tourist Promotion Offices have closed as a result of the Asian economic crisis. For information about Indonesia contact your local embassy or travel agent, or see Online Services below.

Health

Malaria risk exists year-round in Irian Jaya and rural areas of the other islands. There is no risk in the big cities or in the tourist areas of Java and Bali.

There have been recent large outbreaks of dengue fever, so you should take measures to avoid mosquito bites during the day. Food and waterborne diseases do occur, including dysentery and hepatitis, so it is worth paying attention to basic food and water hygiene. Schitsosomiasis (bilharzia) occurs on Sulawesi, and rabies exists on Java, Kalimantan, Sumatra and Sulawesi. Unboiled water should be avoided, but bottled water is available everywhere and many hotels and restaurants provide *air putih* (boiled water) for guests. Take care with ice. Restaurants often provide hygienic, commercially prepared ice, and even roadside food stalls may buy commercial ice – and then chop it up on the side of the road!

Medical standards vary widely. Outside Java, Catholic or missionary hospitals or clinics are often fairly good. In Java and major cities elsewhere, you can often locate a competent doctor, dentist or hospital by asking at hotels, embassies or offices of foreign companies. Jakarta boasts the best medical facilities in the country, but a lot of people still prefer to go to Singapore or Darwin for hospitalisation.

Post & Communications

Indonesia's postal service is quite cheap and has improved enormously, but international mail is quite slow and the domestic mail service is positively glacial. There are post restante services in most major cities, but you'll have to plan well in advance to actually receive anything in time.

The telephone system is better, with 24-hour *kantor Telkom* offices in many cities and towns. Private agencies *(wartel, warpostal* or *warparpostel)* are far more common, but are a bit more expensive. Indonesia has the lowest per capita rate of Internet penetration in Asia (at just 2%), but you will find plenty of opportunities to check and send email or surf the web at post offices in main cities throughout the country. Internet cafes are also popular in the main cities and tourist areas. Indonesian servers are very slow as a rule – it can take forever to log onto popular web sites and email services such as Hotmail.

Money

Costs

Indonesian costs are variable, depending on where you go. If you follow the well beaten tourist track through Bali, Java and Sumatra, you may well find Indonesia to be one of the cheapest countries in South-East Asia. Travellers centres like Danau Toba, Yogyakarta and Bali are superb value for accommodation and food. Elsewhere transport costs rise, budget accommodation can be limited and prices are higher because competition is weaker, especially in the outer provinces. If you confine yourself to Sumatra, Java, Bali and Nusa Tenggara, rock-bottom budget travel will cost around US$10 to US$15 per day. Count on more like US$50 a day if you want air-conditioning, tour guides or souvenirs.

Changing Money

A mix of travellers cheques, cash (preferably US dollars) and credit cards are the way to go in Indonesia. Travellers cheques can be exchanged in all the major centres. Credit cards are accepted by expensive hotels, restaurants and shops, and are a useful way to purchase major items like air tickets. In major centres, you can always find a bank that will advance you cash on Visa or MasterCard. Indonesian banks don't usually charge transaction fees for cash advances on credit cards, but always ask first. Credit card advances through ATMs are possible, but limited. For day-to-day expenses you can't beat cash, but currencies other than US dollars will be hard to change outside the major centres. If you are travelling away from the major cities and tourist areas, change enough money to tide you over until you reach another major centre. For really remote places, carry stacks of rupiah because there won't be anywhere to change foreign cash or travellers cheques.

Online Services

Lonely Planet's *Destination Indonesia* page can be found at www.lonelyplanet. com/dest/sea/indo.htm.

Scouring the links at *Indonesia* (coombs.anu.edu.au/WWWVLPages/IndonPages/WWWVL-Indonesia. html) and the *Indonesian Homepage* (indonesia.elga.net.id/) is a great way to begin an exploration of the archipelago.

The Bali Home Page (www .indo.com) is a lavish virtual tour of the island. *Bali the online travel guide* (werple.mira.net.au/~wreid/bali_p1a .html) is a down-to-earth version, keen to promote independent travel rather than package tours.

Puff the Magic Kretek (discover-jakarta.com/spices/kretek.html) and *The Kretek Page* (www.skypoint.com/ ~gimonca/kretek.html) explore the source of that pungent odour which is 'as much a part of Indonesia as sun and rain' – and which is also partly

responsible for why so many children puke up in minibuses.

Want to order a durian? *717 Trading* (www.gs.com.sg/717trading) can oblige.

TimorNet (www.uc.pt/Timor/ TimorNet. html) offers an historical introduction to East Timor and has links to a news digest and other East Timor web sites. *Indonesian Flight Scheduler* (www.hmorel.com/flight/flight.html) is a nifty way to plan your inter-island hops.

Books

An Empire of the East by Norman Lewis is an informative account of travels through the troublesome parts of the archipelago in 1991, including Aceh and Timor. *Drums of Tonki* by Helen & Frank Schreider is an exhilarating travelogue of island-hopping from Java to Timor.

Islands in the Clouds – Travels in the highlands of New Guinea by Isabella Tree (Lonely Planet) illuminates the tragic consequences of the colonial and postcolonial carve-up on a visit to the highlands of Irian Jaya and Papua New Guinea.

Indonesia in Focus, a Dutch publication edited by Peter Homan et al, has numerous glossy photos and well illustrated articles which explore Indonesia's rich ethnic diversity.

The *Religion of Java* by Clifford Geertz is not only a classic book on Javanese religion, culture and values, but revolutionised the study of social anthropology.

The Year of Living Dangerously by CJ Koch is an evocative reconstruction of Jakarta life during the bloody and chaotic final months of Soekarno's rule, while *Twilight in Jakarta* by

Mochtar Lubis is a scathing account of the political corruption in Indonesia.

A History of Modern Indonesia by MC Ricklefs is a general history concentrating mainly on Java and the Dutch conquest.

Two good illustrated books on Indonesian wildlife are *The Wildlife of Indonesia* by Kathy MacKinnon and *Wild Indonesia* by Tony & Jane Whitten.

Claire Holt's *Art in Indonesia: Continuities and Change* is an excellent introduction to Indonesia's arts, focusing on traditional dance, wayang and literature.

Films

Possibly the best known western film on Indonesia is Peter Weir's *Year of Living Dangerously* (1983). Starring Mel Gibson, it explores the 1965 coup and the subsequent anti-Communist purge.

Manufacturing Consent: Noam Chomsky and the Media (1992) is a documentary containing a discussion of propaganda generated by the US government and big business during the US-backed Indonesian invasion of East Timor.

One of the few domestically produced Indonesian movies is *Enam Djam Di Djogja* (Six Hours in Jogja), a celebration of the recapture of Yogyakarta from the Dutch in 1949, which created international pressure on the Dutch to leave Indonesia.

Entering & Leaving Indonesia

The principal gateways for entry to Indonesia are Jakarta and Bali. Jakarta is serviced by more airlines but, due to its huge tourist trade, Bali gets almost as much traffic. Merpati flights from Darwin to Ambon (Maluku), Ujung Pandang (Sulawesi) and to Biak (Irian Jaya) have opened up eastern Indonesia to Australia. The departure tax on international flights is US$10 from Jakarta and Denpasar, and US$7 from most other airports.

The only open land crossing in Indonesia is from Entikong to Tebedu, between Kalimantan and Sarawak (in Malaysia). Visas are not required and a 60 day visa pass is issued on the spot. Most of the sea connections are on comfortable high-speed ferries which link Malaysia and Sumatra (Penang-Medan, Melaka-Dumai and Tawau-Tarakan), as well as the Philippines and Sulawesi (Davao-Manado). Singapore is accessible from Indonesaa via the Riau Archipelago. Speedboats link Pekanbaru in Sumatra with Batam, and several ships a week link Jakarta with Bintan.

Japan is the subject of more gullible and misguided musings than perhaps any other place in the world – the best way to approach it is to discard your preconceptions. Somewhere between the elegant formality of Japanese manners and the candid, sometimes boisterous exchanges that take place over a few drinks, and between the sanitised shopping malls and the un-expected rural festivals, everyone finds their own vision of Japan. Whether you end up taking photos of an Eiffel Tower replica, surfing an indoor wave, shacking up in a love hotel or kipping down in a capsule, you'll do best to come with an open mind and be prepared to be surprised.

When to Go
Spring (March to May), with its clear skies and cherry blossoms, is probably the most celebrated Japanese season, but it's a holiday period for the Jap-anese as well and many of the more popular travel destinations tend to be flooded with domestic tourists. Au-tumn (September to November) is a great time to travel: the temperatures are pleasant and the autumn colours in the countryside are fantastic. Mid-winter (December to February) can be bitterly cold, while the sticky summer months (June to August) can turn even the briefest excursion out of the air-conditioning into an unpleasant swelter. On the plus side, major tourist attractions will generally be quieter at these times of the year. It's also worth noting peak holiday seasons when you plan your trip. Moving around and finding accommodation during New Year, Golden Week (late April to early May) and the midsummer O-bon Festival can be a real headache.

Highlights
With the notable exception of Mt Fuji, there is no Japanese equivalent of the Taj Mahal or Statue of Liberty. Nevertheless, Japan is crammed with attractions.

AT A GLANCE

Full Country Name: Japan (Nippon)

Area: 377,435 sq km

Population: 125 million

Capital City: Tokyo (pop eight million)

People: 99% Japanese (including indigenous Ainu) and 1% Korean

Languages: Japanese

Religion: 85% Shinto/Buddhist, 11% Shugendo, plus Confucian, Christian, Muslim and new religious fringe groups

Government: Constitutional monarchy

Currency: Yen (¥)

Time Zone: Nine hours ahead of GMT/UTC

International Telephone Code: 81

Electricity: 100V, 50 AC (Tokyo and eastern Japan), 60 AC (western Japan); sockets take two-pin American-style plugs

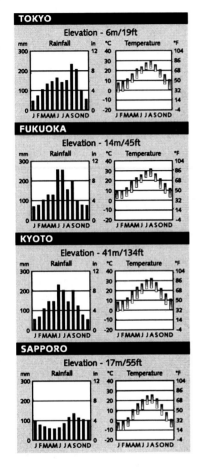

TOKYO
Elevation - 6m/19ft

FUKUOKA
Elevation - 14m/45ft

KYOTO
Elevation - 41m/134ft

SAPPORO
Elevation - 17m/55ft

Castles

The greatest surviving castle is Himeji-jo. Combining elegance and impregnability it soars above the Kansai plain, thus earning the name 'White Egret'. It's an easy day trip from Kyoto. Running a close second is Shikoku's Matsuyama-jo. Other castles worth a visit include Matsumoto-jo in central Honshu; Hirosaki-jo in northern Honshu; Hikone-jo and Inuyama-jo in the Kansai region; Matsue-jo and Bitchu-Matsuyama in western Honshu; and Kumamoto-jo in Kyushu.

Gardens

Japan is justly famed for its beautiful gardens, and whether they are larger Edo 'stroll gardens' or small contemplative Zen gardens, there is always exquisite attention to detail. The 'big three' are Kairaku-en (Mito), Kenroku-en (Kanazawa) and Koraku-en (Okayama). Kyoto has almost too many to mention, including those that virtually define the rock garden and the Zen *kare-sansui* (dry-landscape garden). Among the best smaller Zen gardens outside Kyoto are beautiful Komyo-ji at Dazaifu, Joei-ji in Yamaguchi and Raikyu-ji at Takahashi.

Scenery & Natural Attractions

Despite Japan's population density, it has many areas of great natural beauty. The Japanese rate their three best views as the 'floating' *torii* (entrance gate to a Shinto shrine) of Miya-jima Island, the long sand spit of Amanohashidate (both in western Honshu) and Matsushima-wan Bay (in northern Honshu), with its pine-covered islands. The misty, island-dotted waters of the Inland Sea are one of the most beautiful sights in the country, while spectacular mountain scenery can be found in Nagano-ken (the setting of the Japan Alps) and northern Gifu-ken (Takayama and the Shokawa Valley region). Mt Fuji can actually seem like a Tokyo train station at rush hour, but from a distance it's as beautiful as ever. Hokkaido offers wonderful mountain scenery around Lake Mashu-ko in Daisetsuzan National Park, while the Shiretoko-hanto Peninsula has fine coastal scenery. Kyushu also has some wonderful volcanic scenery, particularly in the immense caldera of Mt Aso, the bleak, volcano-studded Kirishima National Park, and rumbling Sakura-jima near Kagoshima. At the extreme western end of the country, Iriomote-jima Island in the Yaeyama islands has dense jungle and good scuba diving.

Shrines

Shrines are the focus of Japan's indigenous Shinto faith. Ise (Kansai region) has the imperial shrine to Amaterasu, the mythical ancestor of the Japanese imperial line. Nikko has the shrine to Tokugawa Ieyasu, founder of the Tokugawa shogunate, while Izumo Taisha has the largest and, it is claimed, oldest shrine hall in Japan. Kyoto is particularly well endowed with impressive shrines, including Heian-jingu. Other important shrines include the popular Meiji-jingu in Tokyo, the Itsukushima-jinja with its much photographed floating torii on Miya-jima Island, and the hilltop Kotohira-gu in Shikoku.

Temples

The best examples of Buddhist temples are found in Kyoto, Nara and the surrounding Kansai region. Important Kyoto temples include: Daitoku-ji, with its gardens; ancient Kiyomizu-dera with its superb hillside setting; 13th century Sanjusangen-do; and To-ji, established in 794. Nara has the fine Toshodai-ji and Todai-ji, with its Great Buddha. Also in the Kansai region are Kobo Daishi's mountaintop Koya-san, the wonderful Horyu-ji, and Byodo-in in Uji, which is one of the most famous buildings in Japan. Close to Tokyo, Kamakura offers some excellent temple tramping, and Kotoku-in has the country's best known giant Buddha

statue. Although the 88 temples in Kobo Daishi's circuit of Shikoku have no great individual significance, taken together they represent the most important pilgrimage route in Japan.

Historical Japan

Despite the Japanese penchant for knocking down the old and putting up the new, there are other reminders of the country's history. Hakodate, in Hokkaido, is a fascinating old port town with some very interesting Meiji-period western-style buildings. Similar buildings can be seen in the port towns of Nagasaki and Kobe. Takayama, north of Nagoya, has many fine old buildings plus the Hida Folk Village, which consists of more than a dozen farmhouses of the *gassho-zukuri* (hands in prayer) architectural style. Kurashiki is famed for its canal district and old warehouses, while the small town of Chiran in southern Kyushu has an old street of well preserved samurai buildings and a *kamikaze* museum. Hagi in western Honshu is also noted for its samurai quarter, castle ruins, temples and shrines.

Modern Japan

Japan is as much the land of pachinko parlours, love hotels, robot-operated production lines and multistorey buildings filled with nothing but bars. It's the only place in the world to have suffered atomic destruction, and the museums at Hiroshima and Nagasaki should not be avoided. Hiroshima and Osaka are good places to see the modern Japanese industrial machine in peak form, and reams of boisterous bars thrive in their entertainment districts (although Tokyo's Roppongi area and the raunchier Kabuki-cho are perhaps the pinnacle of this dubious artform). In some places there are major enclaves of love hotels – the Dogen-zaka area of Tokyo's Shibuya district is a good example. Further north, Sapporo offers a sense of space unusual in Japanese cities.

Itineraries

Given the high costs of touring Japan, most travellers keep to fairly tight itineraries. Fortunately, Japan's excellent road and rail networks allow you to get around quickly, and public transport is very reliable. To see as much as possible in a short time, organise a JR Rail Pass before you leave home.

ONE WEEK – TOKYO TO KYOTO

The Tokyo-Kyoto route is the most popular Japan primer. For first-time visitors with only a week to look around, a few days in Tokyo sampling the modern Japanese experience and four or five days in the Kansai region exploring the historical sites of Kyoto and Nara are good options. If time is tight, and you have a JR Rail Pass, do the Tokyo-Kyoto journey by *shinkansen* (bullet train), allowing time for a day trip to Nara to sample the delights of Japan's first major capital.

TWO WEEKS TO A MONTH – TOKYO & THE SOUTH-WEST

Kansai, western Honshu and Kyushu are richer in sights than the northern regions of Japan so many travellers tend to head west and south. You could possibly manage everything here in two weeks, but it would be hectic and you'd spend a lot of time on trains. Be selective or allow more time.

Assuming you fly into Tokyo, it's worth spending a few days exploring the city before heading south-west to Kansai. An interesting overnight trip out of Kyoto or Osaka is to the Buddhist mountain sanctuary of Koya-san. From Kansai, take a shinkansen to Fukuoka and then switch to a local express to Nagasaki, which has an interesting cosmopolitan history and a moving museum about the 1945 atomic blast. From Nagasaki it is possible to do a loop through northern Kyushu taking in Kumamoto, hiking at the volcanic Mt Aso and the ultimate in tacky hot-springs re-

sorts, Beppu. South is the balmy port city of Kagoshima. The fastest way to return to Kansai or Tokyo is by plane, but you could take the shinkansen along the Inland Sea side of western Honshu. Stopovers include Hiroshima (from where you can take a cruise through the islands of the Inland Sea) or the castle town Himeji. From Okayama, the seldom visited island of Shikoku is easily accessible. The Japan Sea side of western Honshu is less touristed and more rural – notable attractions are the shrine at Izumo and the small cities of Matsue and Tottori.

ONE MONTH – TOKYO & NORTHERN JAPAN

If you're a nature buff, then Japan's north is the place for you. A good approach from Tokyo is via Matsumoto and Nagano, which are excellent bases for hikes and visits to rural communities such as Kamikochi, the old charms of Takayama and the shrines and temples of Nikko. From Nagano, you could travel up to Niigata and from there to seldom visited Sado-shima Island. On the eastern side of Honshu, the city of Sendai provides easy access to Matsushima, one of Japan's most celebrated scenic outlooks.

Highlights north of Sendai include the cultural centre of Hiraizumi, the samurai houses at Kakunodate, and Aomori, which is a good base for visits to the Towada-Hachimantai National Park and picturesque Lake Towado-ko.

From Aomori to Hokkaido by train involves a ride through the world's longest underwater tunnel. Hokkaido's capital, Sapporo, has the annual February ice festival and is a welcome respite from the frantic cities elsewhere in Japan. Other attractions on Hokkaido are for lovers of the outdoors, such as hiking and skiing in the Daisetsuzan and Shikotsu-Toya national parks or visiting the pristine wilderness at Shiretoko-Hanto Peninsula. If you're short on time, consider returning to Tokyo by plane.

Visa Requirements

Tourist and business visitors of many nationalities are not required to obtain a visa if staying in Japan for less than 90 days. On a business visa, British

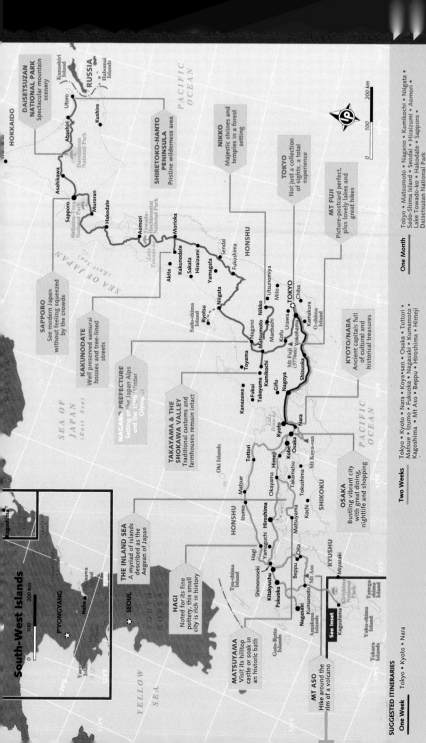

South-West Islands

PYONGYANG

SEOUL

SOUTH KOREA

YELLOW SEA

SEA OF JAPAN (East Sea)

HOKKAIDO

DAISETSUZAN NATIONAL PARK
Spectacular mountain scenery

RUSSIA

Kunashiri Island

Habomai Islands

PACIFIC OCEAN

SHIRETOKO-HANTO PENINSULA
Pristine wilderness area

Utoro

Abashiri

Kushiro

Asahikawa

Asahikawa

Muroran

Sapporo

Hakodate

Daisetsuzan National Park

Shikotsu-Toya Nat'l Park

SAPPORO
See modern Japan without feeling squeezed by the crowds

Aomori

Towada-Hachimantai National Park

Lake Towada-ko

Morioka

Hiraizumi

KAKUNODATE
Well-preserved samurai houses and tree-lined streets

NIKKO
Majestic shrines and temples in a forest setting

Akita

Kakunodate

Sakata

Hiraizumi

Sendai

Yamagata

Fukushima

HONSHU

SEA OF JAPAN (East Sea)

NAGANO PREFECTURE
Setting of the Japan Alps and the 1998 Winter Olympics

Sado-shima Island

Ryotsu

Niigata

Nagano

Nikko

Utsunomiya

TOKYO
Not just a collection of sights, a total experience

TAKAYAMA & THE SHOKAWA VALLEY
Traditional customs and farmhouses remain intact

Toyama

Matsumoto

Maebashi

Mito

TOKYO

Chiba

Kanazawa

Takayama

Kamikochi

Kofu

Urawa

Yokohama

Kamakura

Fukui

Gifu

Nagoya

Mt Fuji (3776m)

Shizuoka

O-shima Island

MT FUJI
Picture-postcard perfect, plus lovely lakes and great hikes

KYOTO/NARA
Ancient capitals full of cultural and historical treasures

Kyoto

Nara

Osaka

Kobe

PACIFIC OCEAN

Lake Biwa-ko

THE INLAND SEA
A myriad of islands described as the Aegean of Japan

Oki Islands

Tottori

Matsue

Izumo

Himeji

Okayama

Takamatsu

Takamatsu

Osaka

Mt Koya-san

HONSHU

Hiroshima

Yamaguchi

Tokushima

OSAKA
Bustling vibrant city with great dining, nightlife and shopping

SHIKOKU

HAGI
Noted for its fine pottery, this small city is rich in history

Hagi

Matsuyama

Kochi

Tsu-shima Island

Shimonoseki

Kitakyushu

Oita

Beppu

MATSUYAMA
Visit its hilltop castle or soak in an historic bath

Fukuoka

Goto-Retto Islands

Nagasaki

Kumamoto

Mt Aso

Amakusa Islands

Miyazaki

KYUSHU

Kagoshima

Naha

Okinawa Island

Iriomote Island

Yaeyama Islands

Miyako-jima Island

Kagoshima

See Inset

Kirishima National Park

Yaku-shima Island

Tanega-shima Island

Tokara Islands

MT ASO
Hike around the rim of a volcano

0   100   200 km

0   100   200 km

0   100   200 km

SUGGESTED ITINERARIES

One Week   Tokyo • Kyoto • Nara

Two Weeks   Tokyo • Kyoto • Nara • Koya-san • Osaka • Tottori • Matsue • Izumo • Fukuoka • Nagasaki • Kumamoto • Kagoshima • Mt Aso • Beppu • Hiroshima • Himeji

One Month   Tokyo • Matsumoto • Nagano • Kamikochi • Niigata • Sado-Shima Island • Sendai • Hiraizumi • Aomori • Lake Towado-ko • Hakodate • Sapporo • Daisetsuzan National Park

citizens can stay for up to six months, and Americans, Australians, Canadians and New Zealanders for three months.

Japanese Embassies

AUSTRALIA
(☎ 02-6273 3244) 112 Empire Circuit, Yarralumla, ACT 2600. Consulates: Brisbane, Melbourne, Perth and Sydney

CANADA
(☎ 613-241-8541) 255 Sussex Drive, Ottawa, Ontario K1N 9E6. Consulates: Edmonton, Montreal, Toronto and Vancouver

NEW ZEALAND
(☎ 04-473 1540) 7th floor, Norwich Insurance House, 3-11 Hunter St, Wellington. Consulate: Auckland

UK
(☎ 020-7465 6500) 43-46 Grosvenor St, London W1X OBA

USA
(☎ 202-939-6700) 2520 Massachusetts Ave, NW Washington, DC 20008-2869. Consulates: Anchorage, Atlanta, Boston, Chicago, Honolulu, Houston, Kansas City, Los Angeles, New Orleans, Portland, New York and San Francisco

Tourist Offices Overseas

The Japan National Tourist Organization (JNTO) maintains a number of overseas offices, including:

AUSTRALIA
(☎ 02-9232 4522) Level 33, The Chifley Tower, 2 Chifley Square, Sydney, NSW 2000

CANADA
(☎ 416-366-7140) 165 University Ave, Toronto, Ontario M5H 3B8

UK
(☎ 020-7734 9638) Heathcoat House, 20 Savile Row, London W1X 1AE

USA
(☎ 213-623-1952) 624 South Grand Ave, Suite 1611, Los Angeles, CA 90017;
(☎ 212-757-5640) 1 Rockefeller Plaza, Suite 1250, New York, NY 10020;
(☎ 415-989-7140) 360 Post St, Suite 601, San Francisco, CA 94108

Health

Looking after your health in Japan should pose few problems. Tap water is safe to drink everywhere, but avoid drinking from mountain streams. Raw freshwater fish and raw wild boar should also be avoided. Health care is excellent but be prepared to pay for it. Dental care also is widely available at steep prices.

Post & Communications

Japan's postal system is very efficient and similarly priced to western countries. Post restante services are not common, but major post offices will hold mail for 30 days before returning it to the sender. The telephone system is world-class, public phones abound (what's more, they almost all work) and international call rates are mostly affordable. Surprisingly, there are not many Internet cafes outside the large cities.

Money

Costs

However you look at it, Japan is a very expensive place to travel. A skeleton daily budget, assuming you stay at the cheapest places (US$22 in a hostel), eat modestly (US$15) and spend only US$15 on short-distance travel, works out at US$50. Add at least US$10 for snacks, drinks, admission fees and entertainment.

Food costs can be kept within reasonable limits by taking set meals for US$3.50 to US$7. Transport is a major expense, although there are ways to limit the damage. The JR Rail Pass is well worth the money if you intend to travel widely in a short space of time. Overnight buses are cheaper than the train, and enable you to save on accommodation. Most cities in Japan have fast, efficient public transport, so you should only need taxis as a last resort.

Changing Money

Cash still rules in Japan, although the use of credit cards is pretty widespread in major cities. The Japanese are used to a very low crime rate and often carry wads of cash for the almost sacred ritual of cash payment. Foreign travellers can safely copy the cash habit, but should still take the usual precautions. You can change cash or travellers cheques at an 'Authorised Foreign Exchange Bank' or at some of the large hotels and stores. US dollars are preferred; trying to exchange Taiwanese or Korean currency is a fruitless task.

Online Services

Lonely Planet's *Destination Japan* page can be found at www.lonelyplanet .com/dest/nea/jap.htm.

Gary's Japan Pages (www2.gol. com/users/garyvabe) shows 'Japan from the gutter up' with itsy-bitsy insights and good photos. Try to allay confusion with handy hints from *Navigating Life in Japan* (www.imasy .or.jp/~eri) and *Rob's Japan FAQ* (www.gol.com/jguide/ rob.html).

The *Japan National Tourist Organization* (www.jnto.go.jp) points to extensive regional information, 'special experiences worth having' and lots more – it's a good site.

Books

Alan Booth's *The Roads to Sata* traces a four month journey on foot from the northern tip of Hokkaido to Sata, the southern tip of Kyushu. *Japan: A Short Cultural History* by George B Sansom, though written some 40 years ago, is still among the best introductions to Japanese history. The best primer on the role of religion in Japanese society is *Japanese Religion: A Cultural Perspective* by Robert S Elwood & Richard Pilgrim. *Inside Japan* by Peter Tasker is an excellent wide-ranging introduction to contemporary Japanese culture, society and the economy. Alex Kerr's *Lost Japan* (Lonely Planet) draws on the author's experiences in Japan over 30 years. Karo Taro Greenfield's *Speedtribes – Children of the Japanese Bubble* is an entertaining foray into the drug-peddling, computer-hacking underworld of the disaffected Japanese youth. Subtle and resonant works by the popular novelist Banana Yoshimoto include *NP* and *Kitchen*.

Films

The 1950s is generally thought of as the golden age of Japanese cinema. Kurosawa Akira took the top prize at the Venice Film Festival in 1951 for *Rashomon*, emerging as Japan's most influential director. His *Shichinin-no-Samurai* (Seven Samurai) gained the ultimate accolade when it was shamelessly ripped off by the Hollywood blockbuster *The Magnificent Seven*. Other Kurosawa classics include *Ran*, an epic historical film.

More modern efforts include Itami Juzo's *Tampopo*, a wonderful comedy weaving vignettes on the themes of food and sex into a story about a Japanese noodle restaurant; and *Marusa-no-Onna* (A Taxing Woman) by the same director, an amusing insight into Japanese-style taxation. Running parallel to the traditional style of film is the animated *manga* style. Famously launched onto the international stage by Katsuhiro Otomo with his 1998 postapocalyptic epic *Akira*, more recent examples include *Bubblegum Crash*, *Nausicaä of the Valley of Wind*, *Ghost in the Shell* plus an American take on manga through Tony Randel's *Fist of the North Star*.

Entering & Leaving Japan

There are flights to Japan from all over the world, usually to Tokyo but also to a number of other airports. Consider arriving elsewhere than Tokyo's impersonal Narita airport – it can be an unpleasant and tedious introduction to Japan. There are a few sea transport options between Japan and South Korea. The cheapest is the Shimonoseki-Pusan ferry which runs nightly in both directions. Between Fukuoka and Pusan there's both an ultra-fast (three hours) hydrofoil and a ferry (15 hours). To China, there are ferries connecting Osaka, Kobe and Nagasaki to Shanghai; there's also a weekly ferry from Kobe to Tanggu (near Tianjin). To Keelung in Taiwan, a weekly ferry leaves from Okinawa. For travellers intending to take the Trans-Siberian Railway to Moscow, there are weekly ferry services between Yokohama and Niigata and the Russian port of Nakhodka near Vladivostok.

LAOS

Laos is the least developed and most enigmatic of the three former French Indochinese states. A ruinous sequence of colonial domination, internecine conflict and dogmatic socialism brought the country to its knees in the 1970s, and almost 10% of the population departed. Now, after 15 years of isolation, this landlocked, sparsely populated country is enjoying peace, stabilising its political and economic structures and admitting foreign visitors. The lack of foreign influence offers contemporary travellers an unparalleled glimpse of traditional South-East Asian life. From the fertile lowlands of the Mekong River valley to the rugged Annamite highlands, travellers who have made it to Laos tend to agree that this country is the highlight of South-East Asia.

When to Go

The best overall time for visiting most of Laos is November to February, when it rains least and is not too hot. If you plan on focusing on the mountainous northern provinces, the hot season (March to May) and early rainy season (June to July) are not bad either, as temperatures are moderate at these higher elevations. The peak months for tourist arrivals are December to February, and August, although the peak season is low-key compared to, say, Chiang Mai in Thailand.

Extensive road travel in remote areas such as Attapeu, Phongsali and Sainyabuli may be impossible during the main rainy season (July to October) when roads are often inundated or washed out for weeks at a time.

River travel makes a good alternative during these months. If you intend to travel extensively by river, November is the best month. Between January and June, boat services on some rivers may be irregular due to low water levels.

AT A GLANCE

Full Country Name: Lao People's Democratic Republic

Area: 236,000 sq km

Population: 4.75 million

Capital City: Vientiane (pop 300,000)

People: 50% Lao Loum, 30% Lao Theung, 10% Lao Sung and 10% tribal Thais

Languages: Lao (closely related to Thai), Lao dialects and French

Religion: 85% Theravada Buddhist, 14% animist, 1% Christian and Muslim

Government: Socialist republic

Currency: Lao Kip (kip); the Thai baht and US dollar are also widely accepted

Time Zone: Seven hours ahead of GMT/UTC

International Telephone Code: 856

Electricity: 220V AC; power outlets most commonly feature two-pronged round or flat sockets

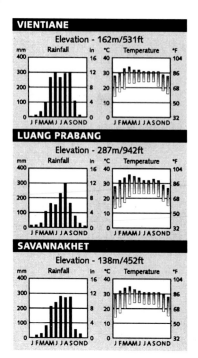

VIENTIANE
Elevation - 162m/531ft

LUANG PRABANG
Elevation - 287m/942ft

SAVANNAKHET
Elevation - 138m/452ft

Highlights

Although Laos is a relatively small country, the lack of travel infrastructure means it pays to be under-ambitious with your plans – transport is prone to long delays. Most visitors begin their journey in Vientiane. If you're short on time, you might want to skip Vientiane until you've seen more interesting parts of the country.

Architecture

The former royal kingdoms of Luang Prabang, Vientiane and Champasak offer the most in terms of classic architecture, from 600-year-old Buddhist temples to French colonial structures. Mysterious Wat Phu dates to the Chenla Kingdom (6th to 8th centuries) and Angkor period (9th to 13th centuries). The enigmatic Plain of Jars near Phonsavan also offers scope for speculation. Colonial architecture is most intact in Luang Prabang, Vientiane, Tha Khaek and Savannakhet.

Handcrafts

Laos' ethnic diversity means a wide range of handcrafts is available for study or purchase throughout the country. Specialities include silverwork, woodcarving, tribal crafts, ceramics, rattan furniture and textiles. North-eastern Laos is famous for Sam Neua-style textiles, which feature rich brocade and dazzling colours. Simple Lao-style cotton fabrics are abundant in the south near Pakse and Don Khong, while Sekong and Attapeu feature their own styles of weaving.

Culture

For mainstream Lao culture your best venues are the towns and villages on or near the Mekong River, which are traditional centres for the lowland Lao. Those interested in Hmong-Mien and Thai tribal cultures should travel to the northern provinces of Luang Nam Tha, Bokeo, Udomxai, Phongsali and Hua Phan. The interior of the south – Salavan, Sekong and Attapeu provinces – is home to Mon-Khmer peoples.

Natural Environment

Laos boasts one of the least disturbed ecosystems in Asia due to its overall lack of development and low population density; but, for much the same reason, access to creatures in the wild is limited. New conservation areas have potential, but visitor facilities are limited. Bring your own camping gear, as it's virtually unavailable in Laos.

Itineraries

ONE WEEK

In one week you can easily take in all the major sights in Vientiane and Luang Prabang, provided you fly between these cities. A popular alternative is to enter the country at Huay Xai in Bokeo Province, opposite Chiang Khong, Thailand, and then to make the river-run to Luang Prabang, continuing south to Vientiane by plane or road. This saves having to backtrack from Luang Prabang to Vientiane.

TWO WEEKS

With two weeks you can add some side trips north of Vientiane to Vang Vieng and north-east to Xieng Khuang Province. If you want to see a bit of the south, substitute an excursion to the area between Pakse and the Cambodian border, taking in Champasak, Wat Phu and the Si Phan Don area. If Vietnam is next on your schedule, consider entering by land via Savannakhet and Lao Bao.

ONE MONTH

A month's sojourn in Laos – which will require a visa extension (see Visa Requirements later) – could begin in the north at Huay Xai and trace a loop through Luang Nam Tha around to Luang Prabang and Xieng Khuang, then on to Vientiane. From there, you can move step by step down the Mekong River valley through the former colonial province capitals of Tha Khaek, Savannakhet and Salavan before heading south-east to remote Sekong and Attapeu provinces. From the latter you could jog back to the Mekong for a laid-back final few days in Si Phan Don before exiting the country at Chong Mek, Thailand, near Pakse.

Visa Requirements

You can get a 15 day visa (US$50 cash) on arrival at Wattay international airport in Vientiane and at the Friendship Bridge border point near Nong Khai in Thailand. A 30 day visa (US$35 to US$50) can be arranged in your home country or most other countries in the region. Vientiane's immigration office is the only place where you can extend your visa (currently US$3 per day).

Lao PDR Embassies

AUSTRALIA
(☎ 02-6286 4595) 1 Dalman Crescent, O'Malley, ACT 2606
USA
(☎ 202-332-6416) 2222 South St NW, Washington, DC 20006

Tourist Offices Overseas

Laos has no overseas tourist offices, but travel agents will be able to supply you with most information. Also check out the web sites listed under Online Services.

Health

Malaria exists year-round in Laos, excluding Vientiane, and there have been recent large outbreaks of dengue fever, so take appropriate precautions against mosquito bites. Food and water-borne diseases, including dysentery, hepatitis and liver flukes occur, so pay attention to basic food and water hygiene. The main risk of liver flukes is from raw or undercooked fish – in particular, avoid eating *päa däek* (fermented fish accompanying rice). Liver flukes can also be acquired by swimming in the Mekong Delta. Rabies is prevalent in Laos (see the Health chapter for more information).

Laos has no facilities for major medical emergencies, and hygiene standards in hospitals are among the poorest in the region. If you are seriously ill, go to Thailand, Malaysia or Singapore.

LAOS HIGHLIGHTS & ITINERARIES

LUANG NAM THA
Rugged hill region with former royal capital and largest variety of tribes

LUANG PRABANG
World Heritage-listed former royal capital with 32 temples

PHONSAVAN
Mysterious Plain of Jars and Indochinese War relics

VIENTIANE
Peaceful riverside capital, with the sacred Pha That Luang, museums and cafes

BOLAVEN PLATEAU
Fertile coffee-growing uplands with tribal villages and waterfalls

WAT PHU CHAMPASAK
Magnificent temple from the Angkor era in mountain setting

ATTAPEU
Wild backwoods province with unusual fauna and Mon-Khmer tribes

KHAMMUA
Scenic rivers dramatic limest country and wate

DON KHONG
Sleepy river archipelago with rare dolphins and mighty Mekong rapids

SUGGESTED ITINERARIES

One Week
① Vientiane • Luang Prabang (air only)
② Huay Xai • Luang Prabang • Vientiane (road)

Two Weeks
① Vientiane • Vang Vieng • Xieng Khuang Province
② Pakse • Champasak • Wat Phu • Si Phan Don • Lao Bao

One Month
Huay Xai • Luang Nam Tha • Luang Prabang • Xieng Khuang • Vientiane • Mekong River Valley • Tha Khaek • Savannakhet • Salavan • Sekong • Attapeu • Si Phan Don • Chong Mek

Post & Communications

Postal rates are much the same as in neighbouring countries, but services are not completely reliable; many travellers wait until they reach Thailand to send their letters and parcels. The service for mail leaving the country is more reliable. There is a post restante service in Vientiane, but ensure the full country name (Lao People's Democratic Republic or Lao PDR) is on the address. The telephone system is improving, but is still poor. Post offices are the first place to go to make international calls, and telephone centres are being built in some towns.

Money

Costs

Staying in Vientiane will cost more than accommodation elsewhere – expect to pay from US$5 in the capital and about US$1.75 in the countryside for a basic room. In a better class tourist hotel you'll pay from about US$25 to US$60 a night. An average meal will set you back less than US$2. All up, you could get by on US$10 a day in the big cities, US$6 a day in the countryside, but that's for the rockiest of rock-bottom budgets. If you want air-con, hot water and foreign food, you'll be paying between US$25 and US$60 a day.

Changing Money

Several local and foreign banks operate in Laos, although outside Vientiane banks are all government-run. Most offer cash advances and withdrawals on credit cards and debit cards (for a fee), but only in kip. Outside Vientiane, credit cards are virtually useless. With some exceptions the best exchange rates are available at banks rather than moneychangers. Apart from Vientiane, Luang Prabang, Savannakhet and Pakse, it can be difficult to change travellers cheques, so carry plenty of cash, preferably in baht and US dollars for large purchases.

Online Services

Lonely Planet's *Destination Laos* page can be found at www.lonelyplanet.com/dest/sea/laos.htm.

Diethelm Travel's Database (www.asiatour.com/laos/content1.htm) is one of the few web sites with information on Laos. Akihito Koriyama's *My Travel in Laos* (www2.gol.com/users/akihito/html/laos.html) is a great big pile of pics accompanied by Akihito's observations of this country. The *Internet Travel Guide to Laos* (www.datacomm.ch/pmgeiser/laos) does a reliable job with travel information.

The Lao Human Rights Council is struggling to have the genocide of Lao people recognised. Read what it's up to at *Genocide in Cambodia and Laos* (home.earthlink.net/~laohumrights/laohdl21.html).

The Hmong Homepage (www.stolaf.edu/people/cdr/hmong) has some excellent information on Hmong culture.

Books

Books on Laos can be difficult to find, but government bookshops in Vientiane are a good place to look once you're there. Overseas, the libraries of universities with Asian studies departments often carry some of the following English-language books. If you can read French, you'll find others as well.

For politics and history try *Contemporary Laos: Studies in the Politics & Society of the Lao People's*

Democratic Republic edited by Martin Stuart-Fox; *Laos: Beyond the Revolution* edited by Joseph Zasloff & Leonard Unger; and *History of Laos* by Maha Sila Viravong.

The Ravens: Pilots of the Secret War of Laos by Christopher Robbins details US involvement in Laos during the Vietnam War. *Air America: The Story of the CIA's Secret Airlines*, also by Robbins, focuses on the infamous gun and drug-running activities of the CIA in Laos. *The Politics of Heroin in South-east Asia* by Alfred W McCoy covers the history, politics and economics of opium in Laos.

Tragic Mountains: The Hmong, the Americans and the Secret Wars for Laos, 1942-1992 by Jane Hamilton-Merritt follows the struggles of the Hmong against the Japanese, the Viet Minh, the Pathet Lao and North Vietnamese.

Entering & Leaving Laos

There are flights from Vientiane's Wattay airport to Bangkok, Hanoi, Ho Chi Minh City (Saigon), Phnom Penh, Singapore, Yangon (Rangoon), and Guangzhou and Kunming in China. There's also a service from Luang Prabang to Chang Mai in Thailand. The departure tax is US$5.

It is now permissable for non-Thai foreigners to cross the Mekong from Thailand into Laos at the following points: Nong Khai (near Vientiane), Nakhon Phanom (opposite Tha Khaek), Chiang Khong (opposite Huay Xai) and Mukdahan (opposite Savannakhet). Use of the bridge spanning the Mekong at Nong Khai is hampered by controls on foreign-registered vehicles, but individual travellers should experience only slight delays.

There is a land border crossing to Thailand at Chong Mek-Ubon Ratchathani, but you must have a visa valid for entry via Chong Mek and Pakse arranged in advance. It's possible to cross to or from Vietnam via Lao Bao if you have a valid Vietnamese visa. Entry to Laos is also possible from China's Yunnan Province at Boten.

MALAYSIA

Malaysia is one of the most pleasant, hassle-free countries to visit in South-East Asia. Several decades of sustained economic growth and political stability have made it one of the most buoyant and wealthy countries in the region. Although political power (Malay) and economic clout (Chinese) are still traditionally divided along racial lines, Malaysia has moved towards a pluralist culture based on a vibrant and interesting fusion of Malay, Chinese, Indian and indigenous cultures and customs. Malaysia has been affected by the Asian economic downturn, but generally it's business as usual.

Most visitors stick to Peninsular Malaysia, where the insane headlong rush of Kuala Lumpur is offset by the soothing Cameron Highlands colonial-era hill station and the hedonistic torpor of Langkawi. Far fewer make it to the Borneo states of Sarawak or Sabah, in East Malaysia, with their spectacular wildlife, longhouses and the awe-inspiring Gunung Kinabalu (4101m).

When to Go
Malaysia is hot and humid year-round so you'll have sunshine and sweat almost any time you visit. It is best to avoid the November to January rainy season on Peninsular Malaysia's east coast if you want to enjoy the beaches. You can see turtles on the east coast between May and September. Malaysia has many colourful festivals, like Thaipusam around January or February, and celebrations are held throughout the year. During public holidays transport is crowded and hotel prices rise in the resorts. The peak holiday times are Chinese New Year (usually February), Hari Raya Puasa (the end of Ramadan, usually January/February) and Christmas. The main beach and hill resorts are also crowded on weekends, but are often deserted during the week. The Muslim month of Ramadan is generally not a problem for travel.

AT A GLANCE

Full Country Name: Federation of Malaysia

Area: 329,750 sq km

Population: 19.7 million

Capital City: Kuala Lumpur (pop 1.2 million)

People: 50% Malay, 33% Chinese, 9% Indian and 8% indigenous groups including the Orang Asli and Iban

Languages: Bahasa Malaysia, English, Chinese dialects, Tamil and indigenous dialects

Religion: 52% Muslim, 17% Buddhist, 12% Taoist, 8% Christian, 8% Hindu and 3% indigenous religions

Government: Constitutional monarchy

Currency: Malaysian ringgit (RM)

Time Zone: Eight hours ahead of GMT/UTC

International Telephone Code: 60

Electricity: 220V to 240V, 50 AC; sockets are almost always the three-pin, square type found in the UK

271

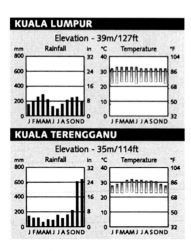

KUALA LUMPUR

Elevation - 39m/127ft

KUALA TERENGGANU

Elevation - 35m/114ft

Highlights

Malaysia has loads to offer the traveller – so much, in fact, that you'll need to have a pretty good idea of what you want to see in order to make the best use of your time.

National Parks

Among the many excellent national parks are Taman Negara (Peninsular Malaysia) with its ancient rainforest; Gunung Mulu (Sarawak), which features pristine rainforest with limestone pinnacles and massive caves; Kinabalu (Sabah) for a trek up the improbably high granite peak of Gunung Kinabalu; and Turtle Islands (Sabah) with the chance to see sea turtles lumbering ashore to lay their eggs.

Wildlife

Sepilok Orang-utan Rehabilitation Centre (Sabah) is one of only four such refuges in the world, while the Sungai Kinabatangan region in Sabah offers arguably the best wildlife spotting in South-East Asia; the animals include proboscis monkeys, macaques,

orang-utans, marbled and flat-headed cats, elephants and giant squirrels, while birdwatchers can expect to see eight species of hornbill and two of pittas, as well as the rarer Oriental darter and Storm's stork, all within a thriving jungle environment.

Islands & Beaches

Of the country's innumerable beaches and islands, perhaps the most beautiful is Pulau Perhentian (Terengganu), with white sand and crystal-clear aquamarine water. Pulau Sipadan (Sabah), Pulau Redang (Terengganu), Pulau Tioman (Pahang) and the islands of the Seribuat Archipelago (Johor) are great for snorkelling and diving, while small Pulau Pangkor (Perak) has some of the best beaches on the west coast. Pulau Langkawi (Kedah) is a lively tourist island with decent beaches and lots of nightlife.

Architecture

The longhouses of East Malaysia display a traditional way of life that has changed little despite the advent of TV and cellular phones. In total contrast, Kuala Lumpur is a bustling, cosmopolitan city with the best food in the country and such modern wonders as the Petronus Towers, the tallest building in the world. Penang is an historic British settlement with strong Chinese influences and colourful temples.

Journeys

Train and river journeys include the 'Jungle Railway' from Tumpat to Gemas (a great way to see the peninsula's mountainous interior without breaking a sweat), while Batang Rejang is Sarawak's longest river and still the main thoroughfare for commerce between the hinterland and the coast, providing the opportunity for riverboat trips.

Itineraries

Travel in Malaysia is easily divided between Peninsular Malaysia, and Sabah and Sarawak across the water. A good look at both halves will take at least a couple of months, but most visitors go only to the peninsula, where travel is easy and you can see a lot in a relatively short time. Travelling in Sarawak and Sabah is more time-consuming, but more rewarding in terms of exotic vistas and destinations that are off the beaten track.

WEST COAST

ONE WEEK

Start at historic Melaka and travel north to Kuala Lumpur, the hill station and tea plantations of the Cameron Highlands, and then to Penang with its vibrant Chinese, Malay and Indian mix. This will give you a good overview, although it might be a bit rushed. If you have to drop one destination, transit through Kuala Lumpur.

TWO WEEKS

The one week itinerary can be done more comfortably in two weeks, with the addition of the island beaches of Pulau Pangkor and Pulau Langkawi, a visit to historic colonial-era Taiping, Kuala Kangsar, or the hill stations of Fraser's Hill or Maxwell Hill.

EAST COAST

ONE WEEK

The main attractions of this Malay-dominated area are the beach resorts strung along the coast and the offshore islands, plus the wonders of Taman Negara National Park. If you are coming from Singapore, start with a visit to Pulau Tioman before heading up the coast via the travellers hang-out of Cherating to Taman Negara. If you're coming from Thailand, spend a couple of days in Kota Bharu for traditional Malay culture and then go to Pulau Perhentian Besar for diving and jungle trekking, before a visit to Taman Negara. Note that it takes the best part of a day each way to get to and from the national park.

TWO WEEKS

Two weeks will allow you to linger at some of the beaches and still leave room for a solid four or five days at Taman Negara. There are good two and three-day walks, but you can trek for up to two weeks if the fancy takes you. If you're coming from Singapore between June and September, stop off at Rantau Abang for the chance to see leatherback turtles laying their eggs. Rather than turning inland at Kuantan, you could continue up the coast, stopping at the sleepy fishing village of Merang, and more developed Marang, before heading inland at Kuala Besat for the journey to Taman Negara.

SARAWAK

ONE WEEK

The longhouse experience is out of reach to all but the most determined (or affluent) travellers nowadays, but Kuching is a real treat. Sarawak also has some of the best national parks in Malaysia. In a week you could fly into Kuching, one of the most pleasant cities in Malaysia; make a day trip to Gunung Gading National Park to see the world's largest flower, the rafflesia; spend a couple of days on the jungle trails of Bako National Park; or take a longhouse tour out of Kuching for two or three days.

TWO WEEKS TO A MONTH

As well as the previous itinerary, you could add a trip to Niah Caves National Park from Kuching (a minimum three day excursion) on the way through to Sabah. You can save some time by flying directly to neighbouring Gunung Mulu National Park, but this will still take a few days. If you have more time, don't miss the week-long riverboat trip up the Batang Rejang to visit longhouses.

SABAH

ONE WEEK

The chief attractions of Sabah are Gunung Kinabalu and Turtle Islands National Park. In a week, undoubtedly the place to go is Gunung Kinabalu, the highest mountain between the Himalaya and the peaks of New

RARIES

PULAU LANGKAWI
Resort island with good restaurants and nightlife; quieter islands a short trip away

PENANG
A colourful mix of colonial and Chinese influences with great food and nightlife

KOTA BHARU
A bastion of Malay culture with the country's best night market

PULAU PERHENTIAN
Two tranquil islands surrounded by crystal-clear waters and white-sand beaches

TAMAN NEGARA NATIONAL PARK
A huge park containing some of the oldest rainforest in the world; great jungle trekking

CAMERON HIGHLANDS
Hill station with jungle walks, tea plantations and gardens

CHERATING
Mellow travellers pitstop with plenty of cheap chalets and a pleasant beach

PULAU PANGKOR
Small island with some of the west coast's best beaches

KUALA LUMPUR
A thriving, multi-ethnic city with something for everyone, including a great Chinatown and night market

MELAKA
Dutch and Portuguese colonial influences linger on in this interesting port town

SUGGESTED ITINERARIES

One Week ❶ Melaka • Kuala Lumpur • Cameron Highlands • Penang
❷ Singapore • Pulau Tioman • Cherating • Taman Negara • Kota Bharu • Pulau Perhentian Besar

Two Weeks ❶ Melaka • Kuala Lumpur • Fraser's Hill • Pulau Pangkor • Cameron Highlands • Taiping • Maxwell Hill • Penang • Pulau Langkawi
❷ Pulau Tioman • Cherating • Taman Negara • Rantau Abang • Merang • Marang • Kuala Besat

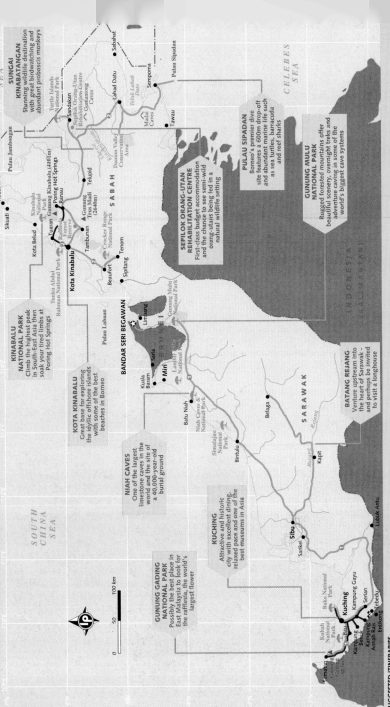

SOUTH CHINA SEA

SEA

CELEBES SEA

INDONESIA (KALIMANTAN)

SABAH

SARAWAK

BRUNEI

GUNUNG GADING NATIONAL PARK
Possibly the best place in East Malaysia to look for the rafflesia, the world's largest flower

KUCHING
Attractive and historic city with excellent dining, relaxed pace and one of the best museums in Asia

NIAH CAVES
One of the largest limestone caves in the world and the site of a 40,000-year-old burial ground

KOTA KINABALU
Great base for exploring the idyllic offshore islands with some of the best beaches in Borneo

KINABALU NATIONAL PARK
Climb the highest peak in South-East Asia then soak your tired limbs at Poring Hot Springs

SUNGAI KINABATANGAN
Stunning wildlife destination with great birdwatching and abundant proboscis monkeys

SEPILOK ORANG-UTAN REHABILITATION CENTRE
First-class budget accommodation and the chance to see semi-wild orang-utans being fed in a natural wildlife setting

PULAU SIPADAN
Borneo's premier dive site features a 600m drop-off and abundant marine life such as sea turtles, barracuda and reef sharks

GUNUNG MULU NATIONAL PARK
Rugged forested mountains offer beautiful scenery, overnight treks and adventure caving in some of the world's biggest cave systems

BATANG REJANG
Venture upstream into the heart of Sarawak - and perhaps be invited to visit a longhouse

BANDAR SERI BEGAWAN

0   50   100 km

SUGGESTED ITINERARIES

One Week ① Kuching • Gunung Gading • Bako National Park
② Kota Kinabalu • Gunung Kinabalu • Turtle Islands National Park • Poring Hot Springs • Tunku Abdul Rahman National Park

Two Weeks to One Month ① Kuching • Gunung Gading • Bako National Park • Batang Rejang • Niah Caves National Park • Mulu National Park
② Kota Kinabalu • Tenom • Gunung Kinabalu • Turtle Islands National Park • Poring Hot Springs • Tunku Abdul Rahman National Park • Rafflesia Forest Reserve • Sepilok Orang-utan Rehabilitation Centre • Danum Valley • Pulau Sipadan

Guinea. Although the climb is only an overnight effort, it is easy to spend a few more days at the park itself and visit the nearby Poring Hot Springs. Access is via Kota Kinabalu, from where the islands and beaches of nearby Tunku Abdul Rahman National Park can be visited as a day trip (or longer if your budget allows).

TWO WEEKS TO A MONTH

In two weeks, you can cover all of western Sabah, also taking in the Rafflesia Forest Reserve, and perhaps the Tenom-Beaufort jungle train, which winds up a scenic mountain range. Eastern Sabah has the Sepilok Orang-utan Rehabilitation Centre, which is a day trip from Sandakan, and Turtle Islands National Park (a three day trip). If you have another week or so, check out the magnificent forest reserve at Danum Valley and the superb marine life of Pulau Sipadan, although these are both expensive destinations.

Visa Requirements

Most Commonwealth citizens do not need a visa to visit Malaysia for up to 60 days. Most other nationalities do not need a visa for a one month visit. Citizens of Israel cannot enter Malaysia. To the east, Sabah and Sarawak are treated in some ways like separate countries. Your passport will be checked on arrival in each state and a new stay permit (usually 30 days) issued. However, if you travel directly from Sabah or Sarawak back to Peninsular Malaysia there are no formalities and you do not start a new entry period, so your 30 day permit from Sabah or Sarawak remains valid (and can be extended).

Malaysian Embassies & High Commissions

AUSTRALIA
(☎ 02-6273 1543) 7 Perth Ave, Yarralumla, ACT 2600

CANADA
(☎ 613-241-5182; fax 241-5214) 360 Boteler St, Ottawa, Ontario K1N 8Y7

NEW ZEALAND
(☎ 04-385 2439) 10 Washington Ave, Brooklyn, Wellington

UK
(☎ 020-7235 8033) 45 Belgrave Square, London SW1X 8QT

USA
(☎ 202-328-2700; fax 483-7661) 2401 Massachusetts Ave NW, Washington, DC 20008

Tourist Offices Overseas

AUSTRALIA
(☎ 02-9299 4441) Ground floor, 65 York St, Sydney, NSW 2000;
(☎ 08-9481 0400) 56 William St, Perth, WA 6000

CANADA
(☎ 604-689-8899) 830 Burrard St, Vancouver, BC V6Z 2K4

UK
(☎ 020-7930 7932) 57 Trafalgar Square, London WC2N 5DU

USA
(☎ 213-689-9702) 818 West 7th St, Los Angeles, CA 90017;
(☎ 212-754-1113) 595 Madison Ave, Suite 1800, New York, NY 10022

Health

Malaysia enjoys good standards of health and cleanliness. You may be required to show proof of cholera vaccination if you are arriving from an infected area, although this is contrary to internationally agreed requirements. The main risk is malaria in the rural hinterlands of Peninsular Malaysia and Sarawak, and throughout Sabah, so take appropriate precautions. Dengue fever also occurs, so it's important to avoid mosquito bites during the day. Tap water is safe to drink in many cities, and bottled water and soft drinks are widely available

Malaysia's hospitals are of a high standard and English is often spoken.

Post & Communications

Peninsular Malaysia's postal and tele-communications infrastructure is among the best in the region. Postal services are efficient and quite cheap for letters and postcards, although parcel services are a bit pricey. There are post restante services in all the major cities. Services are slower and more expensive in Sarawak and Sabah, but still fairly reliable. Telephone services are of a good standard, and charges for local, long-distance and international calls are reasonable. Phonecards can be bought in several denominations for use in public phones. Malaysia continues to move online and there are Internet cafes in some of the large cities, charging from RM7.50 to RM15 per hour.

Money

Costs

Though one of the more expensive countries in South-East Asia, Malaysia is still cheap by world standards and caters well to all budgets. You can get by in Peninsular Malaysia on about US$20 to US$25 a day if you stay in cheaper Chinese hotels, eat in local restaurants or at street stalls and travel mainly by bus. For some luxury, allow around US$65 a day. Note that East Malaysia is more expensive than Peninsular Malaysia, so add about 30% to your budget there.

Changing Money

Malaysian banks are efficient and typically charge around US$2 or US$3 for foreign exchange transactions. Money-changers do not charge a commission but their rates vary, so make sure you know the current rate. All major brands of travellers cheques are acceptable in Malaysia. Cash in major currencies is also readily exchanged, although the US dollar has a slight edge. If you have a credit card with a PIN attached, you can obtain cash advances from ATMs.

Online Services

Lonely Planet's *Destination Malaysia* page is at www.lonelyplanet.com/dest/sea/malay.htm.

Malaysian Information Sources (st-www.cs.uiuc.edu/users/chai/malaysia .html) is as good as its word, providing a good launching pad for numerous sites on Malaysia.

You can get your daily Malaysian news fix from *the Star Online* (thestar .com.my).

For planning a trip, the straightforward travel information at *the Malaysia page* (www.sino.net/asean/malaysia.html) is useful reading. The *Malaysian Tourism Promotion Board* (www.interknowledge.com/malaysia) puts its own spin on this state-by-state Malaysia guide, or check out the *Sarawak Tourism Board* (www.sarawak.gov.my/stb).

The *Sabah, Malaysian Borneo Page* (www.jaring.my/sabah) has good information on off-the-beaten-track locations, wildlife, adventure travel and diving.

Books

Culture Shock: Malaysia by JoAnn Craig explains the customs, cultures and lifestyles of Malaysia's polyglot population. *A Short History of Malaysia, Singapore & Brunei* by CM Turnbull is a straightforward introduction, while *A Stroll Through Borneo* by James Barclay is a delightful tale of a long walking and river trip through Sarawak, Sabah and Kalimantan.

Malaysian-based western fiction includes W Somerset Maugham's *Borneo Stories*, Anthony Burgess' *The Malayan Trilogy*, Paul Theroux's *The Consul's File* and Blanche d'Alpuget's *Turtle Beach*.

Films

The jungles of Sabah and Sarawak have been used by Hollywood and Hong Kong directors as settings for locations as disparate as Vietnam *(Bat 21, Indochine)*, South America *(Fifty/Fifty)*, Sumatra *(Paradise Road)* and South Africa *(Who Am I?)*, as well as for films meant to be set in Malaysia *(Farewell to the King, A Town Like Alice)*. Malaysia does have its own film industry. If you speak some Malay, check out *Bukit Kepong, Kaki Bakar, Litar Kasih* or *Lurah Dendam*.

Entering & Leaving Malaysia

Malaysia's international airport is at Sepang, 50km south of Kuala Lumpur. Most tourists either fly into Sepang or arrive overland from Thailand or Singapore. Penang also accepts international flights, and Kuching in Sarawak and Tawau in Sabah have flights to and from Kalimantan. There is a departure tax of RM40 on international flights, but if you buy your ticket in Malaysia the tax will be included in the ticket price.

There are five border crossings between Thailand and Malaysia – two on the west coast (Sadao-Changlun and Padang Besar), one in the centre (Betong-Keroh) and two on the east coast (Ban Taba-Tumpat and Sungai Kolok). There is also a west coast rail link (crossing at Padang Besar). To get to/from Singapore, you can cross the Causeway at Johor Bahru, catch a ferry or take the train. As well, a daily high-speed catamaran links Singapore with Malaysia's Pulau Tioman. There are three ferry services between Malaysia and Indonesia (Penang-Medan, Melaka-Dumai and, from East Malaysia, Tawau-Tarakan). There's also a difficult road link between Sarawak and Kalimantan at Tebedu-Entikong. The main overland route into Brunei is from Miri in Sarawak to Bandar Seri Begawan. For the Philippines, catch the twice-weekly ferry from Sandakan (Sabah) to Zamboanga (Mindanao).

MONGOLIA

The name 'Mongolia' has always stirred up visions of the untamed and exotic – the warlord Genghis Khan, camels wandering in the Gobi Desert and wild horses galloping across the steppes. Even today, Mongolia seems like the end of the earth – outside Ulaan Baatar you begin to wonder if you've stepped into another century, rather than another country. Mongolia remains one of the last great adventure destinations in Asia. Its survival as an independent nation is little short of miraculous. For the first time in centuries the Mongolians, once rulers of the vast Eurasian steppe, are not colonial subjects of the Russian or Chinese empires. Only a century ago, so few ethinc Mongolians were left that it seemed their ancient, nomadic civilisation might disappear altogether. Today, the country has a constitution, multiparty elections and a ruling democratic coalition.

Travel in Mongolia can be hard, but if you're ready for a tough, invigorating journey, grab your warmest winter coat, steady your stomach and steel your nerves. It's worth the wander into nomad's land.

When to Go
The travel season is typically from May to early October, though Ulaan Baatar can be visited any time of year if you can tolerate the bitter cold. Early July is the best weather for the northern part of the country and is also the time to celebrate the Naadam Festival. Be aware, though, that this is also when Ulaan Baatar's inadequate accommo-dation and creaky transport is stretched to breaking point. September and June are both pleasant times to visit, and attract fewer visitors. The best time to visit the Gobi Desert and not get roasted is September and October. Between mid-October and mid-May sudden snowstorms and extreme cold can ground flights and block roads, causing the transport system to stall.

AT A GLANCE

Full Country Name: Mongolian People's Republic

Area: 1,566,000 sq km

Population: 2.5 million

Capital City: Ulaan Baatar (pop 550,000)

People: 88% Khalkh Mongols, 4% Kazaks, 2% Chinese, 2% Russians, and over a dozen other ethnic groups

Languages: Mongolian, Turkic, Russian and Chinese

Religion: 95% Tibetan Buddhist, 3% Muslim and 2% shamanist

Government: Parliamentary democracy

Currency: Mongolian tögrög (T or MNT)

Time Zone: Eight hours ahead of GMT/UTC (seven hours in the western provinces)

International Telephone Code: 976

Electricity: 220V, 50 AC; power surges and blackouts are common; sockets take European-style two-pin, round plugs

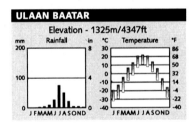

ULAAN BAATAR
Elevation - 1325m/4347ft

Organised Tours

Most travellers visit Mongolia on an organised tour, and this trend is likely to continue as long as visas for independent travellers remain difficult to obtain and to extend. In addition, the roads in the countryside are little more than jeep trails; public transport in the countryside is unreliable, infrequent and uncomfortable; and accommodation can be difficult to find. Tours organised by most travel agencies will take you around Ulaan Baatar and to one or all of the major tourist attractions – the south Gobi, Kharkhorin and Erdene Zuu Khiid (monastery), Khövsgöl Nuur (lake) and Terelj. They will probably include a stay in a *ger* (tent) camp, horse riding and a visit to a nomadic family. If you're short on time or patience, you will still end up seeing a lot more of the country in more comfort and with less hassle than as an independent traveller. But on a tour you will be sheltered in many respects from the 'true' Mongolia and have few opportunities to meet Mongolian people.

Highlights

Mountains & Lakes

Mongolia offers spectacular opportunities for mountain climbing. In the western provinces, there are over 100 glaciers, and 30 to 40 permanently snowcapped mountains. You must have the necessary experience, be fully equipped and hire local guides. The best time to climb is from early July until late August. For camping and general hiking around the mountains, head out to Sutai Uul, Tsast Uul, Mönkh Khairkhan Uul, Tsambagarav Uul, Türgen Uul and, closer to Ulaan Baatar, Bogdkhan Uul and Tsetseegun Uul. For outstanding natural beauty, you would be hard-pressed to find anywhere lovelier than Khövsgöl Nuur.

National Parks

Of the many national parks, the better and more accessible ones are the Uvs Lake Strictly Protected Area which covers the lake and nearby area, the Khan Khentii Strictly Protected Area and, near Ulaan Baatar, the Bogdkhan Mountain Strictly Protected Area and Gorkhi-Terelj National Park. The vast Gobi Desert dominates southern Mongolia and includes five national parks, of which the most accessible is Gurvansaikhan.

Landscapes

The Kharkhiraa Valley and Dadal, with its pine forests and streams, the Orkhon waterfall, and the lakes, sand dunes and animals at Dariganga are all spectacular, and a far cry from the popular and barren Gobi Desert. Other highlights are the sand dunes at Mongol Els and Khongoryn Els, the springs at Khujirt and Shargaljuut, plus the beautiful scenery near Ulaan Baatar at Gachuurt, Terelj and the Bogdkhan Mountain Strictly Protected Area.

Monasteries

The communists did not leave much. Erdene Zuu Khiid is just superb, and Amarbayasgalant Khiid is architecturally

MONGOLIA HIGHLIGHTS & ITINERARIES

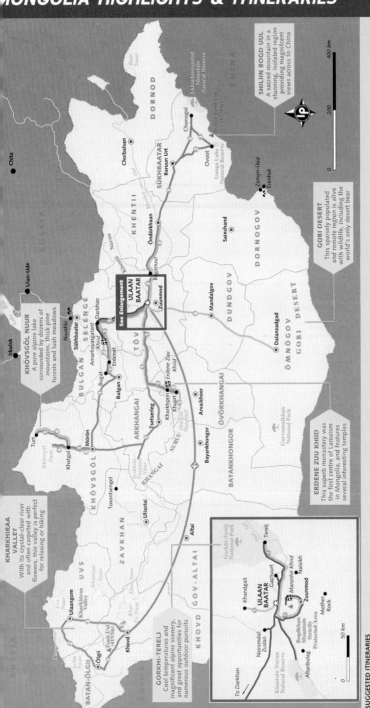

KHARKHIRAA VALLEY
With its crystal-clear river and often carpeted with flowers, this valley is perfect for relaxing or hiking

KHÖVSGÖL NUUR
A pure alpine lake surrounded by dozens of mountains, thick pine forests and lush meadows

GORKHI-TERELJ
Cool temperatures and magnificent alpine scenery, and great opportunities for numerous outdoor pursuits

ERDENE ZUU KHID
This superb monastery was the first centre of Lamaism in Mongolia, and features several interesting temples

SHILIIN BOGD UUL
A sacred mountain in a stunning, isolated region providing magnificent views across to China

GOBI DESERT
This sparsely populated and remote region is alive with wildlife, including the world's only desert bear

SUGGESTED ITINERARIES

Around Ulaan Baatar
Ulaan Baatar • Gachuurt • Terelj • Nairamdal Zuslan • Khustain Nuruu Natural Protected Area • Bogdkhan Mountain Strictly Protected Area • Darkhan • Amarbayasgalant Khiid

Hitching & Public Transport
① Ulaan Baatar • Kharkhorin (Erdene Zuu) • Khujirt
② Ulaan Baatar • Darkhan • Erdenet
③ Ulaan Baatar • Baganuur • Öndörkhaan
④ Ulaan Baatar • Mandalgov • Dalanzadgad

Jeep
① Ulaan Baatar • Amarbayasgalant Khiid • Erdenet • Khövsgöl Nuur • Terkhiin Tsagaan Nuur • Tsetserleg • Kharkhorin • Khujirt • Ulaan Baatar
② Ulaan Baatar • Khovd • Ölgii • Tsast Uul • Ölgii • Achit Nuur • Üüreg Nuur • Ulaangom • Uvs Nuur • Kharkhiraa Valley • Khar Us Nuur
③ Ulaan Baatar • Öndörkhaan • Baruun Urt • Shiliin Bogd Uul • Ganga Lake Natural Reserve

Mountain Bike
① Ulaan Baatar • Terelj • Khandgait • Manzshir Khiid
② Darkhan • Amarbayasgalant Khiid • Erdenet • Bugat
③ Kharkhorin • Khujirt • Orkhon Waterfall
④ Mörön • Khatgal • Turt • Khövsgöl Nuur

special, but remote. Nearer to Ulaan Baatar, Manzshir Khiid is in a delightful location. In Ulaan Baatar, the Winter Palace of Bogd Khaan and the Monastery-Museum of Choijin Lama have great exhibits, but Gandantegchinlen Khiid is the best in the capital.

Ger Camps

If you want a taste of 'traditional' accommodation, the most accessible ger camps are at Terelj; the most useful are in the remote south Gobi, near Dalanzadgad; the most luxurious and expensive (but worth a splurge) is at Bogdkhan Mountain Strictly Protected Area; and the prettiest are at Terelj, the Chandmam camp near Kharkhorin, and at Manzshir Khiid.

Itineraries

ONE WEEK —
AROUND ULAAN BAATAR

If you have limited time, you can base yourself in Ulaan Baatar and take overnight or day trips by jeep or public transport to places such as Gachuurt, Khustain Nuruu Natural Reserve, Nairamdal Zuslan International Children's Centre, Terelj, Manzshir Khiid, the Bogdkhan Mountain Strictly Protected Area, Darkhan and Amarbayasgalant Khiid. Allow one week to see these sights by public transport or three to four days by private jeep.

ONE TO TWO WEEKS — JEEP

If you have a private jeep, and a good driver (driving a jeep yourself around the countryside is not a good idea because the roads are very poor and vehicles prone to regular breakdowns), there are three good routes.

From Ulaan Baatar go to Darkhan, Amarbayasgalant Khiid, Erdenet, Bugat and then to Mörön, and around the area of Khövsgöl Nuur. From the lake, head south to Terkhiin Tsagaan Nuur, and back to Ulaan Baatar via Tsetserleg, Kharkhorin and Khujirt. The total distance is about 2000km, and will take eight to 12 days.

If you fly to Khovd (or to Ulaangom, and do it in reverse), you can visit Khovd city, Kazakh communities, Tsast Uul, Ölgii, Achit Nuur, Üüreg Nuur, Ulaangom, Uvs Nuur, Kharkhiraa Valley and Khar Us Nuur. This is about 1200km; allow at least a week to see it all.

From Ulaan Baatar, Baganuur or Öndörkhaan, travel around the Dariganga district via Baruun Urt, and visit Shiliin Bogd Uul, numerous lakes (including the Ganga Lake Natural Reserve), volcanoes and sand dunes. This will only take a few days.

TWO WEEKS — HITCHING & PUBLIC TRANSPORT

To travel independently in the countryside you will also probably have to hitch, which is generally safe and is a recognised form of transport. From Ulaan Baatar, it is relatively easy to get to Kharkhorin (for Erdene Zuu Khiid) and Khujirt; to Öndörkhaan via Baganuur; and to the big cities of Erdenet and Darkhan. If you fly to Mörön, you can visit Khatgal, but you'll need a jeep to explore Khövsgöl Nuur. A jeep is also essential to get around the south Gobi from Dalanzadgad. You'll need a minimum of two weeks to see all the sights.

ONE MONTH — MOUNTAIN BIKE

Mongolian roads are made for strong bikes and masochistic riders – the roads are rough and villages are few and far between. The best places to try are the trails from Ulaan Baatar to Terelj, Khandgait and/or Manzshir Khiid; from Mörön or Khatgal along either side of Khövsgöl Nuur; from Darkhan to Amarbayasgalant Khiid and on to Erdenet and Bugat; or from Kharkhorin to Khujirt and on to the Orkhon waterfall.

Visa Requirements

Visas are required of all nationalities, but you no longer need to be invited or sponsored by a Mongolian. A 30 day tourist visa can be obtained at the border or airport and costs between US$30 and US$40. For a longer stay, you'll need to arrange your visa before you arrive in the country and supply a letter of invitation. Visas normally take several days, and even up to two weeks to issue. If you need your visa sooner, possibly within 24 hours, you can opt to pay an 'express fee', which is double the normal cost. Many travellers arrange visas at the Mongolian embassy in Beijing.

Mongolian Embassies

CANADA
(☎ 416-865-7776) Suite 1800, BCE Place, 181 Bay St, Toronto, Ontario M5J 2T9

CHINA
(☎ 10-6532 1810) 2 Xiushui Beilu, Jianguomenwai, Beijing. Consulate: Hohhot

UK
(☎ 020-7937 0150) 7 Kensington Court, London W8 5DL

USA
(☎ 202-333-7117) 2833 Main St NW, Washington, DC 20007. Consulate: New York

Tourist Offices Overseas

Mongolia has no official tourist offices overseas. For information about the country, contact your local embassy or consulate, try the sites listed under Online Services, or contact your travel agent.

Health

Except for the possibility of frostbite in winter, Mongolia is generally a healthy country to travel in. The dry, cold climate and sparse human population mean few problems with diseases like malaria and dysentery, but outbreaks of meningococcal meningitis do occur. Travellers diarrhoea will probably hit you at some time during your travels. Mongolian food may not taste very good but generally it is safe to eat, though it's a good idea to boil or purify your water. The main risk is brucellosis

from unboiled milk or home-made cheese, so avoid these products. Be prepared for the cold; dress appropriately and carry basic food supplies.

Medical services are quite basic throughout Mongolia. In Ulaan Baatar, hospitals suffer from shortages of medical supplies and staff. Except in dire emergencies, avoid injections (even if you have your own syringes). If you are injured or really sick, head to Beijing.

Post & Communications

The postal service in Mongolia is fairly reliable, but excruciatingly slow – allow up to three months for delivery. There's a post restante service in Ulaan Baatar. The telephone system is improving all the time and a new mobile network is proving popular, although the land line system is still unreliable. It's very difficult to make calls outside Ulaan Baatar (unless you speak Mongolian or Russian). Post offices are the best places to make calls, but card phones are also popping up throughout the capital. Email services are available at some business centres in Ulaan Baatar. This is the cheapest form of international communication from within Mongolia.

Money

Costs

If you're travelling on an organised tour you'll probably spend about US$100 a day. You can travel independently, see the same sights and stay in the same places for about US$80 a day – or a lot less if you share the cost of a private jeep and camp rather than stay in pricier ger camps. Accommodation and food will cost a minimum of US$10 a day in Ulaan Baatar, but you're better off budgeting closer to twice that amount. In the countryside, allow about US$15 a day if you are using public transport and staying in hotels; if you take a tent and camp, you'll spend about US$7 a day.

Changing Money

Bring US dollar travellers cheques and have some new (post-1996), US dollars in cash – this is the only currency you'll be able to change outside Ulaan Baatar. Only the larger regional towns will even change this, so stock up on tögrögs in Ulaan Baatar before you head into the countryside. Similarly, credit cards are handy at some hotels and at airline offices in Ulaan Baatar, but you won't be able to buy anything on credit outside the capital city.

Online Services

Lonely Planet's *Destination Mongolia* page can be found at www.lonely planet.com/dest/nea/mon.htm.

The United Nations in Mongolia (www.un-mongolia.mn) has a stack of background information, as well as an online version of the *Mongolia Update*.

Find out more about the Mongols at National Geographic's incredibly slick *The Land of Genghis Khan* (www .nationalgeographic.com/features/ 97/genghis/index.html) or the charmingly home-made *Oyunbilig's Great Mongol Home Page* (members.aol.com/ yikhmongol/index.htm).

For Mongol news see *Mongolia Online* (www.visi.com/~bellmyb/story/ index.html). Everything you've ever wanted to know about felt tents is at *Yurt FAQ* (user.aol.com/VirtualMu/ YurtQuest/FAQ.html).

Books

The Secret History of the Mongols, Mongolia's most famous book, has no known author. This epic history records the life and deeds of Genghis Khan. *The Secret History of the Mongols: the Origins of Genghis Khan* by Paul Kahn is regarded as the best study of *The Secret History*.

Written by Charles Bowde, *The Jebtsundampa Khutukhtus of Urga* is a renowned Buddhist history of the greatest Mongolian lamas. *The Lost Country: Mongolia Revealed* by Jasper Becker is an insightful travelogue.

Films

Movies made in Mongolia bring to life the steppe and nomadic way of life. Mongolian directors seldom get a screening outside Mongolia, but video stores may well have the 1991 arthouse hit, *Close to Eden* (also released as *Urga*) by the Russian director Nikita Mikhalkov. Or try *Hei ma* (A Mongolian Tale).

Epic documentaries and feminist fantasies (such as *Johanna D'arc of Mongolia*) by German director Ulrike Ottinger offer an intimate immersion in the life of reindeer herders. Hollywood has produced its fantasies too, with the war epic *Destination Gobi*, plus Orson Welles, Tyrone Power and Herbert Lom starring in *The Black Rose* as Saxon warriors off to meet the great *khaans* (kings).

Entering & Leaving Mongolia

Most people fly into Ulaan Baatar from Beijing, Berlin or Moscow. Organised tours also operate flights from Osaka and Seoul. The international and national carrier is MIAT, which some wags claim stands for 'Maybe I'll Arrive Today'. Delayed and cancelled flights are common, partly due to frequent poor weather conditions. The airport departure tax is around US$10.

The only other way foreigners can enter and leave Mongolia is by train, either on local trains or on the Trans-Mongolian Railway which links Beijing and Moscow. Border crossings are at Erenhot-Zamyn-Üüd on the Chinese-Mongolian border, at and Naushki-Sükh-baatar on the Russian-Mongolian border. Some travellers have reported crossing into Mongolia from Russia and China by jeep or bus, but technically this is illegal.

MYANMAR (BURMA)

Myanmar is far from the easiest country to visit in Asia, but it has some magical sights, incredibly friendly people and offers a glimpse of a bizarre, inept Orwellian society that has withdrawn from contact with the late 20th century. The government's clampdown on outside influences makes Myanmar one of the least western-influenced countries in the world. It has suffered internal strife from a range of dictators, rebels and guerrillas, and is now synonymous in the west with the suppression of democracy and the use of slave labour. If you decide to go, there's no doubt that many of your tourist dollars will bolster the current regime – see the boxed text 'Should You Visit Myanmar?' for a discussion of the issues.

When to Go

The best season for visiting Myanmar is November to February, when it rains least and isn't too hot. If you're hitting the Rakhine coast, try March to May; by contrast, Bagan and Mandalay are intolerable during these months. The

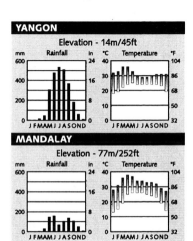

peak months for tourist arrivals are December, February, July and August. Myanmar is least crowded in May, June and September.

Highlights

Try to be underambitious with your travel plans, as flight delays and road travel hassles can quickly turn your trip into a chore. Virtually everyone begins their journey in Yangon, which is a good place to become accustomed to the climate, food and everyday customs before heading upcountry.

Temple Architecture

Myanmar's most magnificent temple ruins are at Bagan, the country's number one tourist attraction. Nearby Salay boasts a little known set of ruins from the same period, easily visited as a day trip from Bagan. Nearly as impressive in form and style are the massive Mrauk U temples near Sittwe in the Rakhine State, which so far have seen few tourists. Mandalay is surrounded by the ancient cities of Ava, Amarapura, Sagaing and Mingun, all easily visited on day trips. Early stupas at the former Pyu capital of Thayekhittaya (Sri Ksetra) near Pyay are the most accessible of all the ancient capitals from Yangon.

Handcrafts

Like most countries in South-East Asia, Myanmar is famed for the range and quality of its handcrafts. Mandalay has been the main handcrafts centre for more than 100 years and sells virtually every type of craft produced in the region, including silverwork, woodcarving, stone sculptures, *kalagas* (embroidered tapestries), marionettes and jadework. Other notable regions include the Shan State (handrolled cigars and embroidered shoulder bags) and Bagan (lacquerware and antiques). Cotton *longyis* (loom-woven lengths of cloth draped around the lower body and legs and tied at the waist) can be found throughout the country and feature considerable regional variation in design.

Beaches

Myanmar's coastline is the longest in mainland South-East Asia, but only those sections north-west of the Ayeyarwady Delta are commonly visited by foreigners. Because of the lengthy travel times, stays of at least one night are necessary at almost all seaside areas. Ngapali, Chaungtha and Letkhokkon have an adequate range of accommodation, so are among the most suitable for overnight visits. By contrast, the beaches and islands south of Mawlamyaing off peninsular Myanmar have incredible recreational potential, but are just beginning to open up, so accommodation is scarce.

Other Highlights

Kyaiktiyo Paya – the postcard-famous, stupa-topped gilded boulder perched on a mountain cliff in the Mon State – is fairly accessible these days to visitors interested in Myanmar's complex, animistic Buddhism. Mt Popa (1520m), near Bagan, holds a similar lure, although the overall atmosphere runs far behind that of Kyaiktiyo. The old Mon capital of Bago, with the second largest reclining Buddha in the country and a highly revered stupa, makes an easy day trip from Yangon or a convenient stopover on the way to Kyaiktiyo. Inle Lake in the Shan State offers the visitor an attractive variety of old Shan temples, boat-tripping and relaxed evenings.

Itineraries

With the exception of the Myeik Peninsula from Mawlamyaing to Kawthoung, Myanmar's asymmetric shape doesn't lend itself to linear north-south or east-west routes. Keep in mind that transport delays are extremely common throughout the country, so always be prepared to alter your itinerary in the face of unforeseen events such as railway repairs, road washouts, cancelled flights and bad weather.

ONE WEEK

For a short Myanmar sampler, start with a two day taste of Yangon's heavily gilded *payas* (religious statues and monuments) and urban intensity, and then travel to Mandalay by bus or plane to see the Mahamuni temples, as well as the royal cities in the region. Then head to Bagan to take in the temple ruins before heading back to Yangon. Alternatively, you could go northeast from Yangon to Bago and then east to the 'golden rock' mountaintop shrine at Kyaiktiyo. One night each will suffice for Bago and Kyaiktiyo, leaving more time for Yangon at the beginning and end of the trip. The more ambitious could continue from Kyaiktiyo to Mawlamyaing – an engaging city of Mon-style payas, historic mosques and algae-trimmed colonial architecture.

TWO WEEKS

Two weeks will allow you to either complete both of the above itineraries, or select one and then head to another part of the country from Yangon. West of the capital is the huge Ayeyarwady Delta, which can be reached by overnight boat. After a night in Pathein, you can go by road to Chaungtha for a couple of nights and then continue north to Ngapali for some beach time, before catching a flight back to Yangon. Alternatively, you could follow a road circuit from Yangon to Pyay, Ngapali, Chaungtha and Pathein, and back to Yangon.

Another option is to visit Mandalay or Bagan and then double back to Meiktila or Thazi by road, before spending a week travelling the eastern road to Inle Lake, stopping at the former British hill station of Kalaw and the extensive limestone Pindaya

Caves, which contain 8094 Buddha images. From Inle you can fly back to Yangon or take the bus. Alternatively, skip Inle and spend a few days in and around Hsipaw (to the north of Mandalay), a charming centre for Shan culture, with a side trip to the Shan/Chinese market town of Lashio.

If you're archaeologically minded, spend the second week at Myanmar's second greatest site of Buddhist ruins, Mrauk U, although you'll have to fly from Yangon.

ONE MONTH

In a month you can sample many of Myanmar's major highlights. After a few days in Yangon head north to Mandalay, with stopovers in the towns of Taungoo, Pyinmana and Bagan. Then go east into the Shan State to take in the Inle circuit or the Pyin U Lwin (a cool former British hill station at 1070m) and Lashio route described under the two week itinerary. With about a week left, fly to Ngapali, enjoy a few days at the beach, and then work your way down the western coast through Chaungtha and Pathein back to Yangon.

If beach resorts don't matter much to you, go for a culture hit by starting with the Bago to Kyaiktiyo one week circuit, then continue south to Mawlamyaing, Dawei and Myeik, one of South-East Asia's most historic ports. You could then fly back to Yangon or head to Kawthoung at Myanmar's south-easternmost tip to cross into Thailand at Ranong by boat.

Visa Requirements

Among the 12 types of visitor visas and border permits (which include gems such as the 'seasonal mahjis permit'), travellers are normally issued a tourist visa valid for 28 days and these are readily available through most Myanmar embassies or consulates. At the embassy in Bangkok you can usually receive a visa the same day you apply. The simple application process requires three passport-size photos and a US$15 to US$20 visa fee. You can receive two extensions of 14 days

THIMPHU

CHINA (Tibet)

Hkakabo Razi (5889m)

Putao (Fort Hertz)

Ledo

Pansan Pass

CHINA (Yunnan)

Khamti

Sumprabum

Pakkhan

MANDALAY
Theatre, monasteries, handcrafts and ancient royal cities

INDIA

Imphal

Lulawgyi Lake

Tamu

Mawlaik

Kalewa

Bhamo

Ruili

Namkham

Mu-se

PYIN U LWIN
Scenic hill-station town, colonial architecture and pony wagons

DHAKA

BAGAN
Vast plain dotted with 800-year-old temples

Hakha

Lashio

Hsipaw

KENGTUNG
Golden Triangle centre, hill tribes, markets, hiking

Monywa

Mingun

Sagaing

Ava

Pyin U Lwin

Mandalay

Amarapura

Kyaukse

Kengtung

VIETNAM

MRAUK U
Impressive 16th century temple ruins

Paletwa

Mt Victoria (3053m)

Pakkoku

Bagan

Nyaung U

Meiktila

Thazi

Pindaya Caves

Heho

Nyaungshwe

Tachilek

Mae Sai

INLE LAKE
Floating gardens, markets, hiking, canoe trips

Teknat

Maungtan

Mrauk U

Minbya

Salay

Kyauk Padaung

Kalaw

Yamethin

Inle Lake

LAOS

Sittwe

NGAPALI BEACH
Attractive sandy beaches and nearby villages to explore

Kyaukpyu

Ramree I

Magwe

Pyinmana

Loikaw

Lawpita

Thanlwin River

Chiang Mai

Cheduba I

Taungup

Remree

Padaung

Pyay

Shwedaung

Paungde

Taungoo

Pasauwng

PYAY
Ancient ruins of the Pyu kingdom

Thandwe

Ngapali

VIENTIANE

PATHEIN
Rich delta culture, seaside villages, beaches

Gwa

Tharrawaddy

Henzada

Bago

Kyaiktiyo

THAILAND

Chaungtha

Pathein

Thaton

Pa-an

Kawkareik

Mae Sot

KYAIKTIYO
Remarkable balancing boulder-shrine

Daedaye

Letkhokkon

YANGON (RANGOON)

Mawlamyaing

YANGON
Shwedagon Paya, teahouses, colonial buildings

Kyaikkami

Thanbyuzayat

BAY OF BENGAL

Mouths of the Ayeyarwady

Gulf of Martaban

Payathonzu

Three Pagodas Pass

Ye

Sangkhlaburi

Yebyu

Dawei

BANGKOK

Andaman Sea

Andaman Islands (INDIA)

Palaw

Myeik

CAMBODIA

Taninthayi

MERGUI ARCHIPELAGO

Bokpyin

Gulf of Thailand

0   100   200 km

Kawthoung

Ranong

each, and if that still isn't enough you can fly to Bangkok and get another one immediately.

Myanmar Embassies

AUSTRALIA
(☎ 02-6273 3811) 22 Arkana St, Yarralumla, ACT 2600

CANADA
(☎ 613-232-6434/6446) 85 Range Rd, Apt 902-903, Sandringham, Ottawa, Ontario K1N 8J6

THAILAND
(☎ 02-233 2237, 234 0320) 132 Sathon Neua Rd, Bangkok 10500

UK
(☎ 020-7629 6966, 7499 8841) 19A Charles St, London W1X 8ER

USA
(☎ 202-332-9044/5/6) 2300 South St NW, Washington, DC 20008

Tourist Offices Overseas

Myanmar maintains very few tourist offices overseas. You would be better served dealing with travel agents and checking out the web sites listed under Online Services.

Health

Malaria risk exists in rural areas, but is not usually a problem in the areas most frequented by foreign travellers. You should take appropriate precautions if travelling to more remote areas. Dengue fever also occurs, and there's a low risk of Japanese encephalitis. Food and waterborne diseases include dysentery, cholera and hepatitis, so be careful with food and drink. All water should be boiled or otherwise treated before consumption – bottled water is available at most tourist destinations.

Myanmar's hospitals and hygiene standards are rudimentary, but hospitals in Yangon are improving. Get

---

SHOULD YOU VISIT MYANMAR?

Myanmar's military regime, led by the State Law & Order Restoration Council (SLORC), allowed a democratic election for a new government in 1990. The National League for Democracy (NLD) won the election but was not permitted to rule. The NLD MPs formed a provisional government in exile called the National Coalition Government of the Union of Burma (NCGUB). From November 1996 to October 1997 SLORC ran a Visit Myanmar Year campaign; the NCGUB made the following statement (which really applies to anyone planning to visit Myanmar at any time):

'Tourists should not engage in activities that will only benefit SLORC's coffers and not the people of Burma. However, responsible individuals and organisations who wish to verify the facts and to publicise the plight of the Burmese people are encouraged to utilise SLORC's more relaxed tourist policies.'

Aung San Suu Kyi, the high-profile representative of the NLD, has said: 'We are totally against the Visit Myanmar campaign.'

Lonely Planet believes it is essential to respect the wishes of the genuine representatives of the people of Myanmar, so potential travellers will need to make their own judgement. If you do decide to travel to Myanmar there are steps you can take to avoid bolstering the government's coffers. For example: avoid staying in government-owned hotels; don't travel with tours operated by Myanmar Travels & Tours (MTT); don't use modes of transport for which the tickets are controlled by MTT (eg the Mandalay Express train and the Mandalay-Bagan tourist boat); use ordinary public transport or charter private vehicles; buy handcrafts directly from the artisans rather than from government shops; and stay at private, locally owned hotels and guesthouses.

yourself to Bangkok or Singapore if you become seriously ill.

Post & Communications

Myanmar's postal system is pretty dodgy, especially away from the cities, although international rates are exceptionally cheap. There is a free poste restante service at the main post office in Yangon. International phone calls are possible, but there are few public facilities outside the main cities and these are in constant demand, so be prepared to wait. Calls can also be made from the better hotels, but at a steep premium. Logging onto the Internet is illegal, so there are no service providers as yet in the country. The government does provide a monopoly email service, but it's prohibitively expensive.

Money

Costs

The official rate of exchange bears no relation to reality. As soon as you exit immigration at Yangon airport, you have to buy US$300 worth of foreign exchange certificates (FEC) at the official rate to pay for officially approved hotel rooms. However, if you travel throughout Myanmar, you'll have to pay in FECs only about half the time; free-market kyats are good for the other half. Accommodation at the free-market exchange rate is a bargain. If you're travelling very cheaply, you can get by on about US$10 a day. If you want your own bathroom and a choice of restaurants, budget on US$25 to US$30 a day. Flying or taking express trains would add around US$5 a day. To stay somewhere fancy will cost you anywhere from US$25 to US$300 a night.

Changing Money

It's illegal to unofficially change US dollars, but you can change FECs with the locals. Changing FECs at the official rate is downright insane. It's safer to change in shops or hotels than on the street, and you should research the going rate before you do your exchange. If you want to change dollars illegally you might get a slightly better rate than for FECs, but the difference is negligible. Very few places accept credit cards.

Online Services

Lonely Planet's *Destination Myanmar* page can be found at www.lonelyplanet .com/dest/sea/myan.htm.

The Burma Project (www.soros .org/burma.html) is 'dedicated to increasing international awareness of conditions in Burma and to helping the country make the transition from a closed to an open society'.

Free Burma (sunsite.unc.edu/free burma/index.html) is a vital collection of interviews, facts and news about Myanmar's current political situation.

The Internet Travel Guide (www .datacomm.ch/pmgeiser/myanmar) has plenty of nitty-gritty travel information if you decide to visit Myanmar.

Frontline's *The Opium Kings* (www.pbs.org/wgbh/pages/frontline/ shows/heroin) includes Adrian Cowell's *30 year chronicle of Burma's heroin trade*, and interviews with an ex-DEA agent in Burma and an ex-US ambassador to Burma.

Books

George Orwell's *Burmese Days* is an interesting, if depressing, novel set in Burma in British colonial times, while Paul Theroux's *The Great Railway*

Bazaar includes chapters on the train trips from Yangon to Mandalay and Mandalay to Pyin U Lwin. *Golden Earth* by Norman Lewis is a delightful tale of a ramble around Burma in the 50s.

Burma by FSV Donnison gives a concise overview of Burmese history up to the 1960s. *Outrage: Burma's Struggle for Democracy* by Bertil Lintner covers the contemporary turmoil, while *Freedom from Fear and Other Writings* is a collection of essays by and about pro-democracy leader Aung San Suu Kyi. There is a chapter on Myanmar in Pico Iyer's *Video Night in Kathmandu*.

Films

Not surprisingly, few dramatic films have been made in or about Myanmar since the 1950s, although a couple of recent documentaries have focused on the plight of pro-democracy citizens under military rule, including John Boorman's graphic *Beyond Rangoon* and Jeanne Hallacy's *Burma Diary*.

Around the WWII period, Burma was a popular setting, particularly for war movies such as *Bombs Over Burma, Objective, Burma!* (one of the best of the genre, starring Errol Flynn) and *Burma Convoy*. Others include *Moon Over Burma*, a Dorothy Lamour romance, and *Escape to Burma*, an adventure flick set in British Burma.

Entering & Leaving Myanmar

Although Myanmar is essentially a 'fly in, fly out' destination, some road border crossings may be open (depending on the mood of the government). You might be able to enter Myanmar overland from Ruili in Yunnan Province, China (Mu-se on the Myanmar side) though you may only be issued a day pass, and day trips can be made from Thailand at Three Pagodas Pass, Mae Sot (Kawkareik) and Mae Sai (Tachilek), or you can take a boat from Kawthoung to Ranong. There are frequent flights to Yangon from Bangkok, Hong Kong, Singapore and Kuala Lumpur, and less frequent flights from the capitals of other neighbouring countries. The departure tax is US$10.

NEPAL ▶▶

Draped along the greatest heights of the Himalaya, the kingdom of Nepal is a land of sublime scenery, time-worn temples, and some of the best walking trails on earth. It's a poor country, but rich in scenic splendour and cultural treasures. Nepal has long exerted a pull on the western imagination and many travellers are drawn back to Nepal, armed the second time round with a greater appreciation of its natural and cultural complexity, a stout pair of walking boots and a desire for improved leg-definition.

When to Go
Climatic factors are very important in deciding when to visit Nepal. October/November, the start of the dry season, is in many ways the best time of year: the weather is balmy, the air is clean, visibility is perfect, and the country is lush following the monsoon. February/April, the tail end of the dry season, is the second best period; visibility is not as good because of dust, but the weather is warm and many of Nepal's wonderful wildflowers are in bloom. In December and January the climate and visibility are good, but it can be chilly: trekkers need to be well prepared for the bitter cold, as do travellers staying in cheap hotels.

The rest of the year is fairly unpleasant for travelling: May and early June are generally too hot and dusty for comfort, and the monsoon from mid-June to September obscures the mountains and turns trails and roads into mud.

AT A GLANCE

Full Country Name: Kingdom of Nepal

Area: 147,181 sq km

Population: 23 million

Capital City: Kathmandu (pop 700,000)

People: A blend of ethnic groups, including Bhotiya, Rai, Limbu, Gurung, Indians, Khas, Magar, Newari, Tharu, Tamong and Tibetan

Languages: Nepali (also called Gurkhali)

Religion: 90% Hindu, 5% Buddhist, 3% Muslim, 2% Christian and Animist

Government: Constitutional democracy

Currency: Nepali rupee (Rs)

Time Zone: Five hours and 45 minutes ahead of GMT/UTC

International Telephone Code: 977

Electricity: Electricity is only found in major towns and some outposts, (eg Namche Bazaar on the Everest Base Camp trail) – when available it's 220V 50 AC; sockets usually take round, three-pin plugs (large or small), but sometimes round two-pin plugs

293

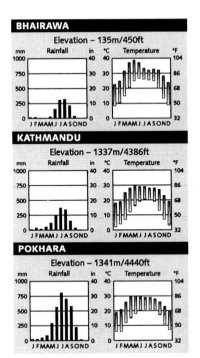

Highlights

Trekking is the number one attraction for most visitors, but Nepal has a lot more to offer, especially in the Kathmandu Valley and the south. If you plan to trek, you'll need to arrange a permit in advance. These are generally only available in Kathmandu and Pokhara.

Kathmandu Valley

Kathmandu is one of the most traveller-friendly cities in Asia. There's plenty of cheap, good-quality food, accommodation, clothing and crafts; you can walk or cycle just about everywhere; and there's plenty to see and do. The downside is that you'll mix with as many fellow travellers as locals, and the locals will all want a piece of you, but it's still a pretty good place to relax, particularly after a long and gruelling trek. The mass of temples in Durbar Square are well worth a day's exploration, but if you go further afield on a bicycle there's also superb architecture to be seen at Patan, Bhaktapur, Swayambhunath, Pashupatinath and Bodhnath.

Mt Everest Region

The classic trek is from Jiri or Lukla to Everest Base Camp. This route takes you through some beautiful scenery in Sagarmatha National Park, a wonderful temple at Tengpoche and finally to the roof of the world. As a bonus, the accommodation is very good and the food palatable. Alternative routes from Namche Bazaar take you to Gokyo or Thami.

Annapurna

The main route through the Annapurna range is known as the 'apple pie' trail because there's electricity all the way along. Together with the laid-back town of Pokhara as the entry and exit point, this makes Annapurna an immensely popular region. Unless you head north to Mustang or east to the Gorkha Loop, you'll share the trail with plenty of others. Don't be put off though, as Annapurna has so many trails that you can tailor a trek to your specific needs and abilities, and the scenery is stunning.

Other Treks

The two week trek to Mustang north of Annapurna comes with many restrictions and is very expensive, but it's well worth seeing this gorgeous area, often described as a piece of Tibet in

Nepal. The Langtang trek is handy to Kathmandu; by contrast, the Jumla to Rara trek will take you well off the beaten track. Possibly the most romantic and rewarding trek in Nepal is the 25 day Humla to Mt Kailas pilgrimage, which takes you across the Chinese border. It's rugged, isolated and expensive, but it reveals a cultural side of Nepal that few travellers see.

The Terai

The Terai is the lowland strip which runs the breadth of the country. It's a fascinating area often overlooked by visitors, and has a great deal to offer. The Royal Chitwan and Royal Bardia national parks offer the chance to see a wide variety of bird and animal life, including the royal Bengal tiger and the rhinoceros, but these parks do receive mixed reviews. Other towns in the Terai, such as Janakpur and Lumbini, are significant religious sites and well worth a visit.

Itineraries

ONE WEEK

Your options will be very limited if you have only a week. The best bet would be to spend three days in the Kathmandu Valley and then fly to Pokhara for some walks in the lower Annapurna range (such as the Ghandruk Loop). Alternatively, you could take a bumpy bus ride down to the Terai and check out the Royal Chitwan National Park and surrounding towns.

TWO WEEKS

Two weeks will give you the opportunity to undertake a decent-length trek, if you wish to do nothing else. Good options here include Jiri to Namche Bazaar (nine days), Barabise to Shivalaya (six days), Annapurna Panorama or Tatopani Loop (both eight days) or Jumla to Rara Lake (nine days).

Alternatively, you could do a loop from the Kathmandu Valley to Bharatpur and Pokhara for a taste of all that Nepal has to offer.

ONE MONTH

This is the most popular length of stay. With four weeks you can spend some time in Kathmandu before and after a good-length trek and also check out the south and laze in Pokhara for a few days. Good treks to consider here include Lukla to Everest Base Camp (15 days), Around Annapurna (16 days), Langtang trek (10 days), Kanchenjunga South in the far east of the country (16 days) and Dunai to Tarap (14 days).

TWO MONTHS

If you have two months, you can get really serious about your trekking. The ultimate is the Humla to Mt Kailas trek (25 days), although the Kanchenjunga North (22 days), Makalu Base Camp (20 days) and Around Manaslu (20 days) treks are pretty solid too. These treks have few creature comforts and you'll be far from assistance, so they are only for fit and reasonably experienced walkers. A better option for inexperienced walkers seeking a long trek is to climb to Everest Base Camp from Jiri (22 days). Alternatively, select several shorter routes around the country, with generous breaks in between to relax.

Visa Requirements

Visas are required by most nationalities (Indians are an exception) and they are available from embassies and consulates abroad, at the border with India or on arrival at Kathmandu's Tribhuvan airport. Single-entry tourist visas are available for 15 or 30 days, and you can also apply for a multiple-entry 60 day visa.

At the airport, and sometimes at border crossings, officials insist on payment in US cash dollars. One passport photo is also required. Outside your home country, the most convenient

NEPAL HIGHLIGHTS & ITINERARIES

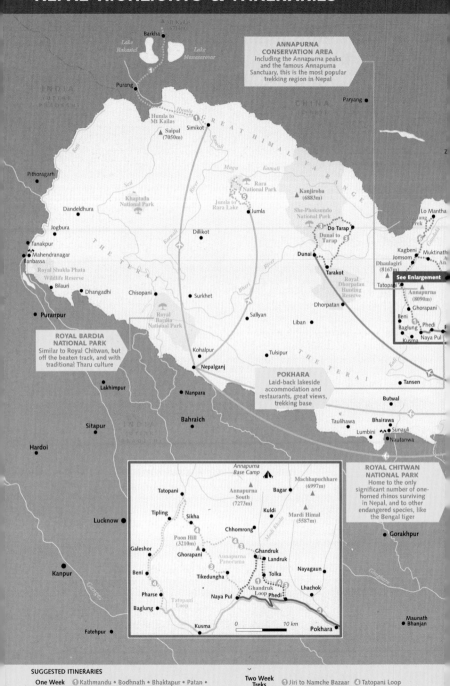

ANNAPURNA CONSERVATION AREA
Including the Annapurna peaks and the famous Annapurna Sanctuary, this is the most popular trekking region in Nepal

POKHARA
Laid-back lakeside accommodation and restaurants, great views, trekking base

ROYAL BARDIA NATIONAL PARK
Similar to Royal Chitwan, but off the beaten track, and with traditional Tharu culture

ROYAL CHITWAN NATIONAL PARK
Home to the only significant number of one-horned rhinos surviving in Nepal, and to other endangered species, like the Bengal tiger

Barkha
Lake Rakastal
Lake Manasarovar
Mt Kailas
INDIA (UTTAR PRADESH)
Purang
Pithoragarh
Dandeldhura
Jogbura
Tanakpur
Mahendranagar
Banbassa
Royal Shukla Phata Wildlife Reserve
Bilauri
Dhangadhi
Puranpur
Lakhimpur
Sitapur
Hardoi
Lucknow
Kanpur
Fatehpur
Chisopani
Khaptada National Park
THE TERAI
Surkhet
Royal Bardia National Park
Kohalpur
Nepalganj
Nanpara
Bahraich
INDIA (UTTAR PRADESH)
Humla to Mt Kailas
Saipal (7050m)
Simikot
GREAT HIMALAYA RANGE
Muga
Kamali
Rara National Park
Jumla to Rara Lake
Jumla
Dillikot
Kanjiroba (6883m)
She-Phoksundo National Park
Do Tarap
Dunai to Tarap
Dunai
Tarakot
Royal Dhorpatan Hunting Reserve
Dhorpatan
Liban
Sallyan
Tulsipur
THE TERAI
CHINA
Paryang
Lo Mantha
Kagbeni
Jomsom
Muktinath
Dhaulagiri (8167m)
See Enlargement
Tatopani
Annapurna (8090m)
Ghorapani
Beni
Baglung
Phedi
Kusma
Naya Pul
Tansen
Butwal
Taulihawa
Bhairawa
Sunauli
Lumbini
Nautanwa
Gorakhpur
Maunath Bhanjan

Annapurna enlargement
Annapurna Base Camp
Machhapuchhare (6997m)
Tatopani
Annapurna South (7273m)
Bagar
Kuldi
Mardi Himal (5587m)
Tipling
Sikha
Chhomrong
Poon Hill (3210m)
Ghorapani
Annapurna Panorama
Ghandruk
Landruk
Galeshor
Tikedungha
Tolka
Nayagaun
Beni
Pharse
Naya Pul
Ghandruk Loop
Phedi
Lhachok
Baglung
Tatopani Loop
Kusma
0   10 km
Pokhara

CHINA (TIBET)

0   50   100 km

Balaju
Dhum Varahi
Bodhnath
Swayambhunath
Pashupatinath
Gokarna Safari Park
Changu Narayan
Jaukhel
KATHMANDU
Thimi
Bode
Gwatala
Bhaktapur
Patan
Koteshwar Mahadev
Jal Binayak

0   3 km

Saga

Shigatse
Lhatse
Sakya

Manaslu (8162m)
Ganesh Himal (7406m)
Around Manaslu
Langtang (7246m)
Langtang Trek
Kyanjin Gompa
Dhunche
Langtang
Langtang National Park
Zhangmu
Kodari
Cho Oyu (8153m)
Gauri Shankar (7146m)
Sagarmatha National Park
Chomolungma, Sagarmatha or Mt Everest (8848m)
Makalu (8475m)
Kanchenjunga (8598m)
Kanchenjunga North
Gunsa

Gorkha
Arughat
Trisuli
See Enlargement
KATHMANDU
Bhaktapur
Patan
Charikot
Barabise to Shivalaya
Jiri to Namche Bazaar
Namche Bazaar
Lukla to Everest Base Camp
Makalu Base Camp
Kanchenjunga South
GREAT HIMALAYA RANGE
INDIA (SIKKIM)

Dumre
Mugling
Naubise
Daman
Barabise
Shivalaya
Lukla
Jiri
Dolalghat
Phaphlu

Bharatpur
Royal Chitwan National Park
Hetauda
Dudh
Phaphlu
Tumlingtar
Taplejung
Kanchenjunga South
Darjeeling

Amlekhganj
THE TERAI
Lamidanda
Basantpur
Hile
Dhankuta
Ilam

Birganj
Raxaul
Laibiti
Chatara
Dharan Bazaar
Itahari
Kakarbhitta
To Siliguri
Bhadrapur

Bettiah
Motihari
Bairagnia
Janakpur
Jaleshwar
Rajbiraj
Biratnagar
Islampur

Sitamarhi
Birpur
Jogbani
Forbesganj
Araria
Kishanganj

Muzaffarpur
Darbhanga
INDIA (BIHAR)
INDIA (WEST BENGAL)

Chapra
Saharsa
Purnia

Atihar

places to get your visa are Bangkok, Calcutta and Delhi. You must use your visa within three months of the date it is issued.

Nepali Embassies

AUSTRALIA
(☎ 02-9233 6161) Level 1, 17 Castlereagh St, Sydney, NSW 2000. Consulates: Melbourne and Perth

CANADA
(☎ 416-865-0200) Box 33, 32nd floor, 200 Bay St, Toronto, Ontario M5J 2W4

INDIA
(☎ 011-332-9969) 1 Barakhamba Rd, New Delhi 110001. Consulate: Calcutta

THAILAND
(☎ 02-391 7240) 189 Sukhumvit Rd, Bangkok 10110

UK
(☎ 020-7229 6231) 12A Kensington Palace Gardens, London W8 4QU

USA
(☎ 202-667-4550) 2131 Leroy Place NW, Washington, DC 20008. Consulate: San Francisco

Tourist Offices Overseas

Nepal maintains few tourist offices overseas. Talk to your travel agent, read guidebooks and check out some of the web sites under Online Services.

Health

The main health concern is the relatively high risk of suffering travellers diarrhoea, a respiratory infection, or an accident while trekking. The risk of malaria is extremely low – it has been reported only in the Terai. Food and waterborne diseases (eg dysentery, hepatitis and typhoid) all occur. Tap water is not safe to drink; also boil or purify all mountain water, and do not eat food which may have been reheated. A meningococcal meningitis vaccination is recommended, especially for trekkers. Trekkers should also be prepared for the cold and be aware of the symptoms and treatment of altitude sickness.

Medical care in Kathmandu is basic but acceptable, but further afield medical facilities are distinctly limited. If you do require serious medical care, head to Bangkok or Singapore.

Post & Communications

Nepal's postal service is generally reliable, but the time it takes varies widely. Parcel post outside the country is expensive and slow, but also reliable. There are poste restante services in Kathmandu and Pokhara, but time might beat you if you're not spending a long time in the country. The telephone system works quite well, and it's easy to make local, STD and international calls from most towns. Email and Internet services are offered by dozens of places in Kathmandu and Pokhara, but elsewhere they are virtually nonexistent.

Money

Costs

If you stay in rock-bottom accommodation and survive on a mainly Nepali diet, you could easily live in Nepal on less than US$15 a day. If you prefer to stay in comfortable lodgings, eat in tourist-oriented restaurants and take the occasional taxi, your living costs are likely to be between US$20 and US$40 a day. On an independent trek between village inns, costs are likely to be between US$10 and US$15 a day, as long as you don't indulge in too many luxury items such as beer, rum and chocolate.

Changing Money

You can exchange cash and travellers cheques at the international terminal at Kathmandu's airport and at banks and/or moneychangers at the various border crossings. Pokhara and the major border towns also have official moneychanging facilities, but changing travellers cheques can be difficult elsewhere in the country. US dollars and pounds sterling are readily accepted, and the Indian rupee is also considered a 'hard' currency. Outside the Kathmandu Valley, it may be hard to get change from large-denomination Nepali notes, so keep a decent portion of your money in small-denomination notes. Major credit cards are widely accepted at mid-range and better hotels, restaurants and fancy shops in the Kathmandu Valley and Pokhara, but not elsewhere.

Online Services

Lonely Planet's *Destination Nepal* page is at www.lonelyplanet.com/dest/ind/nep.htm; try also *Destination Kathmandu* (www.lonelyplanet.com/dest/ind/kat.htm).

Travel sites don't come much better than *Nepal Home Page* (www.info-nepal.com) – good information, pics and a *FAQ page* (www.info-nepal.com/nhp/travel/faq/FAQ.html), while there's good trekking information at *Nepal Trekking* (www.bena.com/nepaltrek/index.html) and *Nepal Himalaya Trekking* (kocsis.mswin.net).

Get your daily news fix from the *Kathmandu Post* (www.south-asia.com/news-ktmpost.html).

William W Greer's *Walking to Rara Lake* (www.gorp.com/gorp/armchair/jumla1.htm) describes a trek in western Nepal, while *Jungle Wildlife in Nepal* (www.gorp.com/gorp/location/asia/nepal/chitbard.htm) covers the lowlands of the Royal Chitwan and Royal Bardia national parks.

The *SINHAS journal* (jhunix.hcf.jhu.edu/deschene/sinhas/index.html) is a multidisciplinary venture for those who seek 'a more complex picture of Nepali society than that provided by guidebooks and travel literature'.

Books

The market is saturated with books on Nepal. Some good general books include Peter Matthiessen's *The Snow Leopard*, a beautifully written account of the author's pilgrimage to Dolpa to track this elusive cat; and Peter Somerville-Large's engagingly dotty *To the Navel of the World*, which chronicles his adventures through some of Nepal's uncharted lands. Also try Pico Iyer's *Video Night in Kathmandu*, a collection of essays which has a chapter on the collision between Nepali tradition and western culture.

Recent histories are limited, but *Fatalism & Development – Nepal's Struggle for Modernisation* by Nepali anthropologist Dor Bahadur Bista is a good place to start. There are more up-to-date books on the country's natural history, including KK Guring's *The Heart of the Jungle*; George Schaller's *Stones of Silence – Journeys in the Himalaya*; and *Birds of Nepal* by Robert Fleming Sr et al.

Mountaineering braggarts include HW Tilman *(Nepal Himalaya)*, Chris Bonington *(Annapurna South Face)* and Mark Anderson *(On the Big Hill)*. These self-congratulatory tomes are devastatingly satirised in *The Ascent of Rum Doodle* by WE Bowman.

Films

There are few Nepali films, due in part to the massive popularity of India's Bollywood productions. Western films made in or about Nepal include

Everest (1998), filmed in IMAX format, which is the dramatic story of an ascent of Everest in the same week as a New Zealand climber made headlines by farewelling his wife via a mobile phone call as he neared death just below the summit.

Powaqqatsi (1988), the disappointing sequel to *Koyaanisqatsi*, is an exploration of third world cultures and their exploitation at the hands of the west. There are some nice scenes in Bhaktapur and Kathmandu. Nepal also features in Ron Fricke's environmental film *Baraka* (1992). Bernado Bertolucci's *Little Emperor* (1993) is pretty dreadful, but beautifully showcases the spectacular scenery of Nepal and Bhutan.

Entering & Leaving Nepal

There are few direct flights to Nepal, which means most travellers from Europe, North America and Australia have to change aircraft and/or airline en route. Nepal's international airport is Kathmandu's Tribhuvan airport. If you want to see the mountains as you fly into Kathmandu, make sure you sit on the right-hand side of the plane. The departure tax for international flights is Rs 700 (Rs 500 to destinations on the Indian subcontinent).

The classic overland routes between Nepal and India are still popular, and buses are usually the quickest and easiest form of transport. The main border crossing points are Sunauli-Bhairawa, Birganj-Raxaul and Kakarbhitta-Siliguri. A few travellers enter Nepal at the Mahendranagar-Banbassa crossing in the extreme west of Nepal, which is handy for travellers coming overland from Delhi wanting to bypass Varanasi. The crossing between Nepal and Tibet via Kodari is open to organised groups, but not to individual travellers. Be prepared with alternative plans if you're thinking about using this route, as landslides can make it impassable during the monsoon.

PAKISTAN ▶▶

Even before the Iranian revolution and the Iran-Iraq and Afghan wars throttled Asian overland travel, Pakistan tended to be seen as simply the last hurdle before reaching India. Few westerners know much about Pakistan beyond media impressions of guns and drugs, communal violence, martial law and cricket, but it contains some of Asia's most mind-blowing landscapes, a multitude of cultures and a deeply hospitable people. It's the site of some of the earliest human settlements, home to an ancient civilisation rivalling those of Egypt and Mesopotamia, and the crucible of Hinduism and Buddhism.

It remains, however, a deeply troubled country. Outside the major centres, lawlessness is rife, making bus, car and motorbike travel very unwise (even with an armed escort). The Highlights section below lists the country's best attractions, while the Itineraries reflect the current parlous situation for travellers and are based on a considerable amount of air or train travel. The situation in Pakistan changes with the wind, so speak with your embassy or high commission before making any firm plans.

When to Go
Generally speaking, the southern parts of Pakistan, including Sind, Baluchistan, Punjab and the southern part of the North-West Frontier Province (NWFP), are best visited in the cooler months between November and April. After that it gets uncomfortably hot. The northern areas such as Azad Jammu and Kashmir, and northern NWFP are best visited during May to October, before the area becomes snowbound. The weather may be a little stormy during this time, but the mountain districts are usually still accessible. Try to avoid Pakistan during Ramadan (normally in December or January).

AT A GLANCE

Full Country Name: Islamic Republic of Pakistan

Area: 887,700 sq km

Population: 124.8 million

Capital City: Islamabad (pop 350,000)

People: 60% Punjabi, plus sizable groups of Pathans, Baluch, Mohajir, Kasmiris, Afghans and Sindhis

Languages: Urdu, Punjabi, English and regional dialects

Religion: 97% Muslim, 3% Christian and Hindu

Government: Parliamentary democracy

Currency: Pakistani rupee (Rs)

Time Zone: Five hours ahead of GMT/UTC

International Telephone Code: 92

Electricity: 220V, 50 AC – some hotels also have 110V shaver outlets; most sockets take round, two-pin plugs, though some hotel sockets will accept a third (earth or ground) pin.

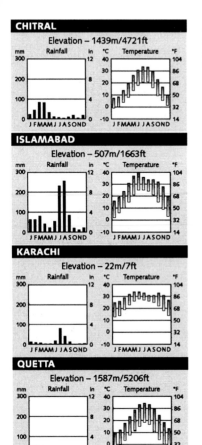

CHITRAL
Elevation – 1439m/4721ft

ISLAMABAD
Elevation – 507m/1663ft

KARACHI
Elevation – 22m/7ft

QUETTA
Elevation – 1587m/5206ft

Highlights

Lahore

The capital of Punjab is Pakistan's cultural, educational and artistic centre and is easily the most visited city in the country. With its refuges of shady parks and gardens, startling Mughal and colonial architecture, and congested streets and bazaars, it's very easy to see why. Its attractions include Lahore Museum, Lahore Fort (packed with stately palaces, halls and gardens), Aitchison College and the Old City, as well as numerous tombs, mosques and mausoleums.

Around Punjab

Punjab is rich in ancient history and is one of the most stable of the country's regions – travellers should encounter few of the problems that occur to the south and north. The prosperous and hospitable town of Bahawalpur is a gentle introduction to the area. From here you can journey into Cholistan – a sandy wasteland dotted with nomadic communities and windswept forts – or the Lal Suhanra National Park, an important wildlife reserve. Further north is Harappa which is, after Moenjodaro, the second most important site of the Indus Valley civilisation. Not far away, Multan is claimed to be the oldest surviving city on the subcontinent, dating back some 4000 years. The Nanga Parbat massif in the southernmost part of the Northern Areas has a 4500m wall that is so steep even the snow refuses to stick.

Karachi

Pakistan's commercial centre and largest city is a sprawling place of bazaars, hi-tech electronic shops, peeling older buildings and modish new hotels. Its sights are spread far and wide so a taxi or rickshaw is necessary to travel between them. Karachi's highlights include the Quaid-i-Azam Mausoleum, the remarkable white-marbled Defence Housing Society Mosque, Honeymoon Lodge (birthplace of the Aga Khan) and the Zoroastrian Towers of Silence, where the dead are traditionally exposed to vultures.

Rawalpindi & Islamabad

Rawalpindi and the country's capital, Islamabad, are twin cities. The former is a patchwork of bustling bazaars while the latter is subdued, suburban and still being built. From here you can visit Taxila, an archaeological repository, and Hasan Abdul, a place of holy pilgrimage.

Quetta

The capital of the parched, barren province of Baluchistan may be light on ancient monuments, but it crackles with a vigorous blend of people, tree-lined boulevards and sterling British architecture. It also has a dramatic setting, with a mountainous backdrop on all sides, and most sights can be easily walked in a day. Make sure you see the Archaeological Museum of Baluchistan, the fort and one of the city's many colourful bazaars. Not far away you'll find the picture-perfect Hanna Lake, picnic spots in Urak Valley, Hazarganji Chiltan National Park and the dramatic Bolan Pass, which can be seen by train.

North-West Frontier Province

Impenetrable mountains, intractable people, and impossibly romantic cities are just some of the reasons why the NWFP is perhaps the most memorable of Pakistan's destinations. Most visits begin in Peshawar, the rough-and-ready provincial capital, with the fabled Khyber Pass nearby, and the long-standing traveller town of Madyan. North of Peshawar is Chitral, a relatively unspoilt area of lush valleys, hot springs and great walks. Vertigo sufferers should steer clear of Indus Kohistan, west of Gilgit, a land of colossal peaks and bottomless canyons and with more good walks.

The Northern Areas

The Northern Areas see few travellers but those that brave the unruly terrain normally end up in Gilgit, the capital. There's not much in the city, but it's an excellent base for alpine walks, trout fishing and strolling around historical ruins in the countryside. Baltistan, once an unexplored dead end, is now privy to world-class mountaineering, fine treks and lovely scenery. More accessible and just as striking – check out the irrigated terraces rippling down the slopes – is the region of Hunza towards the Chinese border.

Itineraries

ONE WEEK

Fly into Lahore and spend a day or two exploring the city, before taking a flight or train to Islamabad and Rawalpindi. Spend a day in these cities before heading to NWFP for the remainder of your stay, spending a day or so in Peshawar with day trips to the Khyber Pass, the Swat region (Madyan) or Chitral. Alternatively, you could fly to Karachi and go to Islamabad via Quetta (to see Hanna Lake, the Urak Valley or Hazarganji Chiltan National Park) or loop back to Karachi via Moenjodaro.

TWO WEEKS

With another seven days you could take your time getting through the one week itinerary from Karachi, perhaps adding visits to the ancient archaeological sites of Moenjodaro, to the north of Hyderabad, or Harappa. The latter is north-east of Multan, which is a good place for an overnight stop. From Islamabad you could also add a visit to Gilgit in the Northern Areas for some short walks into the Karakoram Range. A popular activity from here is a flight over K2, the second highest peak in the world, for some fine views of the whole Karakoram Range. In NWFP, the Chitral Gol National Park is well worth a couple of days exploration.

PAKISTAN HIGHLIGHTS & ITINERARIES

HUNZA
One of Central Asia's most sublime valleys; lush, friendly and presided over by the amazing 7790m Rakaposhi

CHITRAL GOL NATIONAL PARK
High in the Hindukush, this is a beautiful, easily accessible, but rarely visited sanctuary

AROUND K2
Trek into the throne room of the gods, along glaciers and through probably the finest mountain scenery on the planet

MADYAN
Former hippy mecca; a fine place to sit in the sun, chill out and watch the mountains or take leisurely walks to friendly Pashtun villages

PESHAWAR
Bask in the romance of this ancient frontier town which lies at the east end of the legendary Khyber Pass

ISLAMABAD & RAWALPINDI
Twin cities with a gre bazaar plus museum mosques and a nearb national park

QUETTA
Sample the famed hospitality of the tribal peoples who live in this intriguing and relaxing desert outpost

LAHORE
Visit the museums and admire Moghul architect to rival Delhi's and Agra's this grand centre of cultu art and education

BOLAN PASS
Take a train ride to this historic gateway, for some of the most spectacular window views in Pakistan

UCH SHARIF
Famous for its exquisite Sufi shrines and its festive and colourful celebrations

MOENJODARO
Wander among the ruins of one of the most remarkable cities of the ancient world

KARACHI
Go crab-catching, spend a romantic day sailing an outrigger, or comb the bazaars for Pakistan's best shopping

---

SUGGESTED ITINERARIES

One Week
1 Lahore • Islamabad • Rawalpindi • Peshawar • Khyber Pass • Madyan • Chitral
2 Karachi • Quetta • Hanna Lake • Urak Valley • Hazarganji Chiltan National Park • Islamabad

Two Weeks
1 Lahore • Harappa • Multan • Moenjodaro • Hyderabad • Kar
2 Islamabad • Gilgit • K2 • Chitral Gol National Park

One Month
Hunza Valley • Chitral Gol National Park • Baltistan • Nanga Parbat • Ghiza • Uch Sharif

ONE MONTH

A full month will allow keen trekkers to get a good look at Pakistan's stunning northern mountains. Two weeks walking around the Hunza Valley is a very popular option, but there are also excellent trails in Chitral Gol National Park and the regions of Baltistan, Nanga Parbat and Ghizar. Another place worth visiting (it may or may not be open) is the town of Uch Sharif to the south of Multan, which features magnificent Sufi shrines and colourful local festivals.

Visa Requirements

Just about everybody needs a visa to enter Pakistan. With a single-entry tourist visa you can normally enter within six months from the date of issue, and stay for up to three months from the date of entry. You can go almost anywhere except the sensitive border areas, and remote or high-elevation places where you'd need a trekking or mountaineering permit. Pakistan may refuse entry to nationals of Israel. Travellers arriving in Pakistan without a visa may get a transit visa (also called a landing permit), but policies are constantly changing. Immigration officials are authorised to give a month, but you may get as little as 72 hours, so it's more sensible to apply for a visa at a Pakistani embassy or consulate in your home country. Visas from some consular offices, such as that in Hong Kong, are only valid for three months and good for a one month stay.

Pakistani Embassies & High Commissions

AUSTRALIA
(☎ 02-6290 1676) 4 Timbarra Crescent, O'Malley, ACT 2606. Consulate: Sydney

CANADA
(☎ 613-238-7881) 151 Slater St, Suite 608, Ottawa, Ontario K1P 5H3. Consulates: Montreal and Toronto

HONG KONG
(☎ 852-2827 0681) 3806 China Resources Building, 26 Harbour Rd, Hong Kong

INDIA
(☎ 011-600603/5) 2/50-G Shantipath, Chanakyapuri, New Delhi 110021

UK
(☎ 020-7664 9200; recorded visa information ☎ 0891-880 880) 36 Lowndes Square, London SW1X 9JN. Consulates: Bradford, Manchester, Birmingham and Glasgow

USA
(☎ 202-939-6200, consular section ☎ 939-6295) 2315 Massachusetts Ave NW, Washington, DC 20008. Consulates: New York and Los Angeles

Tourist Offices Overseas

The Pakistan Tourism Development Corporation maintains links with several commercial travel agencies overseas. Your best bet is to talk to your travel agent, read guidebooks and check out some of the web sites under Online Services.

Health

Apart from travellers diarrhoea, malaria is the most likely health risk, year-round anywhere below about 2000m (ie well into the hills), so you should take appropriate precautions. Outbreaks of dengue fever have been reported, so avoid mosquito bites at all times. Contaminated food and water may carry many diseases, including typhoid, hepatitis and dysentery. Tap water, ice, salads, unpeeled fruit, milk products, meat and shellfish should all be avoided, but freshly cooked street food will generally be OK. You should be prepared for both hot and cold conditions, while trekkers in northern

Pakistan should be aware of the symptoms and treatment of altitude sickness. Medical care is basic throughout most of Pakistan. If you require serious medical care, go to a major city or leave Pakistan altogether.

Post & Communications

Pakistan's postal service is reliable and reasonably priced, but slow. There are post restante services in all the big cities. Telephone services are more expensive, but are modern and easy to access. Email and Internet services are slowly appearing, but public facilities are still scarce.

Money

Costs

By staying in hostels or dorms and eating like a local you can get by on as little as US$10 to US$15 a day. If, however, you are looking for a moderate touch of luxury, you could spend as much as US$30 to US$40 – this could get you accommodation that included a satellite TV, a desk, a balcony and a spotlessly clean bathroom. Rooms and food are generally cheaper in the north than in the south.

Changing Money

Both travellers cheques and cash are easy to change throughout the country, but commissions on cheques can be high. Apart from top-end hotels, most places won't accept credit cards as payment, although you can often use them for cash advances at western banks. Facilities for validation seem to be better for Visa than for Master-Card. Occasionally a tattered note will be firmly refused as legal tender, and often in smaller towns the appearance of a 500 or 1000 rupee note will

cause consternation, so make sure you get some small denomination notes when you buy your rupees.

Online Services

Lonely Planet's *Destination Pakistan* page is at www.lonelyplanet.com/dest/ind/pak.htm.

Get your daily news from *Dawn* (dawn.com) and the US-based *Pakistan Link* (www.pakistanlink.com).

If it's possible to be glossy online, Pakistan's only monthly e-zine, *Saher* (www.saher.com), achieves it nicely.

Rensselaer Union's *Pakistan Students Association* (www.rpi.edu/dept/union/paksa) discusses Pakistani history and culture. *Shangri-La* (aleph0.clarku.edu/rajs/Shangri_La.html) attempts to keep alive faith in the Himalaya region despite continuing political difficulties.

Colorful Trucks and Buses of Pakistan (www.ee.vt.edu/aak/pakistan/buses_trucks.html) is much more fun than a train timetable. The *Cyber Muslim Information Collective* (www.uoknor.edu/cybermuslim) isn't a bad starting point to learn about Islam.

Books

Brief but descriptive odysseys through Pakistan can be found in *The Great Railway Bazaar* by Paul Theroux, and Danziger's *Travels by Nick Danziger*. Other good travel narratives include *The Golden Peak: Travels in Northern Pakistan* by Kathleen Jamie, *To the Frontier* by Geoffrey Moorhouse and *Full Tilt* by Dervla Murphy.

Pakistan's historical and cultural traditions get a good going over in the excellent *Every Rock, Every Hill: A Plain Tale of the North-West Frontier & Afghanistan* by Victoria Schofield and *Words For My Brother* by John Staley.

Less recent histories are John Keay's *When Men & Mountains Meet*, Sir George Robertson's *Chitral, The Story of a Minor Siege* and Derek Waller's *The Pundits*.

For fiction, don't ignore *Shame*, Salman Rushdie's engrossing tragi-comic fantasy about ZA Bhutto and General Ziaul-Haq. Rudyard Kipling's *The Man Who Would Be King* and *Kim* provide a British colonial perspective and a romping good read.

Films

While nowhere near the scale of India's Bollywood, Pakistan has a strong local film industry that generates a similar level of fanaticism among fans. Recent films include *Kamyabi*, *Dharkan* and *Zar Gul*. An expatriate view of the Pakistani psyche can be found in *My Beautiful Laundrette* by Hanif Kureishi, which explores a romance between an Anglo-Pakistani and a London skin-head. *K2* is a fictional account of an attempt on this famous peak, while *Nusrat! Live at Meany* showcases the spectacular voice of Pakistan's most famous cultural export.

Entering & Leaving Pakistan

Apart from the overland Hippie Trail (where you enter Pakistan from Iran at Mirjave-Taftan – check the current security situation), flying is your best option, although you can catch a train or express bus to and from India. The other overland route is the Karakoram Highway that leaves Pakistan through the northern Khunjerab Pass and takes you through to Kashgar in China's Xinjiang Province (for more details see the Overland Routes section in the Planning chapter at the front of the book).

Most flights from European and Asian centres arrive in Karachi, although a few also go to Islamabad, Lahore, Quetta, Gwadar (Baluchistan) and Peshawar. However, it is much more interesting to use the train. A railway line links Lahore with India through Amritsar (Wagah and Attari are the nearest border towns), and another from Quetta crosses briefly into Iran. Sea passage is a possibility with cargo ships calling at Karachi from the Middle East and Bombay.

THE PHILIPPINES

This 7107 island archipelago is certainly on the established backpacker trail, but attracts far fewer visitors than many mainland Asian countries. It's worth making the flight, however, as the Philippines offers a blend of beautiful beaches, spectacular volcanoes, rich tracts of jungle, a mix of big cities and isolated villages, and some of the most spectacular diving and snorkelling in the region. In addition, English is widely spoken and travel is relatively cheap, although some transport can be time-consuming and unreliable.

The Filipino people have suffered invasions and exploitation for centuries (from both foreign powers and national leaders), but they remain resilient and tolerant towards tourists. The country is still rebuilding after the depredations of the Marcos era and the disappointment of the Aquino years. Fidel Ramos made some social and economic reforms during his stint at the top, and the world is watching keenly to see whether new president, former film star Joseph Estrada, can maintain this momentum.

Mindanao has in recent years been a political trouble spot and a potentially dangerous destination for visitors, with the predominantly Muslim population campaigning for separation from the rest of the country. However, in 1996 a settlement was reached between a Muslim-front organisation and the central government. Mindanao is mostly safe these days, but check with your embassy.

When to Go

The Philippines can be visited and enjoyed year-round, since temperatures are generally warm and even in the wet season it seldom rains all day,

---

AT A GLANCE

Full Country Name: Republic of the Philippines

Area: 300,000 sq km

Population: 73 million

Capital City: Manila (pop 11 million)

People: 87% Malay/Indonesian origin, 11% tribal Filipinos and 1.5% Chinese (plus a significant number of people of mixed Spanish or American heritage, known as Mestizos)

Languages: Tagalog, English, Cebuano, Ilocano, Ilonggo, Bicol, Waray-Waray, Pampango, Pangasinan and Samar-Leyte (although Spain controlled the country for more than 300 years, Spanish is rarely spoken)

Religion: 83% Roman Catholic, 9% Protestant, 5% Muslim and 3% Buddhist

Government: Constitutional republic

Currency: Philippines peso (P)

Time Zone: Eight hours ahead of GMT/UTC

International Telephone Code: 63

Electricity: Mostly 220V 60AC, in some areas 110V; sockets take flat, two-pin

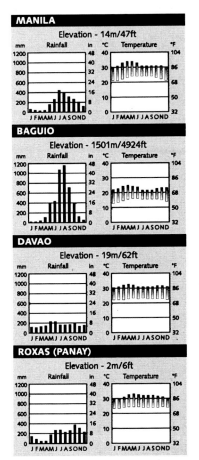

MANILA
Elevation - 14m/47ft

BAGUIO
Elevation - 1501m/4924ft

DAVAO
Elevation - 19m/62ft

ROXAS (PANAY)
Elevation - 2m/6ft

although there is significant regional variation. If you are visiting the western side of Luzon or the islands of Mindoro, Panay, Negros or Palawan, the best months are from November to May, before the onset of typhoons (June to October is a rainy period in these areas). The eastern side of South Luzon and the islands of Samar, Leyte and Mindanao follow a different pattern, receiving heavy rains between

November and January. Other regions have less pronounced seasons and more uniformly distributed rainfall. If you plan to do some island-hopping, then you should avoid Christmas and Easter, when buses and ferries are crowded and cancellations frequent. Even outside these periods, you should make allowances for the unreliability of ferry schedules (with the exception of the 'fastcraft' ferries which seem to operate like clockwork). If you dislike humidity, you can find some relief in the mountain areas, such as Baguio in North Luzon.

Highlights

Manila
The Philippine capital does have a few sights, but many travellers opt to flee this big polluted city at the first opportunity and head for the many attractions elsewhere. If you find yourself with a day or two to kill, check out the Spanish remains in Intramuros (one of the few historic sights to survive the bitter fighting at the end of WWII), the church of San Agustin, the Roman Catholic cathedral and Fort Santiago.

Banaue
The spectacular rice terraces around Banaue and Batad in North Luzon have been described (like a lot of other places) as the eighth wonder of the world, but in this case it's actually true. Carved out of the hillside by Ifugao tribespeople over 2000 years, these remarkable terraces stretch like stepping stones to the sky – some reaching an altitude of 1500m. Access to Batad previously meant a 12km hike from Banaue, but a controversial new road should be finished by the time you read this.

Beaches

The island of Boracay, off the north-western tip of Panay, has long been the accepted 'island to visit' in the Philippines, but unchecked tourist development has caused waste disposal problems. Different environmental tests have declared it both contaminated and safe, but Boracay's beaches certainly look pristine. Puerto Galera on the island of Mindoro is now destined to be *the* place to laze around in the sun. Puraran, on Catanduanes just off Luzon, also has a beautiful beach, reef and surf, but the currents can be dangerous.

Remote Islands

For real Robinson Crusoe fare, try the islands north of Bohol in the Visayas. Alternatively, Gutob Bay (between Culion and Busuanga islands in the west) has the picturesque Dibutonay, Maltatayoc and Horse islands. The Batanes islands in the north and Palawan to the west are surprisingly unspoilt and differ from other islands due to their isolation and the opportunity to visit remote villages.

Vigan

In North Luzon, Vigan displays some precious remnants of the splendid architectural legacy of the Spaniards. The well preserved colonial structures create a 17th century European atmosphere. The town has several museums, as it's the birthplace of a few national heroes.

Viriato

On the island of Samar, in the Visayas, Viriato lies along one of the most scenic coastal roads in the country. The road runs past steep mountains and picturesque boat-filled bays, with islands dotted far out to sea. The town also boasts a large waterfall and good hiking opportunities.

Lake Sebu & Mt Apo National Park

A beautiful inland sea on the island of Mindanao, Lake Sebu sits high within the Tiruray Highlands. The chance to delve into traditional lifestyles and culture, rather than modern attractions, are the highlights in this remote area. The local tribespeople, the T'boli, do not interact much with the outside world and are known for their beautiful brass and fabric products. Their Saturday market is well worth a visit. Further south, Mt Apo National Park offers some rugged hiking and the opportunity to see the rare Philippine monkey-eating eagle.

Other Attractions

There are countless spectacular sights scattered throughout the archipelago, including the strange Chocolate Hills of Bohol in the Visayas; the volcanic crater Lake Taal south of Manila; the burial caves and hanging coffins of Sagada near Bontoc; the easy-going port of Cebu City; and 5000 uninhabited islands to explore.

Itineraries

If time is not a problem, island-hopping can be fun in the Philippines. But if your time is limited, take into account the unreliability of some ferry routes, notably during the rainy season. The possibilities are endless, but here are a few suggested itineraries:

ONE WEEK

Spend a day in Manila and then head north to take in the astonishing rice terraces at Banaue, before making a detour to Central

Cordillera, particularly Sagada for hikes to the burial caves, an underground river and a swimming hole. On the way back to Manila, stop in at the cool highlands of Baguio and the beach resorts near Bauang (or better still, the Hundred islands from the town of Alaminos), or hike up the giant volcano, Mt Pinatubo (1450m).

Alternatively, head south by bus from Manila to Batangas for a ferry to Puerto Galera on Mindoro. The views of the small islands that are sprinkled throughout the Batangas Channel make the ferry ride a delight. At Puerto Galera you can enjoy excellent snorkelling and diving on the northern beaches and visit a Mangyan village in the hills above the town. A day trip to Calapan is a good option, as is hiking in the beautiful jungles of the central mountains.

If you have flown directly to Cebu City, you can catch ferries to several nearby islands in the Visayan archipelago. They offer secluded beaches, wonderful hiking, a tranquil lifestyle and the chance to learn about historical figures such as the explorer Ferdinand Magellan. The islands include Bohol (see the Chocolate Hills or go diving at Alona Beach on nearby Panglao Island), Leyte (linked to Samar by a magnificent 2km-long bridge), Negros and Mindanao (to see Lake Sebu and trek in Mt Apo National Park). You can explore one or more of these islands before returning to Cebu to explore it and Mactan Island.

TWO WEEKS

From Manila, travel to the island of Mindoro and head south to Roxas via Calapan, then island-hop by ferry to the Romblon islands of Boracay, Romblon or Panay. Boracay is a delightful little island for swimming, diving or simple relaxation, but is increasingly touristed. From Kalibo or Iloilo City on Panay, you can fly to Manila or Cebu. There are many permutations to this itinerary using ferries to island-hop within the Visayas, particularly Leyte and Bohol, and to Mindanao (see the one week itineraries for suggestions).

ONE MONTH

From Manila, follow the earlier one week itinerary to Banaue and then do a loop north

to Vigan via San Fernando for a Spanish architecture hit. Return to Manila and head south-east by road to Luzon's rugged and volcanic southern peninsula. Stop off at the mighty Mayon Volcano, near Legaspi, which is said to be the most perfectly symmetrical summit in the world. Continue down to Matnog where you can catch a ferry to Allen at the northern end of Samar and then travel by road down the west coast of Samar, taking in the beautiful scenery near Viriato. Before you cross the bridge to Tacloban, on Leyte, take a detour south and check out the bejewelled-like rock formations of the caves in the Sohoton National Park. After a few days relaxation on Leyte, catch a ferry to Cebu City, which is a transport hub for travel to numerous other islands in the area. A good three to four day trip takes you by plane to Palawan to see the caves, waterfalls and underground river of the St Paul Subterranean National Park near Sabang, and the beautiful Bacuit Peninsula to the north.

This itinerary can be done as quickly or slowly as you wish, and allows ample opportunity for extended walks, days lying on the beach or interacting with the hospitable locals in this area. The journey can of course be undertaken in the reverse order, starting at Cebu City and making your way in an anticlockwise semicircle to Manila.

Visa Requirements

Nationals of most countries (other than India, China and some socialist countries) are allowed to stay for 21 days without a visa. If you are planning to stay longer, you can either obtain a visa from a Philippines embassy or consulate prior to arrival, or obtain an extension (in Manila, Cebu City or Angeles) during the first 21 days after your arrival. An extension to 59 days is straightforward and further extensions are possible.

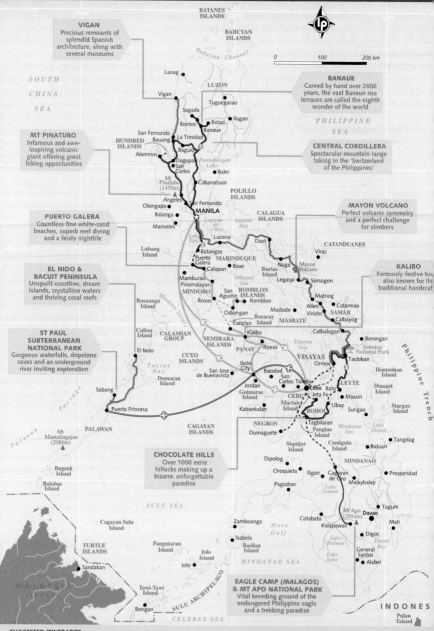

VIGAN
Precious remnants of splendid Spanish architecture, along with several museums

BANAUE
Carved by hand over 2000 years, the vast Banaue rice terraces are called the eighth wonder of the world

MT PINATUBO
Infamous and awe-inspiring volcanic giant offering great hiking opportunities

CENTRAL CORDILLERA
Spectacular mountain range taking in the 'Switzerland of the Philippines'

PUERTO GALERA
Countless fine white-sand beaches, superb reef diving and a feisty nightlife

MAYON VOLCANO
Perfect volcanic symmetry and a perfect challenge for climbers

EL NIDO & BACUIT PENINSULA
Unspoilt coastline, dream islands, crystalline waters and thriving coral reefs

KALIBO
Famously festive town also known for its traditional handcraft

ST PAUL SUBTERRANEAN NATIONAL PARK
Gorgeous waterfalls, dripstone caves and an underground river inviting exploration

CHOCOLATE HILLS
Over 1000 eerie hillocks making up a bizarre, unforgettable paradise

EAGLE CAMP (MALAGOS) & MT APO NATIONAL PARK
Vital breeding ground of the endangered Philippine eagle and a trekking paradise

SUGGESTED ITINERARIES

One Week
① Manila • Banaue • Sagada • Baguio • Bauang • Hundred Islands
② Manila • Batangas • Peurto Galero • Calapan
③ Cebu City • Bohol • Panglao Island • Leyte • Negros • Mindanao • Mt Apo

Two Weeks
Manila • Mindoro • Calapan • Boracay Island • Panay • Kalibo • Roxas • Iloilo City • Cebu

One Month
Manila • Banaue • Vigan • Manila • Mayon Volcano • Matnog • Allen • Samar • Viriato • Sohoton National Park • Leyte • Cebu City • Palawan • Sabang • St Paul Subterranean National Park

Philippine Embassies

AUSTRALIA
(☎ 02-6273 2535) 1 Moonah Place,
Yarralumla, ACT 2600

CANADA
(☎ 613-233-1121) 130 Albert St,
Ottawa, Ontario K1P 5G4

NEW ZEALAND
(☎ 04-472 9921) 50 Hobson St,
Thorndon, Wellington

UK
(☎ 020-7937 1600) 9A Palace Green,
London W84 QE

USA
(☎ 202-467-9300) 1600 Massachusetts
Ave NW, Washington, DC 20036

Tourist Offices Overseas

Department of Tourism (DOT) offices
overseas include:

AUSTRALIA
(☎ 02-9299 6815) Wynyard House,
Suite 703, Level 7, 301 George St,
Sydney, NSW 2000

UK
(☎ 020-7835 1100) 9A Palace Green,
London W84 QE

USA
(☎ 213-487-4527) Suite 216, 3660
Wilshire Blvd, Los Angeles, CA 90010;
(☎ 415-956-4060) Suite 507, 447
Sutter St, San Francisco, CA 94108;
(☎ 212-575-7915) Philippine Center,
556 Fifth Ave, New York, NY 10036

Health

Malaria exists in rural areas, but is not
usually a risk to travellers. There have
been recent large outbreaks of dengue
fever, so take appropriate precautions
to avoid mosquito bites during the
day. Food and waterborne diseases,
including dysentery, hepatitis and liver
flukes, are a risk. You should be particularly wary of eating shellfish, which
are periodically affected by algae ('red
tide'), causing diarrhoea and vomiting,
visual disturbances and even breathing
problems. Schistosomiasis (bilharzia)
occurs in the southern part of the country – avoid bathing or even paddling in
fresh water.

Medical infrastructure can be acceptable in the big cities, but in rural
areas it's almost nonexistent. Give
thought to a flight to Singapore, Hong
Kong or Kuala Lumpur if you are
seriously ill.

Post & Communications

The Philippine mail service is cheap
and reasonably reliable, but if you are
sending film or important documents,
it is best to send it by registered post.
There are post restante services in all
the major cities. The telephone system
is old and prone to breakdown, and
outside of the cities telephones are
a scarce commodity. Local calls are
cheap, but it can take a very long time
to make a connection. International
calls are easier to make, but come at a
high price. Internet and email services
are hardly commonplace, but there's
an increasing number of cybercafes
opening up in the cities and popular
traveller spots.

Money

Costs

Compared with western nations, costs
are low in the Philippines, but not
everything is cheap. You can travel
100km in an air-conditioned bus for a
couple of US dollars, but food and
accommodation tend to be a bit
higher than in many other parts of
South-East Asia. The cheapest areas
are the mountains of North Luzon and
the less popular islands, while the most
expensive are Manila and the more
heavily frequented islands such as
Boracay and Cebu.

Changing Money

The US dollar is the easiest and best currency to change. US dollar travellers cheques are safer and yield a good rate, but you should use the better known brands and cash them in the larger cities. ATMs are found in cities and most towns, and major credit cards are widely accepted. Small-denomination notes are difficult to come by (for locals as well as travellers), so stock up where you can; otherwise you may find it hard to get change from purchases with larger notes.

Online Services

Lonely Planet's *Destination The Philippines* page is at www.lonelyplanet .com/dest/sea/phil.htm.

Tribung Pinoy (www.tribo.org) is a lively 'web journal dedicated to the Philippines, the Filipino People and the Filipino Diaspora', and includes links to a series of personal travelogues (www .mcs.net/~asia1/travel/personal.html).

Get your daily Filipino news from the *Philippine Star* (www.philstar.com) or fortnightly from the *Philippine Reporter* (www.phil-reporter.com).

The *San Francisco Philippine Consulate* (www.filipino.com) has official information on regulations, customs, banking and drug laws, plus details on everything from major attractions down to how much to tip porters at the airport. You'll find more dry but useful travel information at the imaginatively titled *Travel Information of Philippines* page (www.sino .net/asean/philippn .html).

The *Haribon Foundation* (www .haribon.org.ph/indexa.htm) keeps an eye on all things ecological and Filipino. Get the lowdown on the country from someone who knows the turf at

Antoinette's Life in These Islands (www .gsilink.com/~go2net).

Books

A Short History of the Philippines by Teodoro Agoncillo is a general introduction to the country's past. *The Philippines* and *Readings in Philippine History* by Horacio de la Costa are good reads if you're not keen on formal historical analysis. *For Every Tear A Victory* by Hartzell Spence is reckoned to be the best Marcos biography. *Corazon Aquino and the Brushfire Revolution* by Robert Reid & Eileen Guerrero clinically appraises the Aquino presidency.

Timothy Mo's *Brownout on Breadfruit Boulevard* throws light on Manila's murky political twilight zone. Alex Garland brings together three slices of Manila life in *Tesseract.*

Films

There are many films produced in the Philippines, but the quality is uneven. Many deal with violence – the word 'blood' features in a surprisingly large proportion of them – and subtlety is rare. Occasionally a more creative work such as Tahimik's *Mababangong Bangungot* emerges. Screened overseas as *The Perfumed Nightmare*, this film depicts a young Filipino as a sort of innocent in Paris who finds that urban life has its disadvantages. One notable western film shot in the Philippines is *Apocalypse Now.*

Entering & Leaving the Philippines

Although there are many ferries in the waters around the Philippines (routes are often not operating due to pirates in the Celebes Sea), the only realistic way to enter the country is by plane.

There are many airlines flying between the Philippines and other Asian countries, as well as Australia and North America. Most flights terminate in Manila, but Cebu City has become a more pleasant option in recent years. You can also fly in to Laoag in North Luzon (the area from which Marcos originated) or, if you do not mind a little danger, to Davao on Mindanao. Ferry routes include those between Manado in north Sulawesi and Davao, and Sandakan (Sabah) and Zamboanga (Mindanao).

Lying almost on the equator, Singapore is a thriving city-state that has overcome its dearth of natural resources to become one of the juggernaut economies of Asia. A city of concrete, glass and steel, renowned for its hi-tech wizardry, Singapore also offers a taste of the great Asian cultures in a small, easy-to-manage package. In the crowded streets of Chinatown, fortune tellers, calligraphers and temple worshippers are still a part of everyday life. In Little India, you can buy the best sari material, freshly ground spices or a picture of your favourite Hindu god. In the small shops of Arab St, the cry of the imam can be heard from the nearby Sultan Mosque. Singapore may no longer be a rough-and-ready port of rickshaws, opium dens, pearl luggers and pirates, but you can recapture the colonial era with a gin sling under the languorous ceiling fans at the Raffles Hotel, dine out at the renovated quays along the Singapore River and visit the Victorian relics that have survived the city's relentless development. It is this combination of western modernity and a treasured eastern and colonial past that makes Singapore so accessible.

When to Go
Go anytime – climate is not a major consideration, as Singapore gets fairly steady annual rainfall. You may wish to time your visit with a festival – Thaipusam (around February) is one of the most spectacular. If you're after shopping and eating, July is a good time as the Singapore Food Festival and Great Singapore Sale are held then.

AT A GLANCE

Full Country Name: Republic of Singapore

Area: 646 sq km

Population: 3.1 million

Capital City: Singapore

People: 75% Chinese, 15% Malay, 8% Indian, 2% other nationalities

Languages: Mandarin, Malay, Tamil and English

Religion: 65% Buddhist/Taoist/Confucian, 18% Muslim, 9% Christian, 6% Hindu and 2% Sikh

Government: Parliamentary democracy

Currency: Singapore dollar (S$)

Time Zone: Eight hours ahead of GMT/UTC

International Telephone Code: 65

Electricity: 220V to 240V, 50 AC; plugs are the three pronged, square-pin type used in the UK

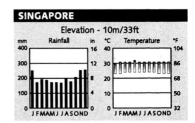

Highlights & Itineraries

The best way to get a feel for Singapore is to wander around the inner city. Though the ethnic areas are quickly becoming dining and drinking venues rather than repositories of traditional culture, Chinatown, Little India and Arab St are still fascinating areas.

SINGAPORE RIVER

One of the most successful redevelopment projects is along the river, worth a wander at any time but especially in the evening when the restaurants and bars are packed. Boat Quay is now Singapore's premier nightspot, while Clarke Quay is more family-oriented, with shopping, children's rides and open-air entertainment. A riverboat tour is an excellent way to view this historic artery through the city.

SENTOSA

Further afield, Sentosa is Singapore's answer to Disneyland, though the comparison is a loose one. This theme-park island has plenty of rides, family attractions and even beaches, while Fort Siloso, Images of Singapore and Underwater World provide more educational entertainment.

ZOOLOGICAL GARDENS & JURONG BIRD PARK

The Singapore Zoo is one of Singapore's most popular attractions. Even if you normally avoid zoos like the plague, the spacious and well designed enclosures make it seem more like an animal resort. Highly recommended is the Night Safari next to the zoo, which allows you to view animals along jungle paths at night. The Jurong Bird Park is another attraction, with beautifully landscaped gardens, an enormous variety of birdlife and well tended enclosures.

GARDENS

Green and clean Singapore has plenty of gardens to visit. The pick of them is the Botanic Gardens, or if you want to walk in the jungle, Bukit Timah Nature Reserve is about as far away from the city as you can get.

ORCHARD ROAD

Last but not least, every visitor ends up on Orchard Rd, and some never get beyond it. It's a dazzling strip of modern delights, with shopping centres, luxury hotels, hundreds of restaurants and a profusion of nightspots strung along it.

Visa Requirements

Citizens of Commonwealth countries (except India), Ireland, the Netherlands, Switzerland and the USA do not need visas for visits of up to 30 days. Citizens of Austria, Belgium, France, Germany, Italy, Japan, Norway, Spain and the Scandinavian countries do not need visas for stays of up to 90 days for social purposes.

Upon arrival, a 14 or 30 day permit is normally issued depending on your stated length of stay. You can easily extend a 14 day permit for another two weeks but you may be asked to show an air ticket out of Singapore and/or sufficient funds to stay. Further extensions are more difficult but in theory most nationalities can extend their permits for up to 90 days.

Singaporean Embassies & High Commissions

AUSTRALIA
(☎ 02-6273 3944) 17 Forster Crescent, Yarralumla, ACT 2600

CANADA
(☎ 604-669-5115) 999 W Hastings St, Vancouver, BC D6C2W2

NEW ZEALAND
(☎ 04-479 2076) 17 Kabul St, Khandallah, Wellington

UK
(☎ 020-7235 8315) 9 Wilton Crescent, London SW1X 8RW

USA
(☎ 202-537-3100) 3501 International Place NW, Washington, DC 20008

Tourist Offices Overseas

The Singapore Tourism Board operates sevral offices overseas, including:

AUSTRALIA
(☎ 02-9290 2888) Level 11, AWA Building, 47 York St, Sydney, NSW 2000;
(☎ 08-9325 8578) 8th floor, St Georges Ct, 16 St Georges Tce, Perth, WA 6000

CANADA
(☎ 416-363-8898) The Standard Life Centre, 121 King St West, Suite 1000, Toronto, Ontario M5H 3T9

UK
(☎ 020-7437 0033) 1st floor, Carrington House, 26-130 Regent St, London W1R 5FE

USA
(☎ 213-852-1901) 8484 Wilshire Blvd, Suite 510, Beverly Hills, CA 90211;
(☎ 212-302-4861) 12th floor, 590 Fifth Ave, New York, NY 10036;
(☎ 312-938-1888) Two Presidential Plaza, 180N Stetson Ave, Suite 1450, Chicago, IL 60601

Health

Dengue fever occurs, so try to avoid mosquito bites. Malaria is not a risk – the cases reported in the media are imported cases, usually in locals returning from a holiday in the neighbouring islands. Singapore's water is potable, its food generally fine and its hospitals among the best in the region.

Post & Communications

Singapore's postal and telecommunications infrastructure is world-class and the costs quite reasonable. There's a post restante service at the Robinson Rd post office. International phone calls can be made practically anywhere, but the many public phones that take phonecards are the cheapest and easiest option. Singapore has plenty of Internet cafes.

Money

Costs

Singapore is far more expensive than the other South-East Asian countries, which may come as a shock if you are travelling on a shoestring budget. You can still stay here, however, without spending too much if you can forego the temptation to run amok in the shops or indulge in luxuries you may have craved while travelling in other Asian countries. It's possible to stay in Singapore for under US$20 a day if you stay in hostels and eat cheaply. If you're staying in mid-range hotels and eating at good restaurants, US$70 is a more realistic daily minimum.

Changing Money

All major credit cards are widely accepted, although you're not going to make yourself too popular after a hard bargaining session for a new camera if you try to pay for it with your Visa card. ATMs are widespread, although it's still a good idea to take cash and travellers cheques for emergencies. You'll find moneychangers in shopping centres all over Singapore. Moneychangers do not charge fees, so you will often get a better overall exchange rate for cash and travellers cheques than at the banks. As well as changing other currencies to Singapore dollars, moneychangers sell a wide variety of currencies and will dazzle you with amazing multiple-currency transactions in the blink of an eye.

Online Services

Lonely Planet's *Destination Singapore* page is at www.lonelyplanet.com/dest/sea/sing.htm.
It wouldn't be Singapore without

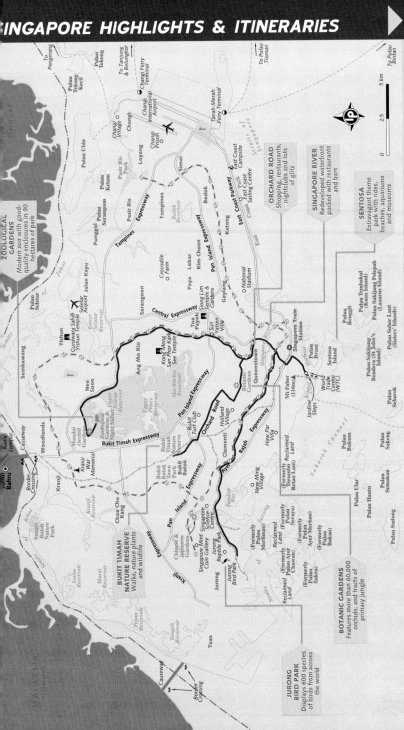

ZOOLOGICAL GARDENS
Modern zoo with good-quality enclosures in 90 hectares of park

ORCHARD ROAD
Shopping, restaurants, nightclubs and lots of glitz

SINGAPORE RIVER
Redeveloped waterfront packed with restaurants and bars

SENTOSA
Extravagant theme park with rides, beaches, aquariums and museums

BUKIT TIMAH NATURE RESERVE
Walks, nature plants and wildlife

BOTANIC GARDENS
Features more than 60,000 orchids, and tracts of primary jungle

JURONG BIRD PARK
Displays 600 species of birds from across the world

SUGGESTED ITINERARIES

One Week Singapore River • Sentosa Island • Jurong Bird Park • Bukit Timah Nature Reserve • Botanic Gardens • Zoological Gardens

a plethora of super-efficient official sites such as *Singapore InfoMap* (www.sg), while doggedly detailed travel information can be found at *Travel Information on Singapore* (www.sino.net/asean/spore.html).

If you're into pink drinks, find out how to concoct a *Singapore Sling* (www.inforamp.net/~stpbyyz/sinsling .html) and for details of what's going on in town, check out the *Straits Times* (straitstimes.asia1.com/).

Four major Singapore museums can be accessed at *Singapore's Online Museum* (www.museum.org.sg), dedicated to 'preserving the heritage of the people of Singapore'.

Books

A History of Singapore by CM Turnbull provides a detailed overview of Singapore's history from prehistory to the present. *Lee Kuan Yew – The Struggle for Singapore* by Alex Josey covers the former prime minister's rise to power and the successful path along which his People's Action Party piloted Singapore. Fictional accounts of Singapore can be found in Joseph Conrad's *Lord Jim*, Paul Theroux's *Saint Jack*, W Somerset Maugham's *Borneo Stories* and James Clavell's *King Rat*.

Fistful of Colours by Suchen Christine Lim (winner of the Singapore Literature Prize) contrasts the differences and discusses the tensions between modern and traditional ethnic communities in Singapore.

Films

During the 1920s, 30s and 40s, Singapore's exotic reputation resulted in a plethora of Hollywood films being set there, including *Across to Singapore* (1928) starring Ramon Novarro and Joan Crawford, *Road to Singapore* (1940) starring Bing Crosby and Bob Hope, *The Blonde From Singapore* (1941) and *Singapore* (1947).

Singapore has a flourishing film industry. Recent local productions include *Ah Tong, The Hainanese Falcon, August, The Cage* (all 1991), *Army Daze* (1996), *Forever Fever* (1998) and

WHAT A FINE COUNTRY

'Singapore is a fine country,' said the taxi driver. 'In Singapore we have fines for everything.' In Singapore a number of activities are frowned upon, and the sometimes draconian methods of dealing with minor transgressions have caused both mirth and dread among visitors. The famous campaign against long hair is now a thing of the past, but it wasn't all that long ago that long-haired men were turned away on arrival at the airport or given a short-back-and-sides on the spot.

Singapore remains tough on a number of other minor 'offences', and the standard way of stamping out un-Singaporean activities is to slap a hefty fine on any offender. Smoking in public places is out. You can smoke at food stalls and on the street (as long as you dispose of your cigarette butt correctly, of course). The move to ban smoking in private cars was eventually quashed because of the difficulty of enforcing it. Jaywalking (walking across the road within 50m of a designated crossing) is also a fineable offence. The successful anti-littering campaign continues, and not surprisingly, Singapore is amazingly clean. The public transport system (the MRT) offers transgressors some particularly heavy fines. Eating, drinking and smoking are forbidden, and watch out if you use the MRT toilet and forget to flush. The sale and importation of chewing gum is now banned and subject to heavy fines, though individual possession is not an offence.

Bailiu Libai (Lucky Number; 1999). *Fatal Reaction: Singapore* (1997) is a documentary on the difficulties that educated, mature Singaporean women can encounter in finding a husband.

Entering & Leaving Singapore

A swag of airlines fly into Singapore's ultramodern Changi international airport (often voted one of the best airports in the world). Lots of visitors combine their stay with a visit to Malaysia, which is just 1km away across the Causeway over the Straits of Johor. You can travel between Malaysia and Singapore very easily by bus or taxi. A vehicle and passenger ferry operates between north Changi in Singapore and Tanjung Belungkor, east of Johor Bahru (Malaysia), and a daily high-speed catamaran links Singapore with Malaysia's Pulau Tioman. Immaculate air-conditioned buses link Singapore to almost all large Malaysian cities; fares are generally inexpensive. Singapore is the southern terminus of Malaysia's rail system and there are four trains a day to Kuala Lumpur.

There are no direct passenger ferries between Singapore and the principal ports of Indonesia, but it is possible to travel between the two countries via the Indonesian islands of the Riau Archipelago, immediately south of Singapore. Modern ferries link Singapore with Batam and Bintan, and speedboats link Batam with Pekanbaru in Sumatra, and several ships a week link Bintan with Jakarta.

SOUTH KOREA

It's a miracle that South Korea still exists. With China looming to its west and Japan nudging it from the east, the country has played unwilling host to centuries of war games. Poking delicately into the East Sea (Sea of Japan), the little peninsula has proved an irresistibly tasty morsel to its hungry neighbours. But no matter how often they try to swallow it, Korea, like plasticine, comes out the other end largely intact. Koreans attribute their indigestible culture to the binding agents of Confucianism, language and pride. Korea's stunning landscape, and the Korean obsession with tramping over every piece of it, has also played a big part in creating a cohesive national identity. Seoul has many attractions, but the rest of the peninsula has lots to see, food and accommodation are plentiful and quite cheap, and transport is reliable and efficient. You may be surprised by what a good time you'll have.

When to Go

If you possibly can, visit in autumn (September to November). It's sunny, the skies are blue, and the autumn foliage is spectacular. Winter (December to March) is cold but dry, and a good time to visit if you like skiing, snow-draped temples, a dearth of tourists, and crisp (ie below freezing) weather. Spring (April to May) can be beautiful, but it's also the most popular time with Japanese tourists and you'll have trouble getting mid-range to top-end accommodation. Summer (June to August) is hot, muggy, crowded, wet, typhoon-prone and expensive.

Highlights

Seoul seems to be an irresistible attraction for many visitors to Korea. It certainly has a lot to recommend it, but make the effort to get out of the city limits and explore the rest of the peninsula. You can literally cross the country in less than five hours, so you can cram a lot into quite a short stay.

AT A GLANCE

Full Country Name: Republic of Korea

Area: 120,540 sq km

Population: 45 million

Capital City: Seoul (pop 12 million)

People: Almost 100% Korean, with a small expat community (mostly American)

Language: Korean

Religion: 47% Buddhist, 28% Christian, 25% Shamanist, Confucian and Ch'ondogyo

Government: Constitutional republic

Currency: Korean won (W)

International Telephone Code: 82

Time Zone: Nine hours ahead of GMT/UTC

Electricity: Both 110V and 220V are common, at 60 AC; the design of the outlet indicates the voltage – two flat pins is 110V and two round pins is 220V

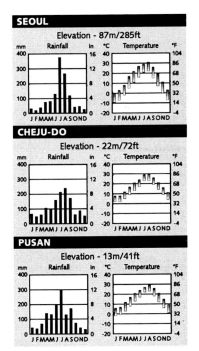

SEOUL

Elevation - 87m/285ft

CHEJU-DO

Elevation - 22m/72ft

PUSAN

Elevation - 13m/41ft

Seoul

Seoul is both mega-modern and appealingly ancient. Flattened in the Korean War, most of the city has been rebuilt since the 1950s. Peeking out from among the 12-lane freeways, Seoul has a hidden history of temples, palaces, pagodas and pleasure gardens. It also has cheap accommodation, excellent public transport, a thriving nightlife and cultural experiences aplenty. Seoul is justifiably famous for its palaces, of which the restored Kyongbokkung and Ch'anggyonggung are the best known.

Korean Folk Village

It sounds ultra-cheesy, but the Korean Folk Village is actually a very tasteful

way to immerse yourself in rural Korean life and is just a day trip away from Seoul. The village has examples of traditional housing styles from all over the country, as well as artisan workshops, a brewery, a Confucian school, a Buddhist temple and a marketplace. This is a real village, not just a tourist show – the people working here also live here. There are buses every 20 minutes from Seoul.

National Parks

The peninsula is dotted with national parks featuring magnificent natural scenery, timeless temples and loads of Koreans checking it all out. At the top of the charts is Soraksan National Park; close to the Demilitarised Zone (DMZ) on the east coast, an area of high craggy peaks, lush forests, boulder-strewn white-water rivers, tremendous waterfalls, beaches and ancient temples. Other popular national parks include Kayasan (which houses Tripitaka Koreana – the complete Buddhist scriptures carved on 80,000 wooden blocks dating from the 14th century), Songnisan (with some of Korea's best hiking and the magnificent temple site of Popchusa), Chirisan (the oldest and still one of the best) and Puk'ansan (an easy day trip from Seoul).

Islands

Korea's coast is littered with islands. To the south, Cheju-do's balmy climate attracts huge numbers of locals fleeing the bitter winter on the mainland; it also features Hallasan National Park, Korea's highest mountain, waterfalls and a culture that's an ancient off-shoot of mainstream Korean culture. Ullungdo, isolated between Korea and Japan, is spectacularly rugged and offers great hiking and superb diving in its frigid waters. Many of Korea's other islands are also national parks, including the 1700 islands which make up Tadohae Haesang National Park on the southern coast.

Itineraries

ONE WEEK
Spend a couple of days sampling Seoul's sights and sounds, before taking the short trip north to Puk'ansan National Park to hike its granite peaks and see the Puk'ansansong mountain fortress which dates from 300 AD. This can be a day trip, but there are plenty of overnight hikes, plus challenging climbs for the serious. Many travellers continue to the DMZ at P'anmunjom, but this is frankly overrated and outrageously expensive. A better option is to take a bus from Seoul to Soraksan National Park to drink in some of South Korea's most spectacular scenery and then, if time permits, flash down the east coast to see the temples, tombs and pagodas at Kyongju, before returning to Seoul for your flight out or continuing to Pusan for a ferry or flight to Japan.

TWO WEEKS
Follow the one week itinerary to the east coast and take a boat from Hup'o to Ullungdo for an overnight visit to this rugged island. Return to P'ohang and continue to Kyongju for a couple of days. There are several national parks within easy striking distance of here, including Kyongju, Kayasan, Chuwangsan, Chirisan and the island-based Hallyo'haesang and Tadohae Haesang national parks. Alternatively take a boat to Cheju-do and spend a few days taking in the sun, exploring the mountains, and battling the hordes of domestic and Japanese tourists. Return to Seoul via the ancient capital of Puyo, a laid-back place with one of the best museums in the country.

ONE MONTH
In four weeks you can take in all of the above sights, with additional side trips to T'ongdosa on the south-east coast – which

features the country's best known temple – and some of the central and west coast national parks, such as Naejangsan, Pyonsan-bando, Woraksan, Songnisan and Togyusan. Other popular options include an overnight boat ride to the nature reserve island of Hongdo, to the west of Mok'po, or a couple of days relaxing at the hot springs at Suanbo.

Visa Requirements
With an onward ticket, citizens of Australia, Canada, New Zealand, the UK and the USA will be granted a transit stay of up to 15 days (nonextendable) without a visa. South Korea has a reciprocal visa-exemption agreement with the UK and Canada which permits stays of 90 days and 180 days respectively. Citizens of all other countries – including Australia, New Zealand and the USA – need visas for stays over 15 days and these must be arranged before you arrive. South Korean embassies are often slow in issuing visas – allow a minimum three working days no matter what they tell you.

South Korean Embassies
AUSTRALIA
(☎ 02-6273 3044) 113 Empire Circuit, Yarralumla, ACT 2600. Consulate: Sydney

CANADA
(☎ 613-232-1715) 5th floor, 151 Slater St, Ottawa, Ontario K1P 5H3. Consulates: Toronto and Vancouver

NEW ZEALAND
(☎ 04-473 9073) 11th floor, ASB Bank, Tower Building, 2 Hunter St, Wellington

UK
(☎ 020-7581 0247) 4 Palace Gate, London W8 5NF

USA
(☎ 202-939-5600) 2450 Massachusetts Ave NW, Washington, DC 20008. Consulates: Agana, Anchorage, Atlanta, Boston, Chicago, Honolulu, Houston, Los Angeles, Miami, New York, San Francisco and Seattle

SOUTH KOREA HIGHLIGHTS & ITINERARIES

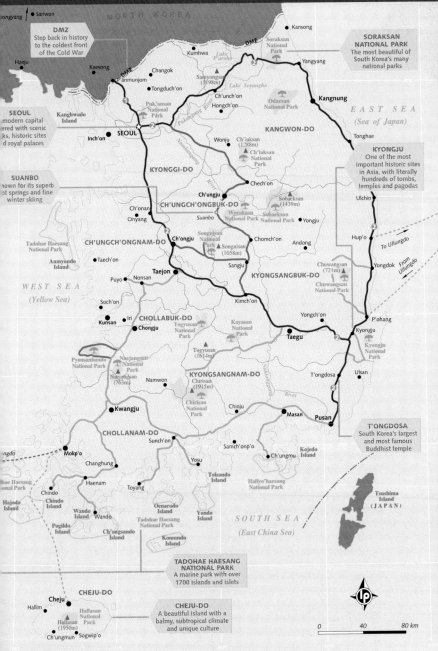

DMZ
Step back in history to the coldest front of the Cold War

SORAKSAN NATIONAL PARK
The most beautiful of South Korea's many national parks

SEOUL
modern capital ...ered with scenic ...ks, historic sites ...d royal palaces

SUANBO
...nown for its superb ...ot springs and fine ...winter skiing

KYONGJU
One of the most important historic sites in Asia, with literally hundreds of tombs, temples and pagodas

T'ONGDOSA
South Korea's largest and most famous Buddhist temple

TADOHAE HAESANG NATIONAL PARK
A marine park with over 1700 islands and islets

CHEJU-DO
A beautiful island with a balmy, subtropical climate and unique culture

NORTH KOREA

...ongyang • Sariwon

Haeju

Kaesong

Kanghwado Island

Inch'on

SEOUL

Kumhwa
Lake P'uroho
Kansong

Changgok
P'anmunjom
Tongduch'on
Samyangsan (1198m)

Puk'ansan National Park

Ch'unch'on
Hongch'on

Lake Soyangho
Sorak san National Park
Yangyang

Odaesan National Park
Kangnung

KANGWON-DO

EAST SEA
(Sea of Japan)

Tonghae

Wonju
Ch'iaksan (1288m)
Ch'iaksan National Park

KYONGGI-DO

Chech'on

Ch'uju
Sobaeksan (1439m)

ULCHIN

CH'UNGCH'ONBUK-DO

Ch'onan
Onyang

Suanbo

Woraksan National Park
Sobaeksan National Park
Yongju

CH'UNGCH'ONGNAM-DO

Ch'ongju

Songnisan National Park
Songnisan (1058m)

Chomch'on
Andong

Hup'o
To Ullungdo

Yongdok
From Ullungdo

Tadohae Haesang National Park
Anmyondo Island

Taech'on

Puyo
Nonsan

Taejon

Sangju

Kimch'on

KYONGSANGBUK-DO

Chuwangsan (721m)
Chuwangsan National Park

P'ohang

WEST SEA
(Yellow Sea)

Soch'on
Iri
Kunsan
Chongju

CHOLLABUK-DO

Togyusan National Park
Kayasan National Park

Yongch'on

Taegu

Kyongju
Kyongju National Park

Pyonsanbando National Park
Naejangsan National Park
Naejangsan (763m)

Namwon

Togyusan (1614m)

Chirisan (1915m)

Chirisan National Park

T'ongdosa
Ulsan

Kwangju

CHOLLANAM-DO

Chinju

Masan
Pusan

Sunch'on

Samch'onp'o

Ch'ungmu
Kojedo Island

Mokp'o

Changhung

Haenam

Toyang

Yosu

Tolsando Island
Yondo Island

Hallyo'haesang National Park

Tsushima Island (JAPAN)

...ngdo
...hae Haesang ...onal Park
Hajodo Island

Chindo

Chindo Island
Wando Island
Wando

Pogildo Island
Ch'ongsando Island

Oenarodo Island

Tadohae Haesang National Park

Komundo Island

SOUTH SEA
(East China Sea)

CHEJU-DO

Cheju

Hallim

Hallasan National Park
Hallasan (1950m)

Ch'ungmun
Sogwip'o

N

0   40   80 km

Tourist Offices Overseas

The Korean National Tourism Office (KNTO) maintains a number of overseas offices. They include:

AUSTRALIA
(☎ 02-9252 4147) 17th floor, Tower Building, Australia Square, George St, Sydney, NSW 2000

CANADA
(☎ 416-348-9056) Suite 406, 480 University Ave, Toronto, Ontario M5G 1V2

UK
(☎ 020-7409 2100) 20 Saint George St, London W1R 9RE

USA
(☎ 213-382-3435) 3435 Wilshire Blvd, Suite 1110, Los Angeles, CA 90010;
(☎ 312-819-2560) 205 North Michigan Ave, Suite 2212, Chicago, IL 60601;
(☎ 201-585-0909) 7th floor, 2 Executive Drive, Fort Lee, NJ 07024;
(☎ 808-521-8066) 1188 Bishop St, Ph 1, Honolulu, Hawaii 96813

Health

You should experience few health problems in South Korea, but take precautions against travellers diarrhoea and other more serious food and waterborne diseases, such as hepatitis and dysentery. Drink only boiled water and eat freshly made, hot food. Shellfish and undercooked meat should be avoided.

Medical care in hospitals is excellent and generally cheap. While Korean pharmacies will dispense almost anything without a prescription, remember that self-treatment can be risky.

Post & Communications

South Korea's postal system is reliable and fast, but not particularly cheap. There are 40% discounts for written matter, but you must seal the envelope or parcel with string. All major cities offer post restante, but only Seoul and Pusan have specific counters – elsewhere it could be difficult if you don't speak Korean. The telephone system is equally good and international calls can be made from most public card phones. Korea has fervently embraced email and the Internet and there are several public cafes in Seoul, Pusan and Taegu.

Money

Costs

South Korea is steadily shouldering its way into the big league when it comes to costs – Japan is about the only place that's still more expensive. If you're slumming it, self-catering and staying in the same place as much as possible, you might be able to get by on US$30 a day. If you've got a few more dollars to throw around, it will make your trip much more enjoyable – for less than US$50 a day you can eat and sleep well, move around a bit, enjoy some nightlife and buy a few souvenirs.

Changing Money

US military bases will let you pay in US dollars (should you feel the need to pick up a stealth bomber or two), but everywhere else you'll need won. Cash US dollars are the easiest to exchange, but any other hard currencies, especially yen, shouldn't pose a problem. You'll get a better rate on travellers cheques than cash – those in US dollars will be more widely accepted. There are ATMs all over Seoul, Pusan and other major cities, but the instructions are in Korean. International credit cards are widely accepted.

Online Services

Lonely Planet's *Destination South Korea* page is at www.lonelyplanet .com/dest/nea/sko.htm.

Travellers' Korea (www.knto.or.kr /index_e.htm) has all the usual tourist information, including accommodation, tours, and convention planning. News is updated every week at *Korea Web Weekly* (www.kimsoft.com/korea.htm), where you'll also find links to other news services.

Korea's mountainous national parks are legendary. Pick a peak and pull on your pack at *National Parks of Korea* (www.npa.or.kr/). Say goodbye antibiotics and hello herbs at *Dr Park's Oriental Medicine of Korea* (members. iWorld.net/cva123/open/estart.html).

It's more than an alphabet, it's an art form. Learn Korean the fun way at *Introduction to Korean* (www.best .com/~nessus/kintro/index.htm).

Books

Korea, Tradition & Transformation by Andrew C Nahm is one of the most up-to-date histories of the peninsula, while *Korea's Cultural Roots* by John Carter Covell is a good primer in Korean culture, covering Shamanism, Confucianism and Buddhism. To understand the heart and soul of Korean Confucianism, read *To Become A Sage – The Ten Diagrams on Sage Learning* by Yi T'oegye.

The entire Choson dynasty is well covered by *The Confucian Transformation of Korea* by Martina Deuchler. The same author also produced a fine earlier work, *Confucian Gentlemen and Barbarian Envoys*, which covers the opening up of Korea to the west

NORTH KOREA

Workers' paradise or totalitarian dictatorship? Your image of North Korea, or the Democratic People's Republic of Korea, may depend on your ideology. While other formerly hardline communist countries are opening up to western-style capitalism, North Korea remains devoutly Marxist. No other country maintains such a rigid Stalinist system.

This may not sound like a travellers paradise. Indeed, it is entirely possible that North Korea hosts fewer foreign tourists than any other country on earth. And those who do manage a visit are restricted to seeing certain places and must be accompanied by a guide the whole time. Visitors will also find that they are subjected to nonstop propaganda – the 'US imperialist aggressors' and 'South Korean puppet stooges' are favourite themes. And finally, North Korea is one of the most expensive countries in the world to visit.

So why go? Simply put, North Korea is fascinating. Tourists are drawn to it out of pure curiosity. Furthermore, it's an education you're not likely to forget – many tourists comment that their visit to North Korea was easily their most memorable journey. Some think of it as a Stalinist theme park, a dictatorship par excellence, almost too surreal to be believable. Regardless of the weird politics, there is no denying that North Korea is a beautiful country that has hardly been touched by tourism.

Some travellers come away from North Korea impressed by its cleanliness and orderliness. Many come away horrified. But the big question is whether or not you'll be able to go at all. North Korea periodically opens and closes its doors to foreign tourists. The government is especially paranoid that tourists will 'pollute' the people's minds with foreign ideas like free enterprise and democracy. In a typical year, North Korea only permits about 200 westerners to visit. Your best bet is to first approach the North Korean visa office in Macau. It is in the business of selling tours and will normally respond much more favourably to travellers than the North Korean embassy in Beijing. Either way, you must pay for the entire trip in advance in hard currency before your visa is issued, and then arrange your own transport to and from North Korea.

between 1875 and 1885. Those interested in the country's economy should pick up a copy of *The Chaebol* by Steers, Shin & Ungson. Finally, *To Dream of Pigs* by Clive Leatherdale is an excellent travelogue of both North and South Korea.

Films

Korea produces plenty of films, but the big problem has been financing them. There are no multimillion dollar budgets as in Hollywood, and consequently no big box office hits. Western films are so popular that the government has felt the need to encourage the production of Korean films by forcing cinemas to limit foreign movies to 60% of the total shown. Most Korean films resemble western-style soap operas – low-budget stories of romance, jealousy, violence (decidedly mild) and people's everyday lives. There is very little sex in Korean movies, largely due to government censorship, though this is now being relaxed. A scant few films are subtitled in English because the producers hope to enter international film festivals – you can occasionally see these films in Seoul, so watch the English-language newspapers for announcements.

Entering & Leaving South Korea

South Korea's principal international airport is in Seoul. The international airports in Pusan and Cheju-do only have flights to and from Japan. Ferries run from Pusan to Shimonoseki and Hakata in Japan, or you can get a combined train-ferry ticket which will take you from Seoul to Osaka. Ferries to Weihai, Qingdao and Tianjin in China go from Inch'on. If you want to sit on a boat for 46 hours, a ferry runs from Pusan to Vladivostok in Russia.

SRI LANKA ▶▶

For quite a small island, Sri Lanka has gathered a lot of names – Serendib, Ceylon, Teardrop of India, Resplendent Isle, Island of Dharma, Pearl of the Orient – an accumulation which reveals its richness and beauty, and the passion it evokes in visitors. For centuries Sri Lanka has seduced travellers, who returned home with enchanting images of a languorous tropical isle of such deep spirituality and serenity that it entered the western imagination as the Tahiti of the East. This, unfortunately, is the same island which for the past 13 years has been traumatised by a ferocious ethnic and religious conflict.

No matter what you want, Sri Lanka is likely to have it – some of the world's finest beaches, a rich cultural life, ancient ruins, beautiful scenery and rare wildlife. All this comes with friendly people, good food, pleasant places to stay and reasonably low costs in a handy, compact package.

When to Go
The driest and best seasons are from December to March on the west and south coasts and in the hill country, and from May to September on the east coast. December to March is when most foreign tourists arrive.

Out-of-season travel has its advantages – not only have the crowds disappeared but many air fares and accommodation prices are very low. Nor does it rain all the time. Reefs may protect a beach area and make swimming quite feasible at places like Hikkaduwa, which during the monsoon can be quite pleasant.

Highlights
In contrast with the rest of the island, Colombo is big, noisy and architecturally uninspiring. There are a few sights, but many travellers don't hang around as there's much more to see elsewhere.

Beaches
If you're looking to laze on the beach, there's a string of beautiful white-sand beaches running south from Colombo

AT A GLANCE

Full Country Name: Democratic Socialist Republic of Sri Lanka

Area: 66,000 sq km

Population: 18 million

Capital City: Colombo (pop 1.2 million)

People: 75% Sinhalese, 18% Tamils and 7% Muslims

Languages: Sinhala, Tamil and English

Religion: 69% Buddhist, 15% Hindu, 8% Muslim and 8% Christian

Government: Constitutional democracy

Currency: Sri Lankan rupee (Rs)

Time Zone: Five-and-a-half hours ahead of GMT/UTC

International Telephone Code: 94

Electricity: 230-240V, 50 AC; plugs have three round pins, as in India

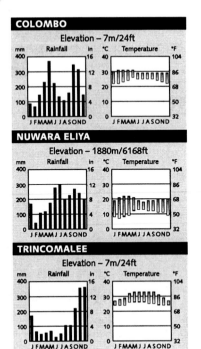

COLOMBO
Elevation – 7m/24ft

NUWARA ELIYA
Elevation – 1880m/6168ft

TRINCOMALEE
Elevation – 7m/24ft

Ancient Cities
The ancient cities in the hills are big drawcards. The ruins of Sri Lanka's first capital, Anuradhapura, evoke the splendour of 1000 years of rule dating from 380 BC, while the spectacular rock fortress of Sigiriya is truly remarkable. Accessible from Kandy is another former capital, Polonnaruwa. Its well preserved ruins, dating back 1000 years, are compact and easily explored by bicycle.

Colonial History
There are also vestiges of the island's colonial past to explore. Nuwara Eliya was once the favourite hill station of the British and retains the flavour of the Empire, while Dutch influence can be clearly observed in the southern port of Galle.

Religion & Culture
The huge number of temples and festivals in Sri Lanka means that you'll be hard-pressed not to absorb some of the country's rich cultural tradition; the laid-back city of Kandy, where the major 10 day Kandy Esala Perahera festival is held in July or August, has some especially fine examples of temple architecture.

all the way around the coast, although some have been crassly developed for the wealthy tourist market. There is good diving, snorkelling and surfing at Hikkaduwa and Unawatuna, plus at a host of other places along the coast.

National Parks
For nature lovers, the good national parks include Yala West with its populations of wild elephants, leopards, bears, crocodiles and monkeys. Nearby, Bundala National Park is Sri Lanka's best spot for birdwatching (especially flamingos), while for trekkers the Peak Wilderness Sanctuary is home to Adam's Peak (2224m). Close by is Horton Plains National Park, which has some good walking trails.

Itineraries

Sri Lanka is not big, so it's easy to take in a wide variety of sights in relatively little time, even for those on a limited budget. Two weeks is generally long enough for a good look at the island, but a longer stay will allow an unhurried tour. Excluding the troubled east and north, Sri Lanka can be divided into three zones: the west coast beaches, the hill country, and the ancient cities.

ONE WEEK
If you have just a week and are travelling by public transport, you could take in a beach

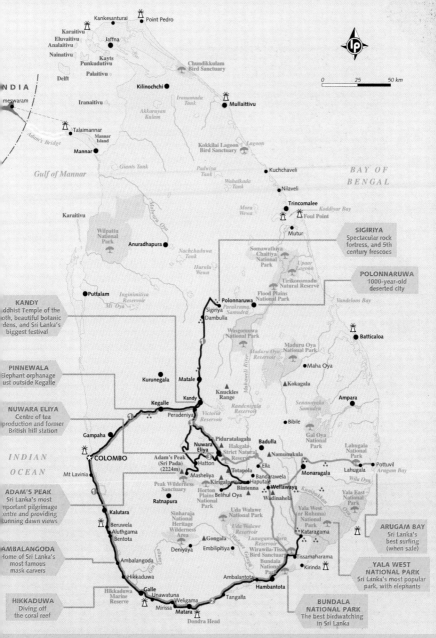

Point Pedro
Kankesanturai
Karaitivu
Eluvaitivu
Analaitivu
Nainativu
Jaffna
Kayts
Punkudutivu
Palaitivu
Delft

INDIA
meswaram

Talaimannar
Mannar Island
Adam's Bridge
Mannar

Gulf of Mannar

Karaitivu

Kilinochchi

Iranamadu Tank

Mullaittivu

Akkarayan Kulam

Chundikkulam Bird Sanctuary

Kokkilai Lagoon Bird Sanctuary
Lagoon

Padviya Tank
Wahalkada Tank

Kuchchaveli
Nilaveli
Trincomalee
Foul Point
Koddiyar Bay
Mutur

BAY OF BENGAL

Giants Tank

Nachchaduwa Tank

Hurulu Wewa

Mora Wewa

Wilpattu National Park

Anuradhapura

Somawathiya Chaitiya National Park
Upaar Lagoon

Tirikonamadu Natural Reserve

Polonnaruwa

SIGIRIYA
Spectacular rock fortress, and 5th century frescoes

POLONNARUWA
1000-year-old deserted city

Flood Plains National Park
Vandeloos Bay

Puttalam

Inginimitiya Reservoir
Mi Oya

KANDY
ddhist Temple of the oth, beautiful botanic dens, and Sri Lanka's biggest festival

Kurunegala
Matale

Wasgomuwa National Park

Maduru Oya Reservoir

Maduru Oya National Park

Batticaloa

Parakrama Samudra
Sigiriya
Dambulla

PINNEWALA
Elephant orphanage ust outside Kegalle

Kegalle
Kandy
Peradeniya

Knuckles Range

Randenigala Reservoir

Mahaweli River

Maha Oya
Kokagala

Senanayaka Samudra

Ampara

NUWARA ELIYA
Centre of tea production and former British hill station

Gampaha

COLOMBO

Victoria Reservoir

Pidurutalagala
Nuwara Eliya
Hakgala Strict Natural Reserve
Badulla

Gal Oya National Park

Bibile

INDIAN OCEAN

Mt Lavinia

Adam's Peak (Sri Pada) (2224m)
Hatton
Masheliya

Peak Wilderness Sanctuary

Kirigalpotta
Totapola
Ella
Bandarawela
Haputale

Namunukula

Monaragala

Lahugala National Park

Lahugala

Pottuvil
Arugam Bay

ADAM'S PEAK
mportant pilgrimage entre and providing tunning dawn views

Kalutara

Ratnapura

Horton Plains National Park
Belihul Oya
Bintenna
Wellawaya
Wadinahela

Wilu Oya

Yala East National Park

Beruwela
Aluthgama
Bentota

Sinharaja National Heritage Wilderness Area

Gongala

Uda Walawe National Park
Uda Walawe Reservoir

Lunuganwehera Reservoir

Yala West (or Ruhuna) National Park

ARUGAM BAY
Sri Lanka's best surfing (when safe)

AMBALANGODA
dome of Sri Lanka's most famous mask carvers

Ambalangoda
Hikkaduwa

Deniyaya

Embilipitiya

Wirawila-Tissa Bird Sanctuary
Bundala National Park

Kataragama

YALA WEST NATIONAL PARK
Sri Lanka's most popular park, with elephants

Hikkaduwa Marine Reserve

Galle
Unawatuna
Weligama
Mirissa
Matara
Dondra Head

Ambalantota
Tangalla
Hambantota

Tissamaharama
Kirinda

HIKKADUWA
Diving off the coral reef

BUNDALA NATIONAL PARK
The best birdwatching in Sri Lanka

at Beruwela or Aluthgama before making a quick visit to Kandy. There are good day trips to the cave temple at Dambulla or the rock fortress of Sigiriya, north of Kandy.

With a car, you could travel down the west coast as far as Tissamaharama, taking in Beruwela and Aluthgama, as well as the birdlife at Bundala National Park and the endangered species (including elephants, leopards and sloth bears) at Yala West National Park. Alternatively, head into the hills to see the ancient city areas, with a climb up Adam's Peak or a walk through Horton Plains National Park.

TWO WEEKS

If you're travelling by public transport, start with a trip through the hill country and the ancient cities before heading down through the former British hill station of Nuwara Eliya to the waterfalls near Ella. Continue either to the beaches at Tangalla or Mirissa on the southern coast, or head east to Arugam Bay (check that it's currently safe), then wander back around the coast to Colombo. Two weeks with a car and driver will allow you to easily accomplish a circuit of the west coast, the south, the hill country and the ancient cities before returning to Colombo.

Visa Requirements

Tourists from 64 countries don't need visas to enter Sri Lanka. Nationals of Australia, New Zealand and the USA are entitled to 90 days upon entry and may extend this by 90 days. Travellers from Canada and the UK are entitled to 30 days upon entry, which can be extended by 60 days.

Sri Lankan Embassies & High Commissions

AUSTRALIA
(☎ 02-6239 7041/2) 35 Empire Circuit, Forrest, ACT 2603

CANADA
(☎ 613-2338-4409) Suite 1204, 333 Lauries Ave West, Ottawa, Ontario KIP ICI

UK
(☎ 020-7262 1841) 13 Hyde Park Gardens, London W2 2LU

USA
(☎ 202-483-4026) 2148 Wyoming Ave NW, Washington, DC 20008

Tourist Offices Overseas

Some embassies maintain Ceylon Tourist Board offices. For details, check with them, talk to your travel agent or look up some of the web site addresses listed under Online Services.

Health

Sri Lanka poses a few health risks. Malaria exists everywhere, except in Colombo and parts of the hill country. Dengue fever, Japanese encephalitis and filariasis all occur in Sri Lanka, so you should avoid mosquito bites. Intestinal worms, including tapeworms and hookworms, are common in rural areas. Hepatitis, typhoid and dysentery can all be transmitted via contaminated food and water. It is not safe to drink tap water anywhere in Sri Lanka; avoid salads and unpeeled fruit, shellfish and undercooked meat. Rabies exists, with monkeys, dogs and bats noted carriers.

If you require medical care, try and get to Colombo, as medical services are poor elsewhere. In Colombo, private hospitals have more facilities and services than the public hospitals.

Post & Communications

Sri Lanka has decent and reasonably priced postal services, but international mail delivery can be slow. There are post restante services in Colombo as well as in major towns. The telephone service is also reasonably good value and you can call internationally with a phonecard from many public phones.

Internet services are springing up in main towns and some tourist destinations such as Hikkaduwa. In Colombo, some top-end hotels have business centres where you can send emails and use the Internet, but these are relatively expensive.

Money

Costs
Sri Lanka is still a pleasantly economical country in which to travel around. Shoestring travellers can exist comfortably on less than US$20 a day by staying in basic share or double rooms, getting around by bus and not lashing out in flash restaurants. Add US$5 to US$10 to kip down in delightful rest houses, or budget on around US$100 a day if you want the full, five star treatment.

Changing Money
You'll have no problem changing travellers cheques at most major banks. There are plenty of moneychangers in Colombo and Hikkaduwa; US dollars are best. ATMs are becoming common, especially in major cities, but outside of Colombo and Kandy they are unlikely to accept international cards. Credit cards are widely accepted, and

Visa and MasterCard cash withdrawals are possible at major banks.

Online Services
Lonely Planet's *Destination Sri Lanka* page is at www.lonelyplanet.com/dest/ind/sri.htm.

The *Sri Lanka Web Server* (www.lanka.net/cgi-bin/index2.html) includes the Ceylon Tourist Board's official site and loads of news links.

You can *Explore Sri Lanka* through the web page of this monthly travel magazine (www.lanka.net/Directory/ExploreSL), while *Welcome to Sri Lanka* (arachnid.cs.cf.ac.uk/Sri_Lanka/sl_home.html) has an eclectic selection of information for anyone not daunted by reading yellow text.

Don't avoid reality by ignoring the *Sri Lanka Human Rights* page (www.derechos.org/saran/lanka.html, which collates reports from Amnesty International and other sources. Daily news is available on *the Daily News* (www.lanka.net/lakehouse), and there are links galore at the *Sri Lanka Info Page* (www.lacnet.org/srilanka).

Books
An idiosyncratic insight into the country can be found in the touching and disarming *Running in the Family*

WARNING

The northern third of Sri Lanka and the eastern coast are off limits to travellers and highly dangerous. The south and south-west areas and the central hill country have generally been calm, but since government troops flushed Tamil Tigers from the Jaffna Peninsula in November 1995, several terrorist attacks have occurred in Colombo, including suicide bomb attacks and train carriage bombings, with heavy losses of life.

Random acts of terrorism are expected to continue as the Tigers seek to prove they are still a force to be reckoned with; most western governments warn visitors to defer nonessential travel to Sri Lanka. Foreign nationals have so far not specifically been targets of attacks, but the Tigers have made it clear that they consider tourism a target. Check with your embassy to see which areas are safe during your visit.

by Michael Ondaatje. *Only Man is Vile: The Tragedy of Sri Lanka* by William McGowan is a brilliant and tragic account of the country's recent ethnic troubles, while Dr KM De Silva's *A History of Sri Lanka* provides a comprehensive overview.

Leonard Woolf's *A Village in the Jungle*, written in 1913, is a sombre and observant account of village life in the early part of this century.

For birdwatchers, GM Henry's *A Guide to the Birds of Ceylon* will help you to identify any bird you see, while elephant fans will want to read *Aliya – Stories of Elephants of Sri Lanka* by Peter Davis & Theresa Cannon.

Films

After a halcyon period during the 1960s and 70s, the output of the Sri Lankan film industry has noticeably slowed, partly under the weight of imported Indian films. A recent effort is *Dorakada Marawa* (Death at the Doorstep), directed by Wasantha Obesekara. Sri Lanka is still a fairly popular shooting location for western directors (films include *Indiana Jones & The Temple of Doom*, *Tarzan* and *The Iron Triangle*).

Entering & Leaving Sri Lanka

The only way to enter Sri Lanka is by air. Colombo is the international gateway for direct flights from Europe, Asia, Australia and the Middle East. Cheap flights are available between Colombo and India (Madras, Trichy, Trivandrum and Mumbai). Departure tax will cost you US$10.

Taiwan is a modern industrialised mega-lopolis clinging to the fringes of an ancient culture, a string of stinking cities at the feet of a glorious mountain range. Taiwan is traditional noodles at a 7-Eleven, aboriginal tribes in mini-skirts, a day of temple rituals followed by water-slide rides. The human tide of Taipei will sweep you off your feet, but if you step outside the city limits you'll discover why Taiwan is known as Ilha Formosa, the beautiful island. Mountain peaks puncturing a sea of clouds, black volcanic coastlines, waterfalls shrouded in mist: Taiwan is a computer-generated Chinese watercolour.

When to Go
Try to avoid major public holidays, especially Chinese New Year (usually early February), when transport will be full, restaurants closed, and hotels expensive. The summer heat can shorten tempers and lift the price of air fares. While October is climatically pleasant, it's also holiday-ridden, so try November instead. Ghost month falls in August/September (when ghosts walk from hell walk the earth), so there'll be no Chinese travellers on the road and temples will be at their most active.

Highlights
Taiwan has loads of attractions, but lots of people to go with them. If you can deal with the crowds, there's much to see and you don't have to travel too

AT A GLANCE

Full Country Name: Republic of China

Area: 35,563 sq km

Population: 21.5 million

Capital City: Taipei (pop 2.63 million)

People: 85% Taiwanese, 13% mainland Chinese and 2% aboriginal groups (Ami, Atayal, Bunun, Paiwan, Puyuma, Rukai, Shao, Saisiat, Tsou and Yami)

Languages: Taiwanese and Mandarin Chinese

Religion: 93% Buddhist, Taoist, Confucian, 4.5% Christian, 2.5% indigenous religions (although the there is a great deal of crossover between all faiths)

Government: Democratic republic

Currency: New Taiwan dollar (NT$)

Time Zone: Eight hours ahead of GMT/UTC

International Telephone Code: 886

Electricity: 110V, 60 AC (the same as North America), although 220V is used in many buildings solely for air-conditioners

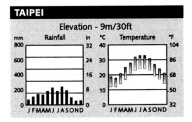

TAIPEI

Elevation - 9m/30ft

far to reach it all. The island's indisputable number one attraction is the National Palace Museum in northern Taipei, which boasts the greatest collection of Chinese art in the world. All visitors should allow at least one full day to explore some of the 720,000 piece collection (only 15,000 pieces are on show at any given time).

Trekking

Taiwan offers many climbing and trekking opportunities, with some challenging peaks such as Yushan, Hsuehshan, Hohuanshan, Nengkaoshan and Kuanshan. Less strenuous hikes can be made in the Alishan and Tungpu areas.

Scenery

For those who prefer to keep to the road, there's plenty of spectacular scenery that can be enjoyed from the comfort of a car or bus. The Central Cross-Island Highway over Hohuanshan offers incredible views (when the weather cooperates). Taroko Gorge on the east coast is an area of superlative beauty with many walking trails, canyons and waterfalls. Hot springs abound in Taiwan – some good areas are Yangmingshan, Chihpen, Antung and Kuantzuling.

Aboriginal Culture

Taiwan still has a strong, if somewhat depleted, aboriginal population and there are many centres where you can gain a good understanding of their cultures. Choose between the more popular and touristy places like Wulai or traditional villages such as Maolin.

Temples

Taiwan features thousands of temples, but Tainan is a standout, with more

than 200 temples providing a true insight into Taiwanese culture and religious ceremonies.

Islands

The islands are great places to get away from the hustle of the cities. In particular, the islands of the Taiwan Straits, some which are only 3km from the Chinese mainland, have fascinating and historical military sites to explore, as well as Kinmen National Park.

Itineraries

THREE DAYS

Three days in Taipei will allow a full-day visit to the National Palace Museum, and two days to explore the many temples and shrines dotted around the city, taking in a colourful night market on one evening. If you want to see some countryside, take a day trip to Wulai (for aboriginal culture) or Yangmingshan National Park, noted for its spectacular cherry blossoms and azalea blooms (February to April) and good hiking.

ONE WEEK

A week is enough to enjoy Taipei's highlights and explore some of Taiwan's spectacular scenery. Spend three days in Taipei before heading to Wulai for the day. A train journey down the east coast to Hualien and Taroko Gorge offers dramatic mountain scenery. From Taroko Gorge you can catch a bus to Lishan, a peaceful mountain retreat, then head for the city of Taichung before returning to Taipei.

TWO WEEKS

Follow the one week itinerary as far as Taroko Gorge National Park and indulge in a little rafting on the Hsiukuluan River. From the gorge continue down the east coast to Taitung, where you can fly to Orchid Island for an insight into a remote aboriginal culture. From Taitung you can visit Chihpen Hot Springs or take a bus to Kenting to check out the beaches and Kenting National Park. From there head north along the coast

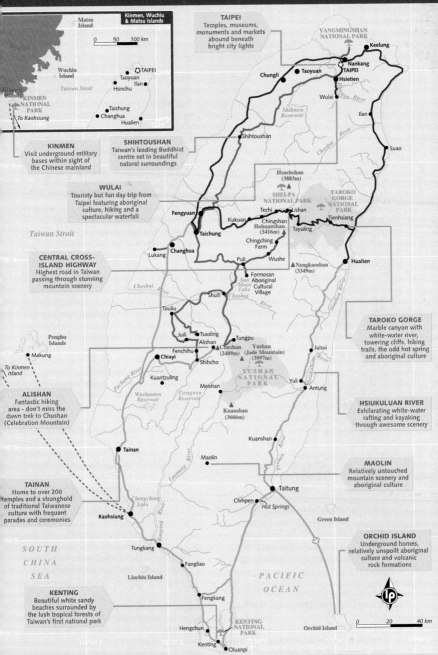

SUGGESTED ITINERARIES

One Week Taipei • Wulai • Hualien • Taroko Gorge • Lishan • Taichung

Two Weeks Taipei • Wulai • Hualien • Taroko Gorge • Taitung • Orchid Island • Chipen Hot Springs • Kenting • Kaohsiung • Tainan • Alishan

One Month Taipei • Wulai • Hualien • Taroko Gorge • Taitung • Orchid Island • Chipen Hot Springs • Kenting • Kaohsiung • Kinmen Island • Tainan • Chiayi • Alishan • Tsaoling • Shuili • Tungpu • Taichung • Shihtoushan

to Kaohsiung and then Tainan. If possible, allow two more days to reach the mountain resort of Alishan before heading back to Taipei.

ONE MONTH

A one month visit will allow you to catch virtually all Taiwan's major sights. Follow the two week itinerary as far as Kaohsiung. Then, if you're visiting during the warmer months, begin an exploration of the islands of the Taiwan Straits – particularly Penghu and Kinmen – which could take up to a week. Return to the mainland to visit the temples of Tainan, followed by Chiayi and Alishan. Returning from Alishan, you could drop into the scenic town of Fenchihu or the isolated village of Juili for some relaxation, before heading to the small city of Touliu to explore the mountains around Tsaoling. Mountain and hot spring enthusiasts can take a bus trip to Shuili, then head on to Tungpu in Yushan National Park. Return to Shuili and visit Sun Moon Lake and the nearby Formosan Aboriginal Cultural Village. From here you can head to Taichung for some nightlife, or go to Puli and catch a bus up to Chingching Farm. Alternatively, hike up to Hohuanshan and take a bus to Taichung the next day.

Using Taichung as a base, take a day trip to the historic port of Lukang and check out some more mountain scenery at Lishan, or head north to Shihtoushan, Taiwan's leading Buddhist centre, before continuing north to Taipei. If you have time, consider flying from Taipei to the sleepy backwater of Matsu, or visiting Yangmingshan National Park.

Visa Requirements

Taiwan allows visa-free stays of up to 14 days for citizens of Australia, Canada, New Zealand, the UK and the USA, as well as most European countries. You must have an onward ticket and six months left on your passport. Visa-free entry is available at the airports at Taoyuan and Kaohsiung and the ports of Keelung and Kaohsiung.

If you wish to stay in Taiwan longer than 14 days – or if you don't qualify for a visa-free stay – you must get a visa. Most westerners will receive a single-entry visa valid for one to two months, that is not extendable.

Taiwanese Embassies

Visas are usually obtained from the embassy of the country you wish to visit, but few countries maintain diplomatic relations with Taiwan, so there are not many ROC embassies in the world. The Taiwanese government gets around this by maintaining a number of 'nongovernmental offices' in many countries, which issue visas. Try any of the following offices:

AUSTRALIA
(☎ 02-6273 3344) Taipei Economic & Cultural Office, Canberra branch, Unit 8, Tourism House, 40 Blackall St, Barton, ACT 2600

CANADA
(☎ 613-231-5080) Taipei Economic & Cultural Office, Ottawa branch, 45 O'Connor St, Ottawa, Ontario KIP1A4

NEW ZEALAND
(☎ 04-473 6474) Taipei Economic & Cultural Office, Wellington branch, PO Box 10250, 105-109 The Terrace, Wellington

UK
(☎ 020-7396 9152) Taipei Representative Office, 50 Grosvenor Gardens, London SWI 0EB

USA
(☎ 202-895-1800) Taipei Economic & Cultural Representative Office (TECRO), Washington branch, 4201 Wisconsin Ave NW, Washington, DC 20016

Tourist Offices Overseas

Taiwan's overseas tourist bureaus are incorporated into the various 'trade offices' that Taiwan maintains around the world. See the earlier Taiwanese

Embassies section for details. Alternatively, consult your travel agent or check out the web sites listed under Online Services.

Health

Except for possible traffic accidents, a visit to Taiwan will present you with few health problems. Outbreaks of dengue fever have occurred during summer in recent years, so you should avoid mosquito bites at all times. Japanese B encephalitis occasionally occurs. Food and waterborne diseases such as typhoid and hepatitis do occur. Tap water should be boiled or purified and, while food standards in Taiwan are fairly high, take care with shellfish and meat dishes.

There are many excellent hospitals and clinics in Taipei and other major cities, and medical services are relatively cheap. Hospitals and clinics can get very crowded, so expect a long wait.

Post & Communications

Taiwan's postal system is quite efficient and reasonably priced, although there is a complex system of rates based on the type of item being sent. All post offices operate post restante services. The telephone system, by contrast, is expensive and standards are variable. Email and Internet services are well established in Taiwan. There are cybercafes in most major cities, but they tend to go out of business without notice.

Money

Costs

As Taiwan's standard of living has increased, the costs of most goods and services have reached the level of many European countries, though Taiwan is still cheaper than Japan (which isn't saying much). If you stay in youth hostels, live on noodles and travel by bus you could get by on US$15 to US$20 a day. If you want a private bathroom, a few souvenirs, a couple of taxi trips and a decent feed or two, budget on US$35 to US$50 a day. Staying in Taipei will cost more than heading into the countryside.

Changing Money

Travellers cheques and cash can be changed at international airports and large banks, but you'll have trouble changing travellers cheques in rural areas. Stick to US dollars for cash and cheques if you can, as other currencies will likely cause you problems. When changing cheques, shop around as commissions can vary widely. There are no legal private moneychangers in Taiwan, but some jewellery shops will change cash. The major international credit cards can be used at big hotels and flash restaurants, or to get cash advances at your card's offices.

Online Services

Lonely Planet's *Destination Taiwan* can be found at www.lonelyplanet .com/dest/nea/tai.htm.

Taiwan Cyberpedia (www.cyber taiwan.com) is functional and funky. For an interesting but pretty dense look at Taiwanese history, try *The History of Taiwan* (www.leksu.com).

It's not the prettiest site on the web, but *Birds of Taiwan* (peacock .tnjc.edu.tw/ADD/bird/bird.home.ht) has plenty to keep the birder happy.

Yam Web (home.yam.org.tw/ index_e.html) is chock-a-block with links on everything from chess to opera, horoscopes to human rights. If you plan to travel around Taiwan by train, check out *Taiwan Railway Administration* (www.railway.gov.tw/taiwan/indexe.html).

For the photographers there are the great photos on *Wee Keng Hor's Homepage* (www.geocities.com/~kenghor/taiwan/taiwan.html).

Books

Books dealing exclusively with Taiwan are scarce. Most people with an interest in this part of the world want to read about China, and Taiwan being only one small province of China (at least officially), it often hardly merits a footnote.

China by Bike: Taiwan, Hong Kong, China's East Coast by Roger Grigsby is a good read covering exactly what the title suggests. *Culture Shock!: Taiwan* by Chris & Ling-Li Bates is a good, entertaining read that will help prepare you for your visit.

The Soong Dynasty by Sterling Seagrave will give you a good understanding of why the Kuomin-tang is in Taiwan and not on mainland China.

For a cultural viewpoint, try *Arts & Culture in Taiwan* by B Kaulbach & B Proksch. *Taiwan with a View* published by the *Independence Evening Post* is a beautifully photographed coffee-table book. The one book you may not be able to do without is *The 100 Best Bars in Taipei* by Jim Ehrhart & Anthony Watts.

Films

Taiwan has a fairly robust film industry, but you have to choose your flicks carefully. Taiwan's most renowned director is Ang Lee. His first feature film was *Pushing Hands*, closely followed by *The Wedding Banquet* and *Eat Drink Man Woman*, which became art-house classics, *Sense and Sensibility* and *The Ice Storm*. Other directors worth viewing include Hou Hsiaohsien and Chu Yen-ping (Kevin Chu), who takes a lowbrow approach to cinema but is consistently popular at the box office.

Entering & Leaving Taiwan

Taiwan has international airports at Taoyuan, near Taipei, and Kaohsiung. You can fly to Taiwan from just about anywhere in the world – except mainland China. Ferries run from Okinawa in Japan to Keelung and Kaohsiung. There are also weekly boats between Kaohsiung and Macau. Departure tax, either for air or sea, is NT$300.

THAILAND ▶▶

There is more visible historical evidence of past eras in Thailand than in any other South-East Asian country, so if you're interested in ruins, temples and deserted cities, this is the place to go. If you're after urban delights, the huge metropolis of Bangkok tends to so charm visitors with its energy and cultural treasures that the steamy soupy diesel mixture which passes for air in this city is more than forgiven.

Thailand is easy to travel in, with efficient transport, cheap accommodation and a delicious national cuisine. The Thais are renowned for their hospitality to strangers; however, while they are often depicted as fun-loving, happy-go-lucky folk (which they certainly can be), they're also very strong-minded and have struggled ceaselessly for centuries to preserve their spirit of independence.

When to Go
The best time for visiting most of Thailand is between November and February – during these months it rains least and is not too hot. The southern part of the country is best visited when the rest of Thailand is miserably hot (March to May), and the weather in the north is best from mid-November to early December, or when it starts warming up again in February. If you plan to spend time in Bangkok, be prepared to roast in April and do some wading in October. The peak tourist months are December and August, and the least crowded months are May, June and September.

Highlights
Thailand's travel scene has many faces, and exploring everything the country has to offer would be a lifetime endeavour. There's so much to see that it pays to be a little under-ambitious with your plans, or your travels may become a bit of a chore.

AT A GLANCE

Full Country Name: Kingdom of Thailand

Area: 517,000 sq km

Population: 57.5 million

Capital: Bangkok (pop six million)

People: 75% Thai, 14% Chinese, 3.5% Malay, plus Mon, Khmer, Phuan and Karen groups

Languages: Thai, plus numerous regional dialects

Religion: 95% Buddhist, 4% Muslim, 1% Christian, Taoist, Hindu and Confucian

Government: Constitutional monarchy

Currency: Thai baht (B)

Time Zone: Seven hours ahead of GMT/UTC

International Telephone Code: 66

Electricity: 220V, 50 AC; most outlets accept round, two-pin plugs, but there are also flat, two-pin plugs

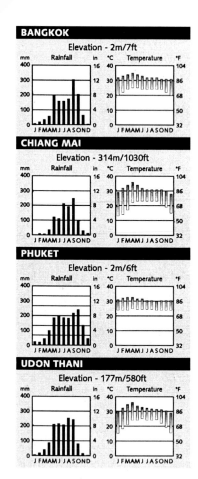

BANGKOK
Elevation - 2m/7ft

CHIANG MAI
Elevation - 314m/1030ft

PHUKET
Elevation - 2m/6ft

UDON THANI
Elevation - 177m/580ft

Temples
The former Thai capitals of Ayuthaya, Lopburi, Kamphaeng Phet, Sukhothai, Si Satchanalai and Chiang Mai offer a wide range of Buddhist temple architecture, mostly from the 11th to 17th centuries. There are dozens of Lao temples along the Mekong River, from Loei Province to Ubon Ratchathani Province.

Handcrafts
Thailand boasts a wide range of handcrafts for study or purchase. Chiang Mai is the oldest tourist centre and you'll find a great variety of hill-tribe and Northern Thai craftwork, as well as materials from Myanmar and Laos. Other places to check out are Nakhon Ratchasima, Ubon Ratchathani, Nakhon Si Thammarat and Songkhla.

Museums
There are many fine museums displaying Thailand's rich cultural heritage. The National Museum in Bangkok is probably the best, with sculpture, pottery, furniture, clothing and musical instruments from across South-East Asia. Also worth visiting are the Chao Sam Phraya Museum and Palace (Ayuthaya), Nan National Museum, Phimai National Museum and Ko Yo Folklore Museum (near Songkhla).

Islands & Beaches
Thailand's coastline boasts some of the finest islands and beaches in Asia. Explore the marine parks at Ko Chang or the Andaman islands; enjoy the comfort, cuisine (and crowds) of Ko Samet, Phuket and Ko Samui; try some exquisite diving at Ko Tao, Ko Phi Phi, Pattaya or the Similan and Surin islands; or laze on the deserted beaches of Songkhla, Pattani and Narathiwat.

National Parks
Thailand boasts nearly 80 national parks which encompass a huge range of vegetation, rare wildlife, hiking trails, vistas and camping opportunities. Some of the best include Kaeng Krachan (large, remote and with populations of gibbons and hornbills), Doi Inthanon (orchids, lichens and nearly 400 bird varieties), Khao Yai (one of the largest intact monsoon

forests in South-East Asia and home to a sizable herd of wild elephants) and Khao Sok (limestone crags, rainforests and jungle streams supporting remnant populations of threatened tigers and clouded leopards).

Itineraries

Most visitors begin their journey in Bangkok. Depending on how much time you have, you might want to save your Bangkok explorations until after you've seen other parts of the country. That way Bangkok won't seem quite so overwhelming as on first arrival. You'll also understand more about the Thai character after travelling around the country, and in Bangkok it pays to be a good judge of character.

ONE WEEK – TEMPLES & GULF BEACHES

Start with a two day taste of Bangkok, then head for Ayuthaya to take in the 400-year-old temple and palace ruins. Transit back through Bangkok and then head south-east to Ko Samet for two or three nights on this all-season island. An alternative one week itinerary would be to make an early morning start for one of the floating markets south-west of Bangkok, such as Damnoen Saduak. Overnight in Nakhon Pathom before heading to Kanchanaburi, then return to Bangkok via Suphanburi and Lopburi.

TWO WEEKS – NORTHERN THAILAND

Begin with either of the one-week itineraries, then take an overnight train (or fly) to Chiang Mai, before moving to Mae Hong Son or Nan for some trekking, and exploring of the national parks and villages.

TWO WEEKS – NORTH-EASTERN THAILAND

Again, start with a one week itinerary, then take a train to Nakhon Ratchasima for the Angkor-period ruins at Phimai. For more Khmer architectural splendour, go to the

Phanom Rung Historical Park in Buriram Province. Finish with a jaunt along the Mekong River – from Chiang Khan to Si Chiangmai if you prefer small towns, or from Nakhon Phanom to Ubon Ratchathani if you like cities.

TWO WEEKS – BANGKOK TO THE MALAYSIAN BORDER

Spend a couple of days in Bangkok and then head for Phetchaburi to spend a day at the late Ayuthaya-period temples and hilltop royal palace. Laze for a day or so on the beaches at Cha-am, Hua Hin or Prachuap Khiri Khan and then visit Khao Sam Roi Yot National Park (considered one of the best spots in the world for viewing the dusky langur). For some serious beach time, zero in on Ko Tao, Ko Pha-Ngan or Ko Samui. Sail back to the mainland and visit Chaiya or Songkhla and follow this with a night or two in Hat Yai. Take the east coast route to Malaysia via Narathiwat for the best natural scenery, or the west coast route if you're in a hurry.

ONE MONTH – TEMPLES, TREKKING & BEACHES

After a few days in Bangkok, take a slow ride north with two-night stopovers in Lopburi, Phitsanulok and Sukhothai for some temple architecture. Then head south-west to Mae Sot and explore the path from Um Phang to Mae Sariang with its waterfalls, trekking, rafting and working elephants. Continue north along the Mae Hong Son loop to Tha Ton on the Kok River, and either boat down the Kok to Chiang Rai or take a ride through the mountains along the Myanmar border to the Yunnanese settlement of Mae Salong. With roughly a week left in your itinerary, choose an island or beach along the upper Gulf of Thailand coast (Pattaya, Ko Samet, Ko Si Chang or Hua Hin), or either the Andaman coast (Phuket, Khao Lak - Lamru National Park, Krabi or Trang) or lower gulf coast (Ko Samui, Ko Pha-Ngan or Ko Tao) if you don't mind an air, road or rail trip. If you have time, make a side trip to Khao Sok National Park.

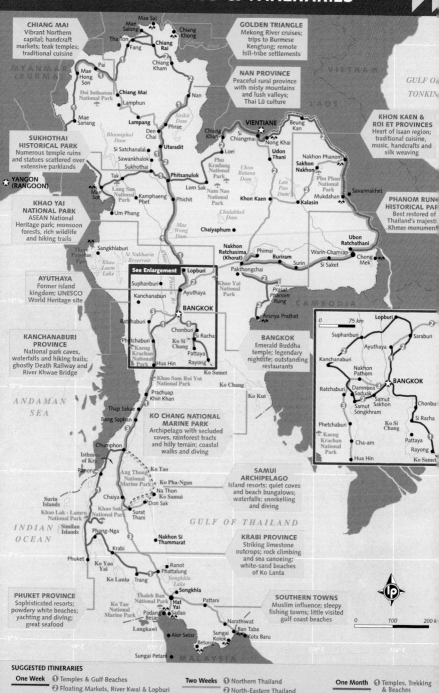

THAILAND HIGHLIGHTS & ITINERARIES

CHIANG MAI
Vibrant Northern capital; handcraft markets; teak temples; traditional cuisine

GOLDEN TRIANGLE
Mekong River cruises; trips to Burmese Kengtung; remote hill-tribe settlements

NAN PROVINCE
Peaceful rural province with misty mountains and lush valleys; Thai Lü culture

KHON KAEN & ROI ET PROVINCES
Heart of Isaan region; traditional cuisine, music, handcrafts and silk weaving

SUKHOTHAI HISTORICAL PARK
Numerous temple ruins and statues scattered over extensive parklands

PHANOM RUNG HISTORICAL PARK
Best restored of Thailand's majestic Khmer monuments

KHAO YAI NATIONAL PARK
ASEAN National Heritage park; monsoon forests, rich wildlife and hiking trails

AYUTHAYA
Former island kingdom; UNESCO World Heritage site

KANCHANABURI PROVINCE
National park caves, waterfalls and hiking trails; ghostly Death Railway and River Khwae Bridge

BANGKOK
Emerald Buddha temple; legendary nightlife; outstanding restaurants

KO CHANG NATIONAL MARINE PARK
Archipelago with secluded coves, rainforest tracts and hilly terrain; coastal walks and diving

SAMUI ARCHIPELAGO
Island resorts; quiet coves and beach bungalows; waterfalls; snorkelling and diving

KRABI PROVINCE
Striking limestone outcrops; rock climbing and sea canoeing; white-sand beaches of Ko Lanta

PHUKET PROVINCE
Sophisticated resorts; powdery white beaches; yachting and diving; great seafood

SOUTHERN TOWNS
Muslim influence; sleepy fishing towns; little visited gulf coast beaches

SUGGESTED ITINERARIES

One Week ① Temples & Gulf Beaches
② Floating Markets, River Kwai & Lopburi

Two Weeks ① Northern Thailand
② North-Eastern Thailand
③ Bangkok to the Malaysian Border

One Month ① Temples, Trekking & Beaches
② North by North-East

ONE MONTH – NORTH BY NORTH-EAST

For a culture hit, start with the Lopburi to Mae Salong route described in the Temples, Trekking & Beaches itinerary, and continue eastward to Nan and Phrae, two of the North's less travelled provinces. Then move on to Loei Province for the Mekong River loop from Chiang Khan to Ubon Ratchathani. If you have time to spare, head into the interior to visit Prasat Hin Phimai and Phanom Rung historical parks. Alternatively, take a whirl along the Cambodian border from Ubon Ratchathani to Aranya Prathet via Surin and Si Saket.

Visa Requirements

The Thai government is reassessing its visa classes and charges, but it currently allows 56 nationalities (including American, Canadian, British and Australian citizens) to enter the country without a visa for 30 days free of charge. New Zealanders receive a free, 90 day visa. Alternatively, go for a tourist visa, good for 60 days (US$15). Three passport photos must accompany all applications and once a visa is issued you must enter Thailand within 90 days. On arrival, you might be required to show an onward ticket and sufficient funds, but this rarely occurs. Dressing neatly will increase your chances of a hassle-free passage.

Thai Embassies

AUSTRALIA
(☎ 02-6273 1149, 6273 2937) 111 Empire Circuit, Yarralumla, ACT 2600

CANADA
(☎ 613-722-4444) 180 Island Park Drive, Ottawa, Ontario K1Y OA2

NEW ZEALAND
(☎ 04-476 8618/9) 2 Cook St, Karori, Wellington 5

UK
(☎ 020-7589 0173) 29-30 Queen's Gate, London SW7 5JB

USA
(☎ 202-944-3600) 1024 Wisconsin Ave NW, Washington, DC 20007

Tourist Offices Overseas

The Tourism Authority of Thailand (TAT) maintains a number of offices overseas. They include:

AUSTRALIA
(☎ 02-9247 7549) Level 2, 75 Pitt Street, Sydney, NSW 2000

UK
(☎ 020-7499 7679) 49 Albemarle St, London W1X 3FE

USA
(☎ 212-432-0433, toll-free ☎ 1-800 THAILAND) 5 World Trade Center, Suite 3443, New York, NY 10048; (☎ 213-461-9814) 1st floor, 611 North Larchmont Blvd, Los Angeles, CA 90004

Health

There have been recent large outbreaks of dengue fever in Thailand, so avoid mosquito bites. Malaria is mostly restricted to a few rural areas, notably the islands of the eastern seaboard (Rayong to Trat) and the provinces of Kanchanaburi, Chaiyaphum, Phetchaburi, Mae Hong Son and Tak. There are small epidemics of Japanese encephalitis in Northern Thailand each rainy season, so consider vaccination if you're planning to spend long periods in there. Food and waterborne diseases (including dysentery, cholera, hepatitis and liver flukes) occur. The main risk of liver flukes is from eating raw or undercooked food, and liver flukes are endemic to villages around Sakon Nakhon Province's Nong Han – do not swim in this lake. HIV/AIDS is the other major risk in Thailand, where it is associated with heterosexual intercourse in more than 80% of cases. Always use condoms (and preferably a brand made outside Thailand).

Thailand's best hospitals are in Bangkok, but there are others of a decent standard in Chiang Mai, Khon Kaen, Hat Yai and Phuket. In remote areas, the best emergency health care can generally be found at military hospitals.

Post & Communications

Thailand's postal service is efficient and relatively cheap, particularly within the country. Bangkok offers a well organised post restante service. Rates for international phone calls from Thailand are reasonable, and between 10 pm and 7 am there is a 66% discount. The Communications Authority of Thailand (CAT) operates telephone offices across the country, and these generally offer the best rates.

Money

Costs

You should be able to get by fairly easily on around US$15 to US$25 a day anywhere in Thailand. Visitors staying in comfortable hotels and eating in restaurants should budget on around US$20 to US$30 a day outside Bangkok and around double that amount in the capital. If money is no object, then you can spend to your heart's content in Bangkok, since it has several of the world's most sumptuous hotels. Your spending levels will be curtailed by the scarcity of luxury accommodation and quality restaurants if you get off the beaten track.

Changing Money

The baht lost 20% of its value overnight in mid-1997, so it's worth keeping an eye on the exchange rates printed daily in the *Bangkok Post*. Banks or legal moneychangers offer the best rates. For buying baht, US dollars are the most readily acceptable currency, though travellers cheques get a better rate than cash. Credit cards are becoming increasingly acceptable in quality shops, hotels and restaurants. Visa is the most useful, followed by MasterCard. ATMs which accept Visa and other credit cards are easily found in the larger cities, and many exchange booths will give you a cash advance on your credit card.

Online Services

Lonely Planet's *Destination Thailand* page can be found at www.lonely planet.com/dest/sea/thai.htm.

Bangkok's Mahidol University (www.mahidol.ac.th/Thailand/Thailand -main.html) has a monster site packed with densely informative articles on Thai history, arts, religion and tourism, while you can get a thumbnail introduction to the hill tribes of Northern Thailand at www.infothai.com/wtcmcr/ hiltribe.htm.

TAT (www.tat.or.th) has very useful information on immigration and customs regulations, transport options from Bangkok airport, social customs, a calendar of events and a copy of the Prostitution Prevention & Suppression Act. The Ministry of Foreign Affairs of Thailand (www.mfa.go.th) has a list of Thai embassies and details of visa requirements.

Get your daily dose of Thai news from the *Bangkok Post* (www.bangkok post.net), or if you're into Thai boxing, check out *Muay Thai World* online magazine (www.siam.net/muaythai/ index.html).

Finally, take a deep breath and dive into the world of Songwut Apirakkhit (www.seas.upenn.edu:80/~

songwut/wut1.shtml), who has an exhaustive index of Thai web sites.

Books

There's a huge volume of western writing about Thailand, encompassing history, culture, people, politics and natural history, as well as travel writing and fiction.

Culture Shock! Thailand & How to Survive It by Robert & Nanthapa Cooper is an interesting outline on getting along with the Thai way of life. One of the more readable general histories written in the latter half of the 20th century is David Wyatt's Thailand: A Short History. Thailand's role in the international narcotics trade is well covered in Alfred McCoy's The Politics of Heroin in Southeast Asia.

Complete with sketches, photos and maps, The Mammals of Thailand by Boonsong Lekagul & Jeffrey McNeely remains the classic on Thai wildlife. If you want detailed information on hill tribes, seek out the hard-to-find The Hill Tribes of Northern Thailand by Gordon Young (Monograph No I, The Siam Society).

Spalding Gray's Swimming to Cambodia includes a humorous account of being on location in Thailand while playing a minor role in The Killing Fields. There's a chapter on Thailand in Pico Iyer's Video Night in Kathmandu.

Works by Thai authors worth checking out include the many science fiction/fantasy/horror books by SP Somtow, rural portraits by Pira Sudham (Siamese Drama and Monsoon Country) and In the Mirror, an excellent collection of translated modern Thai short stories from the 1960s and 1970s.

Films

A number of classic international films have used Thailand either as a subject or as a location – more often the latter. In fact nowadays location shooting in Thailand has become something of a boom industry as the country's jungles, rice fields and islands are used as backdrops for all manner of scripts set in 'exotic' tropical countries.

Hollywood blockbusters include The Bridge on the River Kwai, The Deer Hunter, The Killing Fields, Good Morning Vietnam, Mortal Kombat and Tomorrow Never Dies, while Jean-Claude Van Damme's The Kickboxer brought Thai boxing to the big screen.

The domestic Thai film industry has undergone something of a renaissance in the past decade. Some of the most popular offerings include 2499 antapan krong muang (Dang Bireley and the Young Gangsters), Fun Bar Karaoke and Kalla Khrung Nueng ... Muea Chao Nee (Once Upon a Time ... This Morning).

Entering & Leaving Thailand

Most travellers fly into Bangkok, which has a major international airport. Flights in and out of Thailand are often overbooked so it's imperative to reconfirm ongoing flights as soon as you arrive. The departure tax on international flights is 250B.

Overland travel from Malaysia is popular and there are five border crossings between Thailand and Malaysia – two on the west coast (Sadao and Padang Besar), one in the centre (Betong) and two on the east coast (Ban Taba and Sungai Kolok). It's not possible to buy through-fare tickets for rail journeys between Bangkok and Kuala Lumpur or Singapore, but the trip can be made on express trains via the Thai-Malaysia border at Padang Besar. You can cross into Myanmar at Mae Sai, Mae Sot and Three Pagodas Pass, or take a boat from Ranong to Kawthoung, but the situation changes without notice.

Laos is a little more reliable with crossings at Chiang Khong, Nong Khai, Nakhon Phanom, Mukdahan and Chong Mek, but the only place to enter Cambodia at the moment is at Aranya Prathet. The Cambodian and Myanmar border areas contain a volatile mixture of landmines, bandits, smugglers and rebels, and remain the scene of occasional low-level military stoushes. Contact your embassy before you leave for reports on the current security situation.

Once, the name 'Vietnam' signified not so much a country as brutal jungle warfare or a spectacular failure of American power. However, over recent years, the lifting of Vietnamese government restrictions and the boom in budget travel have enabled more contemporary portraits of the country to be presented to the west.

An understanding of history still goes a long way in Vietnam, since the country has a unique civilisation and a highly cultured people. Most visitors are overwhelmed by Vietnam's sublime natural beauty: the Red River Delta in the North, the Mekong Delta in the South and almost the entire coastal strip are a patchwork of brilliant green rice paddies. Vietnam offers a rare opportunity to see a country of traditional charm taking its first hesitant steps into the modern world.

When to Go

There are no good or bad seasons to visit Vietnam. When one region is wet or cold, or steaming hot, there is always somewhere else that is sunny and warm. Basically, the South has two seasons: the wet (May to November, wettest from June to August) and the dry (December to April). The hottest and most humid time is from late February to May. The central coast is dry from June to October. The North has two seasons: cool, damp winters (November to April) and hot summers (May to October). The highland areas are significantly cooler than the lowlands, and temperatures can drop to freezing in winter. There is the chance of typhoons from July to November, which affect the northern and central areas of the country.

AT A GLANCE

Full Country Name: Socialist Republic of Vietnam

Area: 329,566 sq km

Population: 75 million

Capital City: Hanoi (pop one million)

People: 85% ethnic Vietnamese, 3% ethnic Chinese, plus Khmers, Chams and members of some 60 ethnolinguistic groups

Languages: Vietnamese, Russian, French, Chinese, English, plus Mon-Khmer and Malayo-Polynesian dialects

Religion: 52% Buddhist, 28.5% Taoist and Confucian, 10% Christian, 4% Caodai, 3% animist, 2% Hoa Hao and 0.5% Muslim

Government: Communist People's Republic

Currency: Vietnamese dong (d)

Time Zone: Seven hours ahead of GMT/UTC

International Telephone Code: 84

Electricity: Mostly 220V, 50 AC, but also many 110V; in the South, most outlets take flat, two-pin plugs, while in the North plugs are generally round and two-pin

349

Travellers should take the New Year Tet Festival (late January or early February) into account when planning a trip. Travel (both within and to Vietnam) becomes very difficult, hotels are full and many services close down for at least a week and possibly a lot longer.

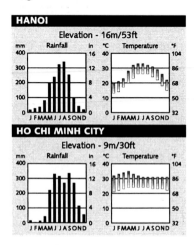

Highlights

Vietnam offers tremendous variety and can suit many different tastes – it's difficult to say just what places should top your list. The following should help you narrow down your choices.

Natural Attractions

Beach lovers will almost certainly want to check out Nha Trang and the more adventurous will appreciate forested Phu Quoc Island, ringed with some of the most beautiful beaches in Vietnam. Dalat – with its park-like setting, waterfalls, ethnic minorities and cool mountain climate – is the jewel (and the kitsch) of the Central Highlands. The splendid limestone formations, sea cliffs and grottoes of Halong Bay could easily rate as one of the wonders of the world. Nearby Cat Ba Island also gets rave reviews. Similar scenery to Halong Bay can be seen at the Perfume Pagoda (on a river, not the sea) and Tam Coc (without any water at all, but with huge rock formations jutting breathtakingly out of the rice paddies). Down south, the pancake-flat but lusciously green Mekong Delta is renowned for its richness, and almost half of it is under cultivation. Popular scenic spots include Cantho, Soc Trang and Chau Doc.

History & Architecture

History and architecture buffs will be attracted to Hué, as it contains splendid tombs of the Nguyen emperors, several notable pagodas and the remains of a 19th century citadel. Hoi An, a picturesque riverside town south of Danang, has some architectural gems from the French colonial period, as well as numerous fine examples of older, traditional architecture. For those fascinated by the American war effort and all its implications, there is no better place to pursue the topic than the old Demilitarised Zone (DMZ).

Cities

Freewheeling Ho Chi Minh City (Saigon), with its dilapidated colonial elegance, outstanding food and bustling nightlife, is a laboratory for Vietnam's economic reforms. Hanoi, with its monuments, parks, lakes and tree-lined boulevards, is the beguiling seat of power in a country trying to decide which direction to head.

Minority Regions

Sapa and nearby Bac Ha offer a glimpse of traditional ethnic lifestyles near the north-west mountains along

VIETNAM HIGHLIGHTS & ITINERARIES

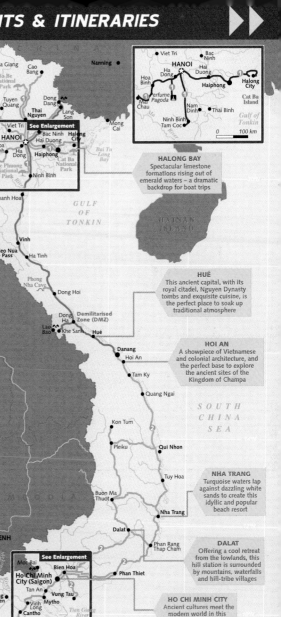

SAPA
Colourful hill-tribe centre renowned for its hiking opportunities and bustling market

HANOI
Lakes and pagodas surround the timeless old quarter of this elegant capital

HALONG BAY
Spectacular limestone formations rising out of emerald waters – a dramatic backdrop for boat trips

HUÉ
This ancient capital, with its royal citadel, Nguyen Dynasty tombs and exquisite cuisine, is the perfect place to soak up traditional atmosphere

HOI AN
A showpiece of Vietnamese and colonial architecture, and the perfect base to explore the ancient sites of the Kingdom of Champa

NHA TRANG
Turquoise waters lap against dazzling white sands to create this idyllic and popular beach resort

DALAT
Offering a cool retreat from the lowlands, this hill station is surrounded by mountains, waterfalls and hill-tribe villages

HO CHI MINH CITY
Ancient cultures meet the modern world in this vibrant and bustling city

SUGGESTED ITINERARIES

One Week
1. Hanoi • Halong Bay • Mai Chau • Perfume Pagoda • Tam Coc
2. Ho Chi Minh City • Cu Chi Tunnels • Mekong Delta • Vung Tau • Long Hai

Two Weeks
1. Hanoi • Sapa • Bac Ha • Cuc Phuong, Ba Be, or Cat Ba National Parks
2. Ho Chi Minh City • Dalat • Nha Trang • Hoi An • Danang

One Month
Hanoi to Ho Chi Minh City (or vice versa) via Danang • Hué • DMZ

Two Months
Mekong Delta • Phu Quoc Island • Phan Thiet • Kon Tum • Phong Nha Cave • Dien Bien Phu • Cao Bang • Bai Tu Long Bay

the Chinese border. Other opportunities for visiting ethnic villages and hiking exist at Mai Chau (also in the north-west). The rugged overland trip to Dien Bien Phu passes through one of Vietnam's most wild and remote areas, which are home to numerous cultural minorities.

Itineraries

ONE WEEK – THE NORTH
From Hanoi make a two day trip to Halong Bay and/or Mai Chau followed by a day trip to the Perfume Pagoda and/or Tam Coc. Spend the remaining time exploring the delights of the capital.

ONE WEEK – THE SOUTH
From Ho Chi Minh City it's possible to do a day trip to the Viet Cong Cu Chi Tunnels, a two or three day tour of the Mekong Delta, and a one or two day trip to the beach resort of Vung Tau or the backpackers retreat of Long Hai on the South China Sea. The rest of the time can be spent sightseeing, eating, shopping and carousing in Ho Chi Minh City.

TWO WEEKS – THE NORTH
Follow the one week itinerary for the North, and then take a spin into the north-west mountains (especially Sapa and Bac Ha) and/or a trip to Cuc Phuong, Ba Be or Cat Ba national parks.

TWO WEEKS – THE SOUTH
A two week visit to the South will allow for the one week itinerary above followed by a trip to Dalat and Nha Trang. If time permits, you could head to Hoi An and fly back to Ho Chi Minh City from Danang.

ONE MONTH
One month is enough time to take in most of the major sights. Starting in the South (this itinerary can also be followed in reverse from Hanoi) follow the two week itinerary as far as Hoi An or Danang before pressing on to Hué. Many people then take

a DMZ tour out of Hué; after that allow some time to cover the two week itinerary for the North, but heading towards Hanoi. You then have the option of flying out of Hanoi or continuing overland to China.

TWO MONTHS
This will allow you to see everything in detail. In addition to the above, you can explore the Mekong Delta more thoroughly, taking in a side trip to lovely Phu Quoc Island. Visit the giant sand dunes at Phan Thiet, south of Nha Trang. A trip to the western part of the Central Highlands should include a visit to relatively unspoiled Kon Tum, with its Montagnard villages. Don't forget Phong Nha Cave, with its thousands of metres of underground passageways, to the north of the DMZ. In the far north, you can explore backwaters such as Dien Bien Phu, Cao Bang and Bai Tu Long Bay.

Visa Requirements
Tourist visas are valid for a single 30 day stay only. To make matters worse, the visa specifies the exact date of arrival and departure, and you cannot arrive even one day earlier than specified. If you change your plans and postpone your trip by two weeks, then you'll only have 16 days remaining on your visa. So, it makes more sense to wait until you enter the region before you obtain your visa, and Bangkok is the most convenient place to do this. Even travel agents from neighbouring countries send the paperwork to Bangkok for processing as it is so much cheaper than dealing with local Vietnamese embassies. In Bangkok, single-entry tourist visas cost about US$40 at budget travel agencies. Processing an application takes five working days in Bangkok, five days in Malaysia, five to 10 days in Hong Kong and 10 working days in Taiwan.

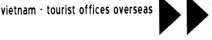
Vietnamese Embassies

AUSTRALIA
(☎ 02-6286 6059) 6 Timbarra Crescent, O'Malley, ACT 2603. Consulate: Sydney

CANADA
(☎ 613-236-0772) 226 Maclaren St, Ottawa, Ontario K2P 0L9

THAILAND
(☎ 02-251 7201, 251 5836) 83/1 Wireless Rd, Bangkok

UK
(☎ 020-7937 1912) 12-14 Victoria Rd, London W8 5RD

USA
(☎ 202-861-0737) 1233 20th St NW, Washington, DC 20036

Tourist Offices Overseas

Vietnam has few overseas tourist offices, but travel agents will be able to supply you with most information. Also check out the web sites listed under Online Services.

Health

There have been recent large outbreaks of dengue fever, so try to avoid mosquito bites. Malaria risk exists year-round in rural areas. Japanese encephalitis, although a small risk to travellers, is endemic in Vietnam, and you may want to consider a vaccination if you are intending to stay for some time, especially in rural areas. Schistosomiasis (bilharzia) is present in the Mekong Delta, so avoid bathing or paddling there. Food and waterborne diseases, including dysentery, cholera and hepatitis, occur so pay attention to basic food and water hygiene rules.

Hospitals in Vietnam's main cities are fairly good, but ensure you're in good health before heading to more remote areas.

Post & Communications

Vietnam's domestic postal rates are amazingly cheap, but international rates are similar to those in western countries. Both Hanoi and Ho Chi Minh City offer post restante services.

Rates for international phone calls from Vietnam are among the highest in the world. Using international call-back services is illegal and carries heavy penalties, so if you have to make a call, you'll pay dearly for the privilege. You can book long-distance calls from hotels or post offices (usually the cheaper alternative).

Money

Costs

Travellers staying in budget accommodation and eating in small cafes should be able to get by on around US$20 per day (not including long-distance transport costs). To stay in mid-range hotels, eat at moderate restaurants, charter occasional taxis and enjoy the nightlife, budget on around US$65 a day. Until recently, many upmarket hotels insisted that you pay in US dollars, but now all businesses (except Vietnam Airlines) must accept payment in dong. In practice, many still display prices in dollars. It's advisable to bring US dollar travellers cheques and a little cash.

Changing Money

There are four ways to exchange currency: at banks, through authorised exchange bureaus, at hotel reception desks, and on the black market. The best rates are offered by the banks, but the exchange bureaus are generally more conveniently located and have longer opening hours. The black market rate is worse than the legal exchange rate, so if you're offered better rates than a bank it's bound to be some sort of scam.

Visa and MasterCard credit cards are accepted in the major cities and towns popular with tourists. It is virtually impossible to exchange foreign currency outside the major cities and tourist areas, so if you're heading off the beaten track you will need to stock up on dong or change money on the black market.

Online Services

Lonely Planet's *Destination Vietnam* page is at www.lonelyplanet.com/dest/sea/vietnam.htm.

The Vietnam Multimedia Archive (sunsite.unc.edu/vietnam/) is a great starting point for those who prefer pics over text. Get the flavour of the country at *Vietnam Online* (www.vietnamonline.net).

The Internet Travel Guide to Vietnam (www.datacomm.ch/pmgeiser/vietnam) does its usual reliable job with travel information.

Although a few years old, Valerie Schumacher's feisty records of her trips to Vietnam make good reading on the *Vietnam Veterans' Home Page* (http://grunt.space.swri.edu/trip95.htm).

The Vietnam Democracy Newsletter (www.fva.org/vndemo.html) aims to provide the news that does not normally filter through to the outside world. All in the name of democracy.

Books

Vietnam: A History by Stanley Kurnow is a very readable account of Vietnam's history from prehistoric times until the fall of Saigon.

Dispatches by Michael Herr takes a cold, hard look at the Vietnam War through the eyes of an American correspondent, while *A Bright Shining Lie* and *Two Cities: Hanoi and Saigon*

by Neil Sheehan cover the war and the personalities of Vietnam's two principal cities.

Vietnamerica, by Thomas Bass, brings the Vietnam War home to America in a more poignant and personal form, following the fortunes of the children fathered by American soldiers in Vietnam.

The Quiet American by Graham Greene is set during the last days of French rule and is probably the most famous western work of fiction on Vietnam, while *The Lover* by Marguerite Duras provides a French perspective on colonial life in Vietnam. *The Great Railway Bazaar* by Paul Theroux includes several chapters on the Trans-Vietnam Railway.

Films

One of Vietnam's first cinematographic efforts was a newsreel of Ho Chi Minh's 1945 Proclamation of Independence. Following this, parts of the Franco-Viet Minh War battle of Dien Bien Phu were restaged for the benefit of movie cameras.

Two contemporary films set in Vietnam are Vietnamese director Tran Anh Hung's *The Scent of Green Papaya* and *Cyclo*, while the book *When Heaven and Earth Changed Places* by Le Ly Hayslip was made into a fascinating movie, *Heaven and Earth*, by Oliver Stone.

Almost all American-made films about Vietnam are about the war, but most were filmed in the Philippines. Some popular war movies include *Rambo, Full Metal Jacket, Platoon, The Deer Hunter, Good Morning Vietnam* and *Air America*. Perhaps the most memorable line about Vietnam was spoken by a captain in *Apocalypse*

Now. 'I love the smell of napalm in the morning'. *Indochine* starring Catherine Deneuve is a French film about that country's colonial experience in South-East Asia.

Entering & Leaving Vietnam

Bangkok, only 80 minutes by air from Ho Chi Minh City, is the main port of embarkation for air travel to Vietnam, followed closely by Hong Kong. There are also direct Bangkok-Hanoi flights. Vietnam Air, the government airline, still has a stranglehold on flights into the country, although other airlines are allowed some access. Consequently, there aren't many bargains available. The departure tax on international flights is US$8 from Ho Chi Minh City and US$7 from Hanoi.

It has become very popular to cross the border into China at Dong Dang, 20km north of Lang Son in north-east Vietnam, to reach Nanning in Guangxi Province. The other popular border crossing is Lao Cai in north-west Vietnam, which lies on the train line between Hanoi and Kunming in China's Yunnan Province (Hanoi-Beijing passenger trains also cross here).

It's possible to enter Laos from Lao Bao and Keo Nua Pass in central Vietnam. The only entry point to Cambodia is at Moc Bai, which is where daily Phnom Penh-Ho Chi Minh City buses cross. Note that Vietnamese visas specify your departure point from the country. If you want to change this you'll have to visit the immigration police or the Foreign Ministry in Hanoi.

Air Fares

Expedia: www.expedia.msn.com/daily/home/default.hts
Flight Info.Com: www.flifo.com
Travelocity: www.travelocity.com

Airlines

Air New Zealand: www.airnz.com
Alitalia: www.alitalia.com/english/index.html
American Airlines: www.americanair.com
Ansett Australia: www.ansett.com.au
British Airways: www.british-airways.com
Canadian Airlines: www.cdnair.ca
Cathay Pacific: www.cathaypacific.com/index.html
Continental Airlines: www.flycontinental.com
International Association of Air Travel Couriers (IAATC): www.courier.org/index.html
Lauda Air: www.laudaair.com
Lufthansa: www.lufthansa.com
Qantas: www.qantas.com
Singapore Airlines: www.newasia-singapore.com; www.singaporeair.com
United Airlines: www.ual.com
Virgin: www.fly.virgin.com

Car & Motorcycle

American Automobile Association: www.aaa.com/vacation/idp.html
Australian Automobile Association: www.aaa.asn.au
British Automobile Association: www.theaa.co.uk/membership/offers/idp.html
Canadian Automobile Association: www.caa.ca/CAAInternet/travelservices/frames14.htm
New Zealand Automobile Association: www.aa.org.nz

Email Accounts

eKno: www.ekno.lonelyplanet.com
Internet Café Guide: www.netcafeguide.com
Opening accounts: www.yahoo.com; www.hotmail.com

Film & Radio

BBC World Service: www.bbc.co.uk/worldservice
Internet Movie Database: www.imdb.com
Radio America: www.voa.gov
Radio Australia: www.abc.net.au/ra

Health

Altitude Sickness: www.princeton.edu/~oa/altitude.html; www.gorgr.net/hamg/AMS.html
American Society of Tropical Medicine & Hygiene: www.astmh.org
British Airways Travel Clinics: www.britishairways.com/travelqa/fyi/health/health.html
CDC (US Centers for Disease Control & Prevention): www.cdc.gov/travel/travel.html
International Association for Medical Assistance to Travellers (Canada): www.sentex.net

The International Planned Parenthood Federation: www.ippf.org
International Society of Travel Medicine: www.istm.org
Lariam Action USA: www.suggskelly.com/lariam
Marie Stopes: www.mariestopes.org/uk
MASTA (Medical Advisory Services for Travellers): www.masta.org
Medical College of Wisconsin Travelers Clinic: www.intmed.mcw/travel.html
Mefloquine: www.travelhealth.com/mefloqui.htm; www.geocities.com/TheTropics/6913/
    lariam.htm
Shorelands: www.tripprep.com
Travel Health Information Service: www.travelhealth.com
Travellers Medical and Vaccination Centre: www.tmvc.com.au/info.html
WHO (World Health Organization): www.who.ch

Magazines & Newspapers

Action Asia Magazine: www.actionasia.com
Bicycling: www.bicyclingmagazine.com
Big World Magazine: www.bigworld.com
Chicago Tribune: www.chicagotribune.com
LA Times: www.latimes.com
Mountain Bike: www.mountainbike.com
National Geographic: www.nationalgeographic.com
New York Times: www.nytimes.com
Outside: outside.starwave.com
San Francisco Examiner: www.examiner.com
Southern Cross (UK): www.southerncross.co.uk
Surfer Magazine: www.surfermag.com
Sydney Morning Herald: www.smh.com.au
The Age (Melbourne): www.theage.com.au
The Australian: www.news.com.au
The Globe & Mail (Toronto): www.theglobeandmail.com
The Independent (UK): www.independent.co.uk
The Times: www.the-times.co.uk
Time Out: www.timeout.com/london
TNT: www.tntmag.co.uk
Traveller Magazine: www.travelmag.co.uk
Vancouver Sun: www.vancouversun.com

Maps

Hagstrom Map and Travel Center: www.hagstromstore.com
Mapquest Mapstore: www.mapquest.com
Rand McNally – The Map & Travel Store: www.randmcnallystore.com
World of Maps & Travel Books: www.worldofmaps.com

Money Matters

Credit cards: www.mastercard.com/atm or www.visa.com/
    cgi-bin/vee/pd/atm/main.html?2+0 ou
Oanda online currency converter: www.oanda.com/site/cc_index.html

Passports & Visas

General: www2.travel.com.au/cgi-bin/clcgi?E=bevisreq
Passports Australia, Department of Foreign Affairs & Trade: www.dfat.gov.au/passports/
    passports_faq_contents.html

Passport Office, Department of Foreign Affairs & International Trade (Canada): www
.dfait-maeci.gc.ca/passport/paspr-2.htm
Passport Office, Department of Internal Affairs (New Zealand):
inform.dia.govt.nz/internal_affairs/businesses/doni_pro/fees.html
Passport Services, the State Department (USA): travel.state.gov/passport_services.html
UK Passport Agency, The Home Office: www.open.gov.uk/ukpass/ukpass.htm

Teaching Resources

EFL in Asia: www.geocities.com/Tokyo/flats/7947/elfasia.htm
English Expert Page: www.englishexpert.com
Hong Kong School Board: www.info.gov.hk/ed/teacher/elt.net.htm
International House: www.international-house.org
PADI: www.padi.com
TEFL Job Centre: www.jobs.edunet.com

Travel Advisories

British Foreign & Commonwealth Office: www.fco.gov.uk
Conservation International's Ecotravel Center: www.ecotour.org/ecotour.htm
Council Travel: www.counciltravel.com
Ecotour: www.ecotour.org/ecotour.htm
The Ecotourism Association of Australia: www.wttc.org
Encounter: www.encounter.co.uk
Exodus: www.exodustravels.co.uk
Global Exchange: www.globalexchange.org
Intrepid Travel: www.intrepidtravel.com.au
Journeys International: www.journeys-intl.com
Monkey Business: www.monkeyshrine.com
The Russia Experience: www.travel.world.co.uk
Serious Sports: www.serioussports.com/core.html
STA Travel: www.sta-travel.com
Tourism Offices Worldwide Directory: www.towd.com
Trailfinders: www.trailfinder.com
Travel CUTS: www.travelcuts.com

Travel Equipment

Karrimor: www.karrimor.co.uk
Macpac: www.macpac.co.nz
REI: www.REI.com

Travellers With Disabilities

Mobility International USA: www.miusa.org
Society for the Advancement of Travel for the Handicapped (SATH): sath.org/index.html
Global Access: www.geocities.com/Paris/1052
Royal Association for Disability & Rehabilitation (RADAR): www.radar.org.uk

Volunteer Organisations

Australian Volunteers International: www.ozvol.org.au
Earthwatch Institute: www.earthwatch.org/australia/html;
www.earthwatch.org/t/Toeuropehome.htm
Global Volunteers: www.globalvolunteers.org
International Voluntary Service: www.ivsgbn.demon.co.uk
Oxfam International: www.oxfaminternational.org
Peace Corps of the USA: www.peacecorps.gov

Voluntary Service Overseas (VSO): www.oneworld.org/vso
Volunteer Service Abroad: www.tcol.co.uk/comorg/vsa.htm

Other Useful Sites

Federation of International Youth Travel Organisations: www.fiyto.org/index-old.html
Gay Asia Compass: www.asiancompass.com
Hiking & Walking Homepage: www.teleport.com/-walking/hiking.html
Hostelling International: www.iyhf.org
International Student Travel Confederation: www.isic.org/index.htm
Internet Guide to Hostelling: www.hostels.com
Internet Traveller Information Service: www.itisnet.com
Lonely Planet: www.lonelyplanet.com
Photo.net: www.photo.net/photo
Rain or Shine: www.rainorshine.com
Travelocity: www.travelocity.com
US State Department Travel Warnings & Consular Information Sheets: travel.state.gov/
    travel_warnings.html
Utopia Asian Gay & Lesbian Resources: www.utopia.com
World Events Calendar: www.travel.epicurious.com
World Tourism Organization: www.world-tourism.org/ows-doc/wtich.htm
Zen study: www.zendo.com/eiheiji.html

GLOSSARY

COMMON WORDS

AIR PUTIH – boiled water (Indonesia)

AUTO – auto-rickshaw (India)

AYURVEDA – Indian herbal medicine (practised also in Sri Lanka)

BAJAJ – auto-rickshaw (Indonesia)

BATIK – coloured cloth made by a waxing and dyeing process (Bali)

BECAK – bicycle rickshaw (Indonesia)

BEMO – pick-up truck or minibus popular in Indonesia; also known as an *angkot*

BUUZ – steamed mutton dumplings consumed during the Tsagaan Sar festival (Mongolia)

CYCLO – pedicab (Vietnam)

DAL BHAT – rice and lentil meal (Nepal)

DERA – temple (Japan)

DHOTI – like a sarong, with the cloth pulled up between the legs (worn by men; India)

DIM SUM – series of small dishes; often steamed (Hong Kong)

DMZ – Demilitarised Zone (South Korea and Vietnam)

DO – island (South Korea)

DOKAR – two-wheeled horse-drawn cart (Indonesia)

DZONG – fort-monastery (Bhutan)

ELS – sand dunes (Mongolia)

EN – garden (Japan)

FACE – a mixture of pride, reputation and dignity that is gained by display of personal wealth or power and lost via personal embarrassment or public humiliation; it's particularly important in North-East and South-East Asian cultures.

GASSHO-ZUKURI – 'hands in prayer' traditional farmhouse architectural style (Japan)

GER – traditional tent (Mongolia)

GINSENG – aromatic roots used medicinally throughout the region

GOEMBA – monastery of the Mahayana Buddhist sect

GOMPA – monastery of the Tibetan-Buddhist sect

GUANYIN – Chinese name for the Buddhist Goddess of Mercy

GULAL – a coloured powder thrown around to celebrate the Holi festival (India)

GUNUNG – mountain (Indonesia and Malaysia)

GURU RIMPOCHE – the common name of Admasambhava, the founder of Mahayana Buddhism

HANAMI – cherry blossom viewing season (Japan)

IKAT – cloth in which the pattern is produced by dyeing individual threads prior to weaving (Indonesia)

JEEPNEY – small bus (Philippines)

JI – temple (Japan)

JINGU/JINJA – shrine (Japan)

KALAGA – an embroidered tapestry (Myanmar)

KANTOR TELKOM – government-run telephone offices (Indonesia)

KHAAN – king (Mongolia)

KHIID – monastery (Mongolia)

KHLONG – canal (Thailand)

KRIS – knives (Malaysia)

LONGYI – loom-woven length of cotton cloth draped around the lower body and legs and tied at the waist (Myanmar)

LOSMEN – basic accommodation or guesthouse (Indonesia)

MANDI – bathing facility (Indonesia)

MANGA – Japanese comics

MINSHUKU – simple traditional inn (Japan)

MONTAGNARDS – literally 'mountain people'; a French term for ethnic minorities living in remote areas of Vietnam

MUAY THAI – Thai boxing

NAMASTE – Nepali greeting

NUUR – lake (Mongolia)

OGOH-OGOH – a huge doll to which offerings are made during the Hindu New Year (Bali)

PĂA DĂEK – fermented fish accompanying rice (Laos)

PACHINKO – vertical pinball game that is a Japanese craze

PAYA – religious statue or monument (Myanmar)

QI – the life energy, relating to traditional Chinese medicine

ROCKET – steamer (Bangladesh)

RYOKAN – traditional inn (Japan)

SADHU – ascetic, holy person; one who is trying to achieve enlightenment (India)

SAMLOR – auto-rickshaw (Thailand)

SHINKANSEN – ultra-fast 'bullet' train (Japan)

SHOGUNATE – governed by a shogun (military ruler of old Japan)

SONGKET – gold thread (Malaysia)

STUPA – hemispherical Buddhist religious structure that houses relics

SUNGAI – river (Indonesia and Malaysia)

SUSHI – dish made from rice and raw fish (Japan)

TEMPO – small bus (Nepal)

THANGKA – painted or embroidered religious picture (Bhutan and Nepal)

TORII – entrance gate to a Shinto shrine (Japan)

TSECHU – festivals honouring Guru Rimpoche (Bhutan)

TUK-TUK – auto-rickshaw (Thailand)

UUL – mountain (Mongolia)

VIHARA – Buddhist religious building

WARTEL – private telephone agencies (Indonesia; also warpostal or warparpostel)

WARUNG – food stall or cheap restaurant (Indonesia)

WASHI – Japanese paper

WAT – Buddhist temple-monastery (South-East Asia)

WAYANG KULIT – shadow puppets (Indonesia)

YOGWAN – simple, traditional guesthouse; also known as *yoinsuk* (Korea)

ZAMINDAR – landlord (Bangladesh)

AIR TRAVEL TERMS

BAGGAGE ALLOWANCE – Written on your ticket and usually includes one 20kg item to go in the hold, plus one item of hand luggage.

BUCKET SHOPS – Unbonded travel agencies specialising in discounted plane tickets.

CANCELLATION PENALTIES – If you have to cancel or change a discounted ticket, there are often heavy penalties involved; insurance can sometimes be taken out against these penalties. Some airlines impose penalties on regular tickets as well, particularly against 'no-show' passengers.

CHECK-IN – If you fail to check in on time (usually one to two hours before departure time on international flights) and the flight is overbooked, the airline can cancel your booking.

CONFIRMATION – Having a ticket written out with the flight and date you want doesn't mean you have a seat until the agent has checked with the airline that your status is 'OK' or confirmed.

FULL FARES – Airlines generally offer 1st class (coded F), business class (J) and economy class (Y) tickets. With so many promotional and discounted fares around, few passengers pay full economy fare.

ITX – An ITX, or 'independent inclusive tour excursion', is often available on tickets to popular holiday destinations. Officially it's a package deal combined with hotel accommodation, but many agents will sell you one of these for the flight only and give you phoney hotel vouchers in the unlikely event that you're challenged at the airport.

LOST TICKETS – If you lose your plane ticket an airline will usually treat it like a travellers cheque and, after inquiries, issue you with another one. Legally, however, an airline is entitled to treat it like cash and if you lose it then it's gone forever.

MCO – An MCO, or 'miscellaneous charge order', is a voucher that looks like a plane ticket but carries no destination or date. It can be exchanged through any International Association of Travel Agents (IATA) airline for a ticket on a specific flight. It's a useful alternative to an onward ticket in those countries that demand one, and is more flexible than an ordinary ticket if you're unsure of your route.

NO-SHOWS – These are passengers who fail to show up for their flight. Full-fare passengers who fail to turn up are sometimes entitled to travel on a later flight. The rest are penalised.

ON REQUEST – An unconfirmed booking for a flight.

ONWARD TICKETS – An entry requirement for many countries is that you have a ticket out of the country. If you're unsure of your next move, the easiest solution is to buy the cheapest onward ticket to a neighbouring country or a ticket from a reliable airline which can later be refunded if you don't use it.

OPEN-JAW TICKETS – Return tickets where you fly into one place but out of another.

OVERBOOKING – Since every flight has some passengers who fail to show up, airlines often book

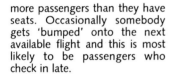

more passengers than they have seats. Occasionally somebody gets 'bumped' onto the next available flight and this is most likely to be passengers who check in late.

POINT-TO-POINT TICKETS – Discount tickets that can be bought on some routes in return for passengers waiving their rights to a stopover.

PROMOTIONAL FARES – Officially discounted fares bought from travel agencies or directly from the airline.

RECONFIRMATION – If you don't reconfirm your flight at least 72 hours prior to departure, the airline may delete your name from the passenger list.

RESTRICTIONS – Discounted tickets often have various restrictions on them such as needing to be paid for in advance, incurring a penalty to be altered, or restrictions on the minimum and maximum period you must be away.

ROUND-THE-WORLD TICKETS – RTW tickets give you a limited period (usually a year) in which to circumnavigate the globe. You can go anywhere the carrying airlines go, as long as you don't backtrack. The number of stopovers or total number of separate flights is decided before you set off and they usually cost a bit more than a basic return flight.

STAND-BY – A discounted ticket where you only fly if there is a seat free at the last moment, and usually available only on domestic routes.

TRANSFERRED TICKETS – Plane tickets cannot be transferred from one person to another. Travellers sometimes try to sell the return half of their ticket, but officials can ask you to prove that you are the person named on the ticket. This is less likely to happen on domestic flights, but on an international flight tickets are compared with passports.

TRAVEL PERIODS – Ticket prices vary depending on the time of year – low (off-peak) season, high (peak) season or shoulder season. Usually the fare depends on your outward flight – if you depart in the high season and return in the low season, you pay the high-season fare.

INDEX

Italics indicates maps

FREE Lonely Planet Newsletters

We love hearing from you and think you'd like to hear from us.

Planet Talk

Our FREE quarterly printed newsletter is full of tips from travellers and anecdotes from Lonely Planet guidebook authors. Every issue is packed with up-to-date travel news and advice, and includes:

- a postcard from Lonely Planet co-founder Tony Wheeler
- a swag of mail from travellers
- a look at life on the road through the eyes of a Lonely Planet author
- topical health advice
- prizes for the best travel yarn
- news about forthcoming Lonely Planet events
- a complete list of Lonely Planet books and other titles

To join our mailing list, residents of the UK, Europe and Africa can email us at go@lonelyplanet.co.uk; residents of North and South America can email us at info@lonelyplanet.com; the rest of the world can email us at talk2us@lonelyplanet.com.au, or contact any Lonely Planet office.

Comet

Our FREE monthly email newsletter brings you all the latest travel news, features, interviews, competitions, destination ideas, travellers' tips & tales, Q&As, raging debates and related links. Find out what's new on the Lonely Planet Web site and which books are about to hit the shelves.

Subscribe from your desktop:
www.lonelyplanet.com/comet

LONELY PLANET

Guides by Region

L onely Planet is known worldwide for publishing practical, reliable and no-nonsense travel information in our guides and on our web site. The Lonely Planet list covers just about every accessible part of the world. Currently there are nine series: travel guides, shoestring guides, walking guides, city guides, phrasebooks, audio packs, travel atlases, diving and snorkelling guides and travel literature.

AFRICA Africa – the South ● Africa on a shoestring ● Arabic (Egyptian) phrasebook ● Arabic (Moroccan) phrasebook ● Cairo ● Cape Town ● Central Africa ● East Africa ● Egypt ● Egypt travel atlas ● Ethiopian (Amharic) phrasebook ● The Gambia & Senegal ● Kenya ● Kenya travel atlas ● Malawi, Mozambique & Zambia ● Morocco ● North Africa ● South Africa, Lesotho & Swaziland ● South Africa, Lesotho & Swaziland travel atlas ● Swahili phrasebook ● Tanzania, Zanzibar & Pemba ● Trekking in East Africa ● Tunisia ● West Africa ● Zimbabwe, Botswana & Namibia ● Zimbabwe, Botswana & Namibia travel atlas

Travel Literature: The Rainbird: A Central African Journey ● Songs to an African Sunset: A Zimbabwean Story ● Mali Blues: Traveling to an African Beat

AUSTRALIA & THE PACIFIC Australia ● Australian phrasebook ● Bushwalking in Australia ● Bushwalking in Papua New Guinea ● Fiji ● Fijian phrasebook ● Islands of Australia's Great Barrier Reef ● Melbourne ● Micronesia ● New Caledonia ● New South Wales & the ACT ● New Zealand ● Northern Territory ● Outback Australia ● Papua New Guinea ● Papua New Guinea (Pidgin) phrasebook ● Queensland ● Rarotonga & the Cook Islands ● Samoa ● Solomon Islands ● South Australia ● South Pacific Languages phrasebook ● Sydney ● Tahiti & French Polynesia ● Tasmania ● Tonga ● Tramping in New Zealand ● Vanuatu ● Victoria ● Western Australia

Travel Literature: Islands in the Clouds ● Sean & David's Long Drive

CENTRAL AMERICA & THE CARIBBEAN Bahamas and Turks & Caicos ● Barcelona ● Bermuda ● Central America on a shoestring ● Costa Rica ● Cuba ● Dominican Republic & Haiti ● Eastern Caribbean ● Guatemala, Belize & Yucatán: La Ruta Maya ● Jamaica ● Mexico ● Mexico City ● Panama
Travel Literature: Green Dreams: Travels in Central America

EUROPE Amsterdam ● Andalucía ● Austria ● Baltic States phrasebook ● Barcelona ● Berlin ● Britain ● British phrasebook ● Canary Islands ● Central Europe ● Central Europe phrasebook ● Corsica ● Croatia ● Czech & Slovak Republics ● Denmark ● Dublin ● Eastern Europe ● Eastern Europe phrasebook ● Edinburgh ● Estonia, Latvia & Lithuania ● Europe ● Finland ● France ● French phrasebook ● Germany ● German phrasebook ● Greece ● Greek phrasebook ● Hungary ● Iceland, Greenland & the Faroe Islands ● Ireland ● Italian phrasebook ● Italy ● Lisbon ● London ● Mediterranean Europe ● Mediterranean Europe phrasebook ● Norway ● Paris ● Poland ● Portugal ● Portugal travel atlas ● Prague ● Provence & the Côte d'Azur ● Romania & Moldova ● Rome ● Russia, Ukraine & Belarus ● Russian phrasebook ● Scandinavian & Baltic Europe ● Scandinavian Europe phrasebook ● Scotland ● Slovenia ● Spain ● Spanish phrasebook ● St Petersburg ● Switzerland ● Trekking in Spain ● Ukrainian phrasebook ● Vienna ● Walking in Britain ● Walking in Italy ● Walking in Ireland ● Walking in Switzerland ● Western Europe ● Western Europe phrasebook

Travel Literature: The Olive Grove: Travels in Greece

INDIAN SUBCONTINENT Bangladesh ● Bengali phrasebook ● Bhutan ● Delhi ● Goa ● Hindi/Urdu phrasebook ● India ● India & Bangladesh travel atlas ● Indian Himalaya ● Karakoram Highway ● Nepal ● Nepali phrasebook ● Pakistan ● Rajasthan ● South India ● Sri Lanka ● Sri Lanka phrasebook ● Trekking in the Indian Himalaya ● Trekking in the Karakoram & Hindukush ● Trekking in the Nepal Himalaya

Travel Literature: In Rajasthan ● Shopping for Buddhas

LONELY PLANET

Mail Order

Lonely Planet products are distributed worldwide.They are also available by mail order from Lonely Planet, so if you have difficulty finding a title please write to us. North and South American residents should write to 150 Linden St, Oakland CA 94607, USA; European and African residents should write to 10a Spring Place, London, NW5 3BH; and residents of other countries to PO Box 617, Hawthorn, Victoria 3122, Australia.

ISLANDS OF THE INDIAN OCEAN Madagascar & Comoros • Maldives • Mauritius, Réunion & Seychelles

MIDDLE EAST & CENTRAL ASIA Arab Gulf States • Central Asia • Central Asia phrasebook • Iran • Israel & the Palestinian Territories • Israel & the Palestinian Territories travel atlas • Istanbul • Jerusalem • Jordan & Syria • Jordan, Syria & Lebanon travel atlas • Lebanon • Middle East on a shoestring • Turkey • Turkish phrasebook • Turkey travel atlas • Yemen

Travel Literature: The Gates of Damascus • Kingdom of the Film Stars: Journey into Jordan

NORTH AMERICA Alaska • Backpacking in Alaska • Baja California • California & Nevada • Canada • Chicago • Florida • Hawaii • Honolulu • Los Angeles • Louisiana • Miami • New England USA • New Orleans • New York City • New York, New Jersey & Pennsylvania • Pacific Northwest USA • Puerto Rico • Rocky Mountain States • San Francisco • Seattle • Southwest USA • Texas • USA • USA phrasebook • Vancouver • Washington, DC & the Capital Region

Travel Literature: Drive Thru America

NORTH-EAST ASIA Beijing • Cantonese phrasebook • China • Hong Kong • Hong Kong, Macau & Guangzhou • Japan • Japanese phrasebook • Japanese audio pack • Korea • Korean phrasebook • Kyoto • Mandarin phrasebook • Mongolia • Mongolian phrasebook • Seoul • South-West China • Taiwan • Tibet • Tibetan phrasebook • Tokyo

Travel Literature: Lost Japan

SOUTH AMERICA Argentina, Uruguay & Paraguay • Bolivia • Brazil • Brazilian phrasebook • Buenos Aires • Chile & Easter Island • Chile & Easter Island travel atlas • Colombia • Ecuador & the Galapagos Islands • Latin American Spanish phrasebook • Peru • Quechua phrasebook • Rio de Janeiro • South America on a shoestring • Trekking in the Patagonian Andes • Venezuela

Travel Literature: Full Circle: A South American Journey

SOUTH-EAST ASIA Bali & Lombok • Bangkok • Burmese phrasebook • Cambodia • Hanoi • Hill Tribes phrasebook • Ho Chi Minh City • Indonesia • Indonesia's Eastern Islands • Indonesian phrasebook • Indonesian audio pack • Jakarta • Java • Laos • Lao phrasebook • Laos travel atlas • Malay phrasebook • Malaysia, Singapore & Brunei • Myanmar (Burma) • Philippines • Pilipino (Tagalog) phrasebook • Singapore • South-East Asia on a shoestring • South-East Asia phrasebook • Thailand • Thailand's Islands & Beaches • Thailand travel atlas • Thai phrasebook • Thai audio pack • Vietnam • Vietnamese phrasebook • Vietnam travel atlas

ALSO AVAILABLE: Antarctica • Brief Encounters: Stories of Love, Sex & Travel • Chasing Rickshaws • Sacred India • Not the Only Planet: Travel Stories from Science Fiction • Travel with Children • Traveller's Tales • Healthy Travel Asia & India • Healthy Travel Africa • Lonely Planet Travel Journal

TRAVEL GUIDES

Travel Guides explore a destination in depth, with options to suit a range of budgets. With reliable, practical advice on getting around, restaurants and accommodation, these easy-to-use guides also include numerous detailed maps, colour photographs, extensive background material and coverage of sights both on and off the beaten track.

PHRASEBOOKS

Lonely Planet phrasebooks cover essential words and phrases travellers need to effectively communicate. With colour tabs for quick reference, extensive vocabulary lists, use of local scripts and easy to follow pronunciation keys, these handy, pocket size language guides cover most situations a traveller is likely to encounter.

PISCES BOOKS

Beautifully illustrated with full-colour photos, Lonely Planet's Pisces Books explore the world's best diving and snorkelling areas and prepare divers for what to expect when they get there, both topside and underwater. Dive sites are described in detail with specifics on depths, visibility, level of difficulty, special conditions, underwater photography tips and common and unusual marine life present.

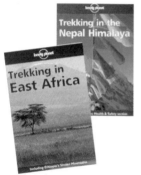

WALKING

With detailed descriptions ranging from family walks to hard high-level routes, advice on when to and how to do it, detailed and reliable maps and background information, these informative walking guides are an invaluable resource for both independent walkers and those in an organised group - in fact, for anyone who believes that the best way to see the world is on foot.

CITY MAPS

Lonely Planet's City Map series covers the world's great cities, both on and off the beaten track. This full-colour and easy-to-use product contains downtown and metropolitan maps, transit routes, unique walking tours, and essential information (including phone numbers), plus a complete index of streets and sights. The information is up-to-date and accurate, and the maps are plastic-coated for extra durability.

TRAVEL ATLASES

Lonely Planet's Travel Atlases are thoroughly researched and fact-checked by the guidebook authors to ensure they complement the guidebooks. And the booklet format means none of the holes, wrinkles, tears or constant folding and refolding characteristic of large sheet maps.

LONELY PLANET ONLINE

Lonely Planet's award-winning web site has insider info on hundreds of destinations from Amsterdam to Zimbabwe, complete with interactive maps and colour photographs. You'll also find the latest travel news, recent reports from travellers on the road, guidebook upgrades and a lively bulletin board where you can meet fellow travellers, swap recommendations and seek advice. www.lonelyplanet.com or AOL keyword: lp

UPGRADES

Lonely Planet publishes online Upgrades of some of our most popular guidebooks. Upgrades are regular reports from Lonely Planet authors summarising important information gathered since the book was published. Designed as supplements to current editions of selected Lonely Planet guidebooks, Upgrades can be downloaded for free from the Lonely Planet web site, at: www.lonelyplanet.com/upgrades

COMMUNICATION CARD

It's midnight. You've been on the road for 16 hours and you've just arrived in another new country – you've just had the most incredible journey and you have to call home to tell them all about it. But your pockets are empty – no loose change and no one speaks your language. No worries – you've got eKno.

Cheaper international phone calls

You can currently make calls at budget rates from over 40 countries and growing all the time. This is similar to using a calling card. It's simple, just dial the access number of the country you are in and then follow the voice prompts.

Voicemail

You can send, leave and receive voice messages – so friends can leave you messages from home or on the road and you can reply or even forward the message to others. Give your eKno number to your friends and family or swap eKno numbers with friends you make on the road – this way you can always keep in touch.

You can also listen to your voice messages via the web for free.

Free email

Get a free email address that works anywhere in the world. All you have to do is log onto a computer and pick up your email via your eKno address.

Travel information

Comet, Lonely Planet's online newsletter, is full of up to date travel information, and can be delivered straight to your eKno email account.

If you are a Read This First user, you can join eKno and get 10% bonus free usage.

To get your bonus, all you need to do is to provide the code RTGIV2699 when you register on line or with customer service.

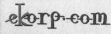